Re:ZeRo
-Starting Life in Another World-
Chapter 4: The Sanctuary and the Witch of Greed

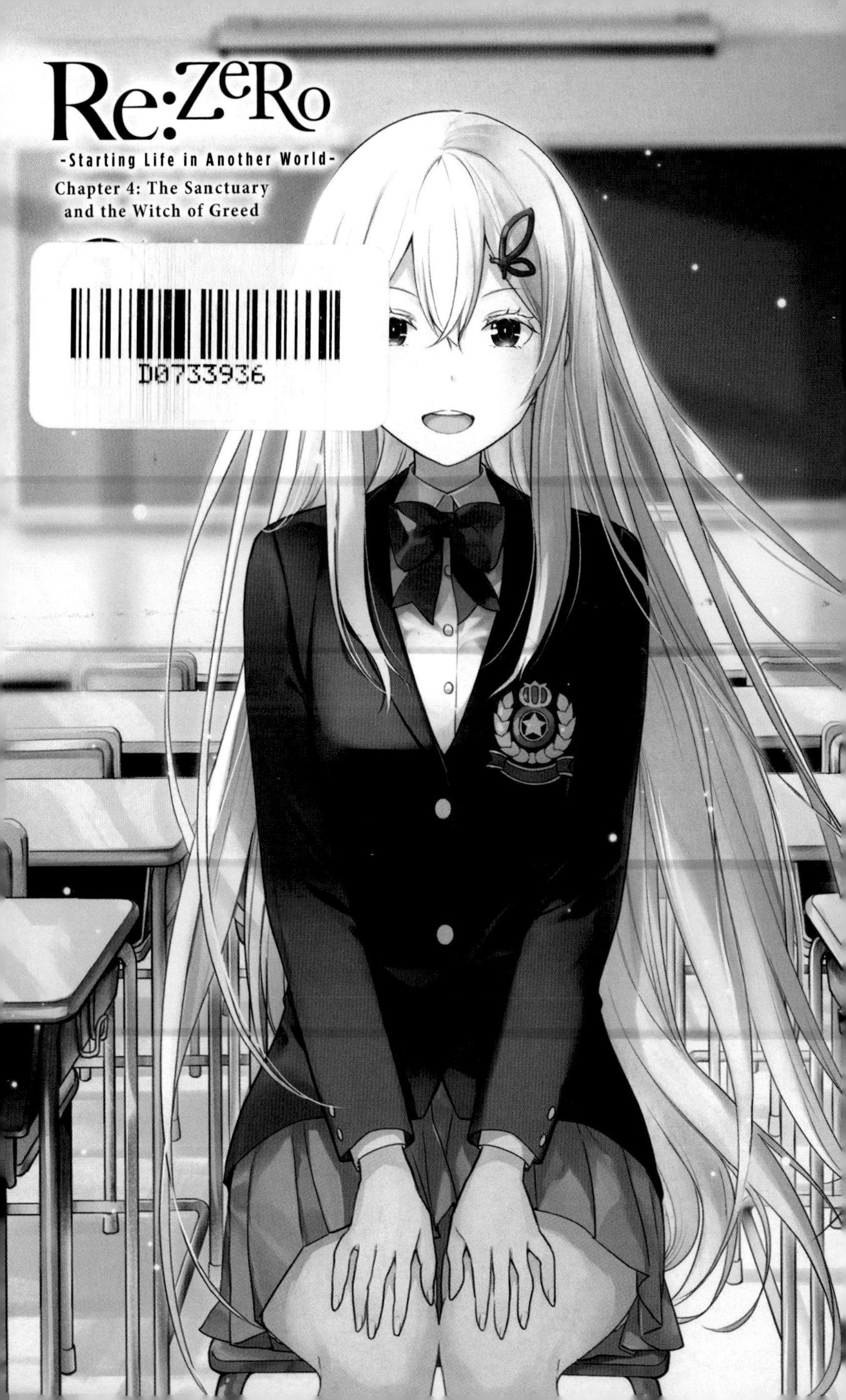

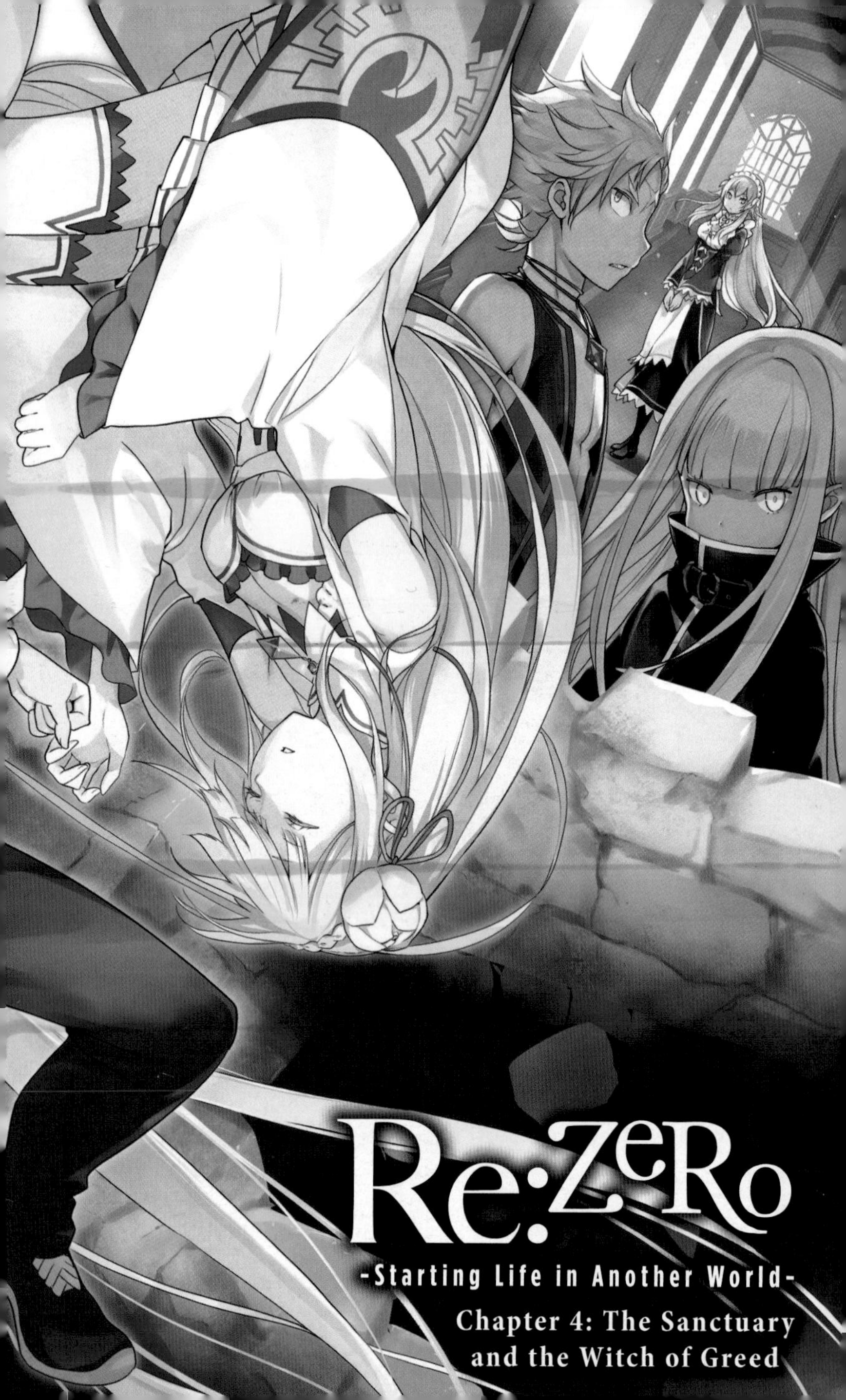
Re:ZeRo
-Starting Life in Another World-
Chapter 4: The Sanctuary and the Witch of Greed

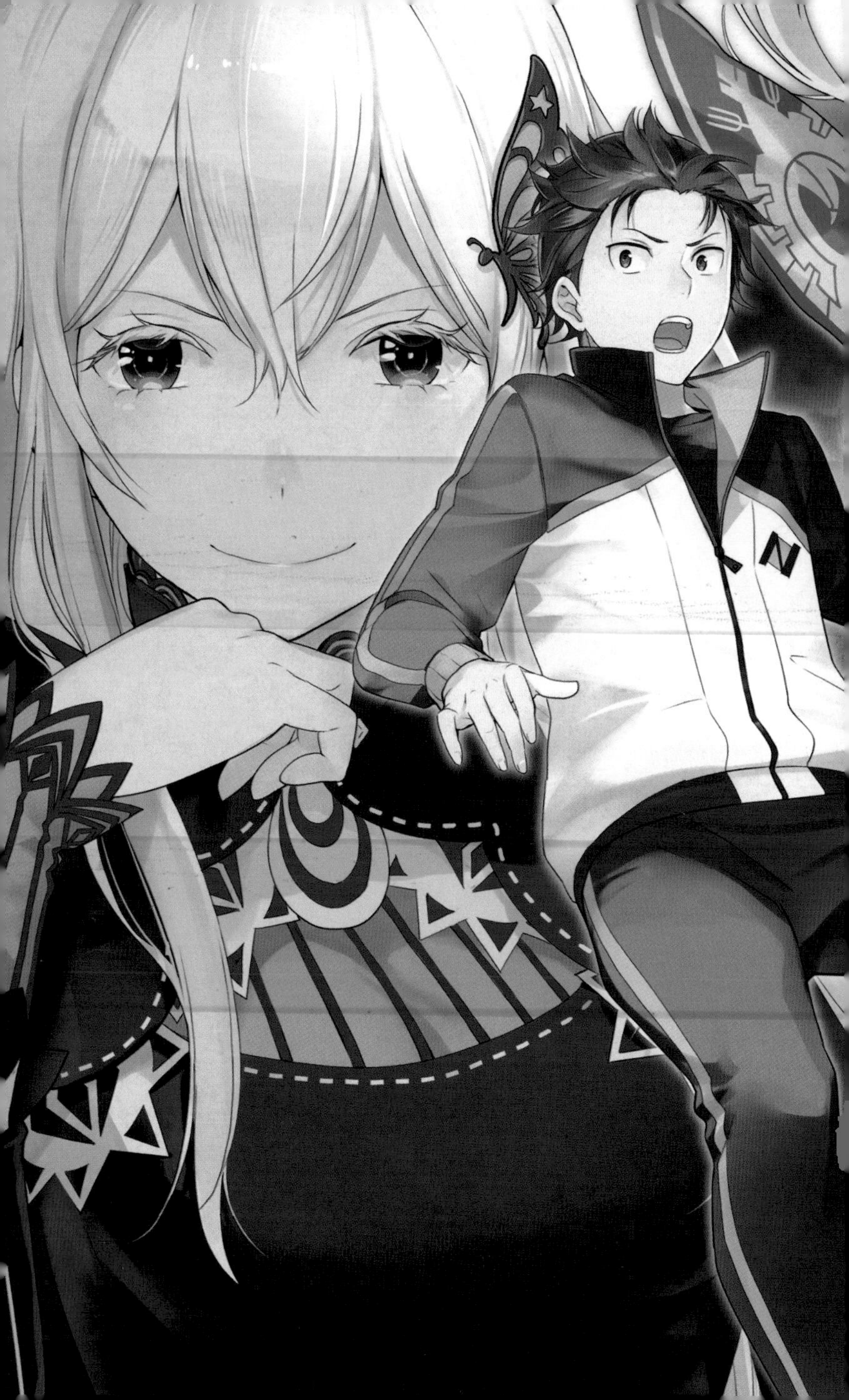

CONTENTS

Re:ZeRo

-Starting Life in Another World-

Chapter 4: The Sanctuary
and the Witch of Greed

SUMMARY

On the way back from a convenience store, high school student Subaru Natsuki was suddenly summoned to another world.
The one ability the powerless boy gains is Return by Death, rewinding time upon his demise.
He strives to use this power for the happiness of those close to him.

When the barrier protecting the Sanctuary activates, Subaru has an unexpected encounter with Echidna, the Witch of Greed.

Faltering before her bizarre sense of presence, he sits at her so-called Tea Party, hearing about the Sanctuary and the Witch, and receiving a particular "souvenir" before returning safe and sound.

Along the way, he encounters the very Garfiel that Frederica told him to be wary of, but Emilia and company safely enter the Sanctuary, and Subaru is reunited with Ram and the rest of the residents of Earlham Village. Afterward, Roswaal explains the situation in the Sanctuary, circumstances no one could have expected ——

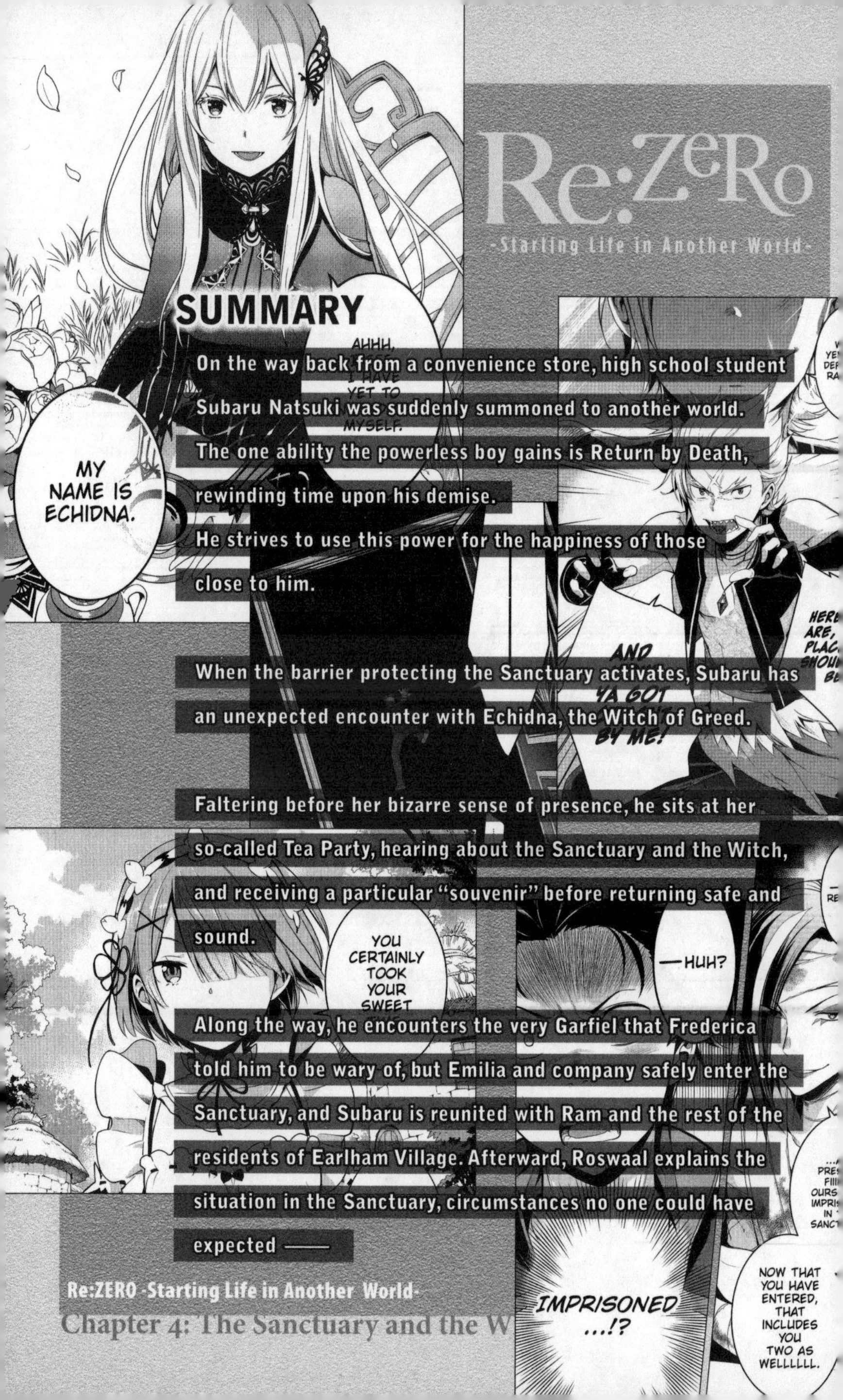
Re:ZeRo
-Starting Life in Another World-
MY NAME IS ECHIDNA.
—HUH?
NOW THAT YOU HAVE ENTERED, THAT INCLUDES YOU TWO AS WELLLLLL.
IMPRISONED ...!?
Re:ZERO -Starting Life in Another World-
Chapter 4: The Sanctuary and the W

CHARACTERS

Re:ZERO –Starting Life in Another World–

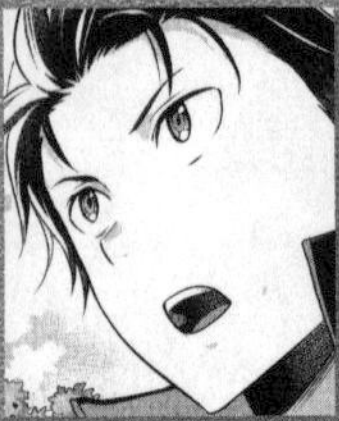

Subaru Natsuki

Modern Japanese boy transported to another world. Strives to use his only power, Return by Death, for the sake of those close to him.

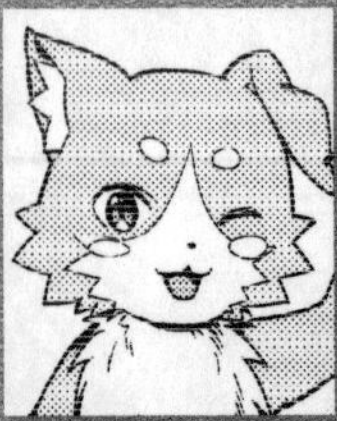

Puck

Spirit in cat form acting in concert with Emilia, who watches over her like a parent. In contrast to his appearance, he wields very powerful magic.

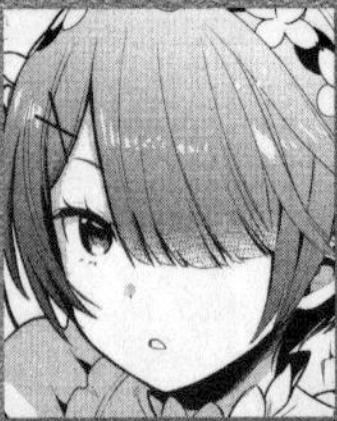

Ram

As a maid of Roswaal Manor, she runs the mansion alongside her twin sister, Rem. She is arrogant and foul-mouthed, but her gentle disposition runs deep.

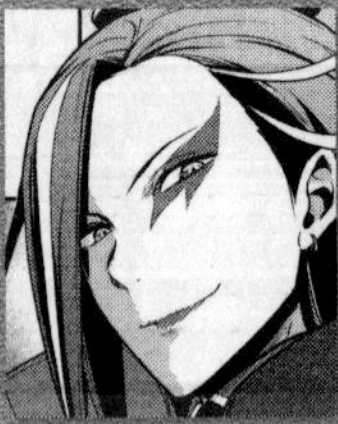

Roswaal L. Mathers

Holds the title of Marquis. Upper-ranking noble of the Kingdom of Lugunica. Sponsor of Emilia in the royal selection. A famous eccentric, he wears clown-like makeup and bizarre outfits.

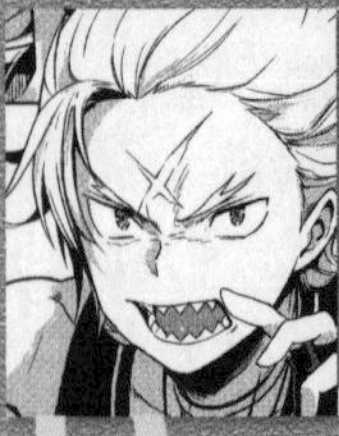

Garfiel Tinzel

A young man with a foul look, sharp fangs, and a short temper and barbaric personality to match. The limit of his combat ability is unknown, but he can easily hurl a land dragon weighing hundreds of kilograms.

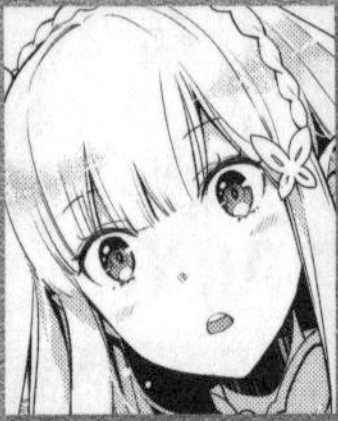

Emilia

Beautiful half-elf girl. Spirit mage served by the cat-form spirit Puck, one of those seeking to become the next Queen of Lugunica.

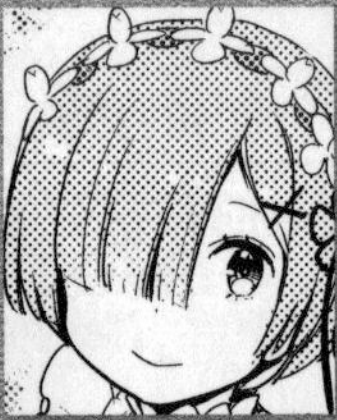

Rem

Demon girl working as a maid at Roswaal Manor where Emilia resides. After the battle with the Witch Cult's Archbishop, she vanished from the memories of others and became a so-called Sleeping Princess.

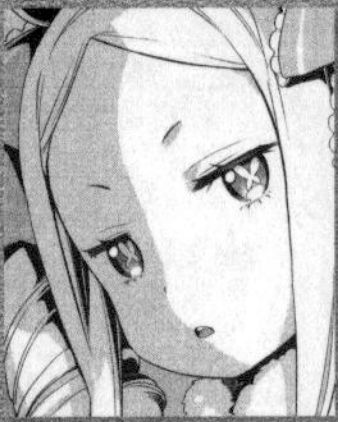

Beatrice

Calls herself the Librarian of the Archive of Forbidden Books at Roswaal Manor. A girl wearing an extravagant dress, she is an exceptionally high-end user of Dark Magic, allowing her to move freely throughout the mansion.

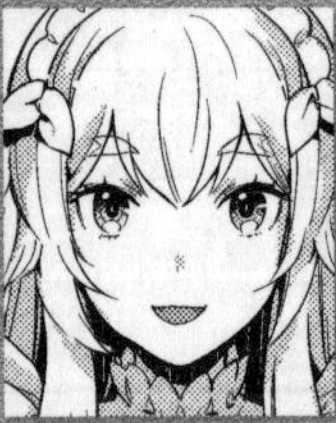

Frederica Baumann

Eldest maid of Roswaal Manor. Formerly on leave for personal reasons, she was summoned back by Ram.

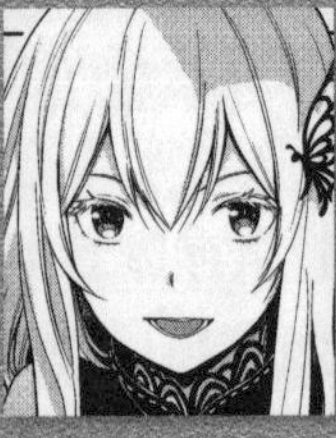

Echidna

One of the seven Witches, dubbed the Witch of Greed for craving all of the knowledge of the world. Destroyed by the Witch of Jealousy, her soul is presently captive in the Sanctuary's tomb.

Re:ZeRo -Starting Life in Another World-

Chapter 4: The Sanctuary and the Witch of Greed

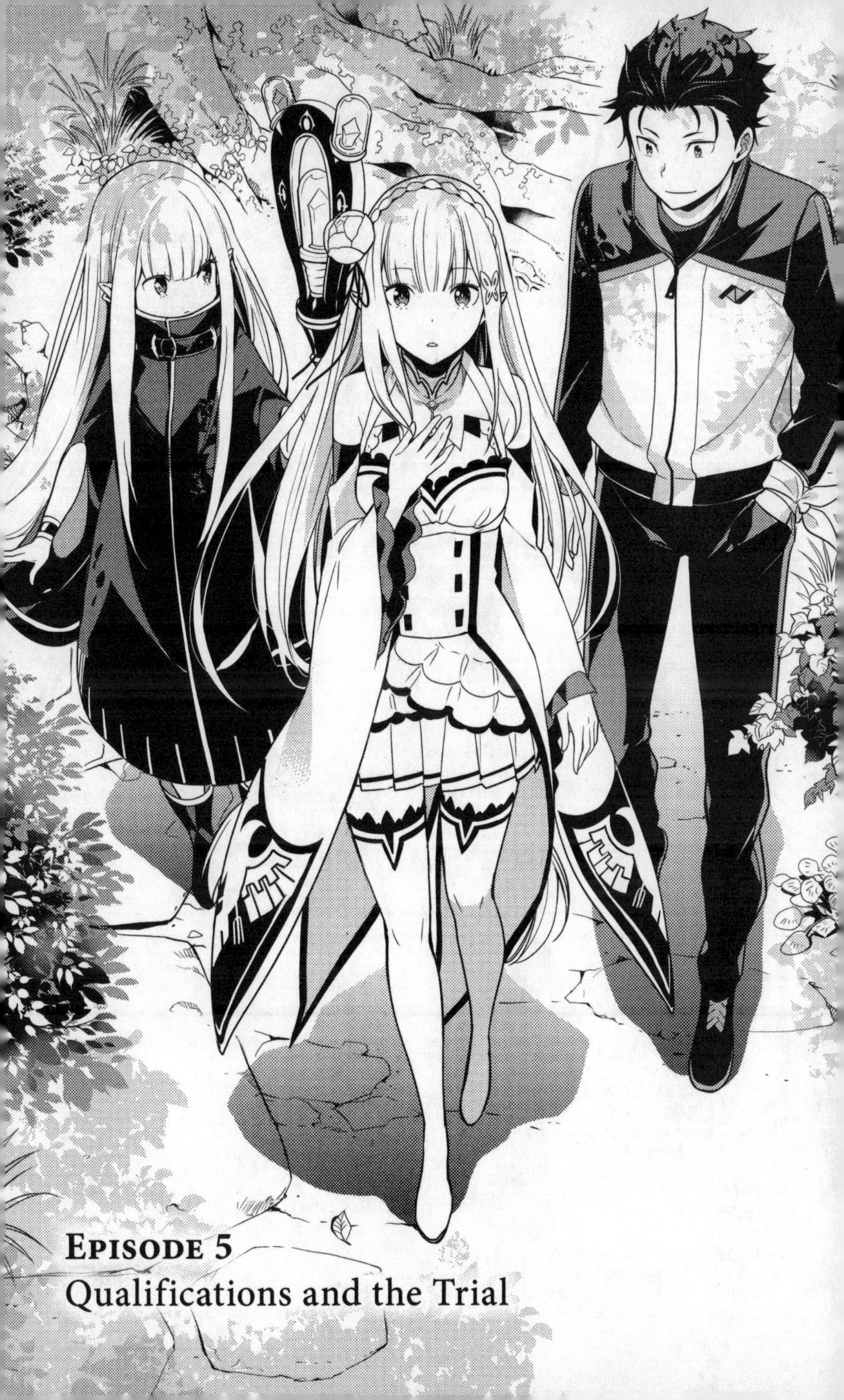

Episode 5
Qualifications and the Trial

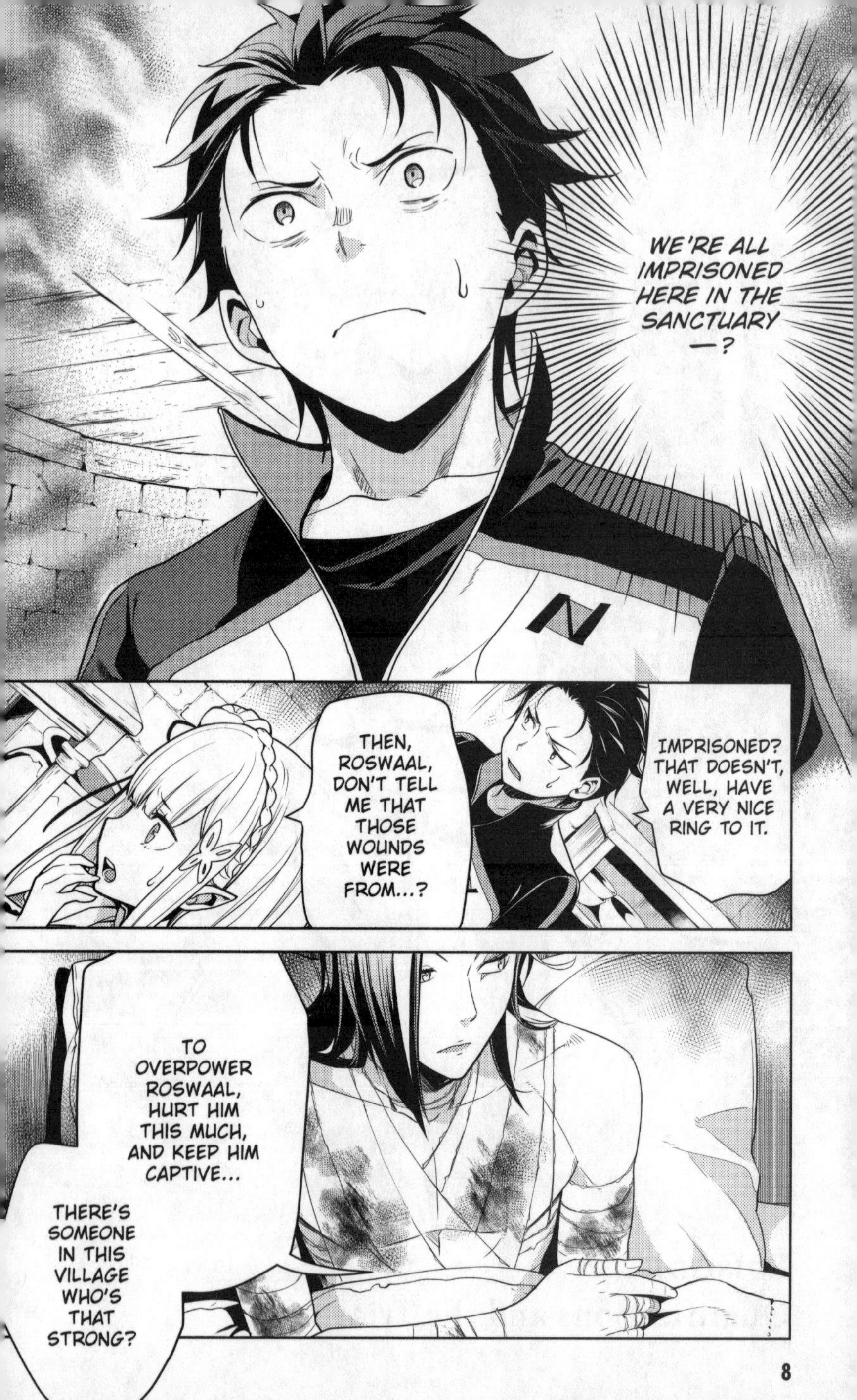
WE'RE ALL IMPRISONED HERE IN THE SANCTUARY —?
IMPRISONED? THAT DOESN'T, WELL, HAVE A VERY NICE RING TO IT.
THEN, ROSWAAL, DON'T TELL ME THAT THOSE WOUNDS WERE FROM...?
TO OVERPOWER ROSWAAL, HURT HIM THIS MUCH, AND KEEP HIM CAPTIVE...
THERE'S SOMEONE IN THIS VILLAGE WHO'S THAT STRONG?

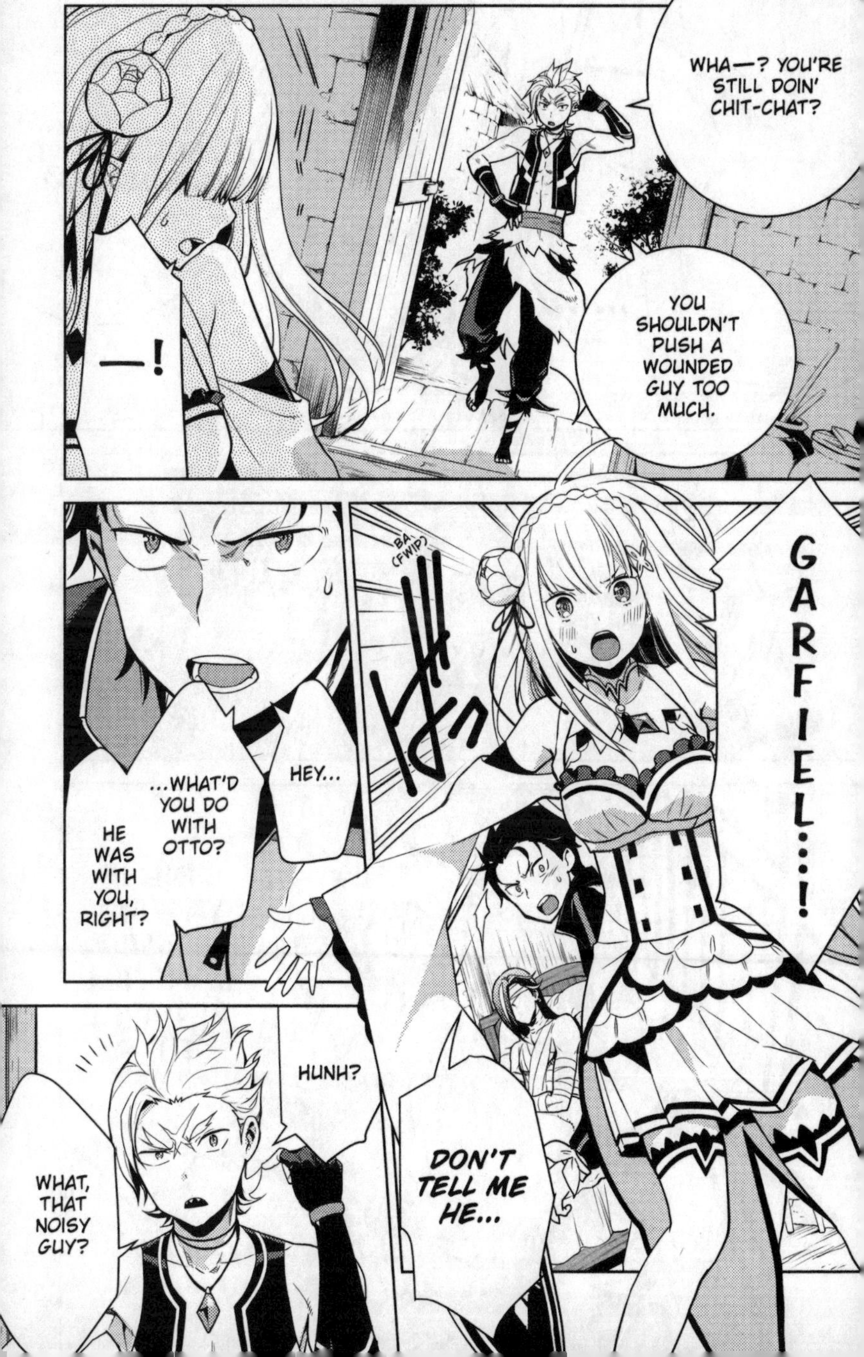
WHA—? YOU'RE STILL DOIN' CHIT-CHAT?
YOU SHOULDN'T PUSH A WOUNDED GUY TOO MUCH.
—!
GARFIEL...!
BA (FWIP)
HEY...
...WHAT'D YOU DO WITH OTTO?
HE WAS WITH YOU, RIGHT?
DON'T TELL ME HE...
HUNH?
WHAT, THAT NOISY GUY?

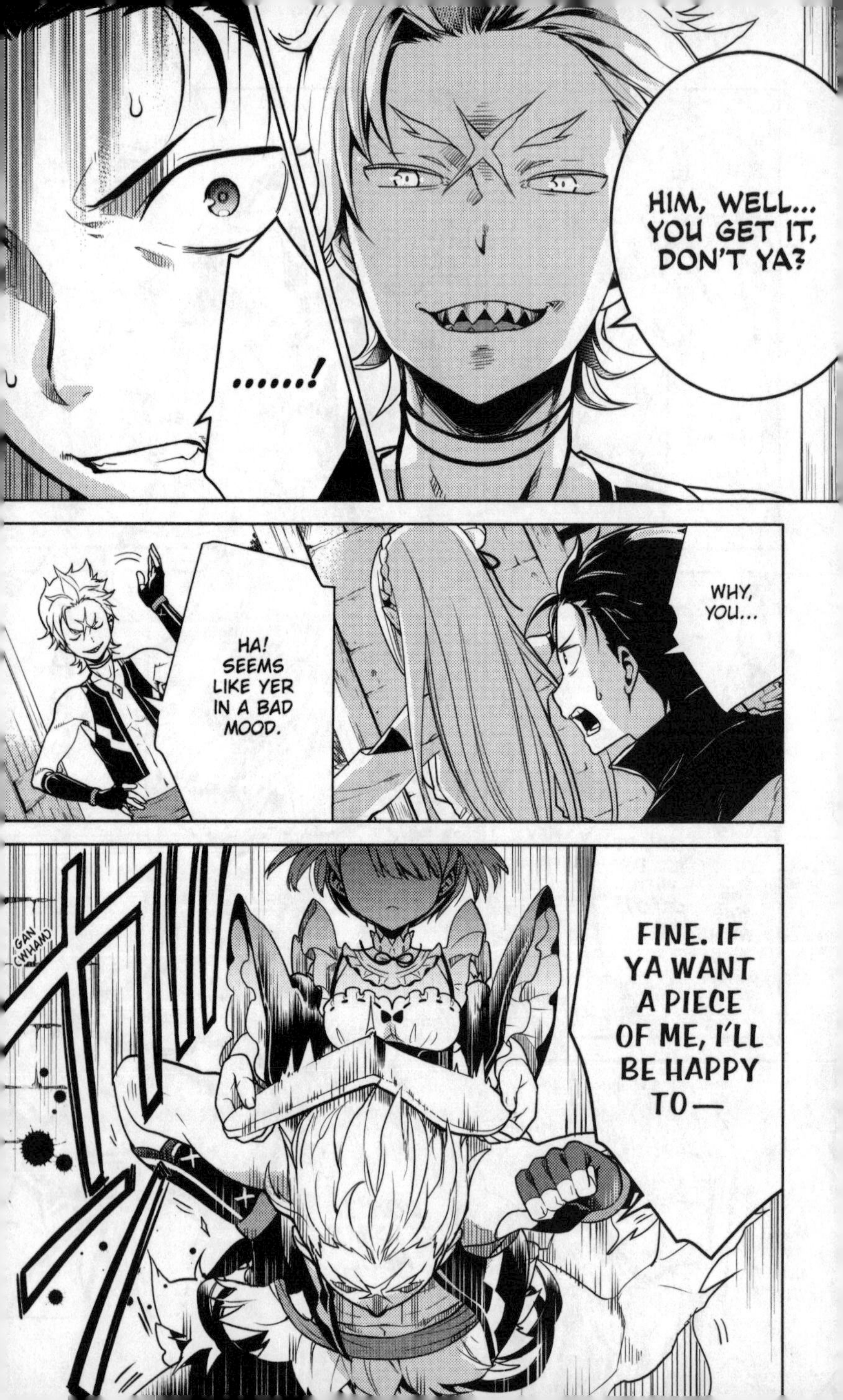
HIM, WELL... YOU GET IT, DON'T YA?
......!
WHY, YOU...
HA! SEEMS LIKE YER IN A BAD MOOD.
FINE. IF YA WANT A PIECE OF ME, I'LL BE HAPPY TO—
GAN (WHAM)

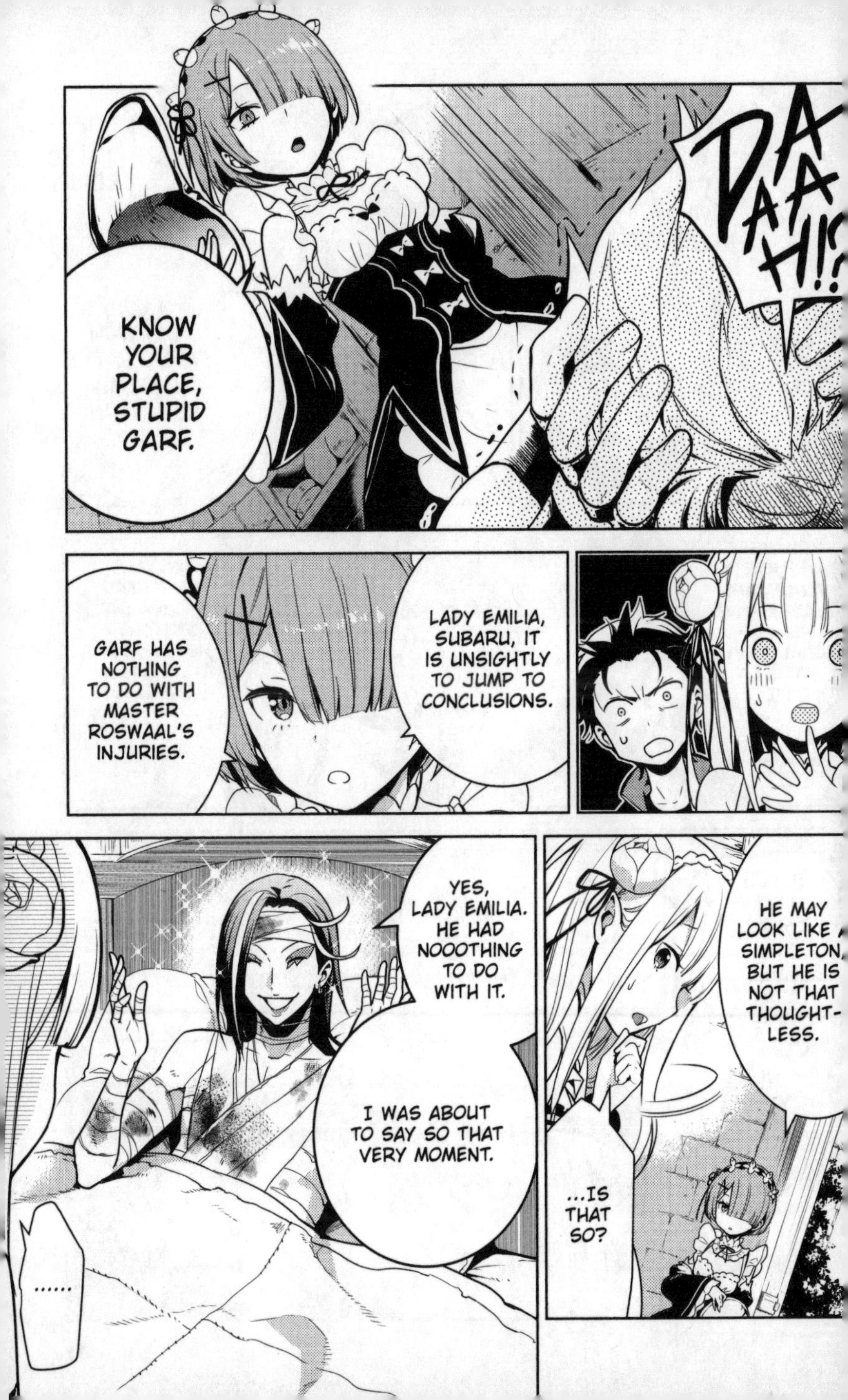
DAAAH!?
KNOW YOUR PLACE, STUPID GARF.
LADY EMILIA, SUBARU, IT IS UNSIGHTLY TO JUMP TO CONCLUSIONS.
GARF HAS NOTHING TO DO WITH MASTER ROSWAAL'S INJURIES.
HE MAY LOOK LIKE A SIMPLETON, BUT HE IS NOT THAT THOUGHTLESS.
...IS THAT SO?
YES, LADY EMILIA. HE HAD NOOOTHING TO DO WITH IT.
I WAS ABOUT TO SAY SO THAT VERY MOMENT.
......

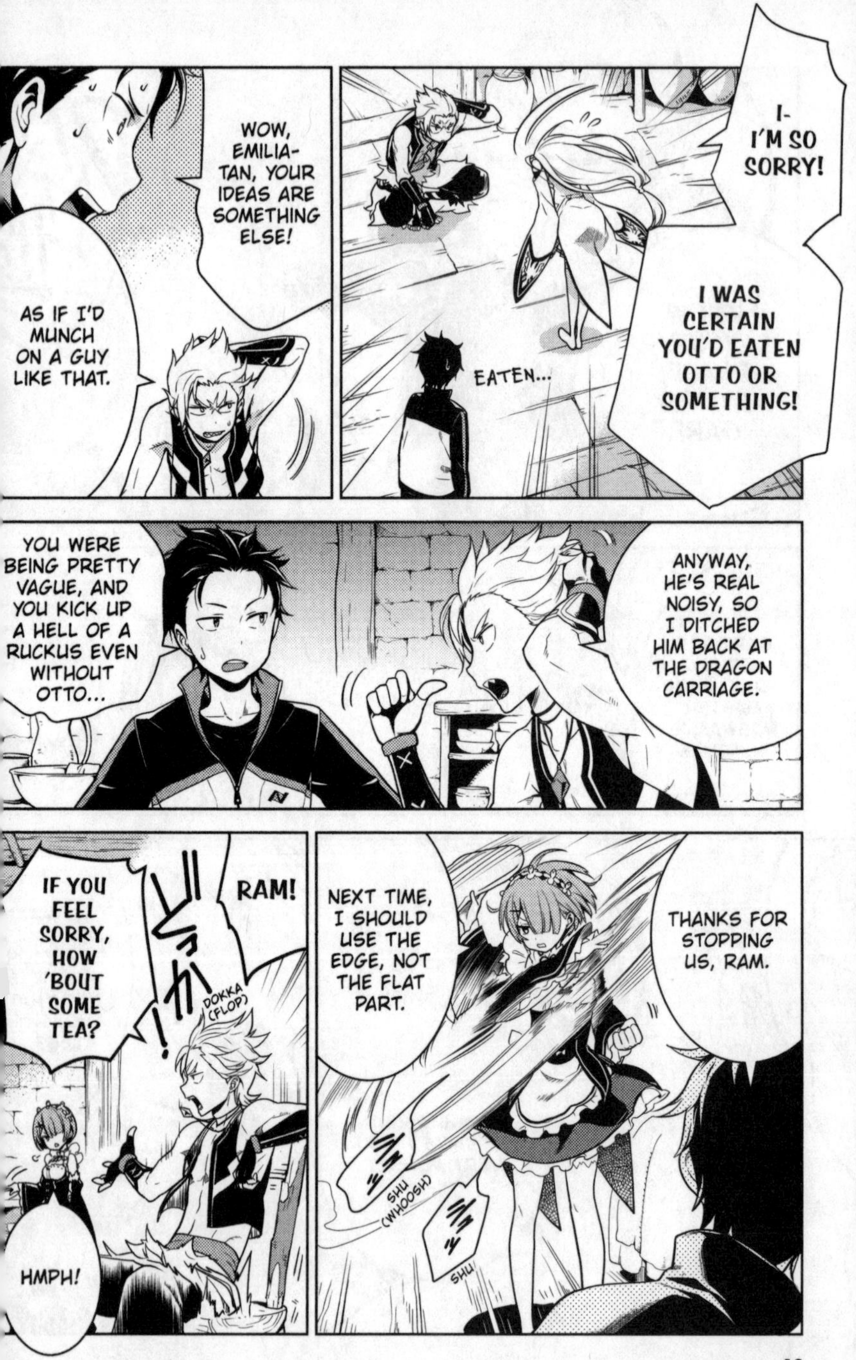
I- I'M SO SORRY!
I WAS CERTAIN YOU'D EATEN OTTO OR SOMETHING!
EATEN...
WOW, EMILIA-TAN, YOUR IDEAS ARE SOMETHING ELSE!
AS IF I'D MUNCH ON A GUY LIKE THAT.
ANYWAY, HE'S REAL NOISY, SO I DITCHED HIM BACK AT THE DRAGON CARRIAGE.
YOU WERE BEING PRETTY VAGUE, AND YOU KICK UP A HELL OF A RUCKUS EVEN WITHOUT OTTO...
THANKS FOR STOPPING US, RAM.
NEXT TIME, I SHOULD USE THE EDGE, NOT THE FLAT PART.
SHU (WHOOSH)
SHU
RAM!
DOKKA (FLOP)
IF YOU FEEL SORRY, HOW 'BOUT SOME TEA?
HMPH!

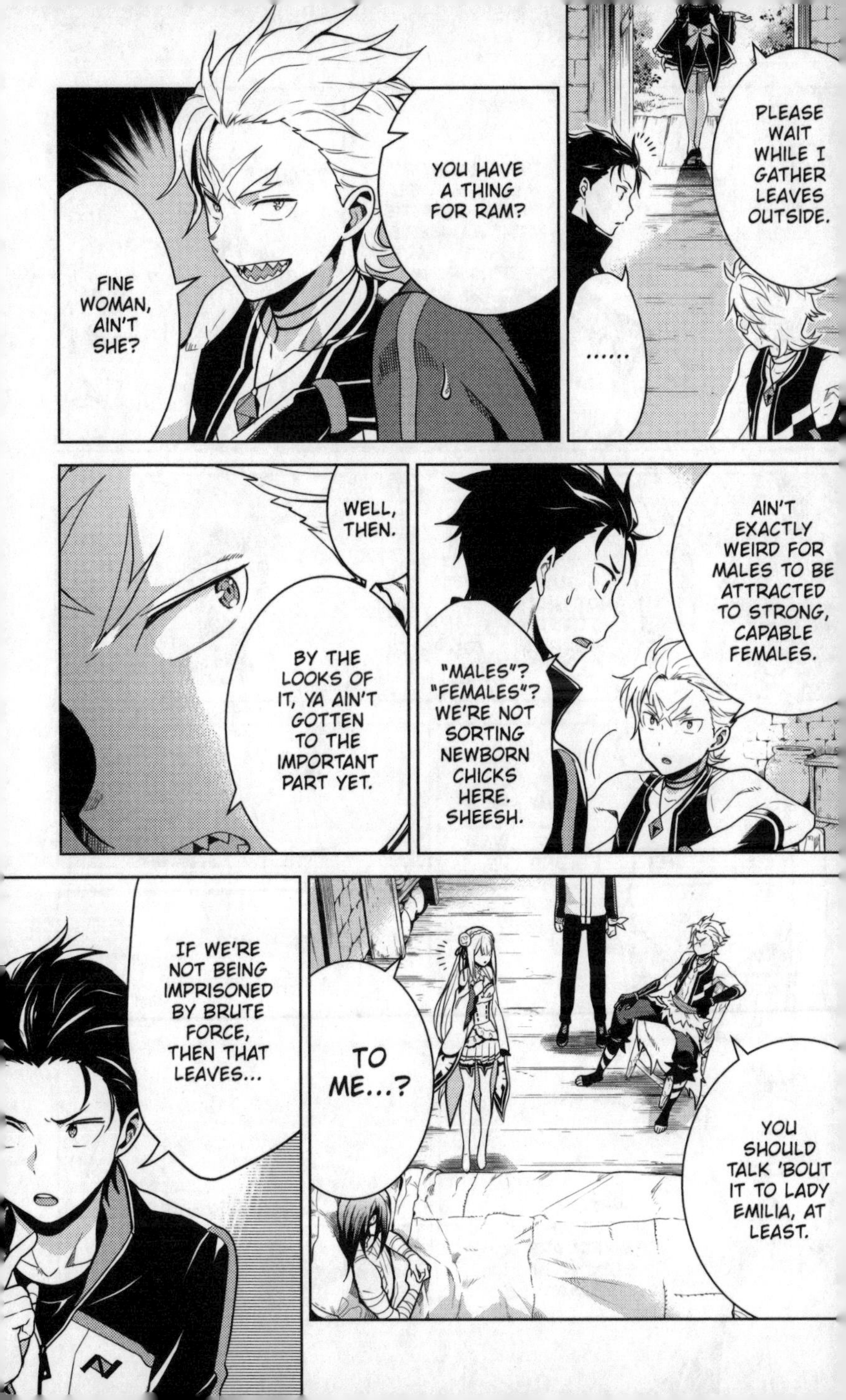

PLEASE WAIT WHILE I GATHER LEAVES OUTSIDE.
......
YOU HAVE A THING FOR RAM?
FINE WOMAN, AIN'T SHE?
AIN'T EXACTLY WEIRD FOR MALES TO BE ATTRACTED TO STRONG, CAPABLE FEMALES.
"MALES"? "FEMALES"? WE'RE NOT SORTING NEWBORN CHICKS HERE. SHEESH.
WELL, THEN.
BY THE LOOKS OF IT, YA AIN'T GOTTEN TO THE IMPORTANT PART YET.
YOU SHOULD TALK 'BOUT IT TO LADY EMILIA, AT LEAST.
TO ME...?
IF WE'RE NOT BEING IMPRISONED BY BRUTE FORCE, THEN THAT LEAVES...

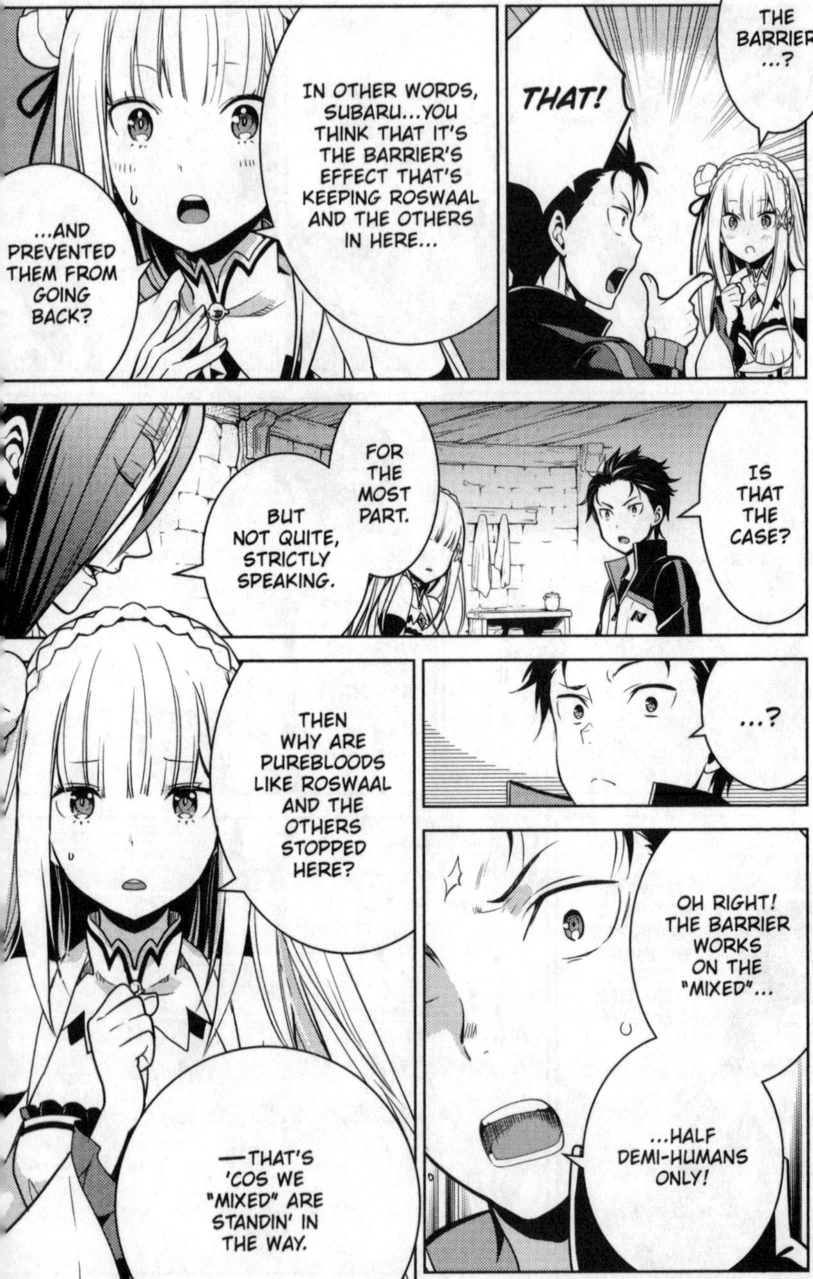
THE BARRIER ...?
THAT!
IN OTHER WORDS, SUBARU...YOU THINK THAT IT'S THE BARRIER'S EFFECT THAT'S KEEPING ROSWAAL AND THE OTHERS IN HERE...
...AND PREVENTED THEM FROM GOING BACK?
IS THAT THE CASE?
FOR THE MOST PART.
BUT NOT QUITE, STRICTLY SPEAKING.
...?
OH RIGHT! THE BARRIER WORKS ON THE "MIXED"...
...HALF DEMI-HUMANS ONLY!
THEN WHY ARE PUREBLOODS LIKE ROSWAAL AND THE OTHERS STOPPED HERE?
—THAT'S 'COS WE "MIXED" ARE STANDIN' IN THE WAY.

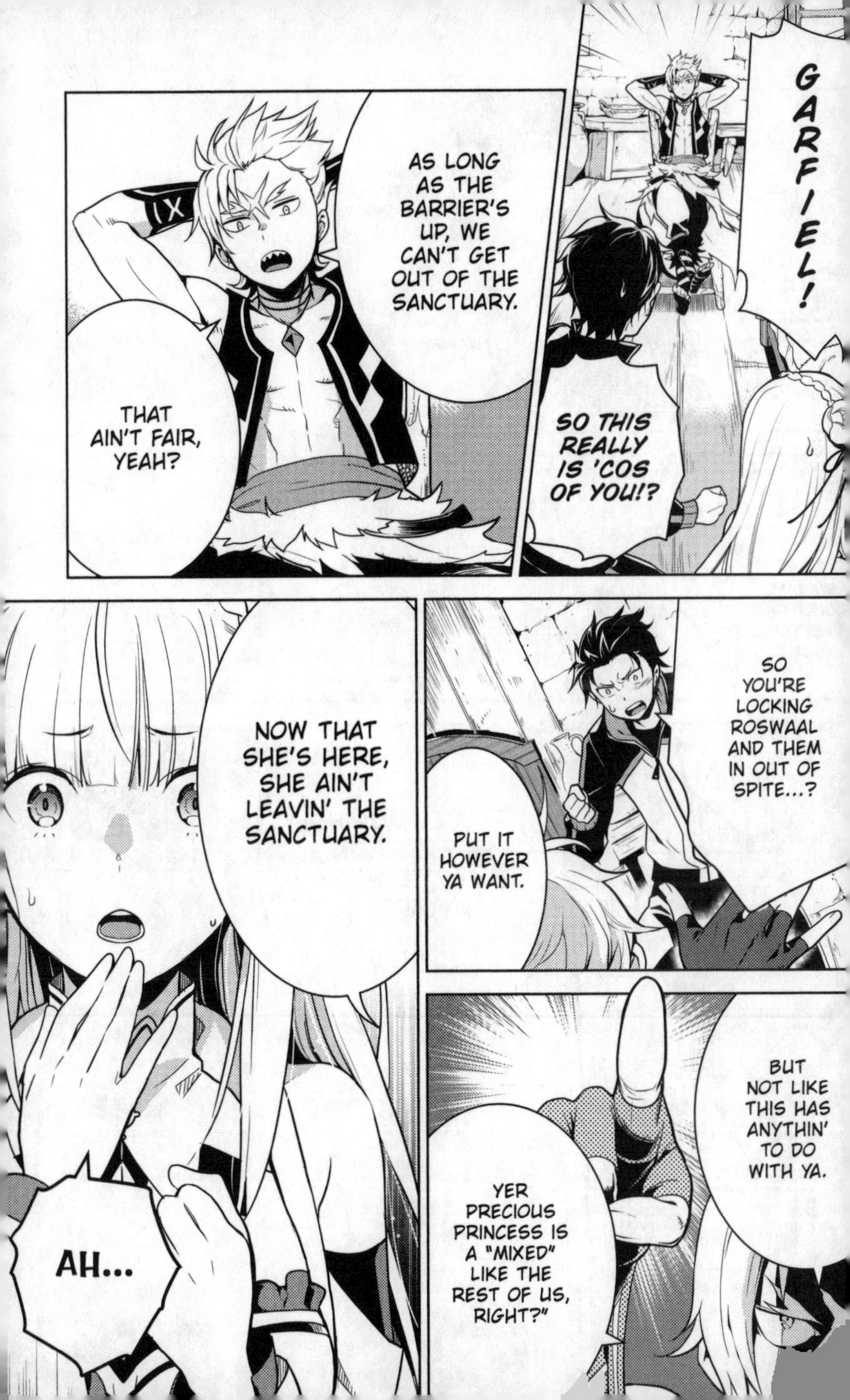
GARFIEL!
SO THIS REALLY IS 'COS OF YOU!?
AS LONG AS THE BARRIER'S UP, WE CAN'T GET OUT OF THE SANCTUARY.
THAT AIN'T FAIR, YEAH?
SO YOU'RE LOCKING ROSWAAL AND THEM IN OUT OF SPITE...?
PUT IT HOWEVER YA WANT.
BUT NOT LIKE THIS HAS ANYTHIN' TO DO WITH YA.
YER PRECIOUS PRINCESS IS A "MIXED" LIKE THE REST OF US, RIGHT?"
NOW THAT SHE'S HERE, SHE AIN'T LEAVIN' THE SANCTUARY.
AH...

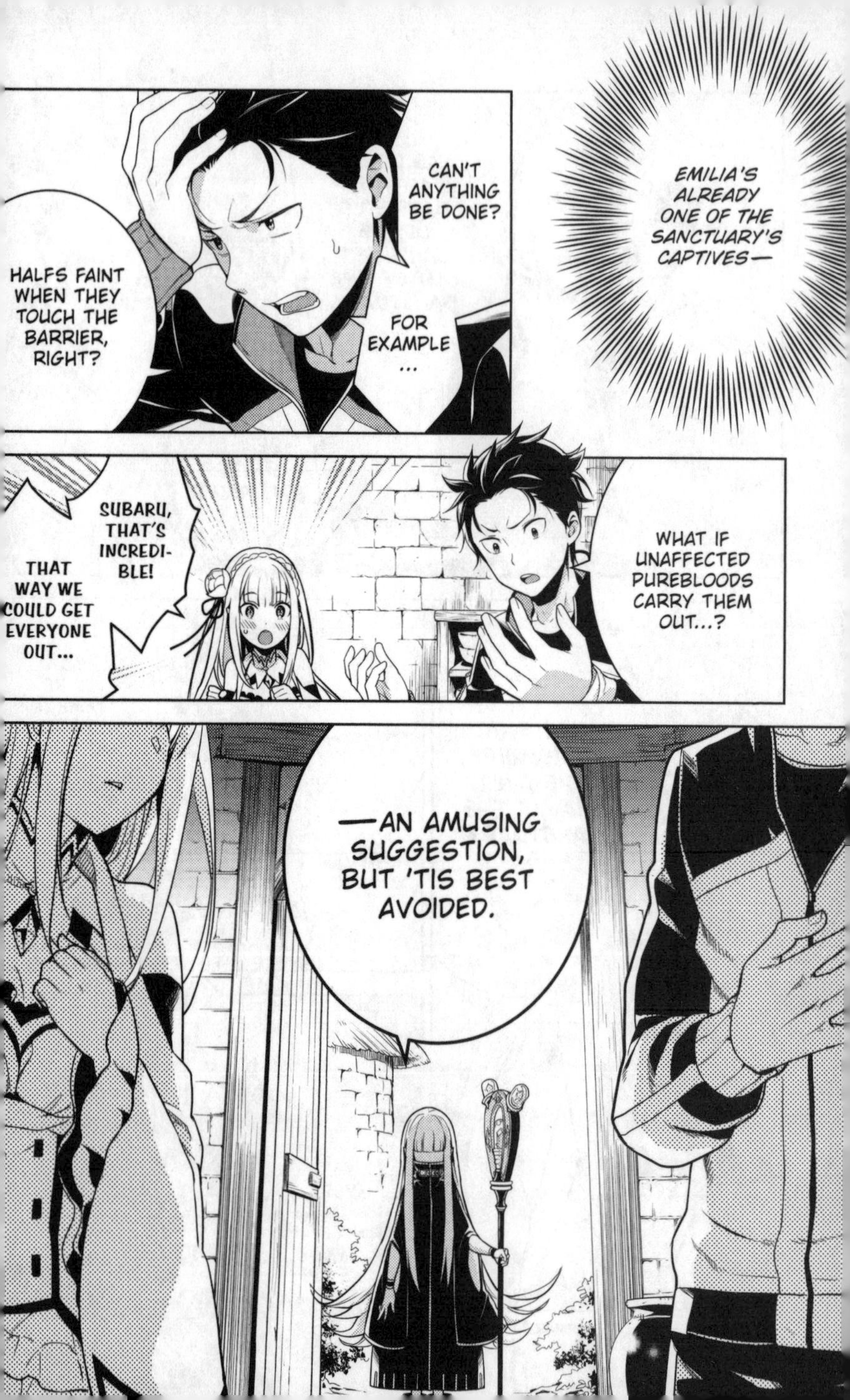
EMILIA'S ALREADY ONE OF THE SANCTUARY'S CAPTIVES—
CAN'T ANYTHING BE DONE?
FOR EXAMPLE...
HALFS FAINT WHEN THEY TOUCH THE BARRIER, RIGHT?
WHAT IF UNAFFECTED PUREBLOODS CARRY THEM OUT...?
SUBARU, THAT'S INCREDI-BLE!
THAT WAY WE COULD GET EVERYONE OUT...
—AN AMUSING SUGGESTION, BUT 'TIS BEST AVOIDED.

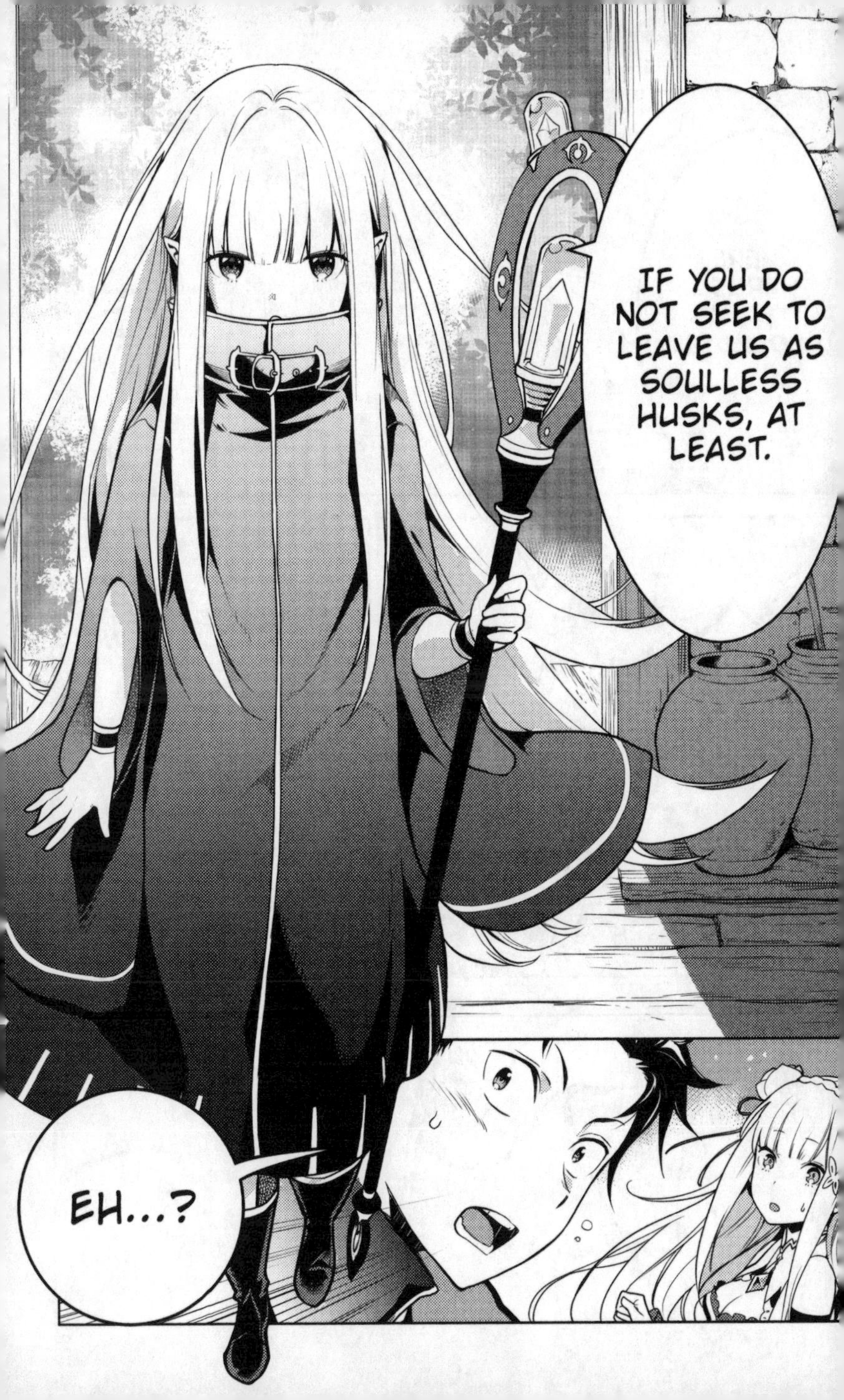
IF YOU DO NOT SEEK TO LEAVE US AS SOULLESS HUSKS, AT LEAST.
EH...?

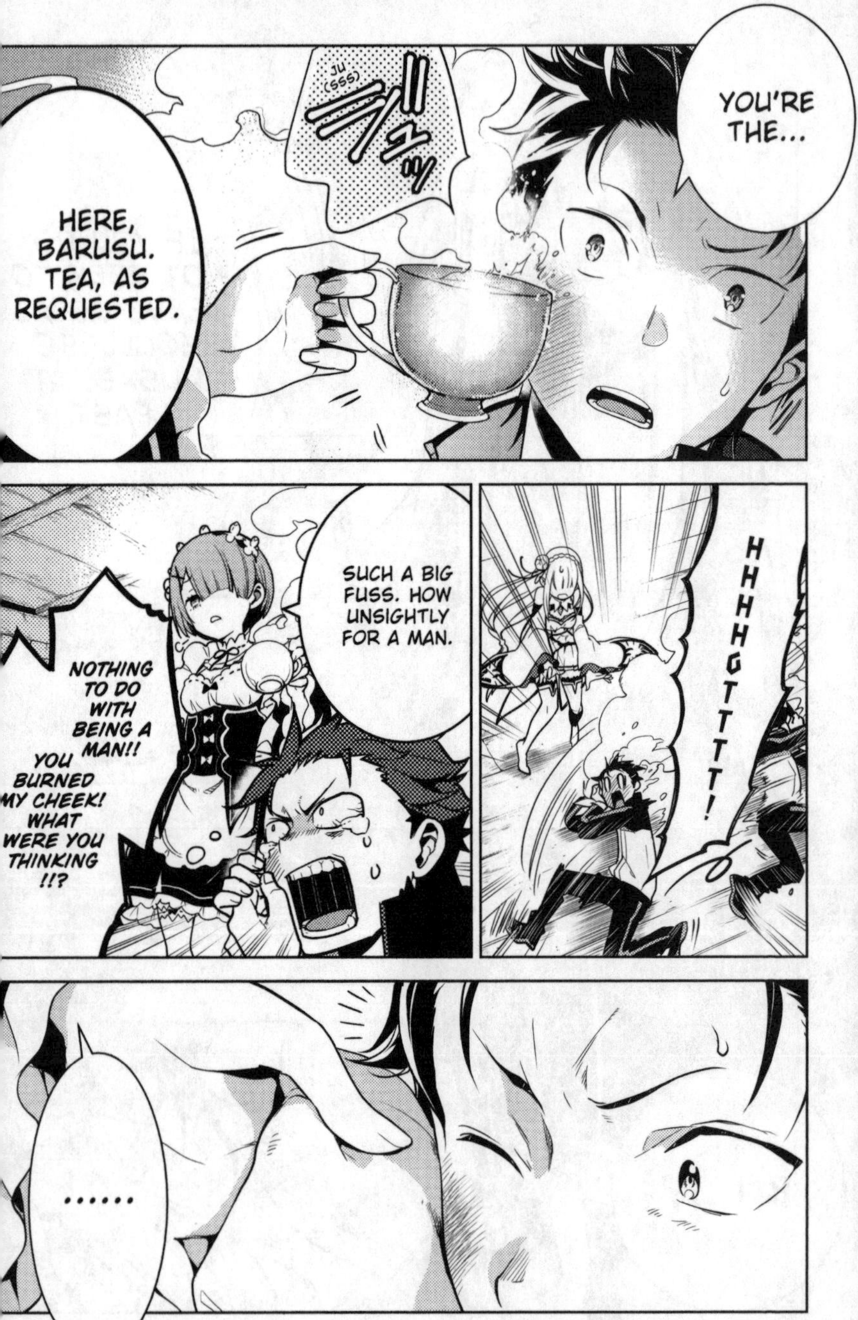
YOU'RE THE...
JU (SSS)
HERE, BARUSU. TEA, AS REQUESTED.
HHHHGTTTT!
SUCH A BIG FUSS. HOW UNSIGHTLY FOR A MAN.
NOTHING TO DO WITH BEING A MAN!! YOU BURNED MY CHEEK! WHAT WERE YOU THINKING!!?
......

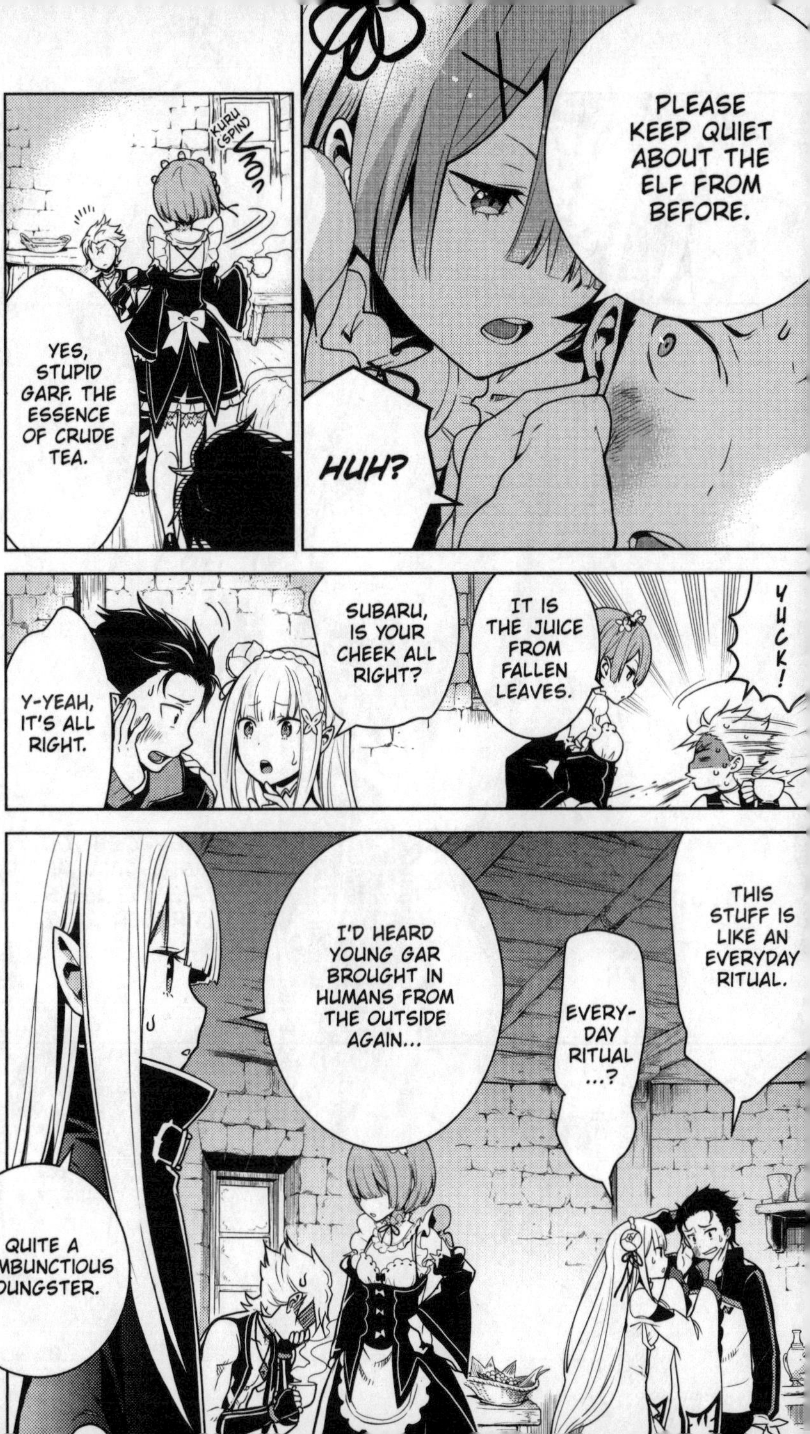
PLEASE KEEP QUIET ABOUT THE ELF FROM BEFORE.
HUH?
KURU (SPIN)
YES, STUPID GARF. THE ESSENCE OF CRUDE TEA.
YUCK!
IT IS THE JUICE FROM FALLEN LEAVES.
SUBARU, IS YOUR CHEEK ALL RIGHT?
Y-YEAH, IT'S ALL RIGHT.
THIS STUFF IS LIKE AN EVERYDAY RITUAL.
EVERY-DAY RITUAL ...?
I'D HEARD YOUNG GAR BROUGHT IN HUMANS FROM THE OUTSIDE AGAIN...
QUITE A RAMBUNCTIOUS YOUNGSTER.

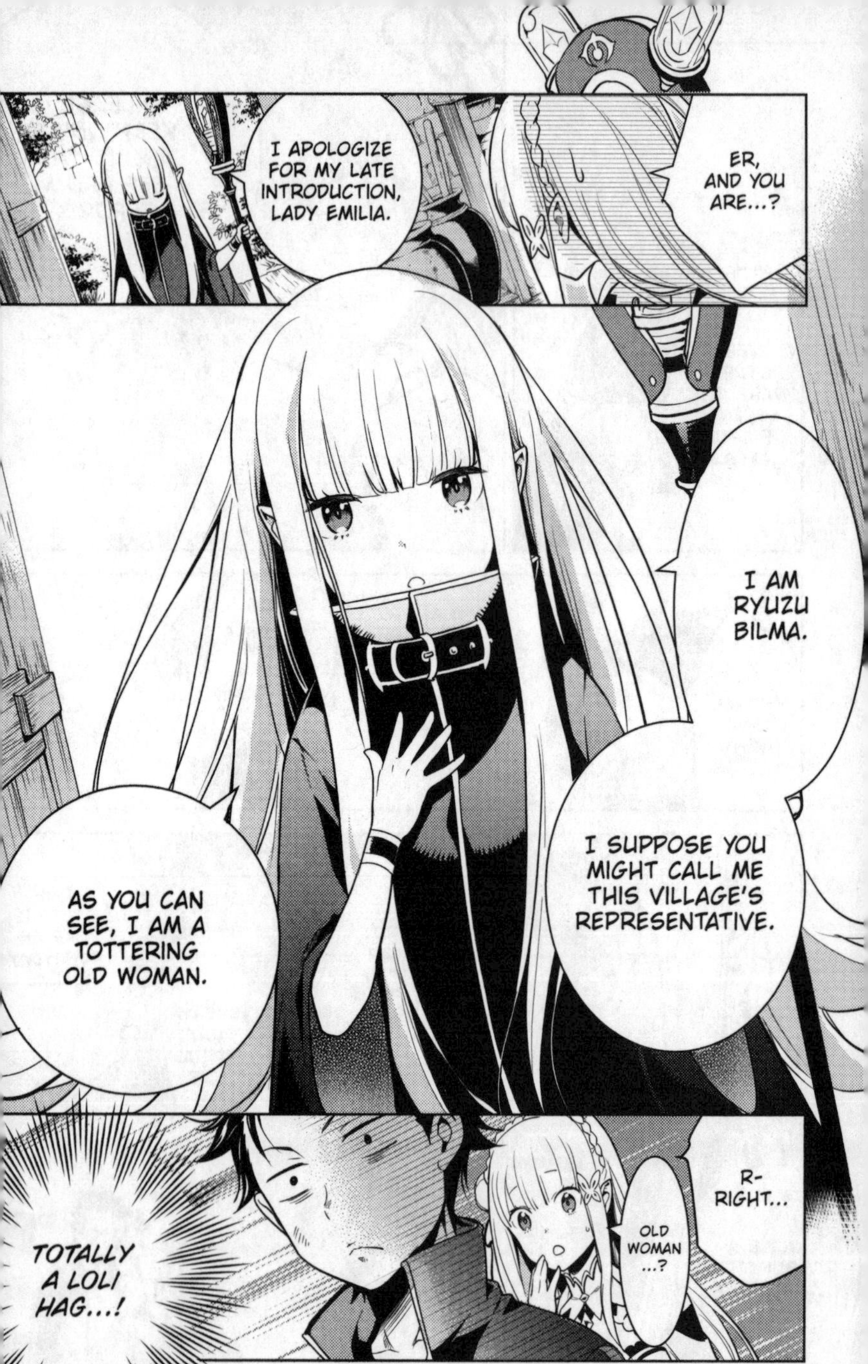
ER, AND YOU ARE...?
I APOLOGIZE FOR MY LATE INTRODUCTION, LADY EMILIA.
I AM RYUZU BILMA.
I SUPPOSE YOU MIGHT CALL ME THIS VILLAGE'S REPRESENTATIVE.
AS YOU CAN SEE, I AM A TOTTERING OLD WOMAN.
R-RIGHT...
OLD WOMAN ...?
TOTALLY A LOLI HAG...!

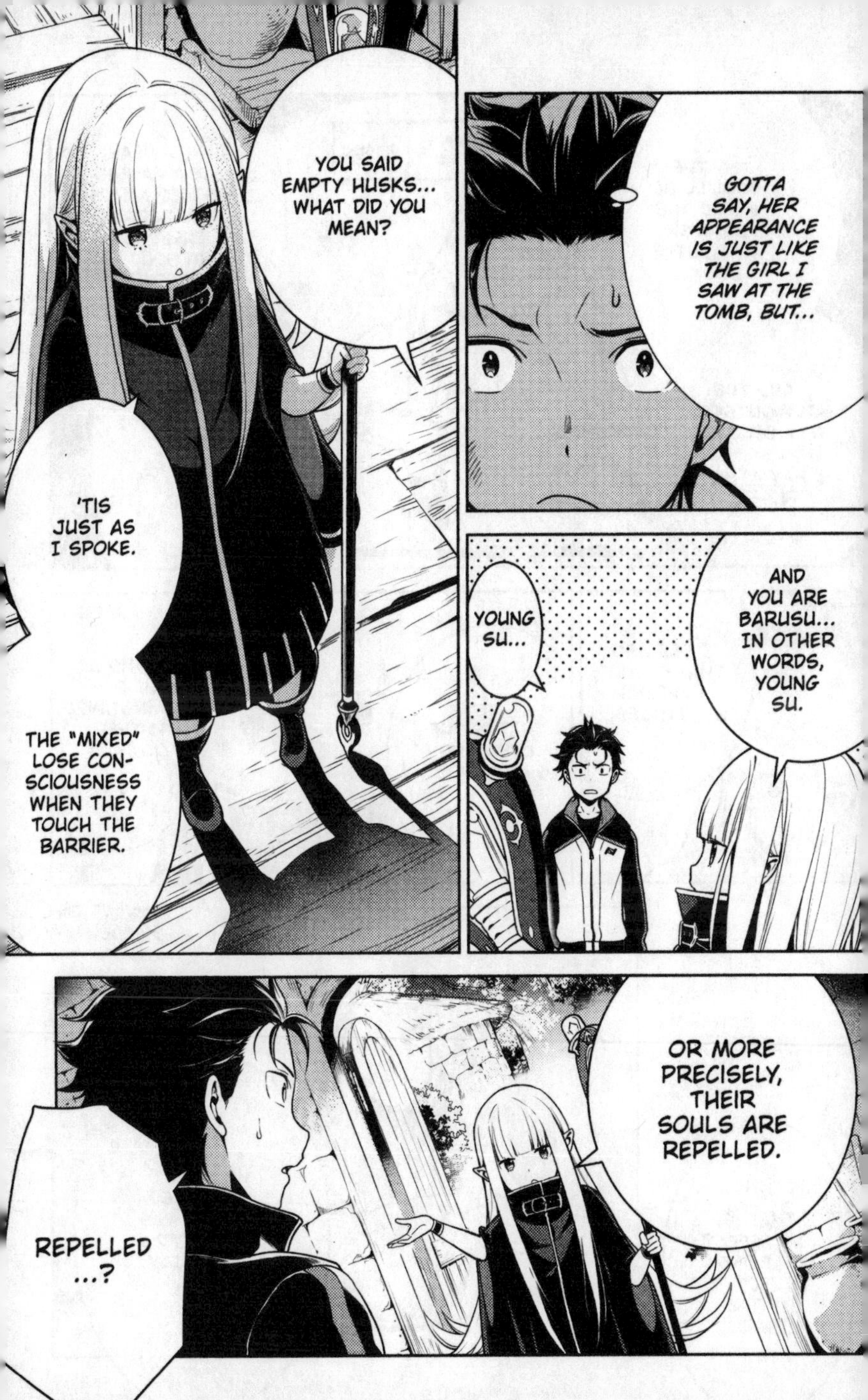
GOTTA SAY, HER APPEARANCE IS JUST LIKE THE GIRL I SAW AT THE TOMB, BUT...
AND YOU ARE BARUSU... IN OTHER WORDS, YOUNG SU.
YOUNG SU...
YOU SAID EMPTY HUSKS... WHAT DID YOU MEAN?
'TIS JUST AS I SPOKE.
THE "MIXED" LOSE CON-SCIOUSNESS WHEN THEY TOUCH THE BARRIER.
OR MORE PRECISELY, THEIR SOULS ARE REPELLED.
REPELLED ...?

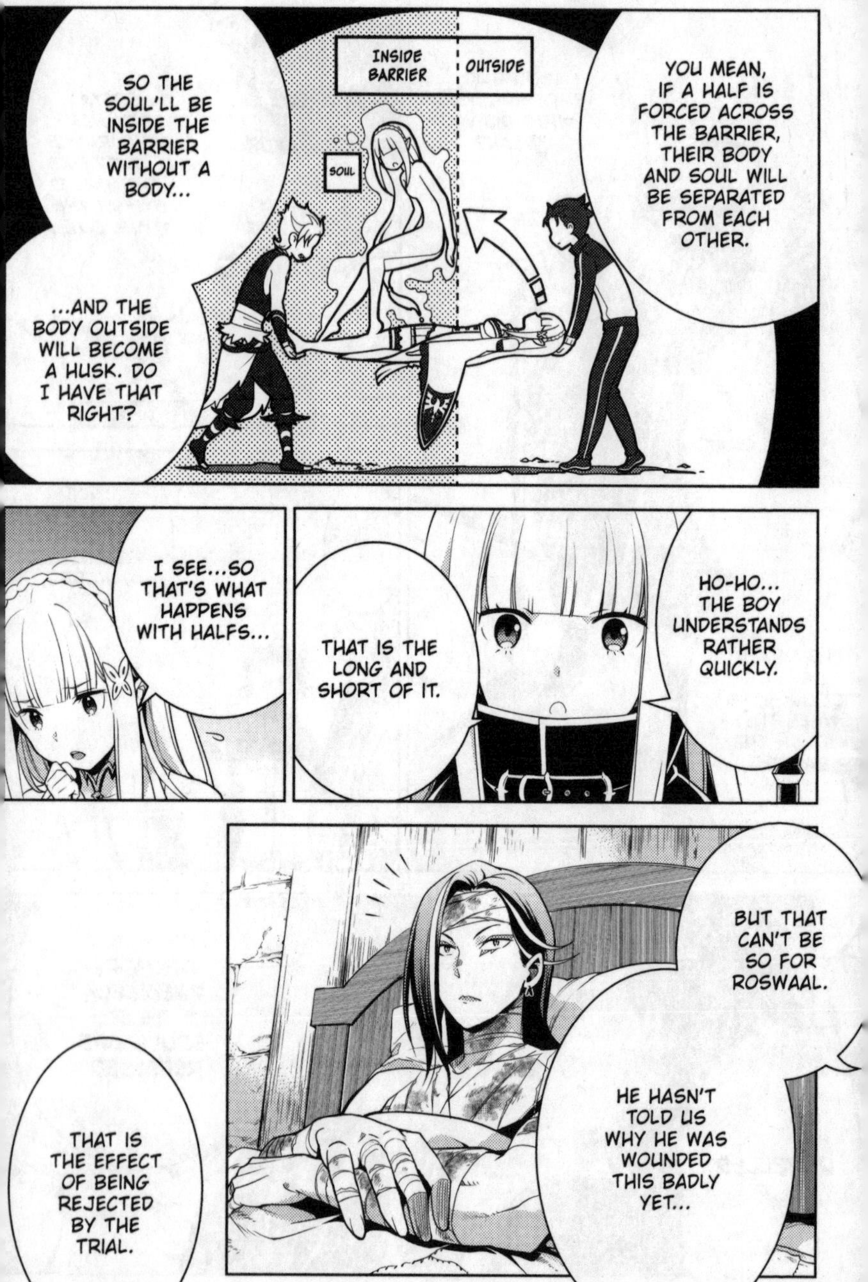
YOU MEAN, IF A HALF IS FORCED ACROSS THE BARRIER, THEIR BODY AND SOUL WILL BE SEPARATED FROM EACH OTHER.
OUTSIDE
INSIDE BARRIER
SOUL
SO THE SOUL'LL BE INSIDE THE BARRIER WITHOUT A BODY...
...AND THE BODY OUTSIDE WILL BECOME A HUSK. DO I HAVE THAT RIGHT?
HO-HO... THE BOY UNDERSTANDS RATHER QUICKLY.
THAT IS THE LONG AND SHORT OF IT.
I SEE...SO THAT'S WHAT HAPPENS WITH HALFS...
BUT THAT CAN'T BE SO FOR ROSWAAL.
HE HASN'T TOLD US WHY HE WAS WOUNDED THIS BADLY YET...
THAT IS THE EFFECT OF BEING REJECTED BY THE TRIAL.

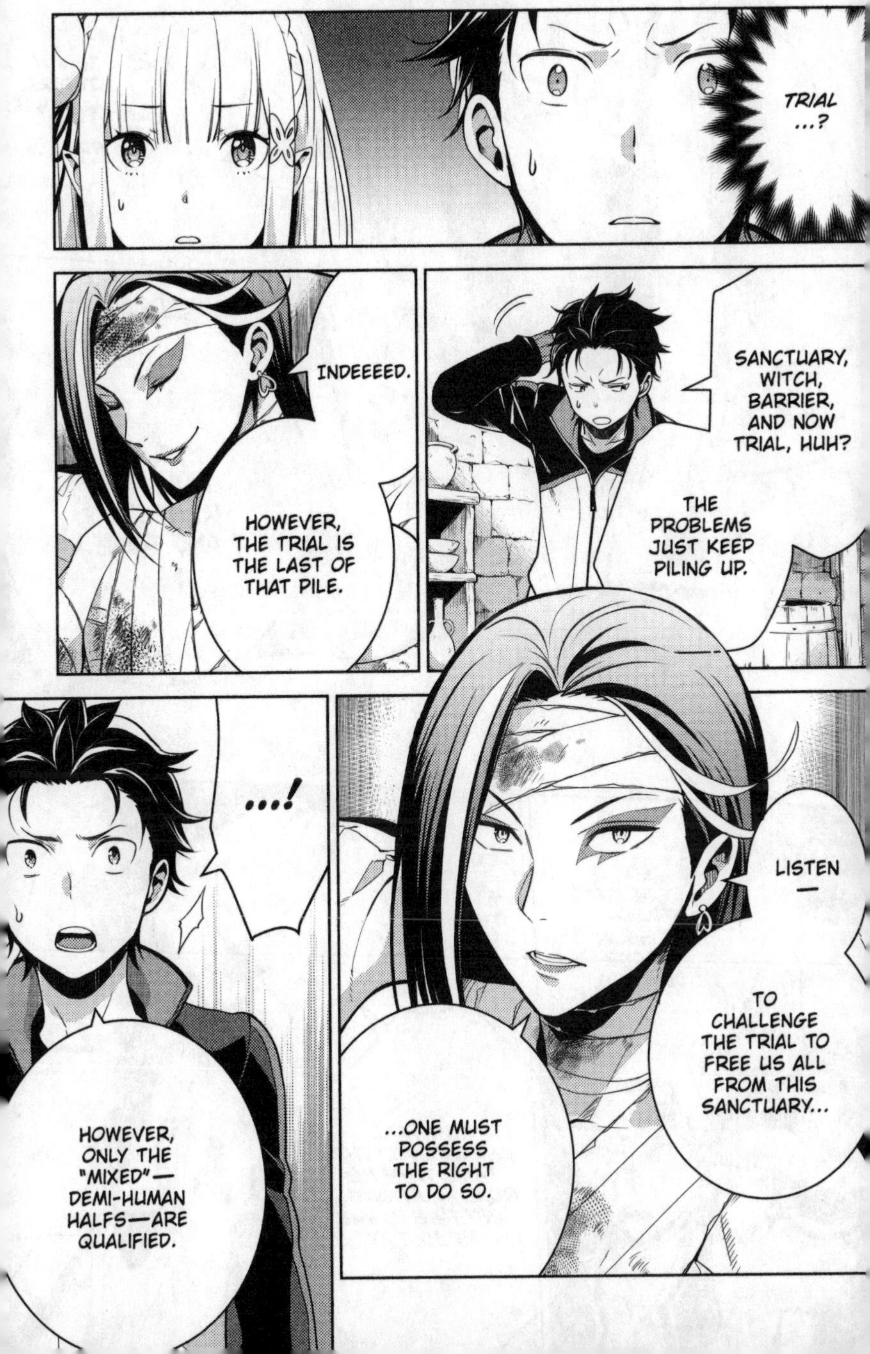
TRIAL ...?
SANCTUARY, WITCH, BARRIER, AND NOW TRIAL, HUH?
THE PROBLEMS JUST KEEP PILING UP.
INDEEEED.
HOWEVER, THE TRIAL IS THE LAST OF THAT PILE.
LISTEN—
TO CHALLENGE THE TRIAL TO FREE US ALL FROM THIS SANCTUARY...
...ONE MUST POSSESS THE RIGHT TO DO SO.
...!
HOWEVER, ONLY THE "MIXED"—DEMI-HUMAN HALFS—ARE QUALIFIED.

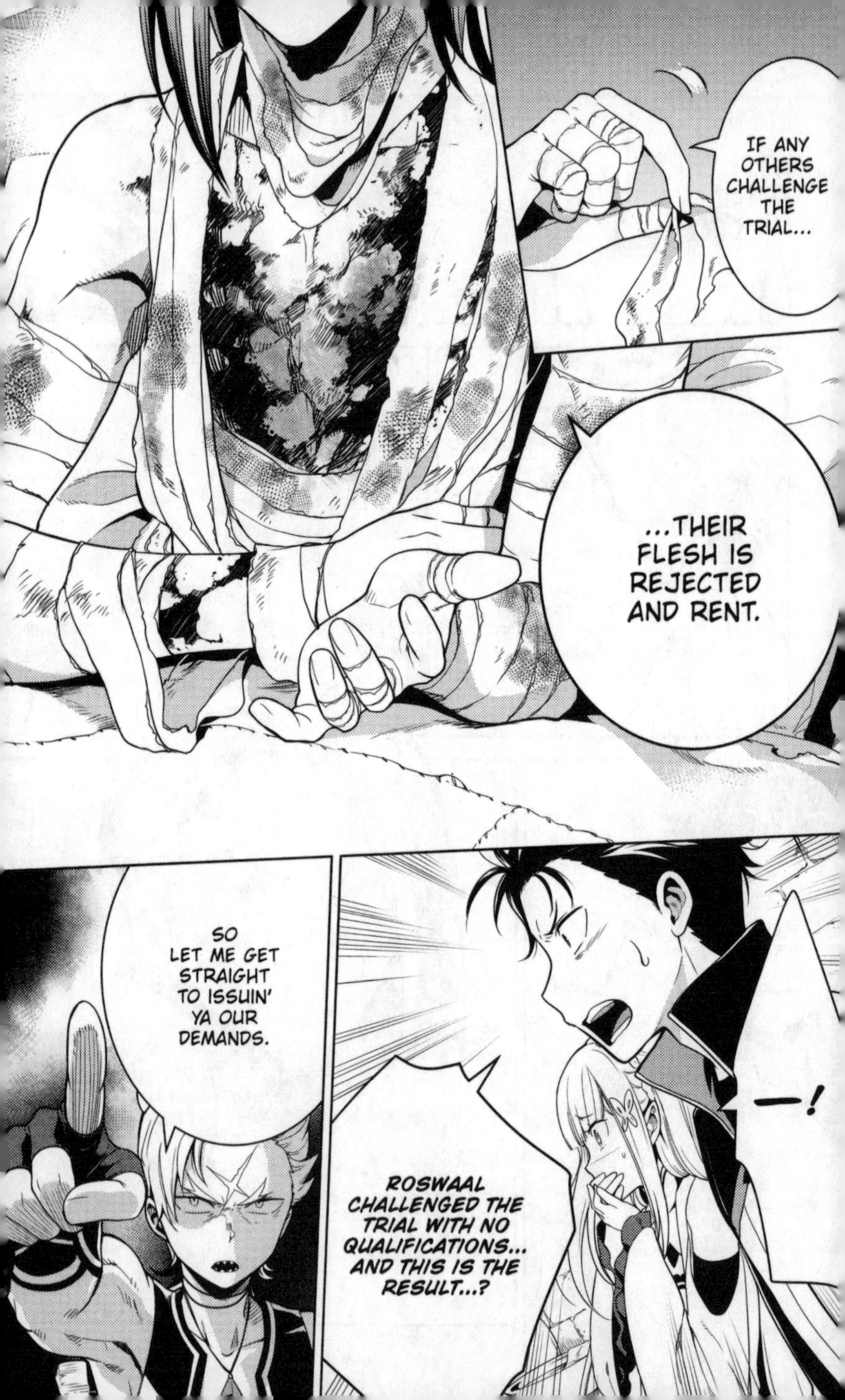
IF ANY OTHERS CHALLENGE THE TRIAL...
...THEIR FLESH IS REJECTED AND RENT.
—!
ROSWAAL CHALLENGED THE TRIAL WITH NO QUALIFICATIONS... AND THIS IS THE RESULT...?
SO LET ME GET STRAIGHT TO ISSUIN' YA OUR DEMANDS.

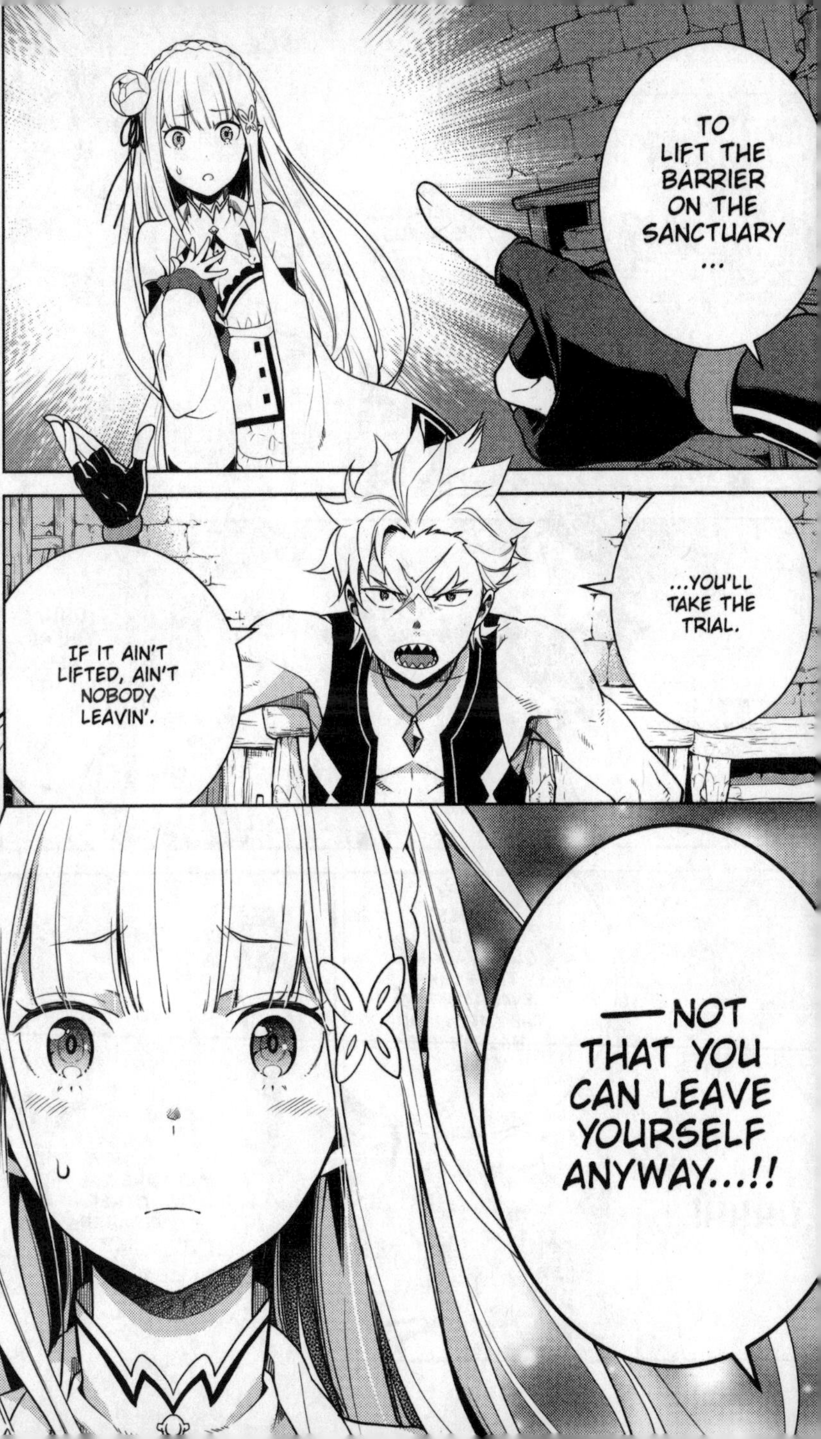
TO LIFT THE BARRIER ON THE SANCTUARY...
...YOU'LL TAKE THE TRIAL.
IF IT AIN'T LIFTED, AIN'T NOBODY LEAVIN'.
—NOT THAT YOU CAN LEAVE YOURSELF ANYWAY...!!

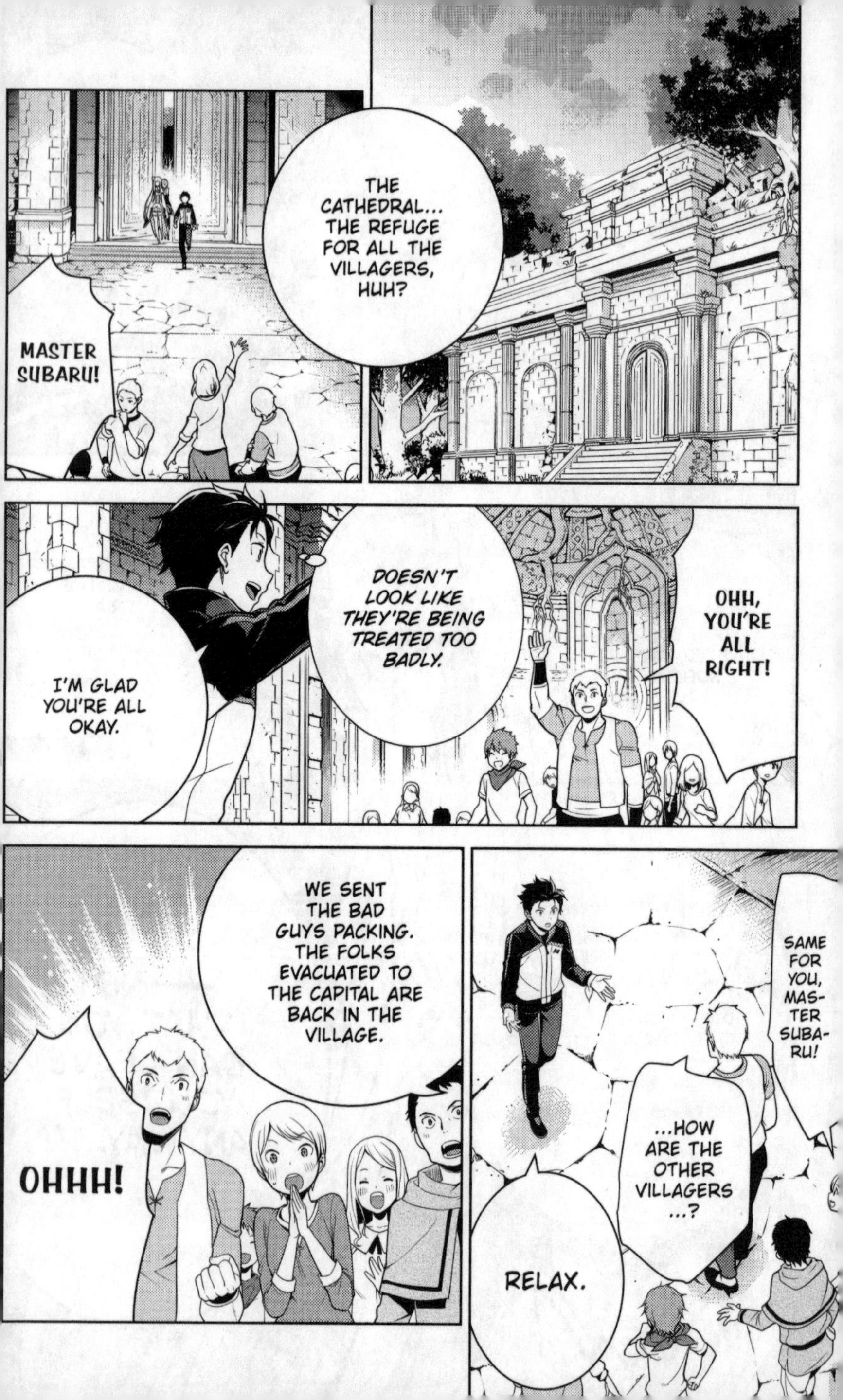
THE CATHEDRAL... THE REFUGE FOR ALL THE VILLAGERS, HUH?
MASTER SUBARU!
OHH, YOU'RE ALL RIGHT!
DOESN'T LOOK LIKE THEY'RE BEING TREATED TOO BADLY.
I'M GLAD YOU'RE ALL OKAY.
SAME FOR YOU, MAS-TER SUBA-RU!
...HOW ARE THE OTHER VILLAGERS ...?
RELAX.
WE SENT THE BAD GUYS PACKING. THE FOLKS EVACUATED TO THE CAPITAL ARE BACK IN THE VILLAGE.
OHHH!

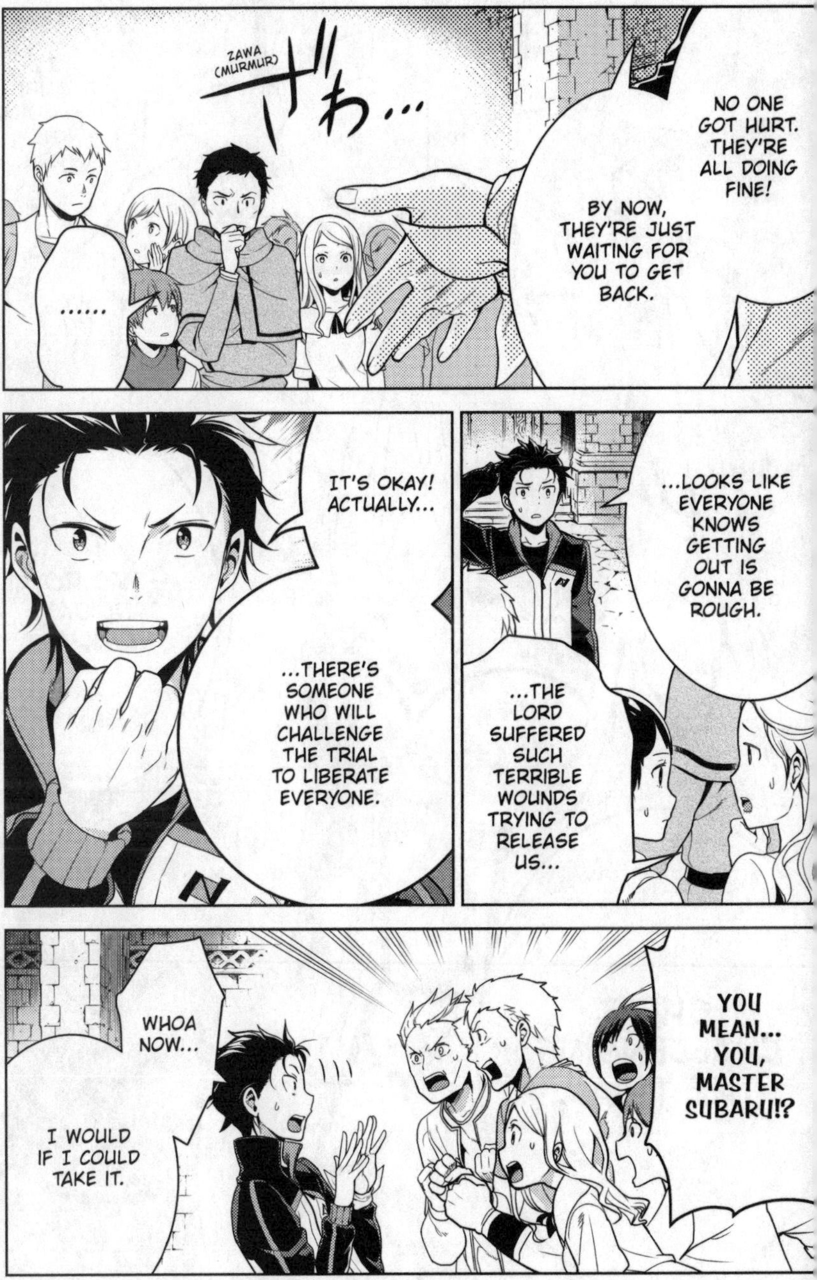
NO ONE GOT HURT. THEY'RE ALL DOING FINE!
BY NOW, THEY'RE JUST WAITING FOR YOU TO GET BACK.
ざわ…
ZAWA (MURMUR)
......
...LOOKS LIKE EVERYONE KNOWS GETTING OUT IS GONNA BE ROUGH.
...THE LORD SUFFERED SUCH TERRIBLE WOUNDS TRYING TO RELEASE US...
IT'S OKAY! ACTUALLY...
...THERE'S SOMEONE WHO WILL CHALLENGE THE TRIAL TO LIBERATE EVERYONE.
YOU MEAN... YOU, MASTER SUBARU!?
WHOA NOW...
I WOULD IF I COULD TAKE IT.

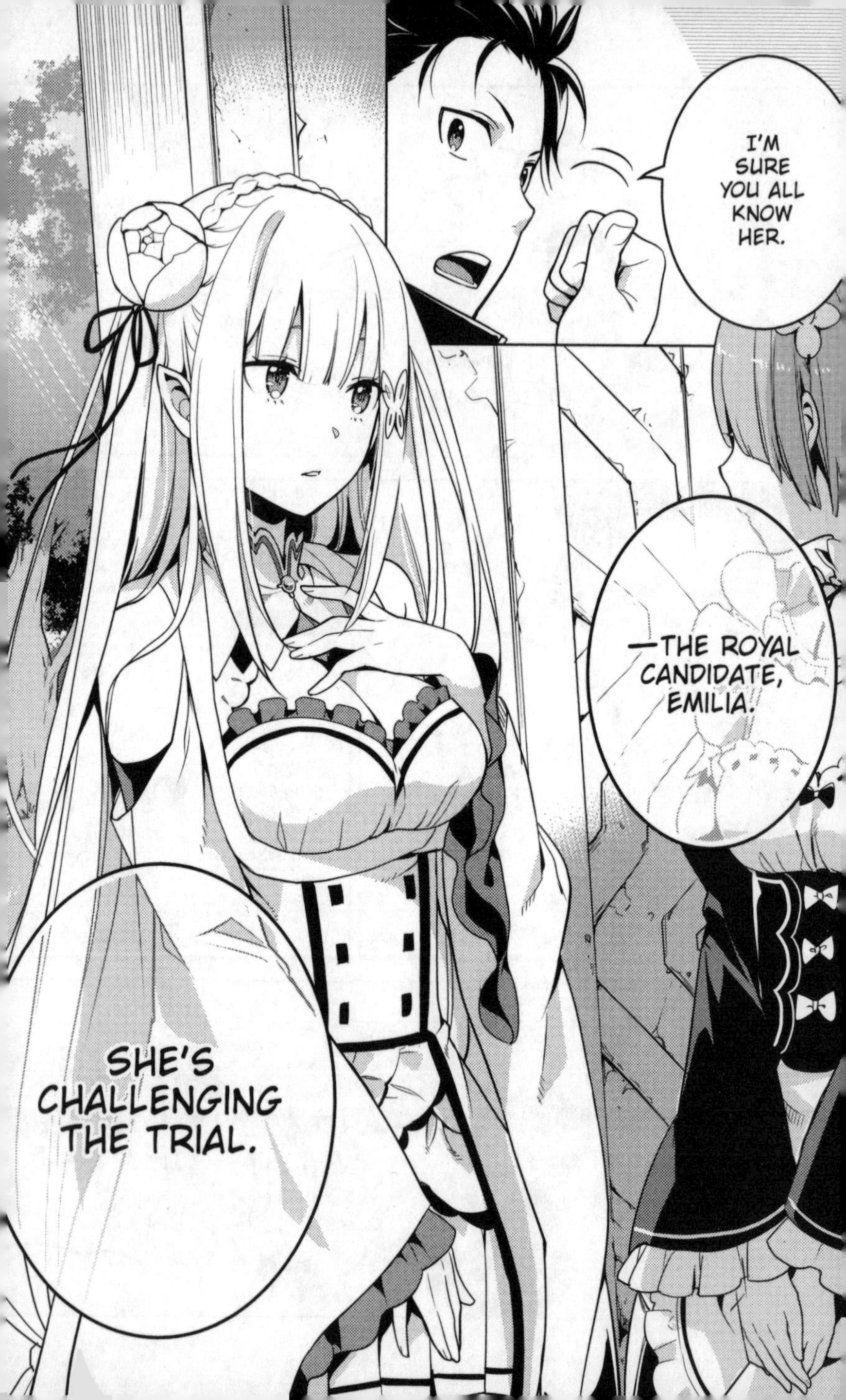
I'M SURE YOU ALL KNOW HER.
—THE ROYAL CANDIDATE, EMILIA.
SHE'S CHALLENGING THE TRIAL.

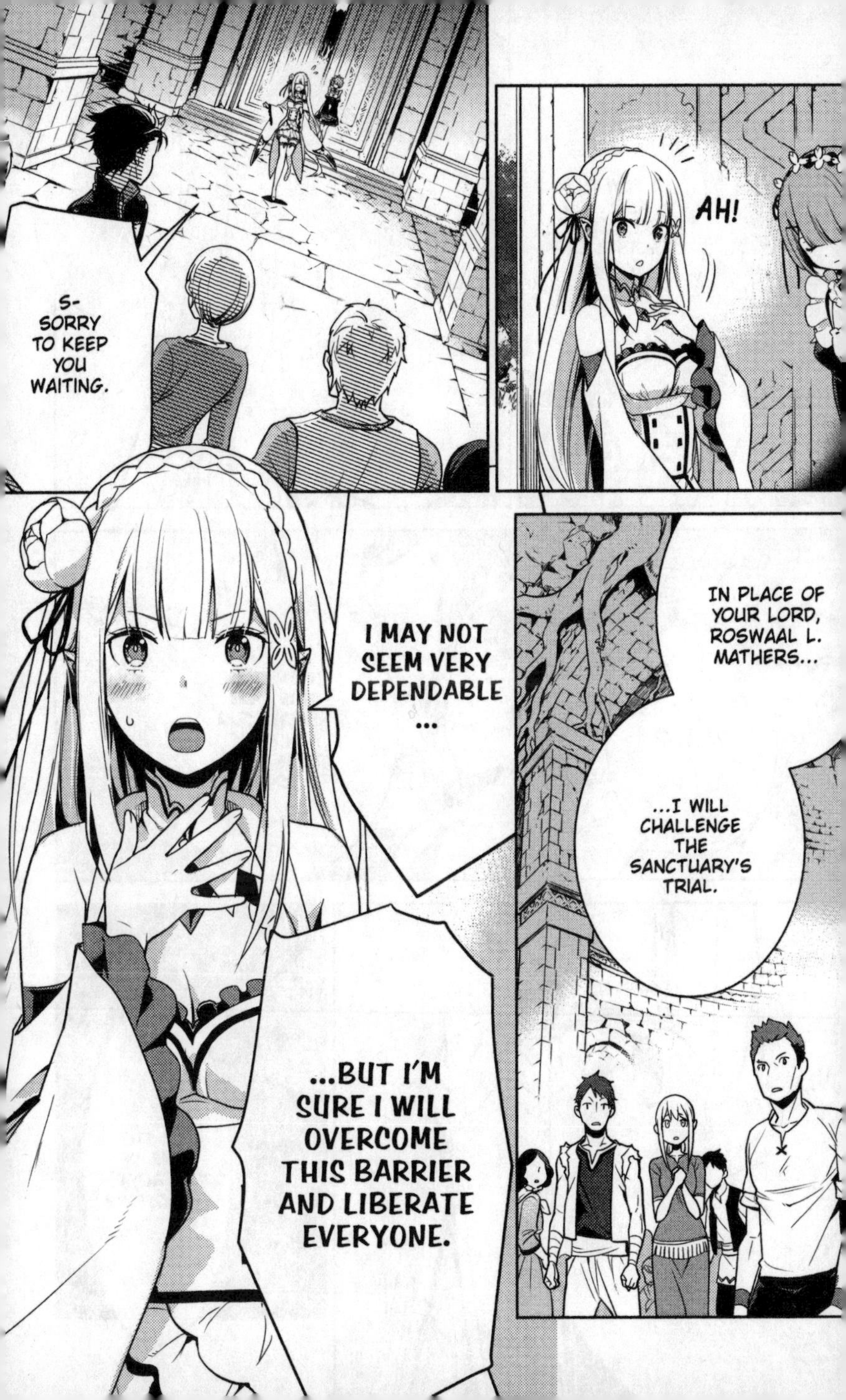
AH!
S-SORRY TO KEEP YOU WAITING.
IN PLACE OF YOUR LORD, ROSWAAL L. MATHERS...
...I WILL CHALLENGE THE SANCTUARY'S TRIAL.
I MAY NOT SEEM VERY DEPENDABLE...
...BUT I'M SURE I WILL OVERCOME THIS BARRIER AND LIBERATE EVERYONE.

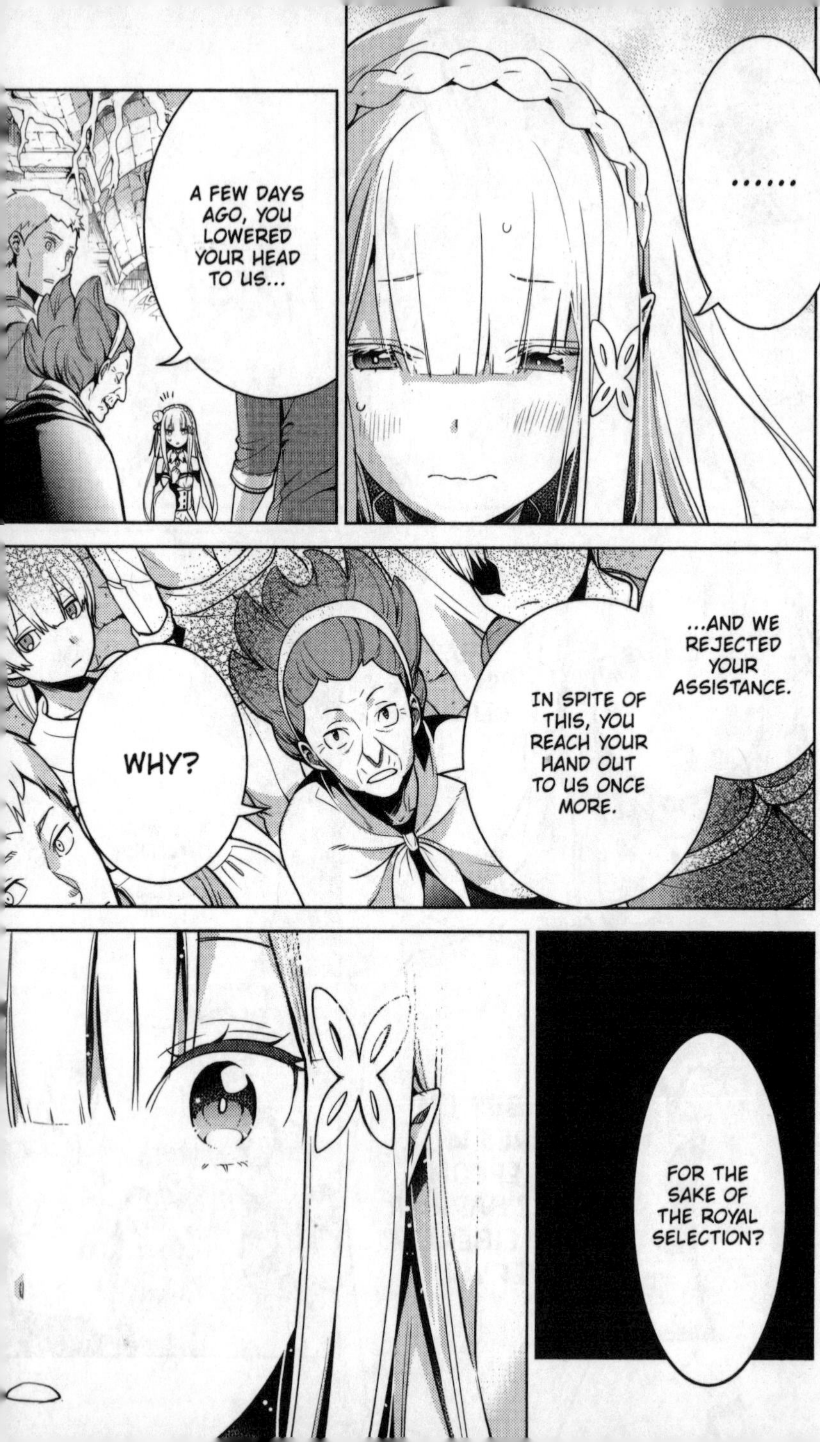
......
A FEW DAYS AGO, YOU LOWERED YOUR HEAD TO US...
...AND WE REJECTED YOUR ASSISTANCE.
IN SPITE OF THIS, YOU REACH YOUR HAND OUT TO US ONCE MORE.
WHY?
FOR THE SAKE OF THE ROYAL SELECTION?

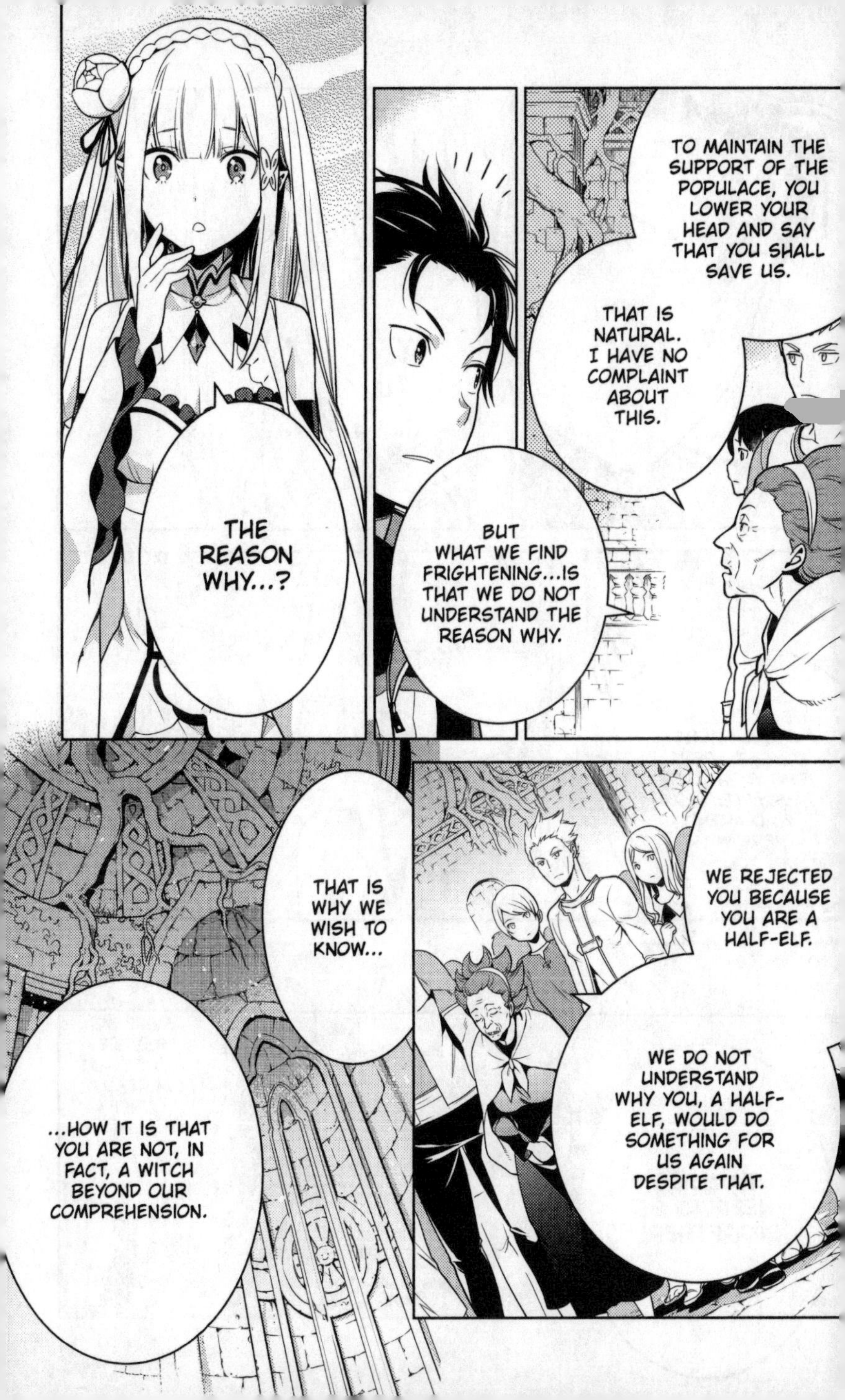
TO MAINTAIN THE SUPPORT OF THE POPULACE, YOU LOWER YOUR HEAD AND SAY THAT YOU SHALL SAVE US.
THAT IS NATURAL. I HAVE NO COMPLAINT ABOUT THIS.
BUT WHAT WE FIND FRIGHTENING...IS THAT WE DO NOT UNDERSTAND THE REASON WHY.
THE REASON WHY...?
WE REJECTED YOU BECAUSE YOU ARE A HALF-ELF.
WE DO NOT UNDERSTAND WHY YOU, A HALF-ELF, WOULD DO SOMETHING FOR US AGAIN DESPITE THAT.
THAT IS WHY WE WISH TO KNOW...
...HOW IT IS THAT YOU ARE NOT, IN FACT, A WITCH BEYOND OUR COMPREHENSION.

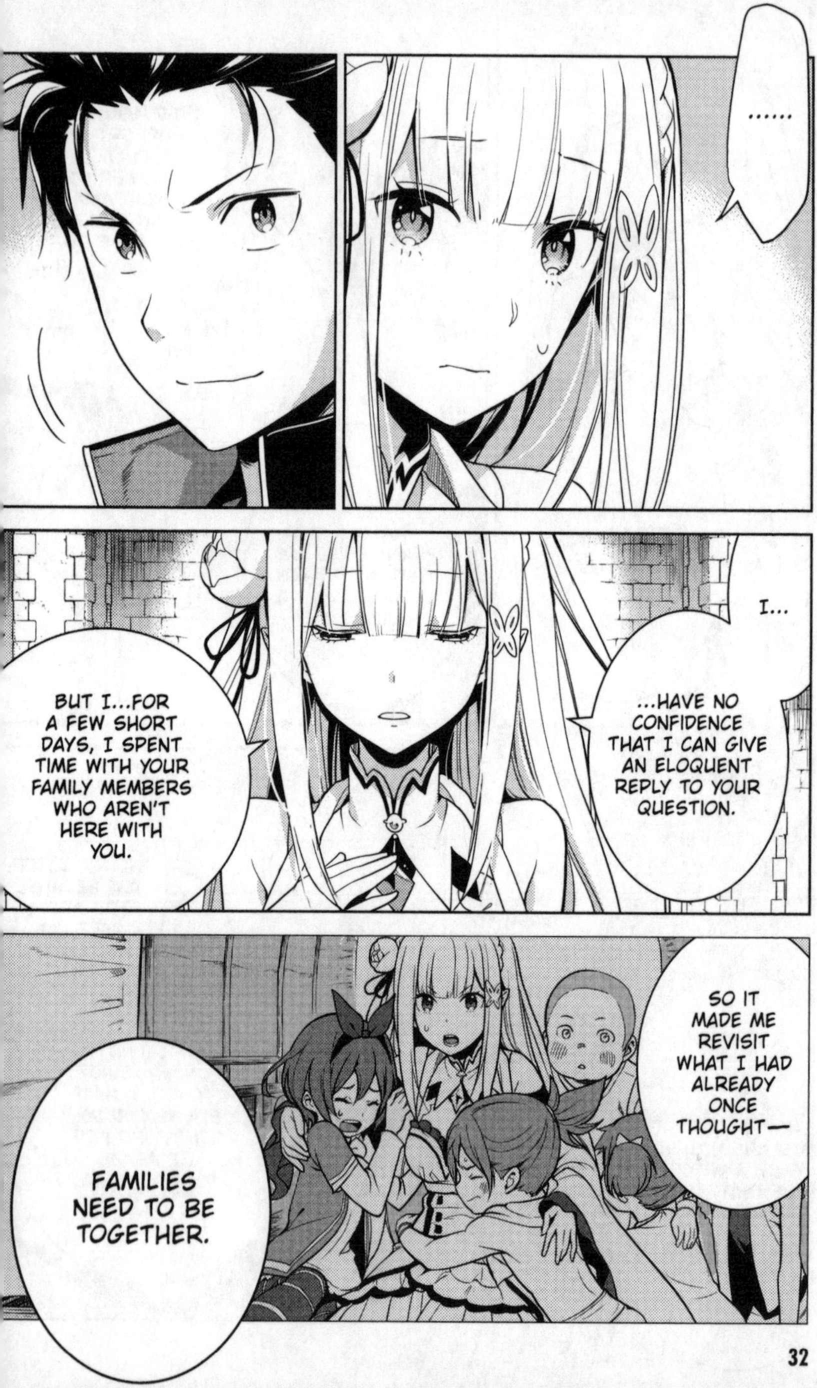
......
I...
...HAVE NO CONFIDENCE THAT I CAN GIVE AN ELOQUENT REPLY TO YOUR QUESTION.
BUT I...FOR A FEW SHORT DAYS, I SPENT TIME WITH YOUR FAMILY MEMBERS WHO AREN'T HERE WITH YOU.
SO IT MADE ME REVISIT WHAT I HAD ALREADY ONCE THOUGHT—
FAMILIES NEED TO BE TOGETHER.

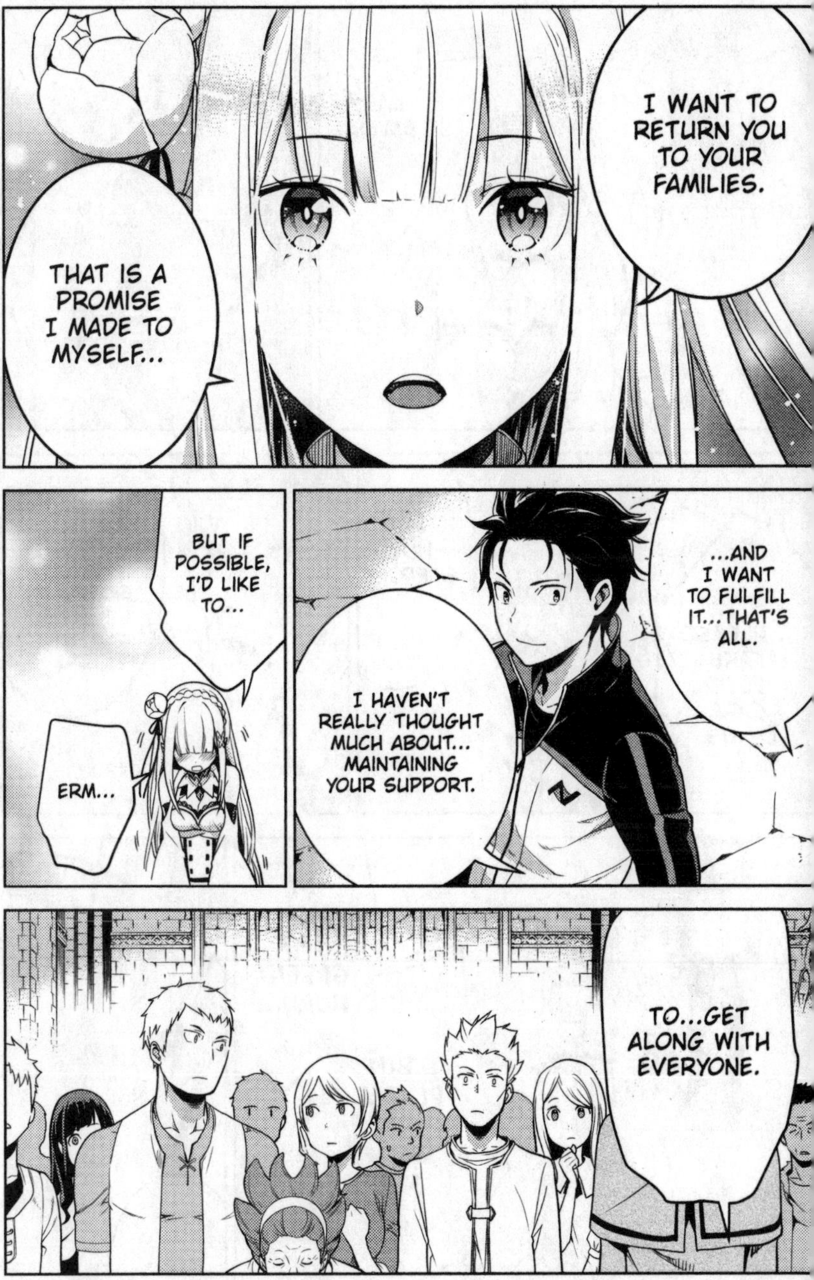
I WANT TO RETURN YOU TO YOUR FAMILIES.
THAT IS A PROMISE I MADE TO MYSELF...
...AND I WANT TO FULFILL IT...THAT'S ALL.
I HAVEN'T REALLY THOUGHT MUCH ABOUT... MAINTAINING YOUR SUPPORT.
BUT IF POSSIBLE, I'D LIKE TO...
ERM...
TO...GET ALONG WITH EVERYONE.

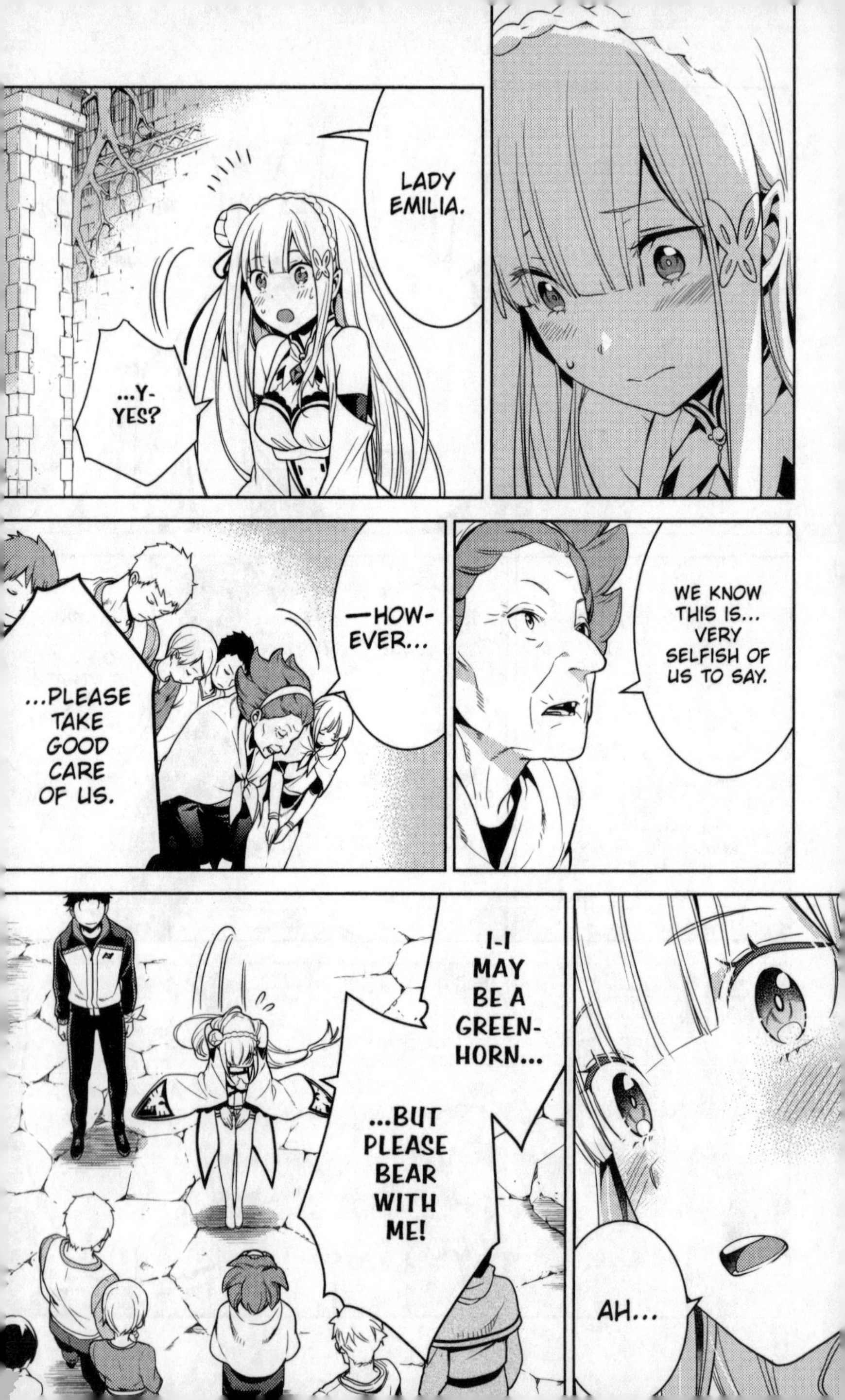
LADY EMILIA.
...Y-YES?
WE KNOW THIS IS... VERY SELFISH OF US TO SAY.
—HOW-EVER...
...PLEASE TAKE GOOD CARE OF US.
AH...
I-I MAY BE A GREEN-HORN...
...BUT PLEASE BEAR WITH ME!

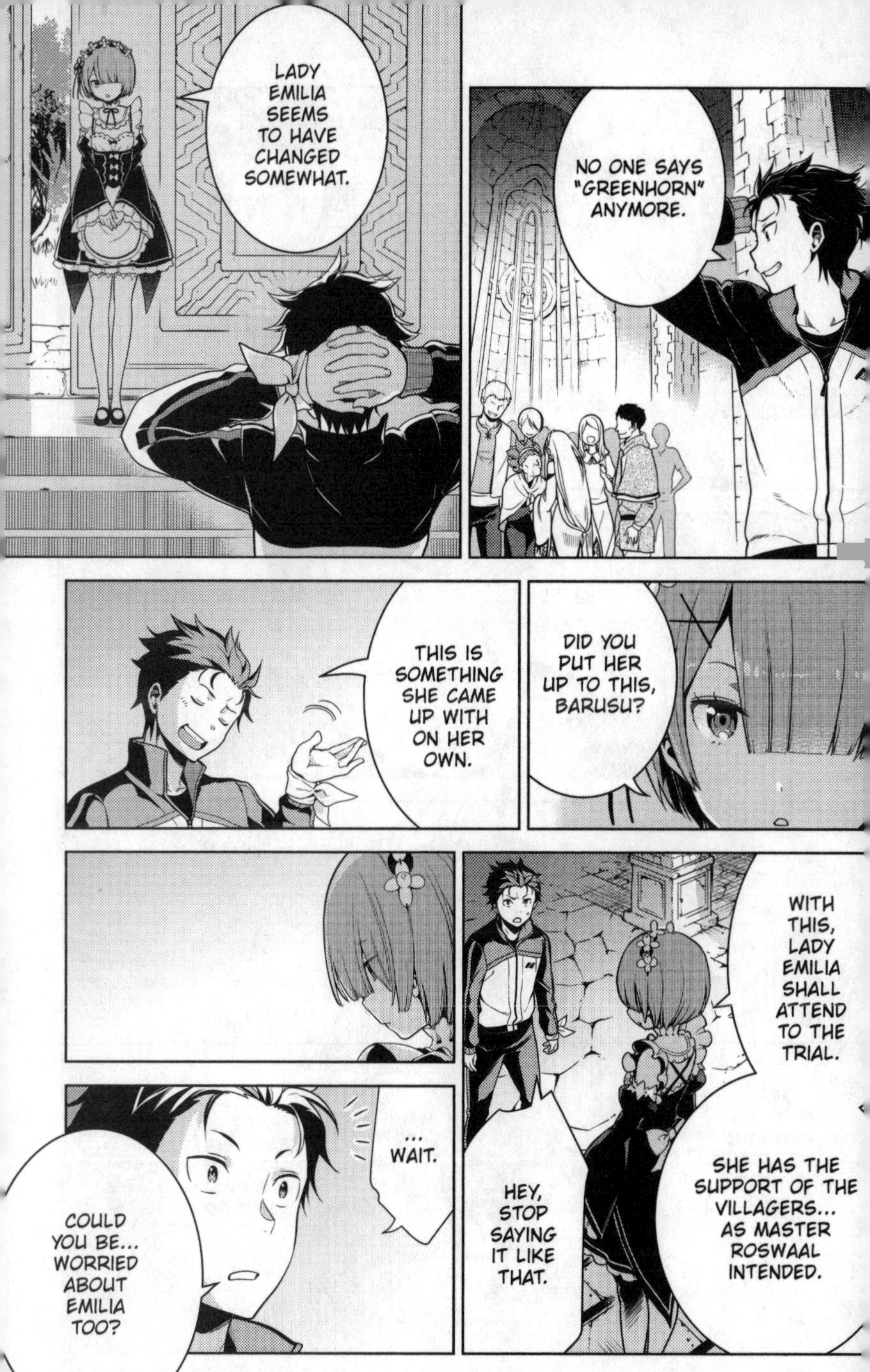
NO ONE SAYS "GREENHORN" ANYMORE.
LADY EMILIA SEEMS TO HAVE CHANGED SOMEWHAT.
DID YOU PUT HER UP TO THIS, BARUSU?
THIS IS SOMETHING SHE CAME UP WITH ON HER OWN.
WITH THIS, LADY EMILIA SHALL ATTEND TO THE TRIAL.
SHE HAS THE SUPPORT OF THE VILLAGERS... AS MASTER ROSWAAL INTENDED.
HEY, STOP SAYING IT LIKE THAT.
...WAIT.
COULD YOU BE... WORRIED ABOUT EMILIA TOO?

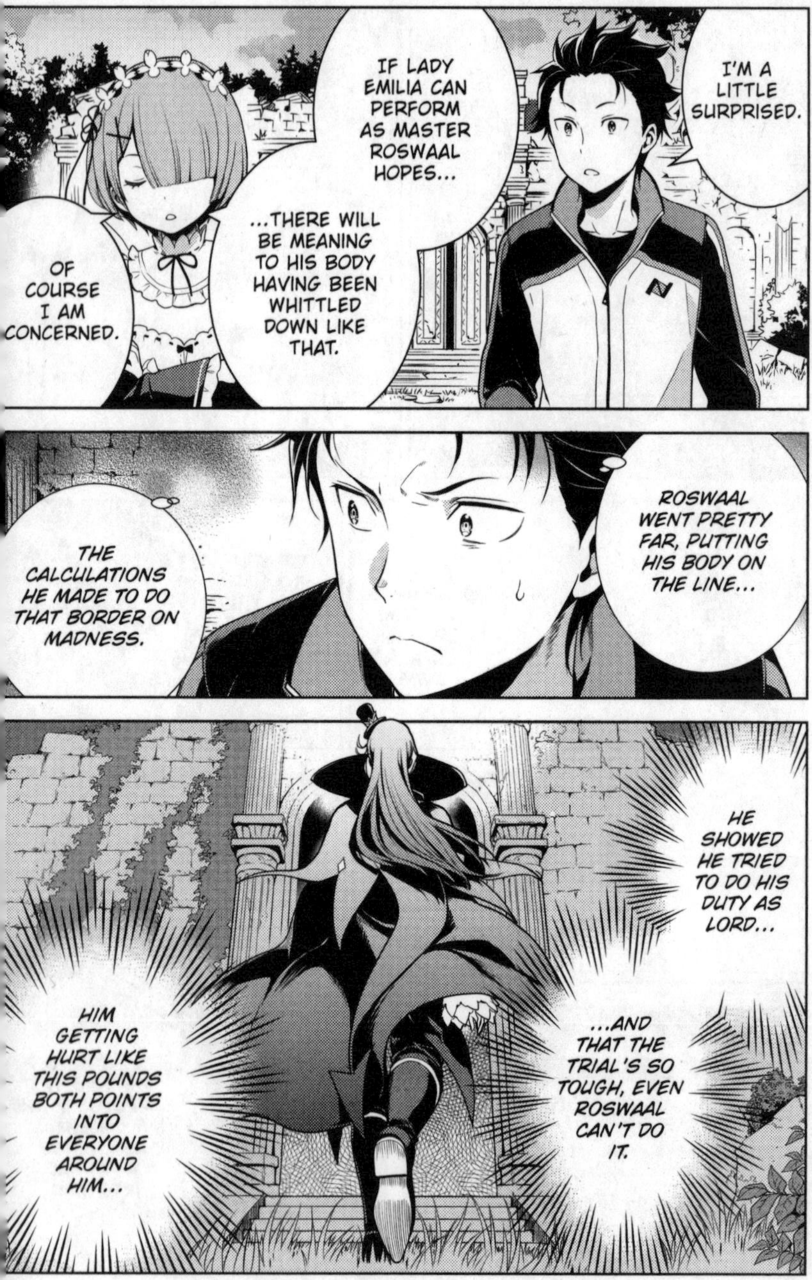
I'M A LITTLE SURPRISED.
IF LADY EMILIA CAN PERFORM AS MASTER ROSWAAL HOPES...
...THERE WILL BE MEANING TO HIS BODY HAVING BEEN WHITTLED DOWN LIKE THAT.
OF COURSE I AM CONCERNED.
ROSWAAL WENT PRETTY FAR, PUTTING HIS BODY ON THE LINE...
THE CALCULATIONS HE MADE TO DO THAT BORDER ON MADNESS.
HE SHOWED HE TRIED TO DO HIS DUTY AS LORD...
...AND THAT THE TRIAL'S SO TOUGH, EVEN ROSWAAL CAN'T DO IT.
HIM GETTING HURT LIKE THIS POUNDS BOTH POINTS INTO EVERYONE AROUND HIM...

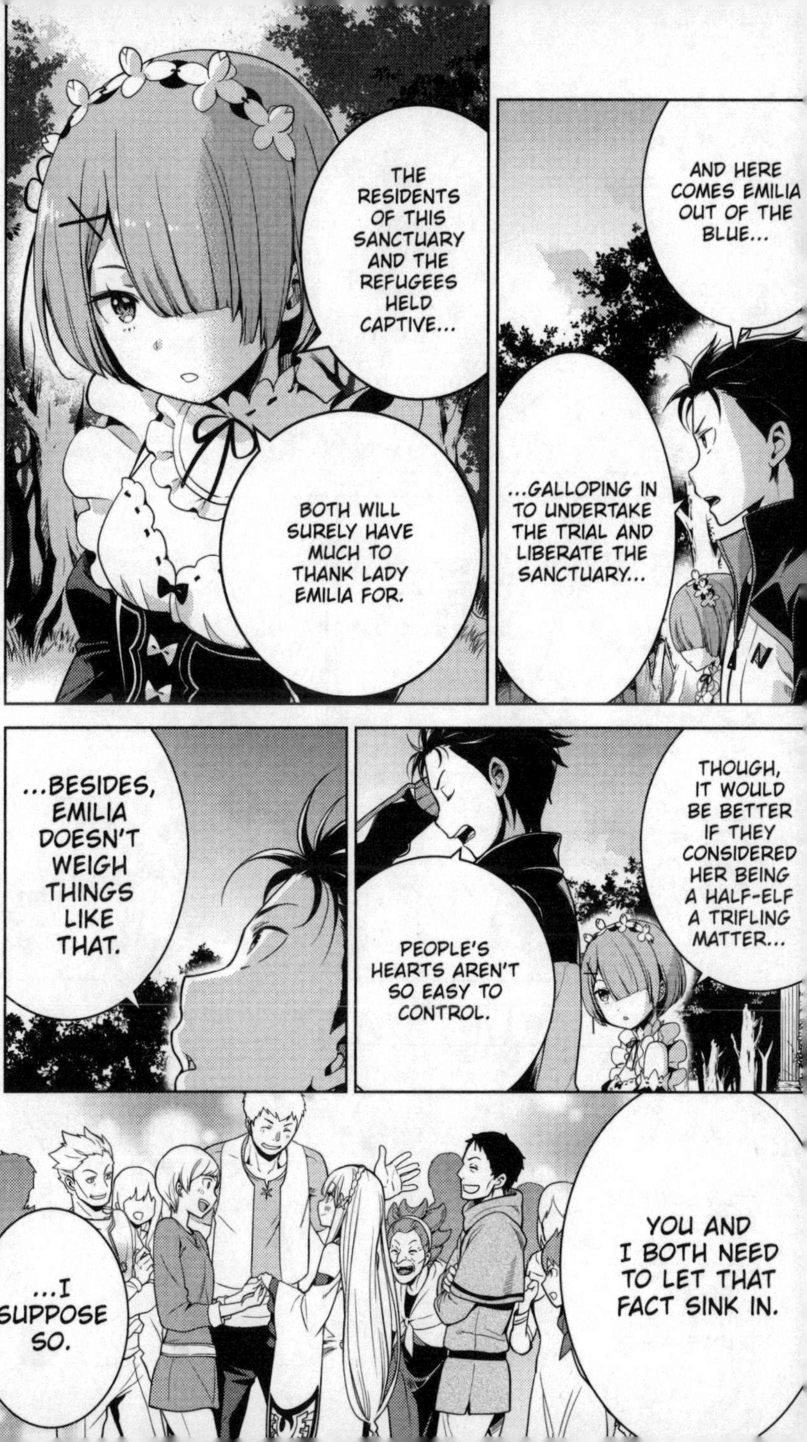
AND HERE COMES EMILIA OUT OF THE BLUE...
...GALLOPING IN TO UNDERTAKE THE TRIAL AND LIBERATE THE SANCTUARY...
THE RESIDENTS OF THIS SANCTUARY AND THE REFUGEES HELD CAPTIVE...
BOTH WILL SURELY HAVE MUCH TO THANK LADY EMILIA FOR.
THOUGH, IT WOULD BE BETTER IF THEY CONSIDERED HER BEING A HALF-ELF A TRIFLING MATTER...
PEOPLE'S HEARTS AREN'T SO EASY TO CONTROL.
...BESIDES, EMILIA DOESN'T WEIGH THINGS LIKE THAT.
YOU AND I BOTH NEED TO LET THAT FACT SINK IN.
...I SUPPOSE SO.

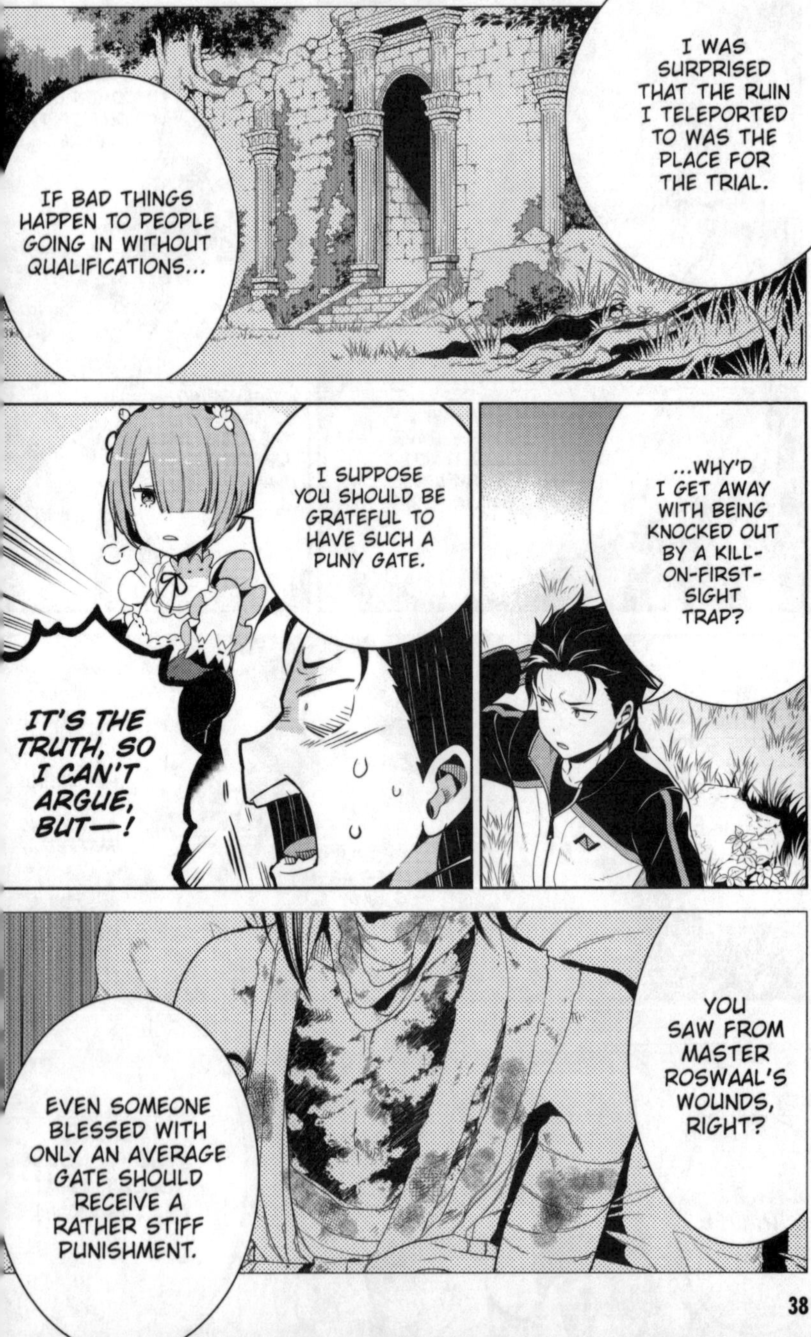
I WAS SURPRISED THAT THE RUIN I TELEPORTED TO WAS THE PLACE FOR THE TRIAL.
IF BAD THINGS HAPPEN TO PEOPLE GOING IN WITHOUT QUALIFICATIONS...
...WHY'D I GET AWAY WITH BEING KNOCKED OUT BY A KILL-ON-FIRST-SIGHT TRAP?
I SUPPOSE YOU SHOULD BE GRATEFUL TO HAVE SUCH A PUNY GATE.
IT'S THE TRUTH, SO I CAN'T ARGUE, BUT—!
YOU SAW FROM MASTER ROSWAAL'S WOUNDS, RIGHT?
EVEN SOMEONE BLESSED WITH ONLY AN AVERAGE GATE SHOULD RECEIVE A RATHER STIFF PUNISHMENT.

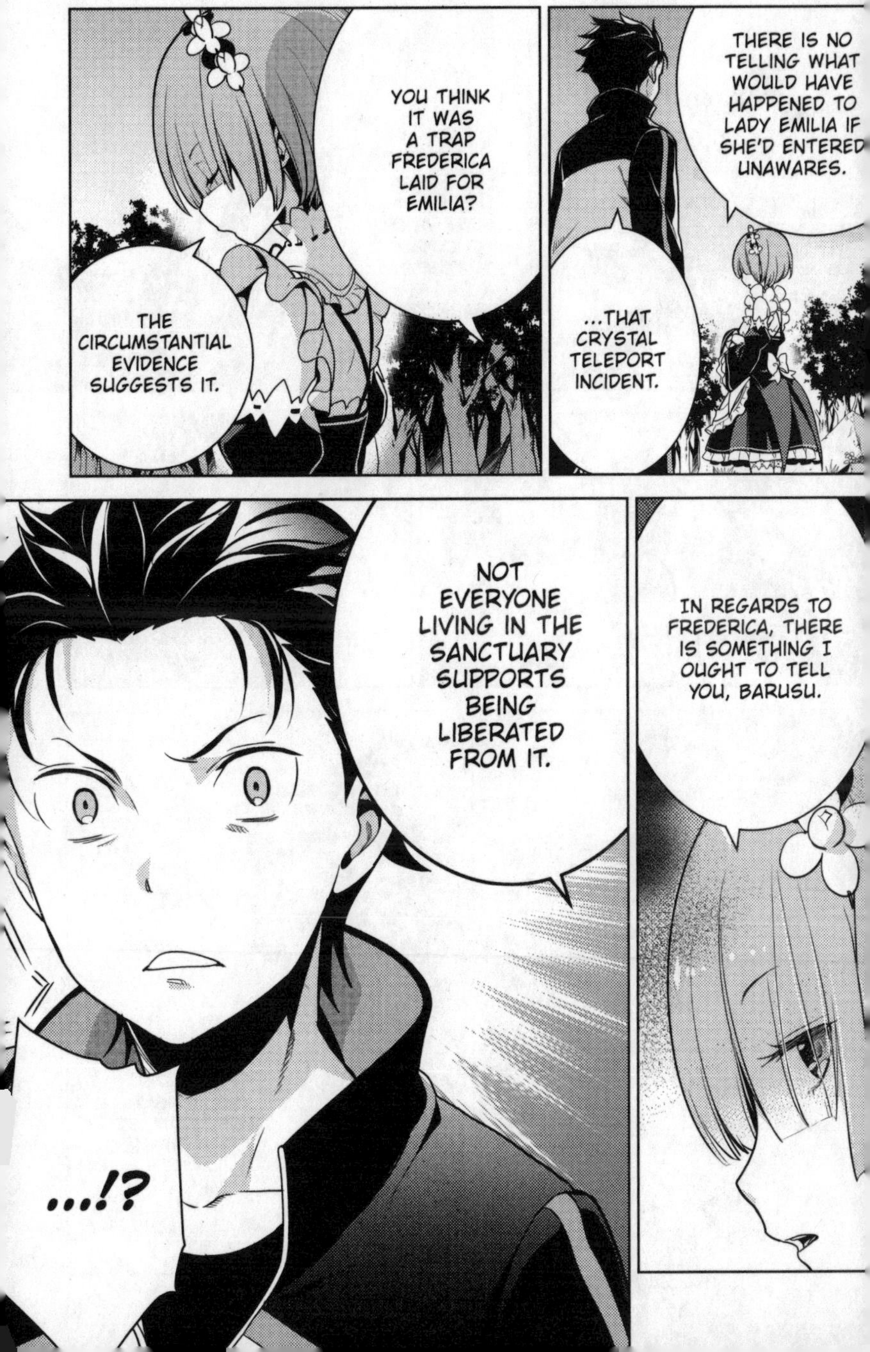
THERE IS NO TELLING WHAT WOULD HAVE HAPPENED TO LADY EMILIA IF SHE'D ENTERED UNAWARES.
...THAT CRYSTAL TELEPORT INCIDENT.
YOU THINK IT WAS A TRAP FREDERICA LAID FOR EMILIA?
THE CIRCUMSTANTIAL EVIDENCE SUGGESTS IT.
IN REGARDS TO FREDERICA, THERE IS SOMETHING I OUGHT TO TELL YOU, BARUSU.
NOT EVERYONE LIVING IN THE SANCTUARY SUPPORTS BEING LIBERATED FROM IT.
...!?

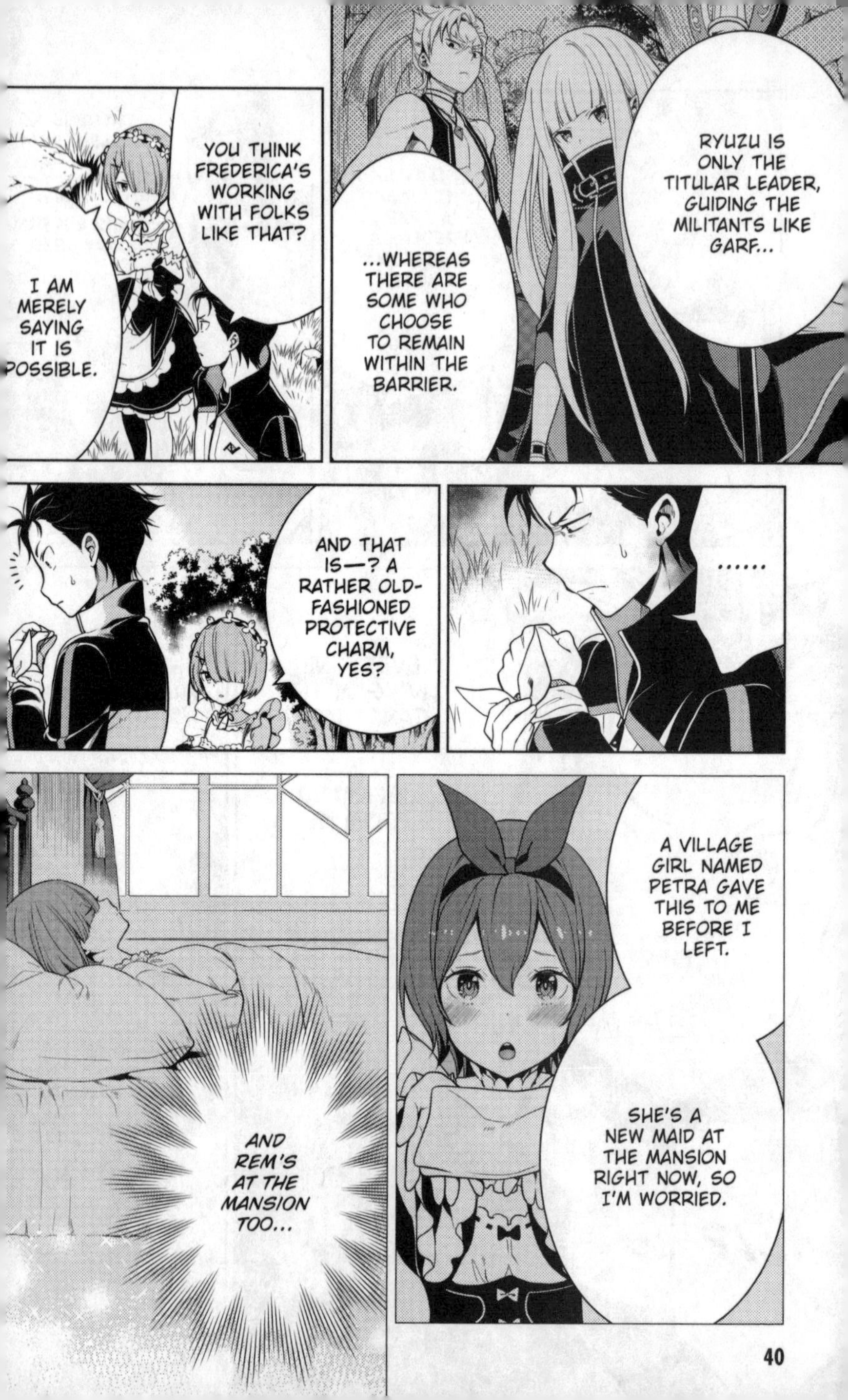
RYUZU IS ONLY THE TITULAR LEADER, GUIDING THE MILITANTS LIKE GARF...
...WHEREAS THERE ARE SOME WHO CHOOSE TO REMAIN WITHIN THE BARRIER.
YOU THINK FREDERICA'S WORKING WITH FOLKS LIKE THAT?
I AM MERELY SAYING IT IS POSSIBLE.
......
AND THAT IS—? A RATHER OLD-FASHIONED PROTECTIVE CHARM, YES?
A VILLAGE GIRL NAMED PETRA GAVE THIS TO ME BEFORE I LEFT.
SHE'S A NEW MAID AT THE MANSION RIGHT NOW, SO I'M WORRIED.
AND REM'S AT THE MANSION TOO...

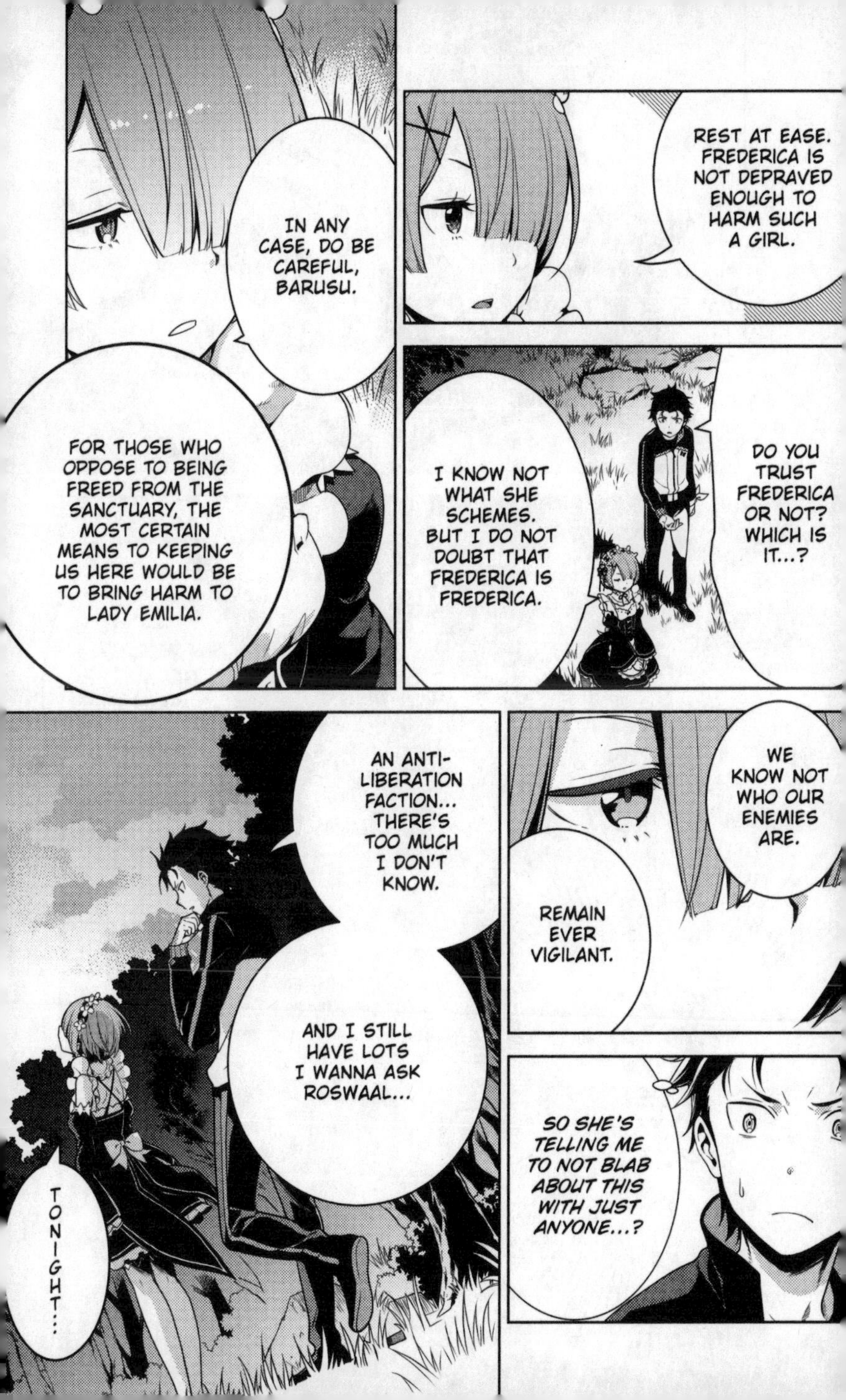
REST AT EASE. FREDERICA IS NOT DEPRAVED ENOUGH TO HARM SUCH A GIRL.
DO YOU TRUST FREDERICA OR NOT? WHICH IS IT...?
I KNOW NOT WHAT SHE SCHEMES. BUT I DO NOT DOUBT THAT FREDERICA IS FREDERICA.
IN ANY CASE, DO BE CAREFUL, BARUSU.
FOR THOSE WHO OPPOSE TO BEING FREED FROM THE SANCTUARY, THE MOST CERTAIN MEANS TO KEEPING US HERE WOULD BE TO BRING HARM TO LADY EMILIA.
WE KNOW NOT WHO OUR ENEMIES ARE.
REMAIN EVER VIGILANT.
SO SHE'S TELLING ME TO NOT BLAB ABOUT THIS WITH JUST ANYONE...?
AN ANTI-LIBERATION FACTION... THERE'S TOO MUCH I DON'T KNOW.
AND I STILL HAVE LOTS I WANNA ASK ROSWAAL...
TONIGHT...

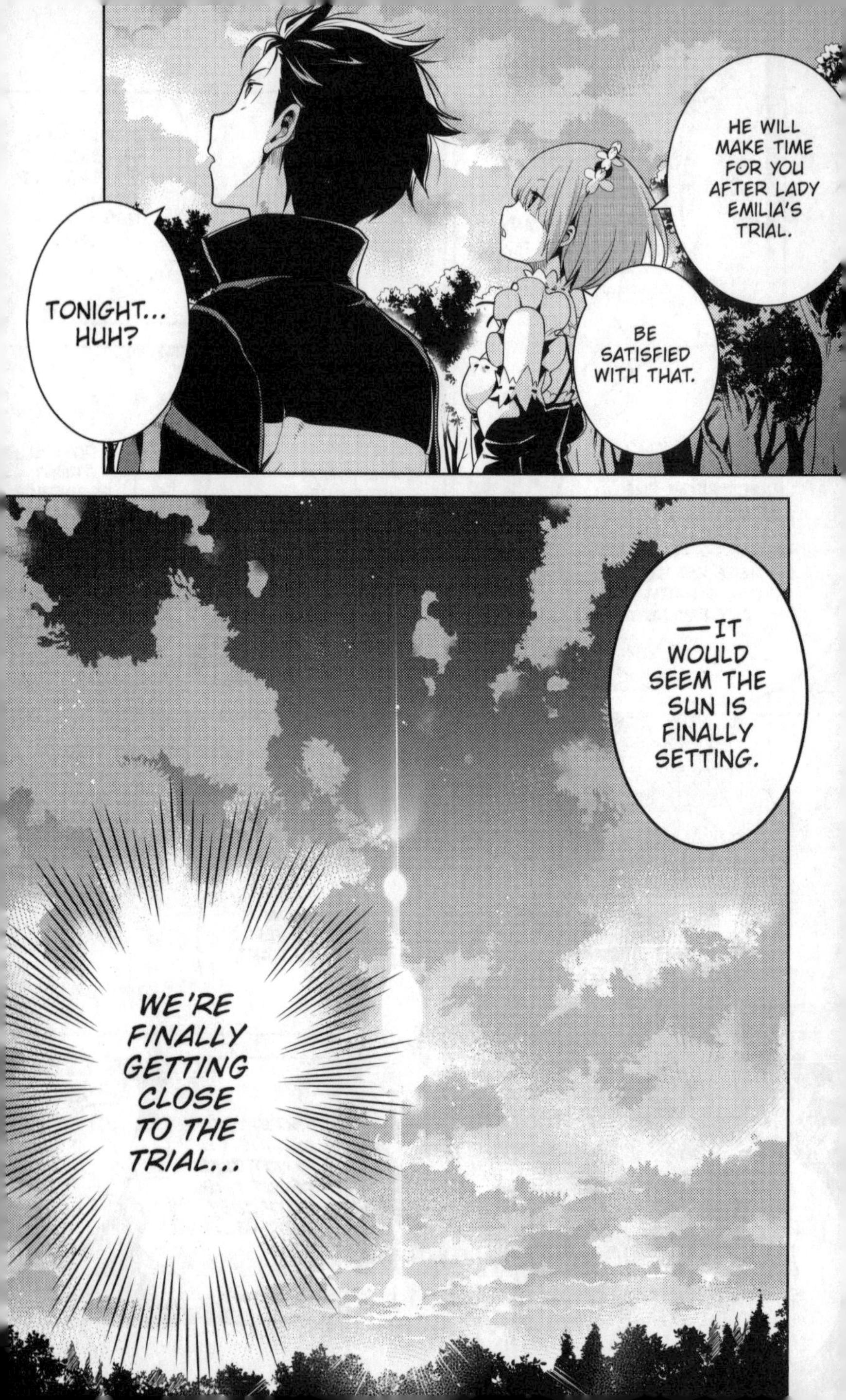
HE WILL MAKE TIME FOR YOU AFTER LADY EMILIA'S TRIAL.
BE SATISFIED WITH THAT.
TONIGHT... HUH?
—IT WOULD SEEM THE SUN IS FINALLY SETTING.
WE'RE FINALLY GETTING CLOSE TO THE TRIAL...

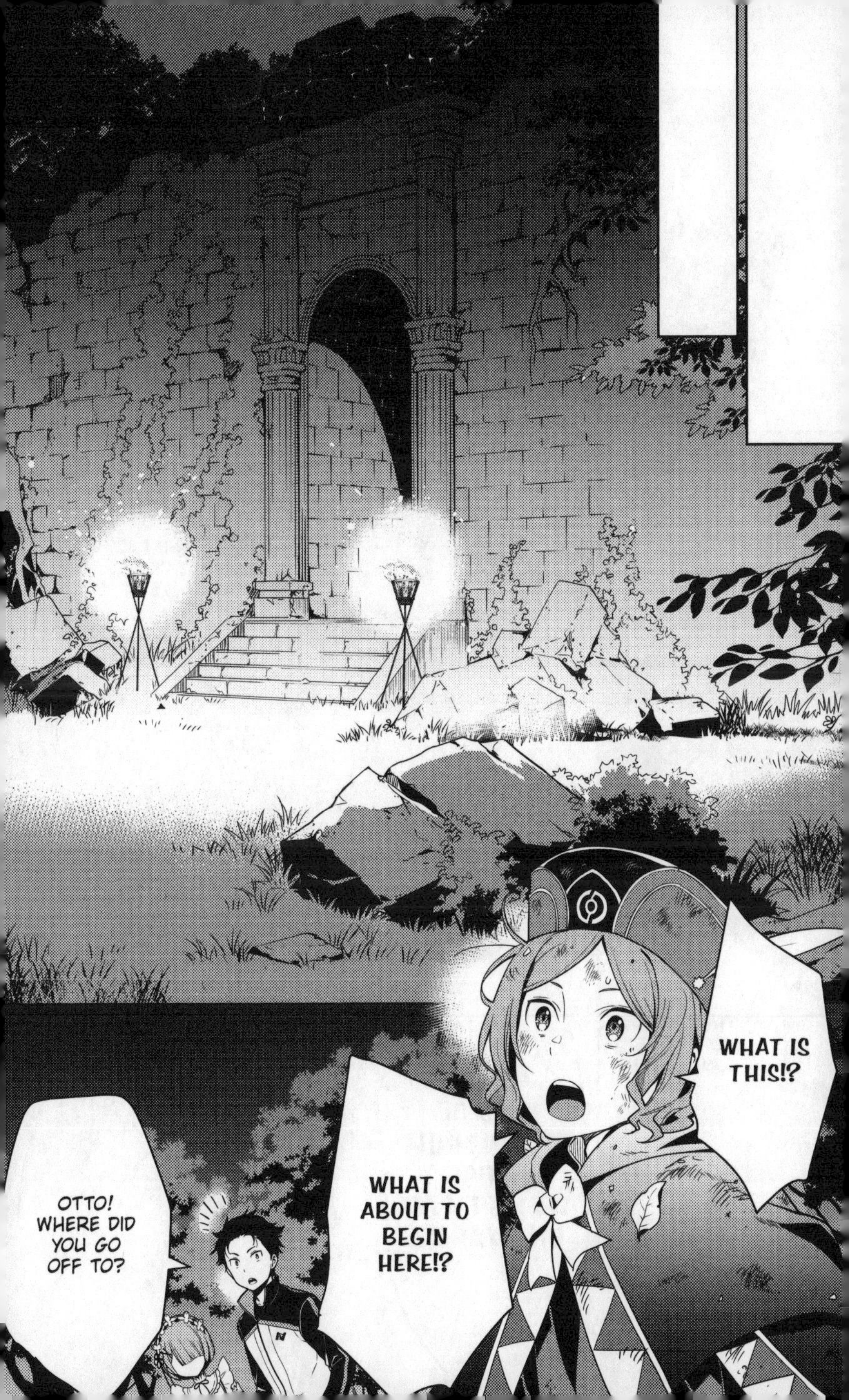
WHAT IS THIS!?
WHAT IS ABOUT TO BEGIN HERE!?
OTTO! WHERE DID YOU GO OFF TO?

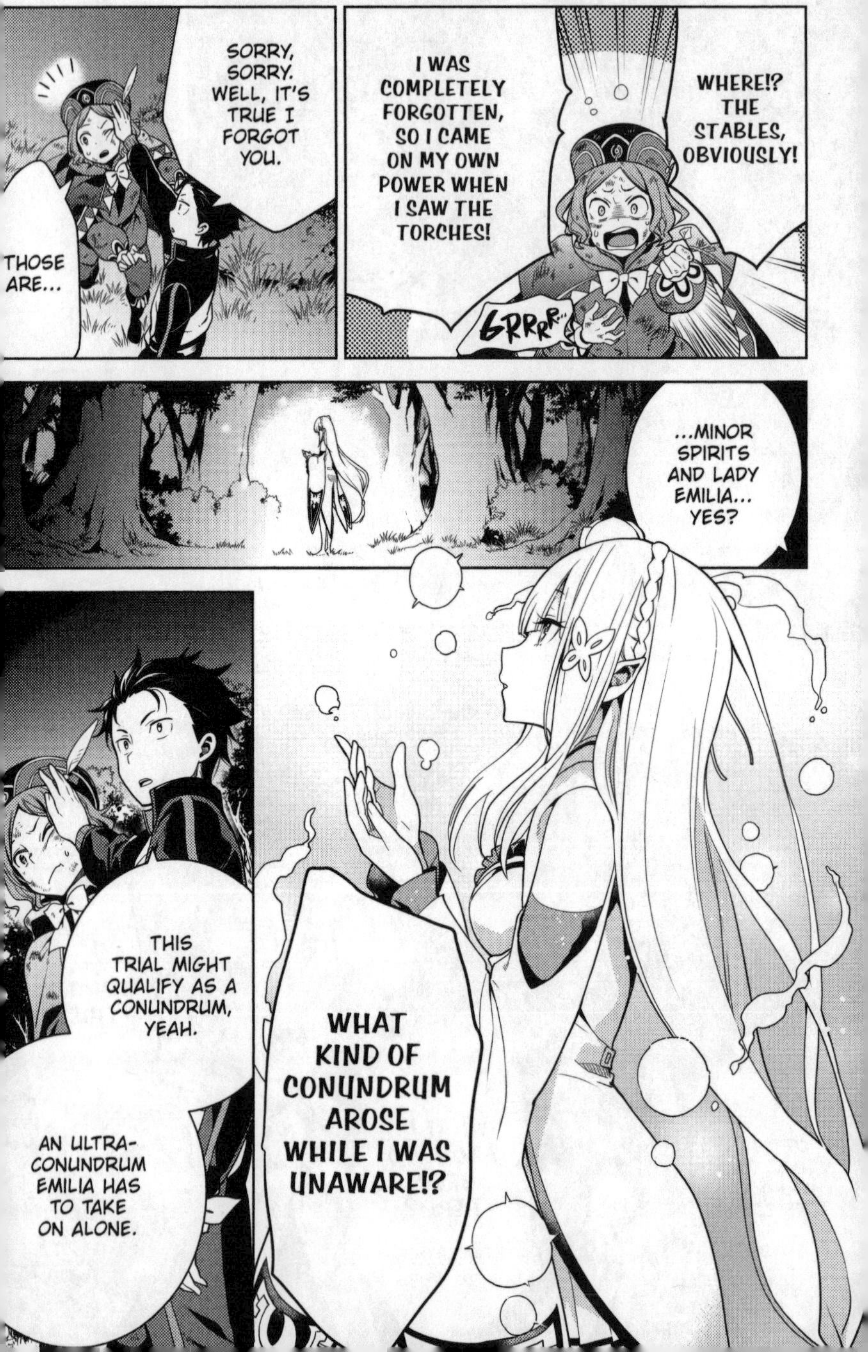

WHERE!? THE STABLES, OBVIOUSLY!
I WAS COMPLETELY FORGOTTEN, SO I CAME ON MY OWN POWER WHEN I SAW THE TORCHES!
GRRRR...
SORRY, SORRY. WELL, IT'S TRUE I FORGOT YOU.
THOSE ARE...
...MINOR SPIRITS AND LADY EMILIA... YES?
WHAT KIND OF CONUNDRUM AROSE WHILE I WAS UNAWARE!?
THIS TRIAL MIGHT QUALIFY AS A CONUNDRUM, YEAH.
AN ULTRA-CONUNDRUM EMILIA HAS TO TAKE ON ALONE.

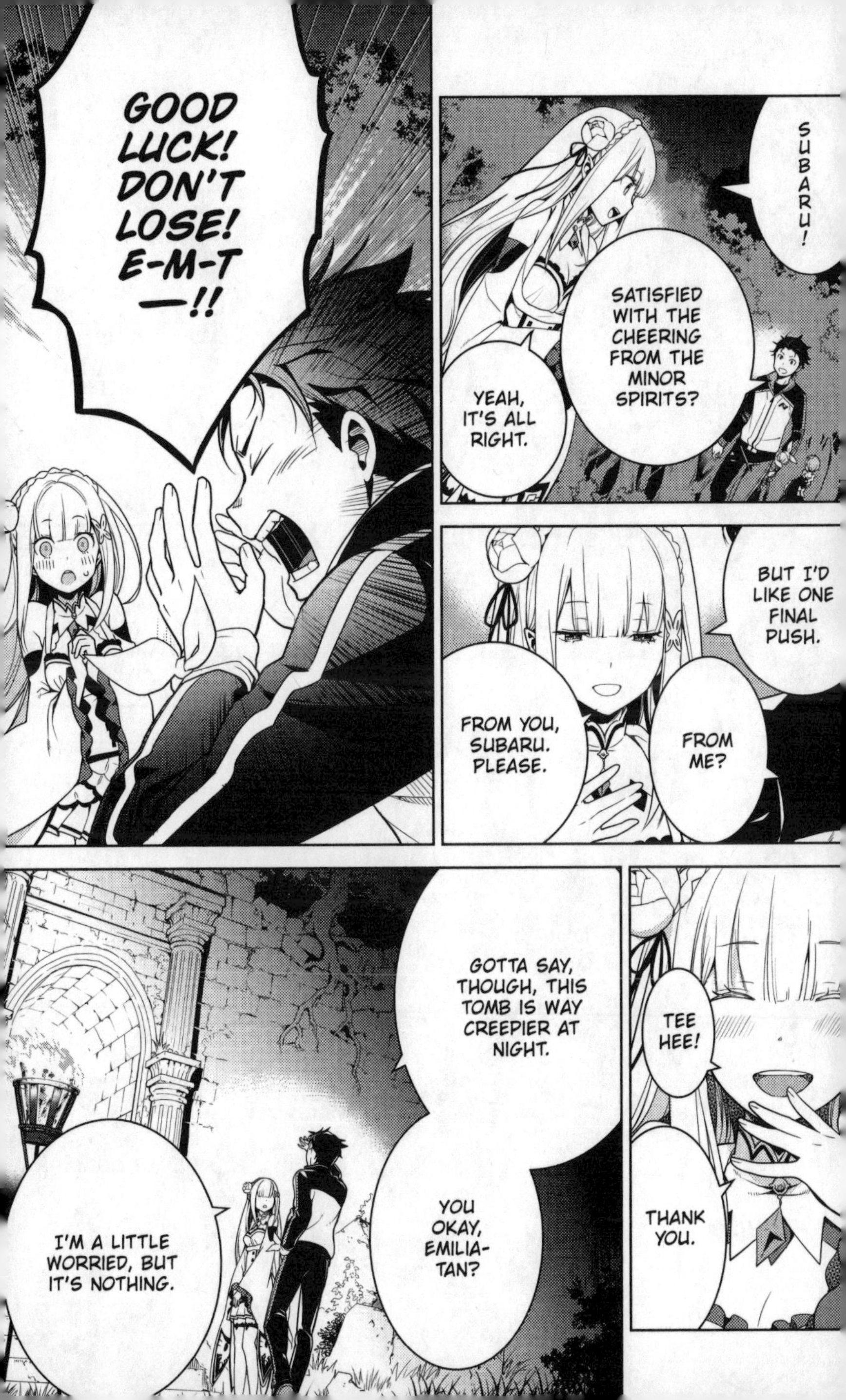
SUBARU!
SATISFIED WITH THE CHEERING FROM THE MINOR SPIRITS?
YEAH, IT'S ALL RIGHT.
BUT I'D LIKE ONE FINAL PUSH.
FROM ME?
FROM YOU, SUBARU. PLEASE.
GOOD LUCK! DON'T LOSE! E-M-T—!!
TEE HEE!
THANK YOU.
GOTTA SAY, THOUGH, THIS TOMB IS WAY CREEPIER AT NIGHT.
YOU OKAY, EMILIA-TAN?
I'M A LITTLE WORRIED, BUT IT'S NOTHING.

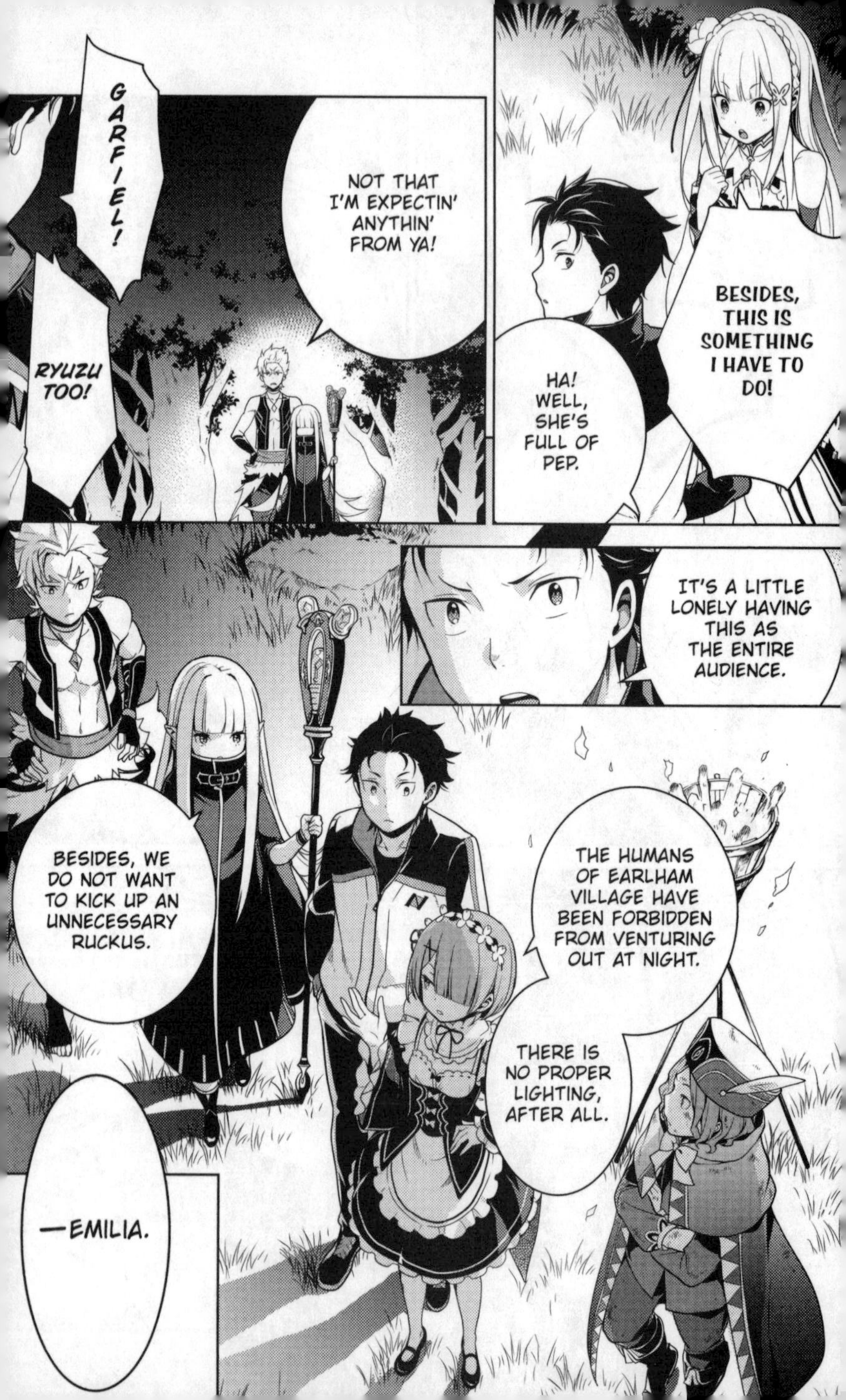

BESIDES, THIS IS SOMETHING I HAVE TO DO!
HA! WELL, SHE'S FULL OF PEP.
NOT THAT I'M EXPECTIN' ANYTHIN' FROM YA!
GARFIEL!
RYUZU TOO!
IT'S A LITTLE LONELY HAVING THIS AS THE ENTIRE AUDIENCE.
THE HUMANS OF EARLHAM VILLAGE HAVE BEEN FORBIDDEN FROM VENTURING OUT AT NIGHT.
THERE IS NO PROPER LIGHTING, AFTER ALL.
BESIDES, WE DO NOT WANT TO KICK UP AN UNNECESSARY RUCKUS.
—EMILIA.

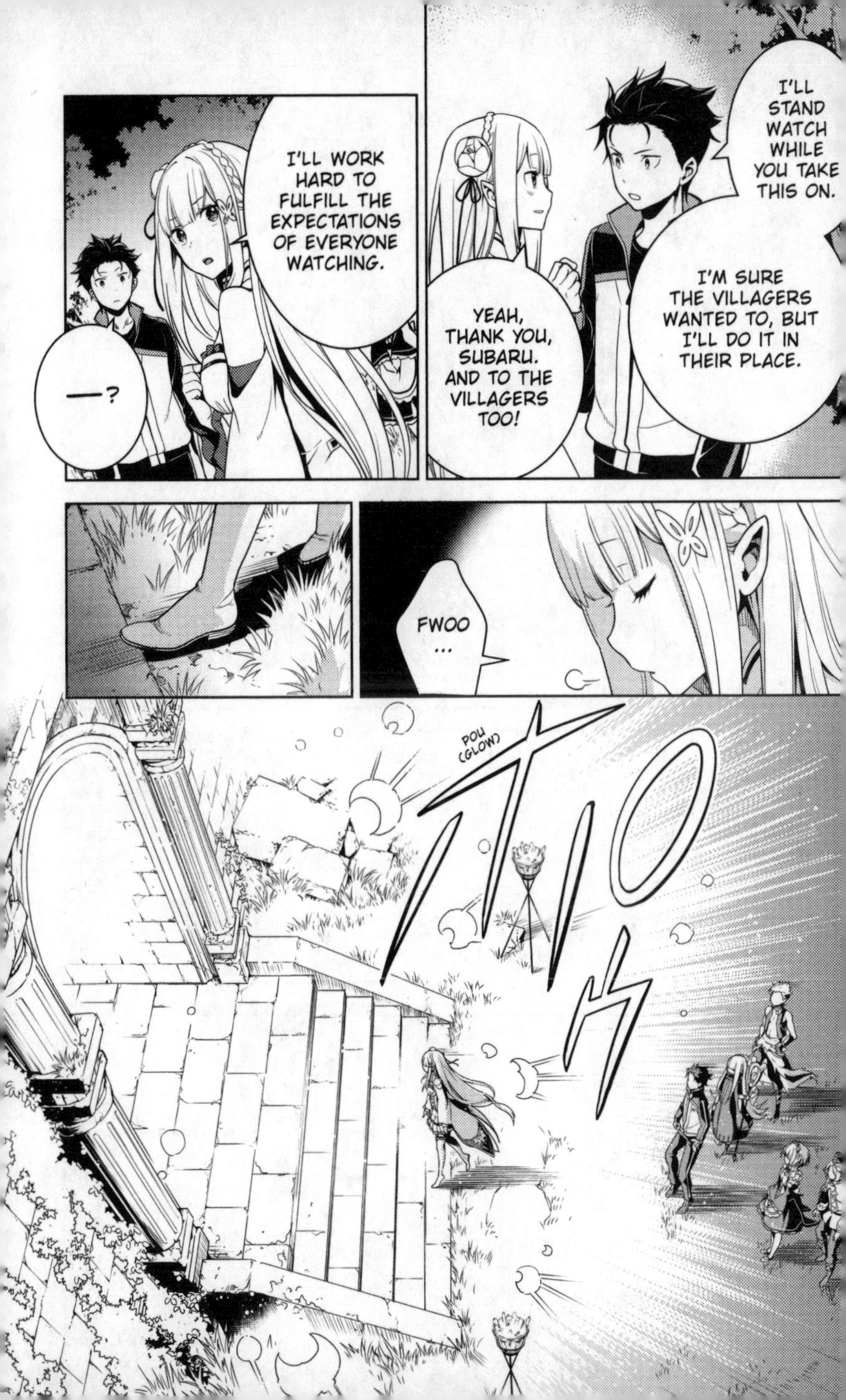
I'LL STAND WATCH WHILE YOU TAKE THIS ON.
I'M SURE THE VILLAGERS WANTED TO, BUT I'LL DO IT IN THEIR PLACE.
YEAH, THANK YOU, SUBARU. AND TO THE VILLAGERS TOO!
I'LL WORK HARD TO FULFILL THE EXPECTATIONS OF EVERYONE WATCHING.
—?
FWOO...
POU (GLOW)

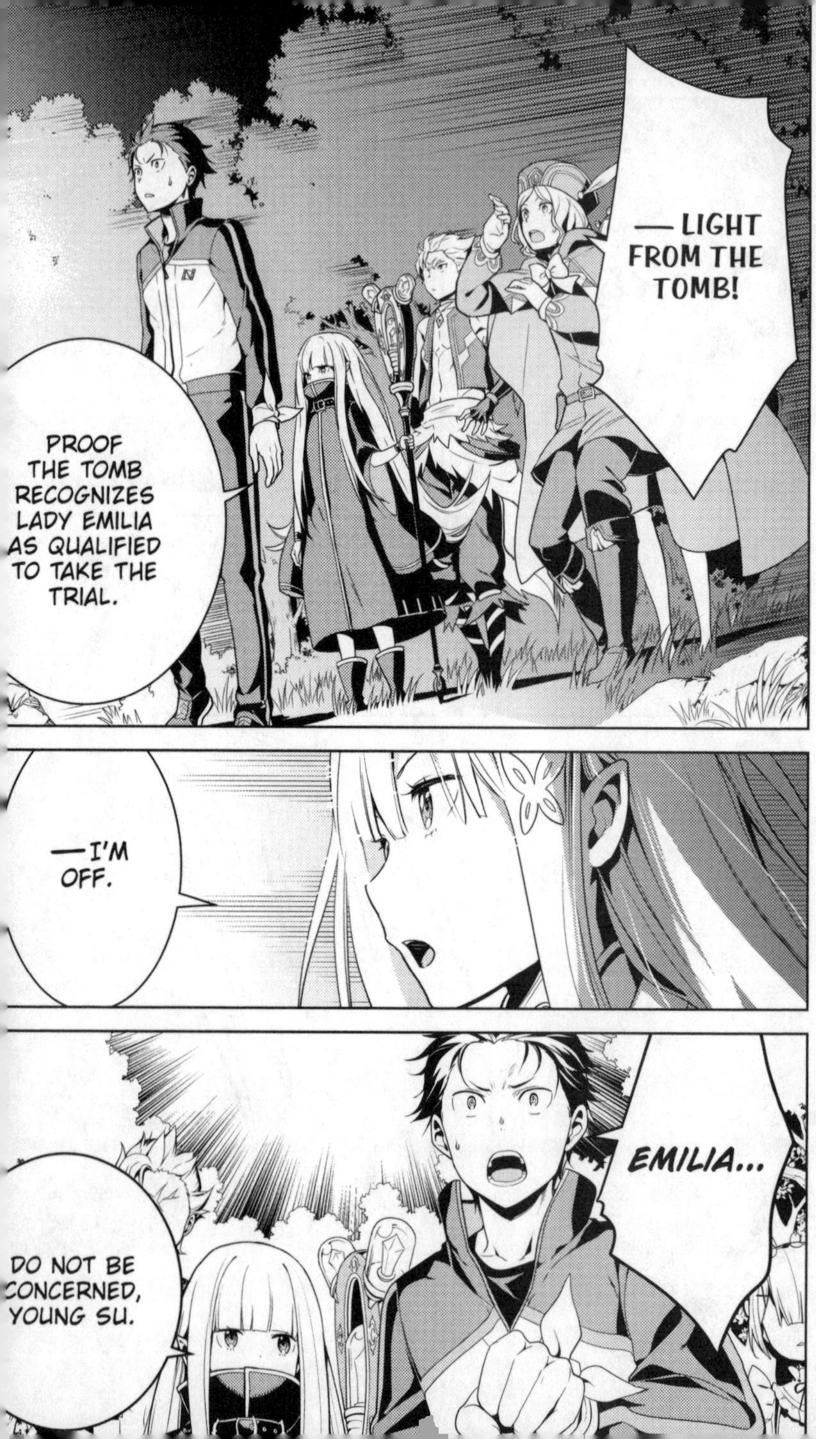
— LIGHT FROM THE TOMB!
PROOF THE TOMB RECOGNIZES LADY EMILIA AS QUALIFIED TO TAKE THE TRIAL.
—I'M OFF.
EMILIA...
DO NOT BE CONCERNED, YOUNG SU.

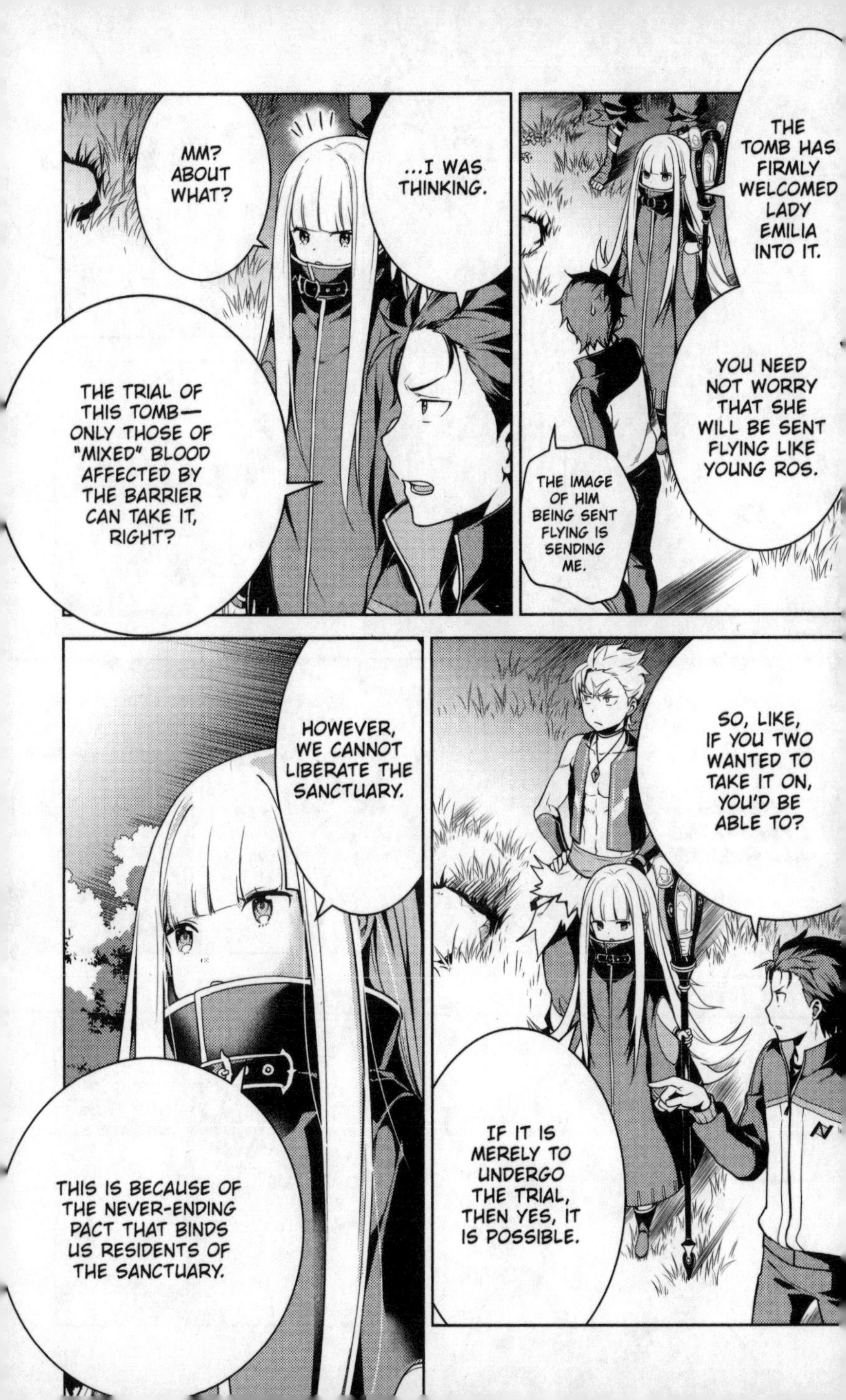
THE TOMB HAS FIRMLY WELCOMED LADY EMILIA INTO IT.
YOU NEED NOT WORRY THAT SHE WILL BE SENT FLYING LIKE YOUNG ROS.
THE IMAGE OF HIM BEING SENT FLYING IS SENDING ME.
...I WAS THINKING.
MM? ABOUT WHAT?
THE TRIAL OF THIS TOMB—ONLY THOSE OF "MIXED" BLOOD AFFECTED BY THE BARRIER CAN TAKE IT, RIGHT?
SO, LIKE, IF YOU TWO WANTED TO TAKE IT ON, YOU'D BE ABLE TO?
IF IT IS MERELY TO UNDERGO THE TRIAL, THEN YES, IT IS POSSIBLE.
HOWEVER, WE CANNOT LIBERATE THE SANCTUARY.
THIS IS BECAUSE OF THE NEVER-ENDING PACT THAT BINDS US RESIDENTS OF THE SANCTUARY.

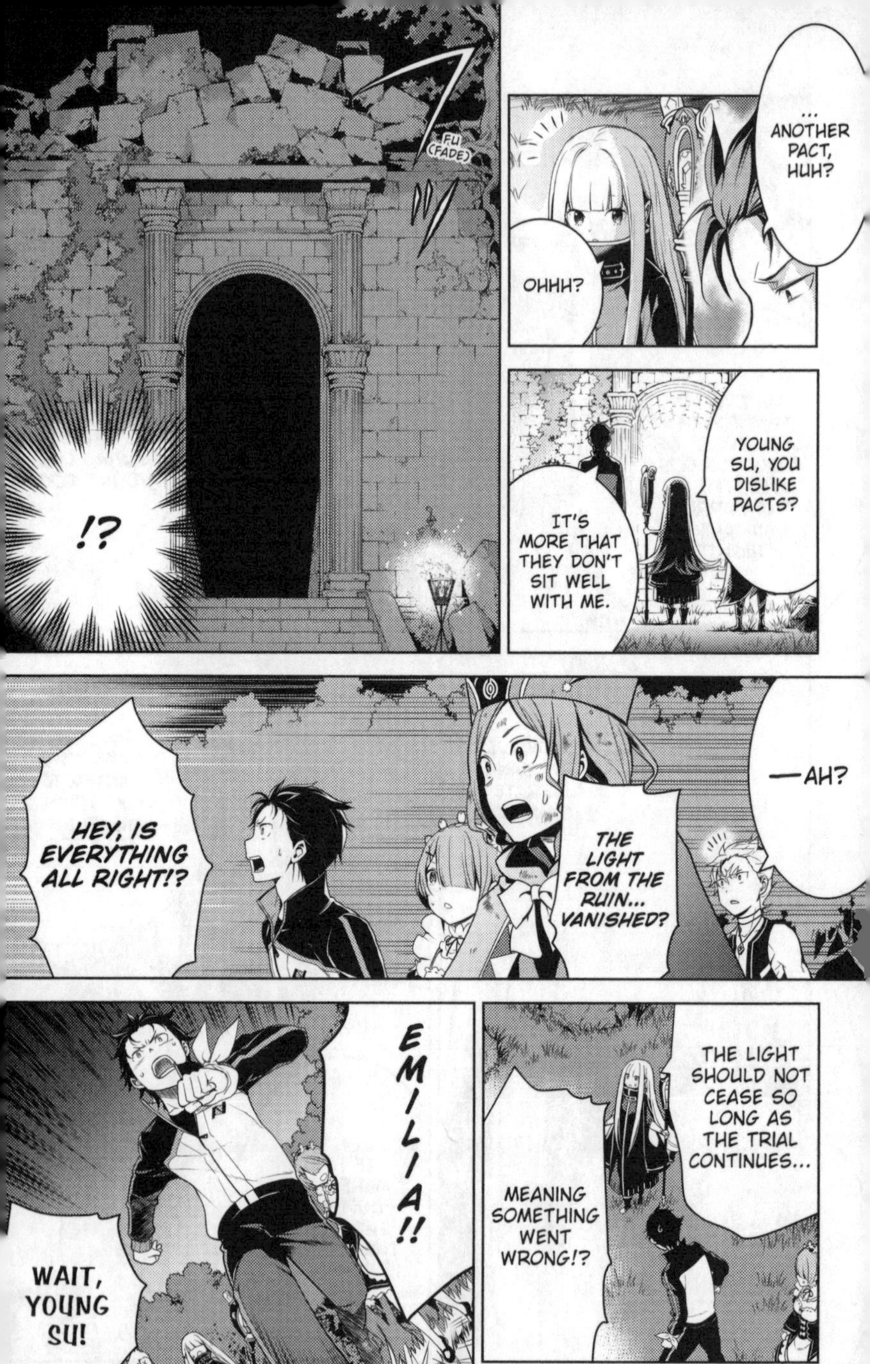
...ANOTHER PACT, HUH?
OHHH?
YOUNG SU, YOU DISLIKE PACTS?
IT'S MORE THAT THEY DON'T SIT WELL WITH ME.
FU (FADE)
!?
—AH?
THE LIGHT FROM THE RUIN... VANISHED?
HEY, IS EVERYTHING ALL RIGHT!?
THE LIGHT SHOULD NOT CEASE SO LONG AS THE TRIAL CONTINUES...
MEANING SOMETHING WENT WRONG!?
EMILIA!!
WAIT, YOUNG SU!

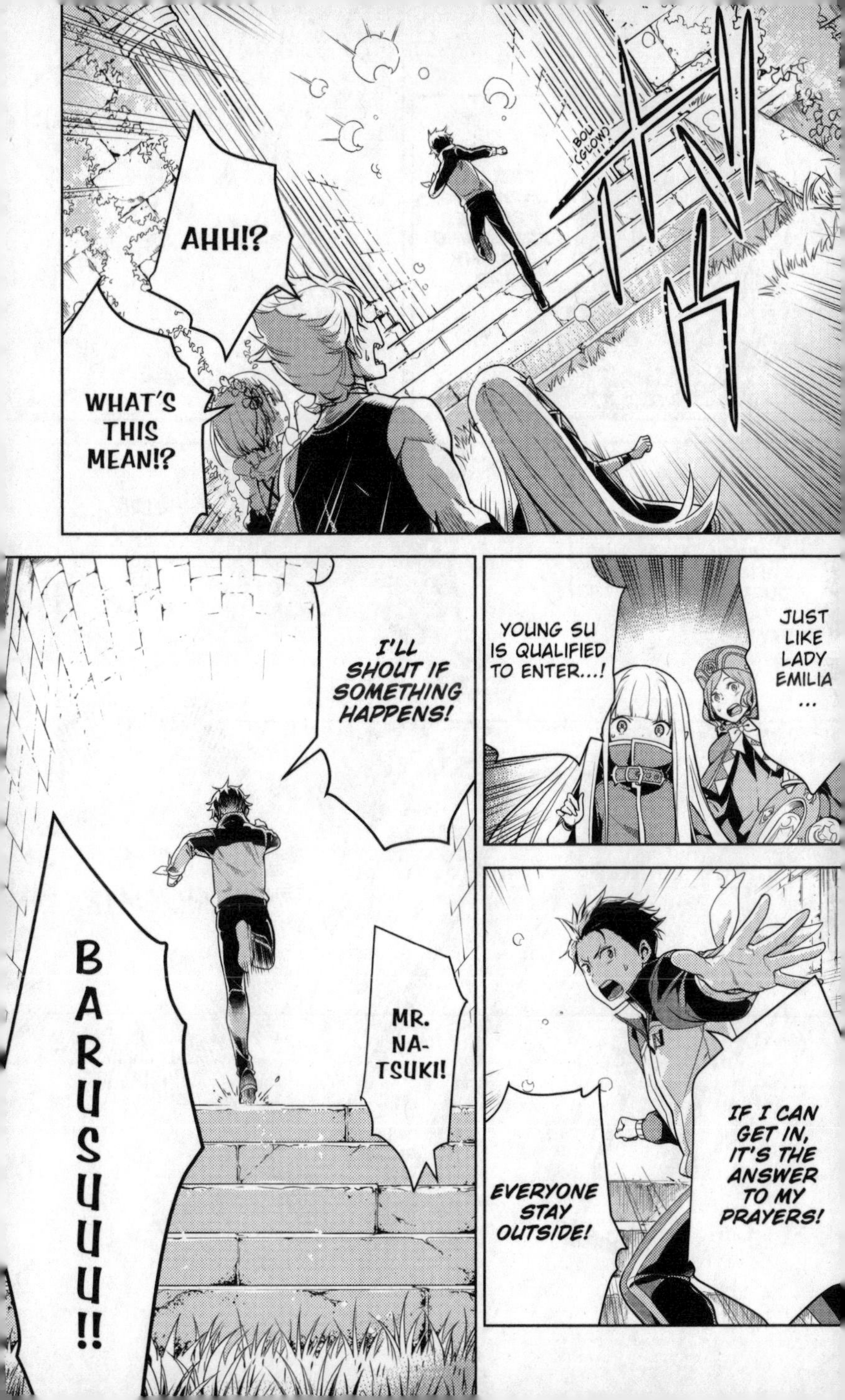
BOU (GLOW)
AHH!?
WHAT'S THIS MEAN!?
JUST LIKE LADY EMILIA ...
YOUNG SU IS QUALIFIED TO ENTER...!
IF I CAN GET IN, IT'S THE ANSWER TO MY PRAYERS!
EVERYONE STAY OUTSIDE!
I'LL SHOUT IF SOMETHING HAPPENS!
MR. NA-TSUKI!
BARUSUUU!!

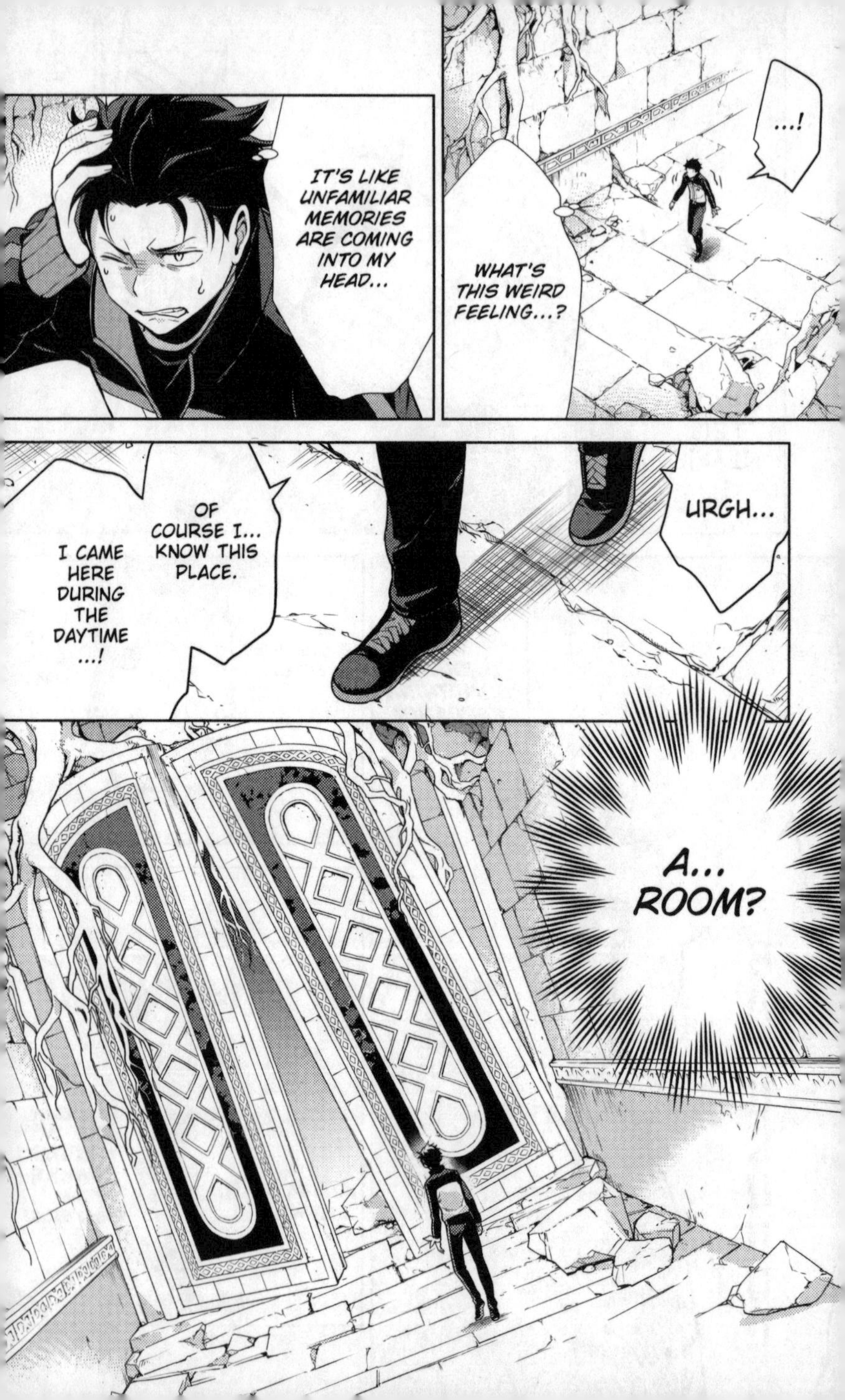
...!
WHAT'S THIS WEIRD FEELING...?
IT'S LIKE UNFAMILIAR MEMORIES ARE COMING INTO MY HEAD...
URGH...
OF COURSE I... KNOW THIS PLACE.
I CAME HERE DURING THE DAYTIME ...!
A... ROOM?

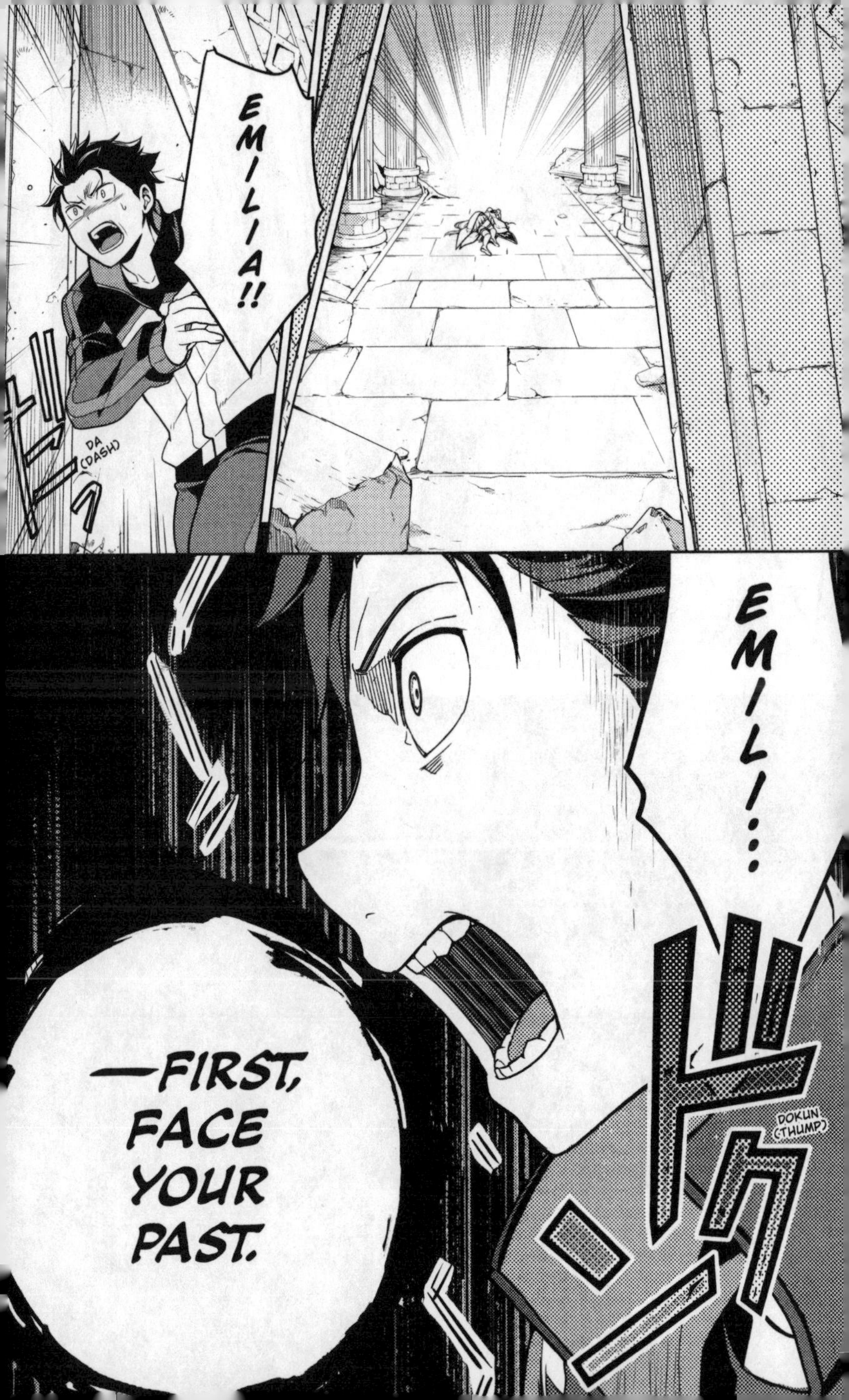
EMILIA!!
DA (DASH)
EMILI...
DOKUN (THUMP)
—FIRST, FACE YOUR PAST.

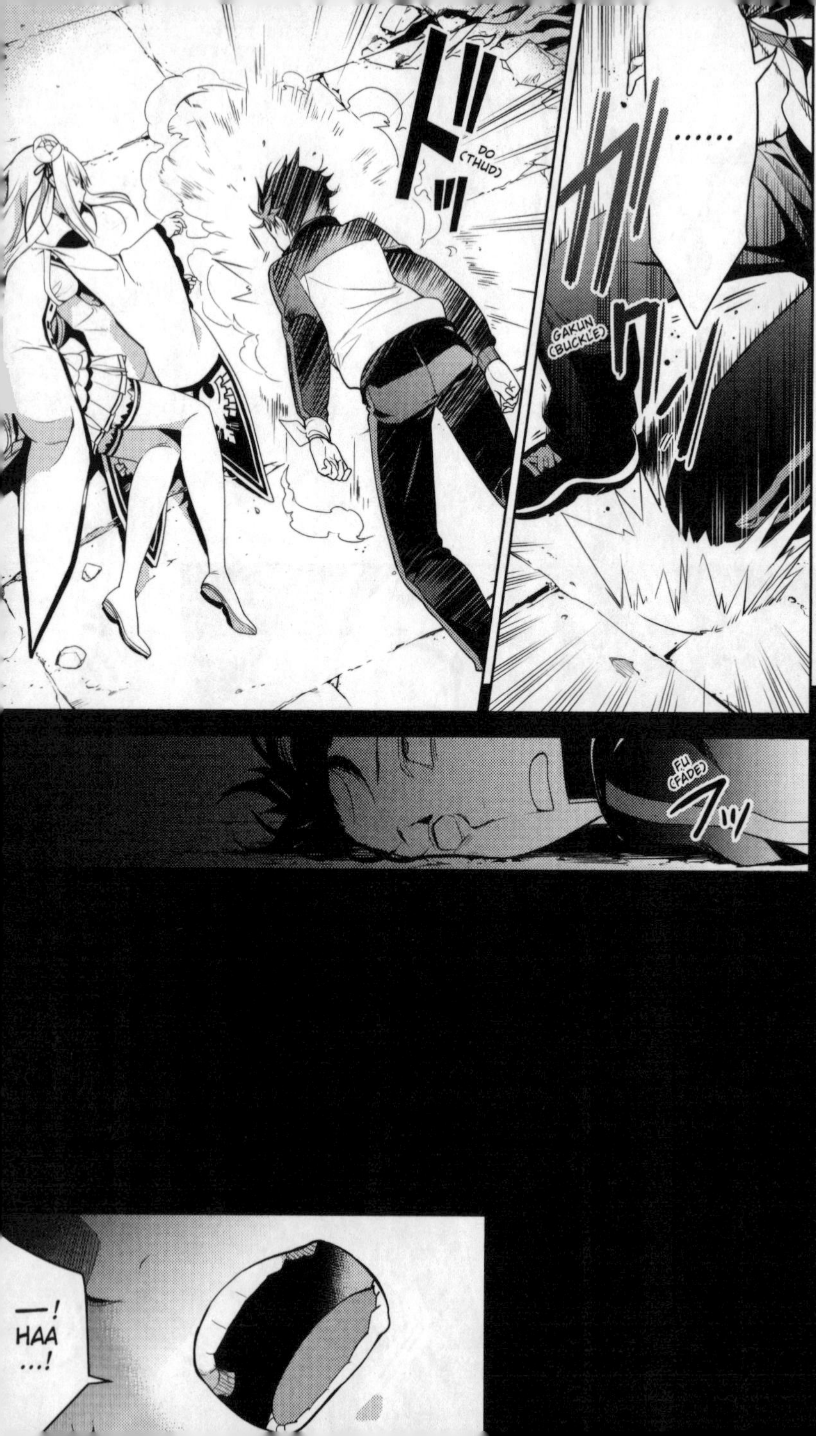
......
GAKUN (BUCKLE)
DO (THUD)
FU (FADE)
—! HAA ...!

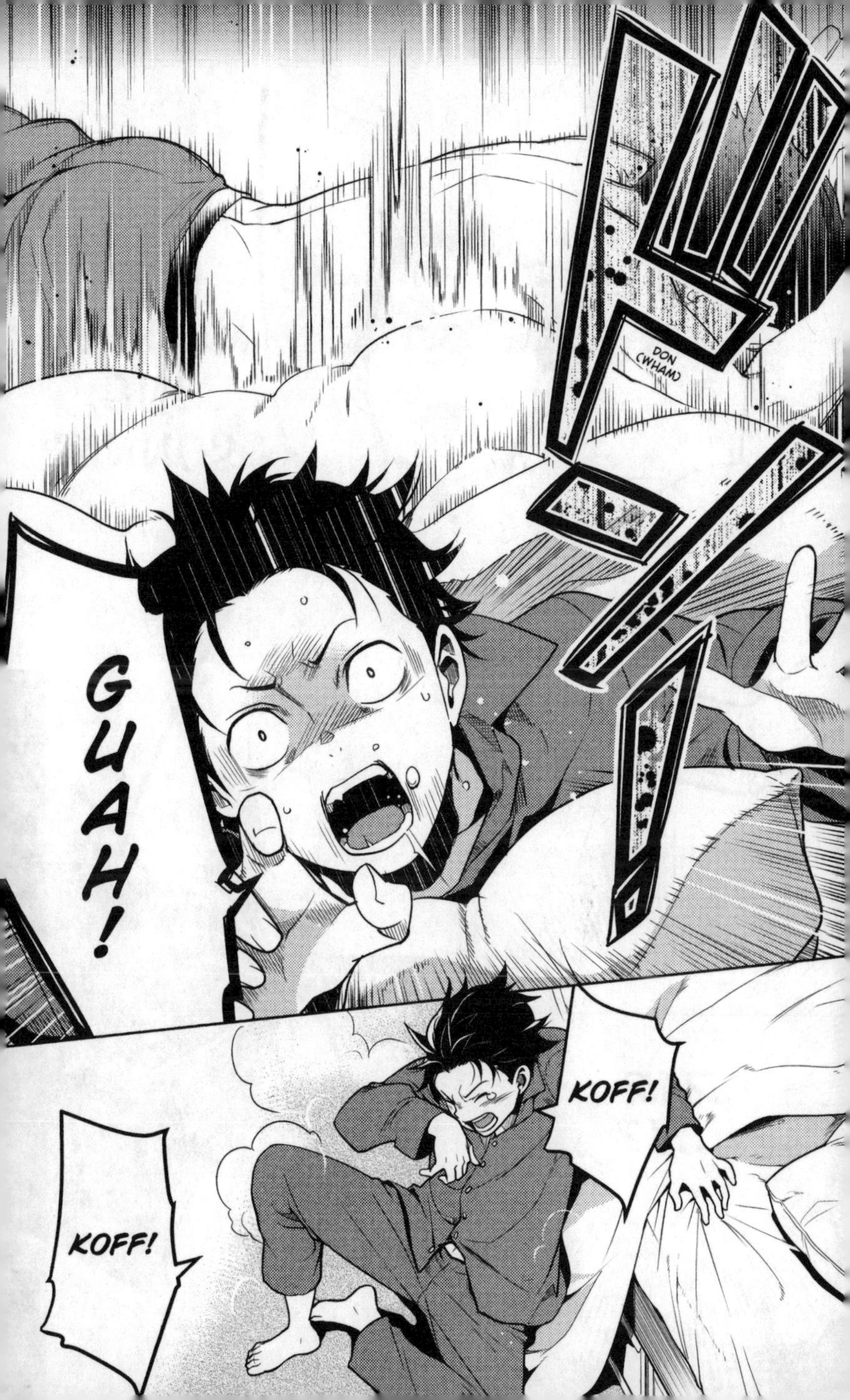
DON (WHAM)
GUAH!
KOFF!
KOFF!

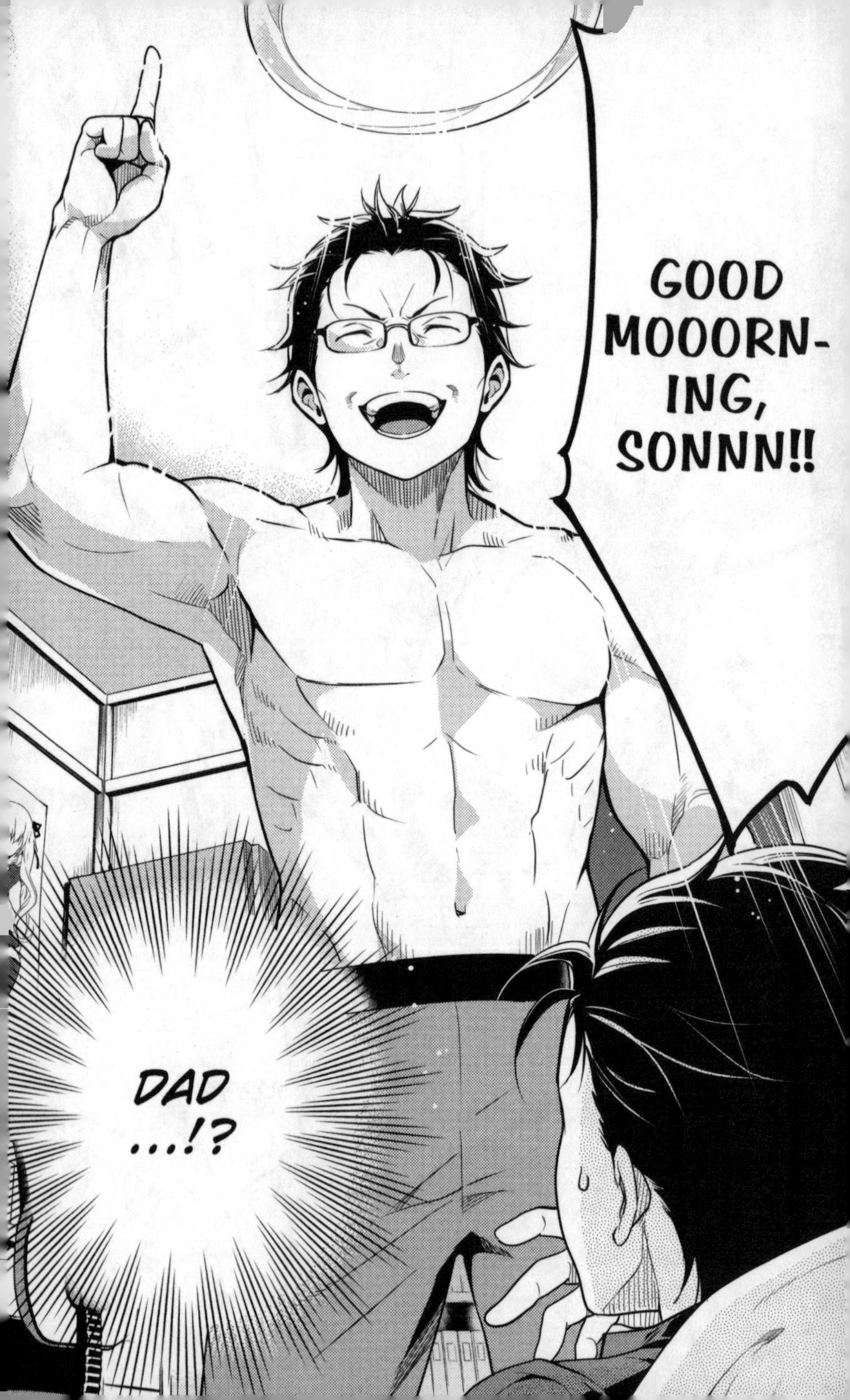
GOOD MOOORN-ING, SONNN!!
DAD ...!?

The only ability Subaru Natsuki gets when he's
summoned to another world is time travel via his own death.
But to save her, he'll die as many times as it takes.

Re:ZERO

-Starting Life in Another World-

Re:ZERO -Starting Life in Another World-

Chapter 4: The Sanctuary and the Witch of Greed

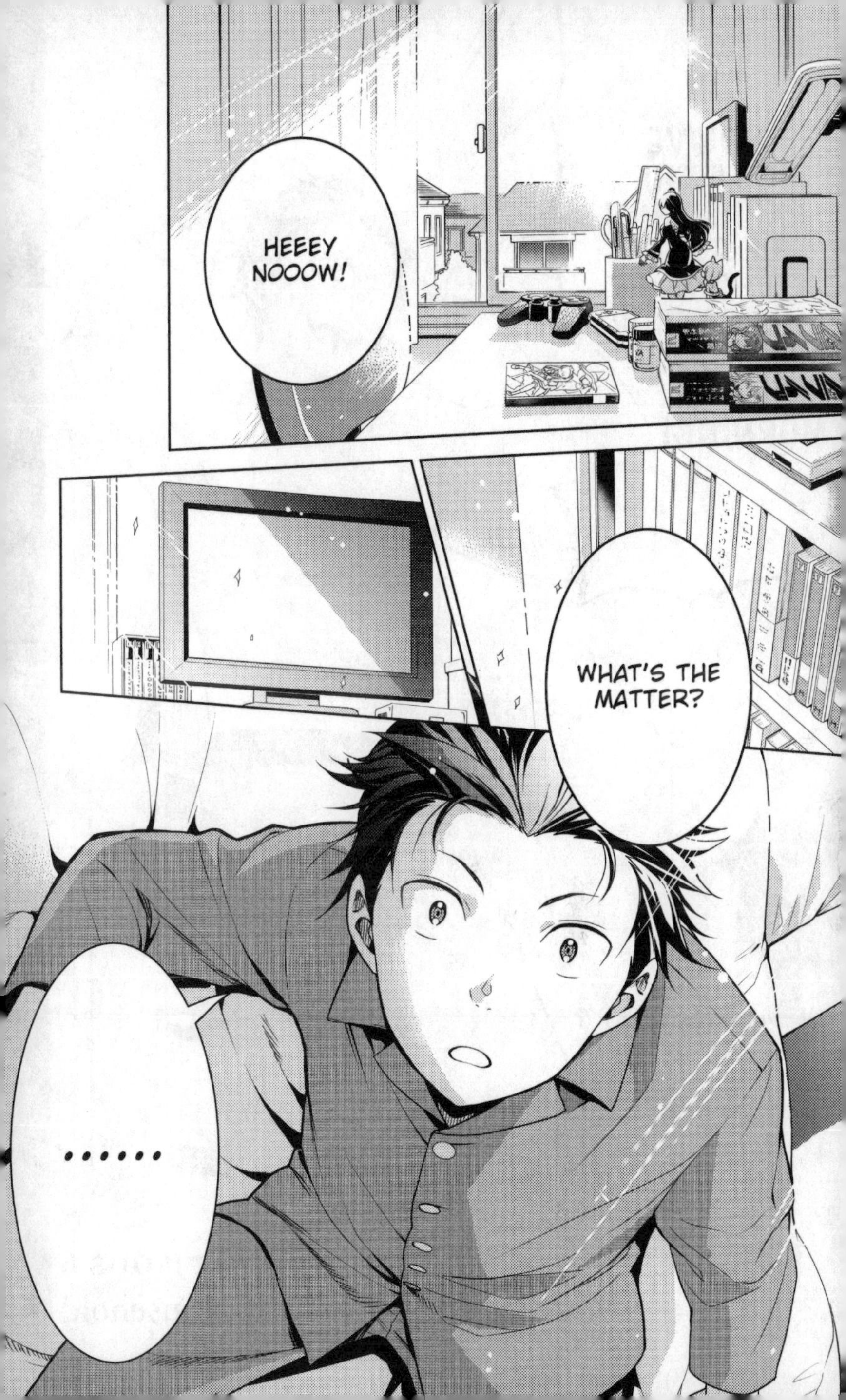
HEEEY NOOOW!
WHAT'S THE MATTER?
......

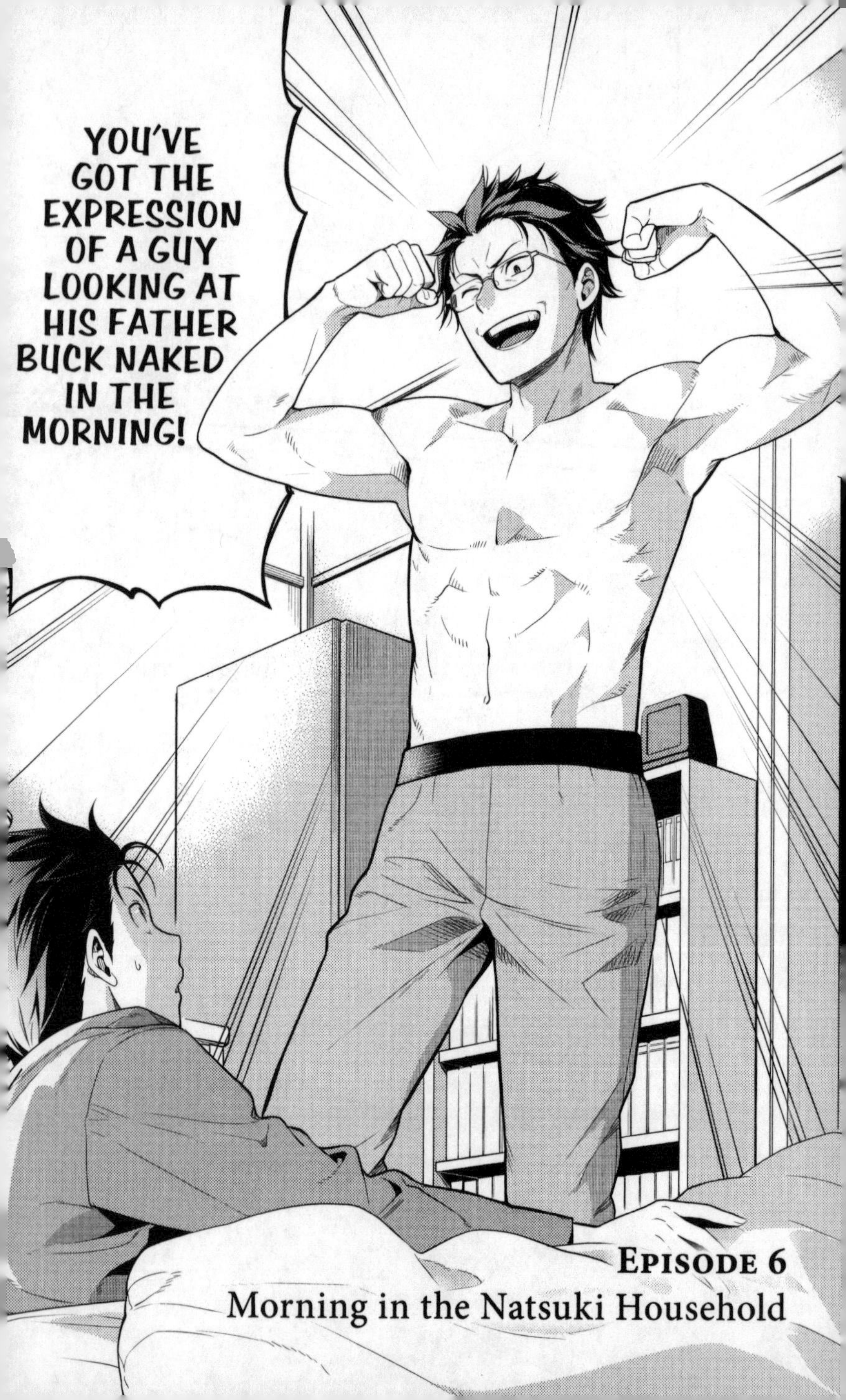
YOU'VE GOT THE EXPRESSION OF A GUY LOOKING AT HIS FATHER BUCK NAKED IN THE MORNING!

Episode 6
Morning in the Natsuki Household

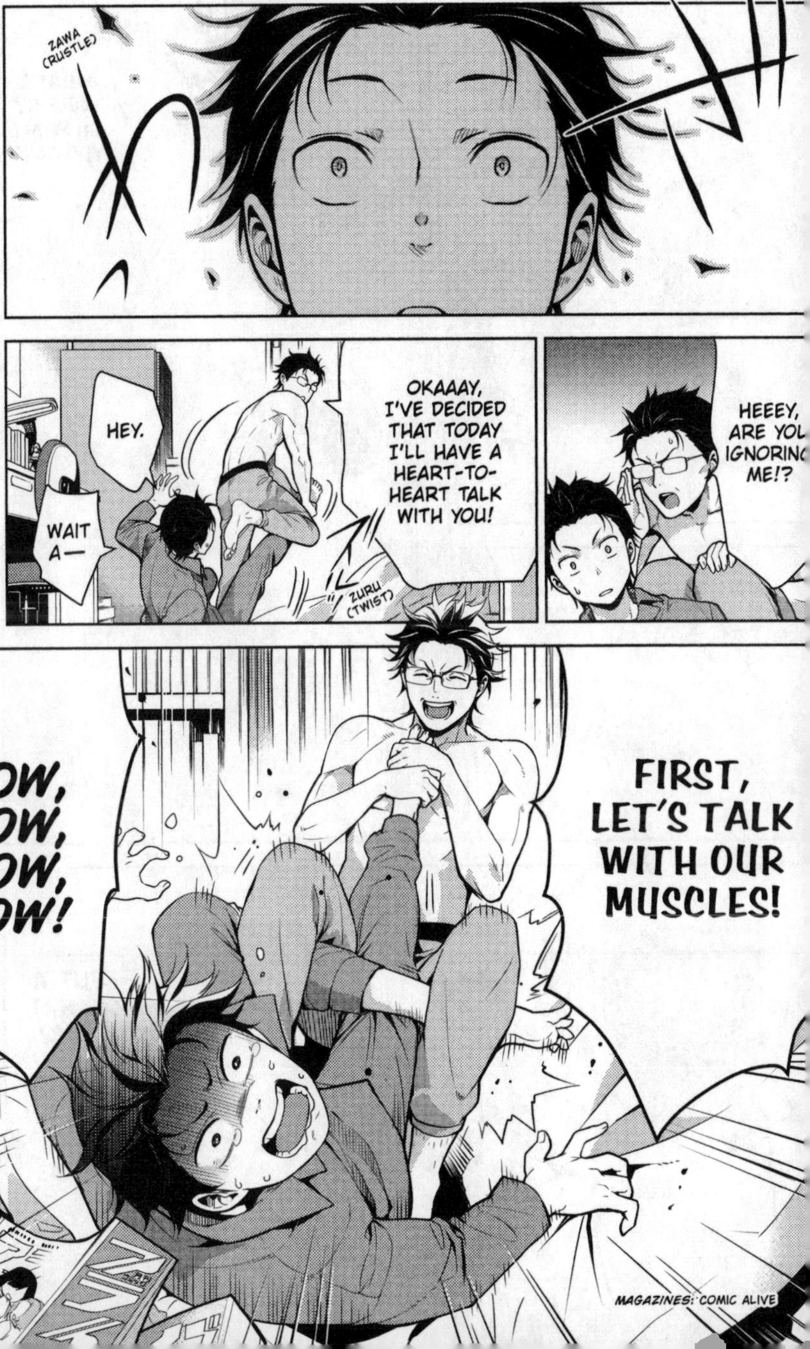
ZAWA (RUSTLE)
HEEEY, ARE YOU IGNORING ME!?
OKAAAY, I'VE DECIDED THAT TODAY I'LL HAVE A HEART-TO-HEART TALK WITH YOU!
ZURU (TWIST)
HEY.
WAIT A—
FIRST, LET'S TALK WITH OUR MUSCLES!
OW, OW, OW, OW!
MAGAZINES: COMIC ALIVE

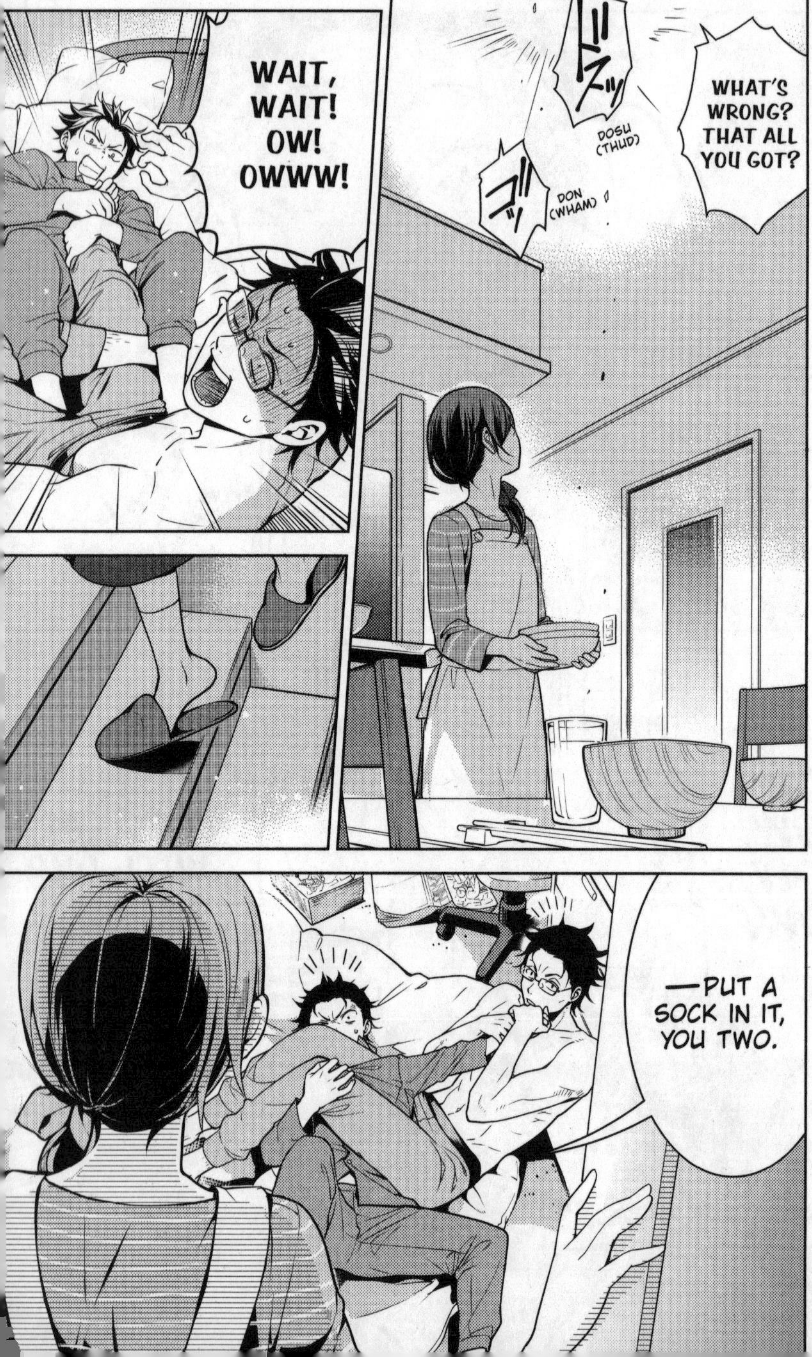
WHAT'S WRONG? THAT ALL YOU GOT?
DOSU (THUD)
DON (WHAM)
WAIT, WAIT! OW! OWWW!
—PUT A SOCK IN IT, YOU TWO.

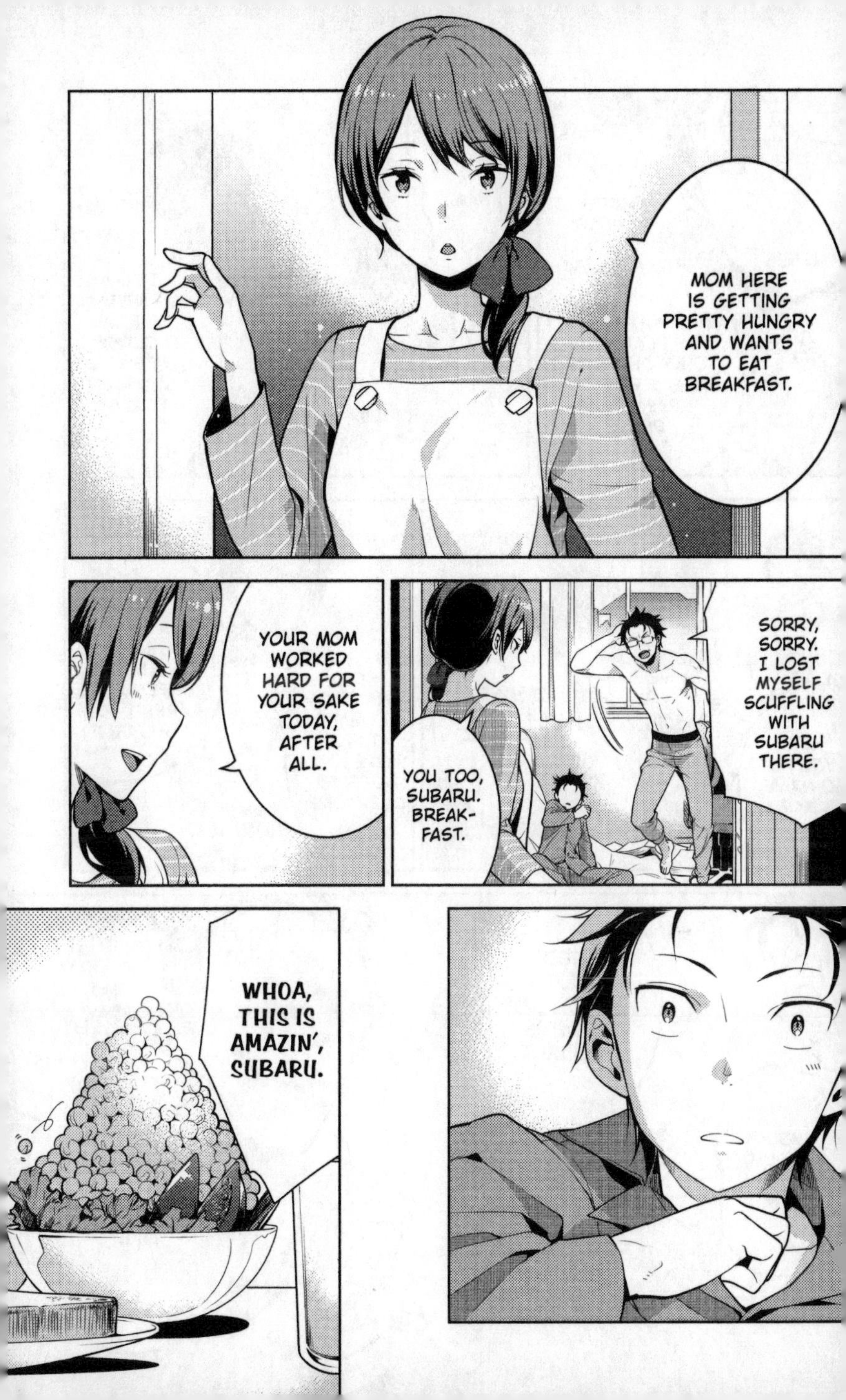
MOM HERE IS GETTING PRETTY HUNGRY AND WANTS TO EAT BREAKFAST.
SORRY, SORRY. I LOST MYSELF SCUFFLING WITH SUBARU THERE.
YOU TOO, SUBARU. BREAK-FAST.
YOUR MOM WORKED HARD FOR YOUR SAKE TODAY, AFTER ALL.
WHOA, THIS IS AMAZIN', SUBARU.

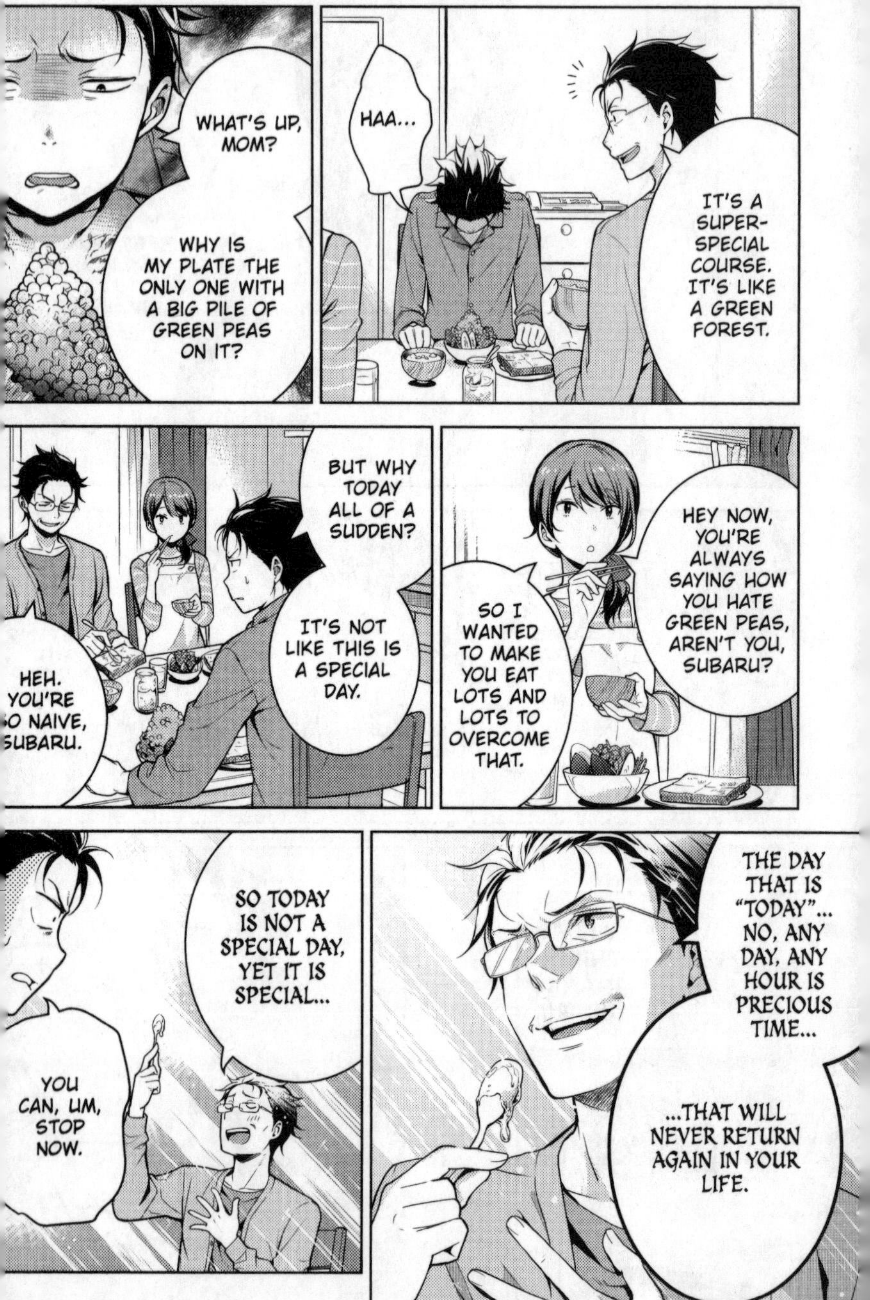
IT'S A SUPER-SPECIAL COURSE. IT'S LIKE A GREEN FOREST.
HAA...
WHAT'S UP, MOM?
WHY IS MY PLATE THE ONLY ONE WITH A BIG PILE OF GREEN PEAS ON IT?
HEY NOW, YOU'RE ALWAYS SAYING HOW YOU HATE GREEN PEAS, AREN'T YOU, SUBARU?
SO I WANTED TO MAKE YOU EAT LOTS AND LOTS TO OVERCOME THAT.
BUT WHY TODAY ALL OF A SUDDEN?
IT'S NOT LIKE THIS IS A SPECIAL DAY.
HEH. YOU'RE O NAIVE, UBARU.
THE DAY THAT IS "TODAY"... NO, ANY DAY, ANY HOUR IS PRECIOUS TIME...
...THAT WILL NEVER RETURN AGAIN IN YOUR LIFE.
SO TODAY IS NOT A SPECIAL DAY, YET IT IS SPECIAL...
YOU CAN, UM, STOP NOW.

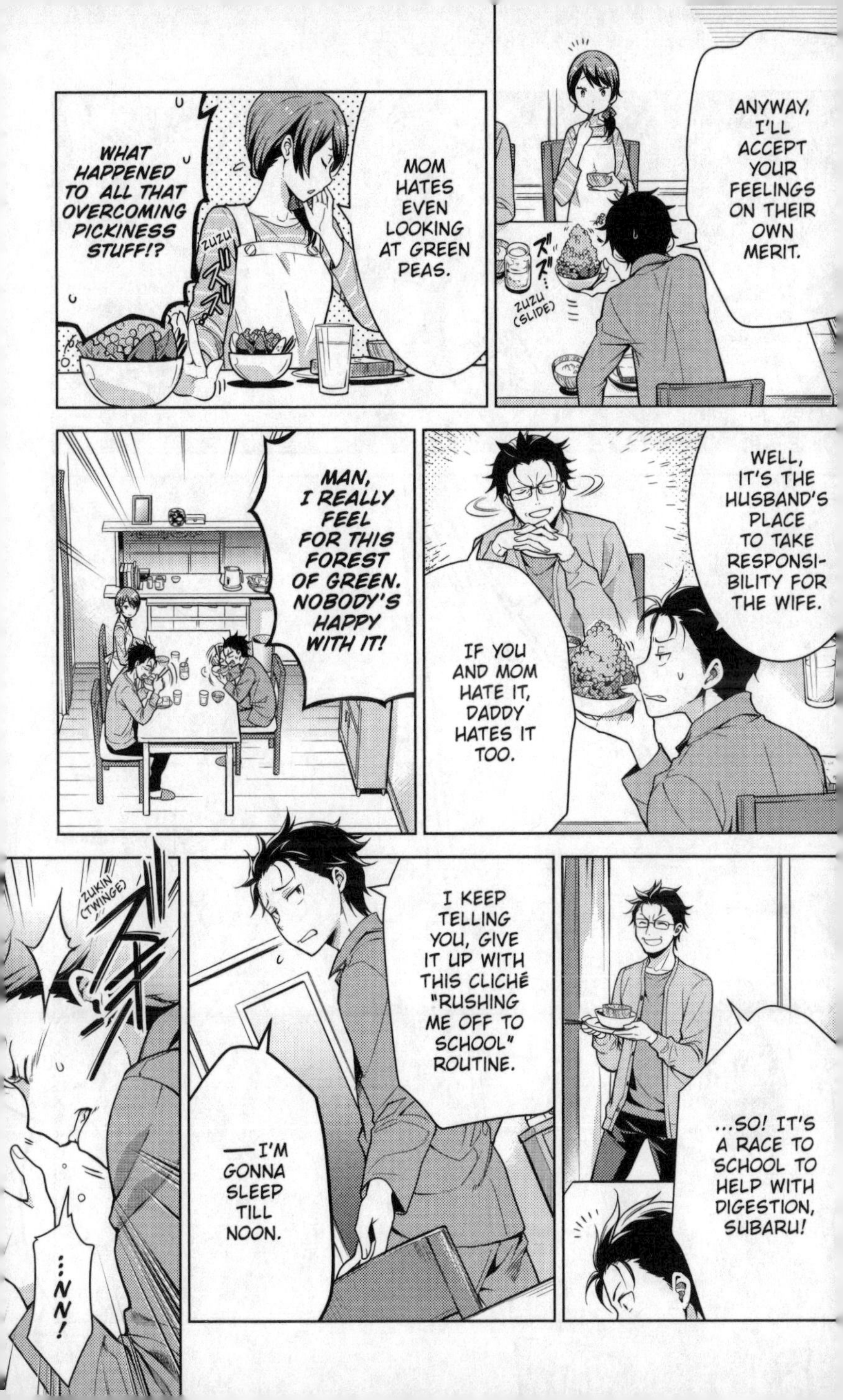
ANYWAY, I'LL ACCEPT YOUR FEELINGS ON THEIR OWN MERIT.
ZUZU (SLIDE)
MOM HATES EVEN LOOKING AT GREEN PEAS.
WHAT HAPPENED TO ALL THAT OVERCOMING PICKINESS STUFF!?
ZUZU
WELL, IT'S THE HUSBAND'S PLACE TO TAKE RESPONSIBILITY FOR THE WIFE.
IF YOU AND MOM HATE IT, DADDY HATES IT TOO.
MAN, I REALLY FEEL FOR THIS FOREST OF GREEN. NOBODY'S HAPPY WITH IT!
...SO! IT'S A RACE TO SCHOOL TO HELP WITH DIGESTION, SUBARU!
I KEEP TELLING YOU, GIVE IT UP WITH THIS CLICHÉ "RUSHING ME OFF TO SCHOOL" ROUTINE.
—I'M GONNA SLEEP TILL NOON.
ZUKIN (TWINGE)
...NN!

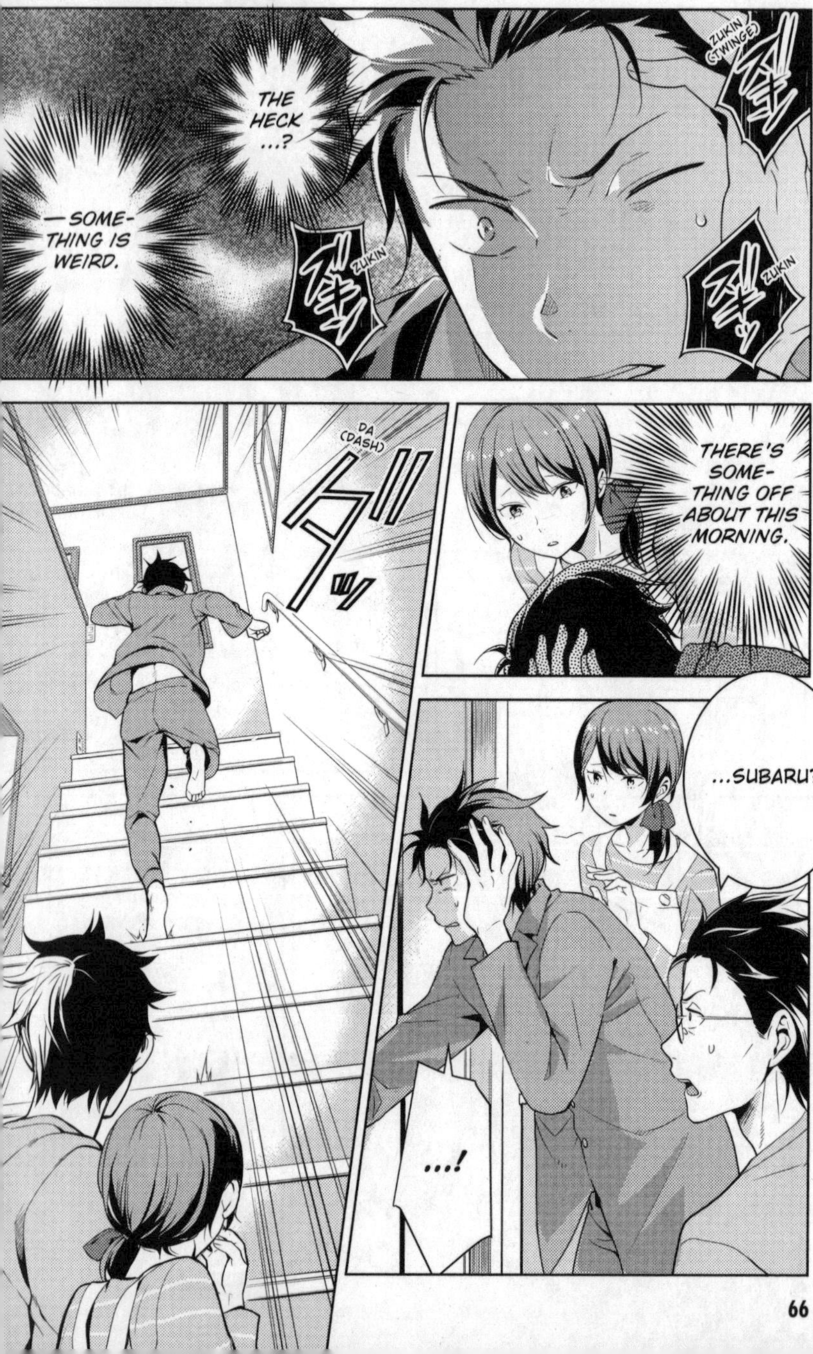

ZUKIN (TWINGE)
THE HECK ...?
ZUKIN
ZUKIN
—SOME-THING IS WEIRD.
THERE'S SOME-THING OFF ABOUT THIS MORNING.
...SUBARU?
...!
DA (DASH)

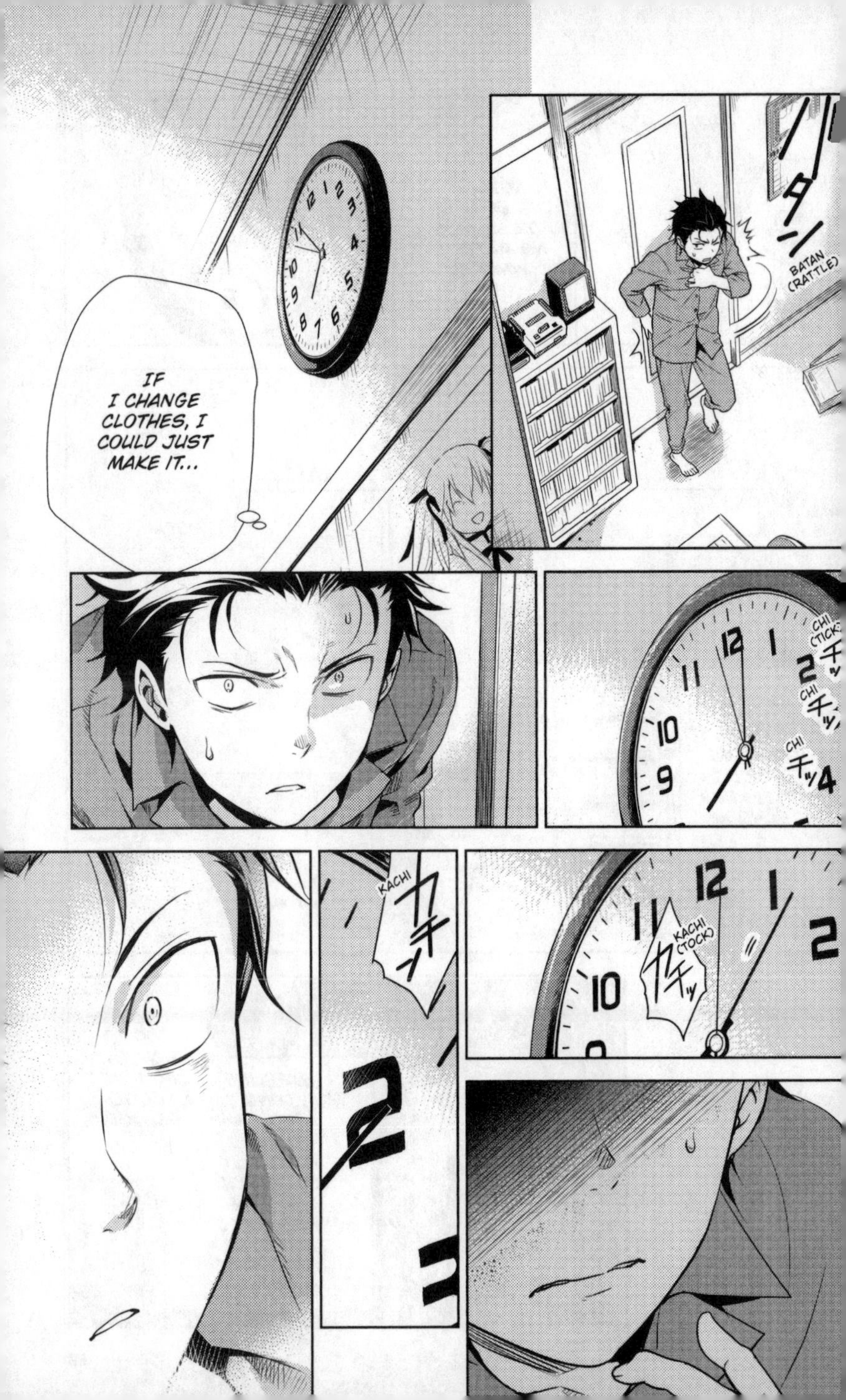
バタン
BATAN (RATTLE)
IF I CHANGE CLOTHES, I COULD JUST MAKE IT...
CHI (TICK)
CHI
CHI
KACHI (TOCK)
KACHI

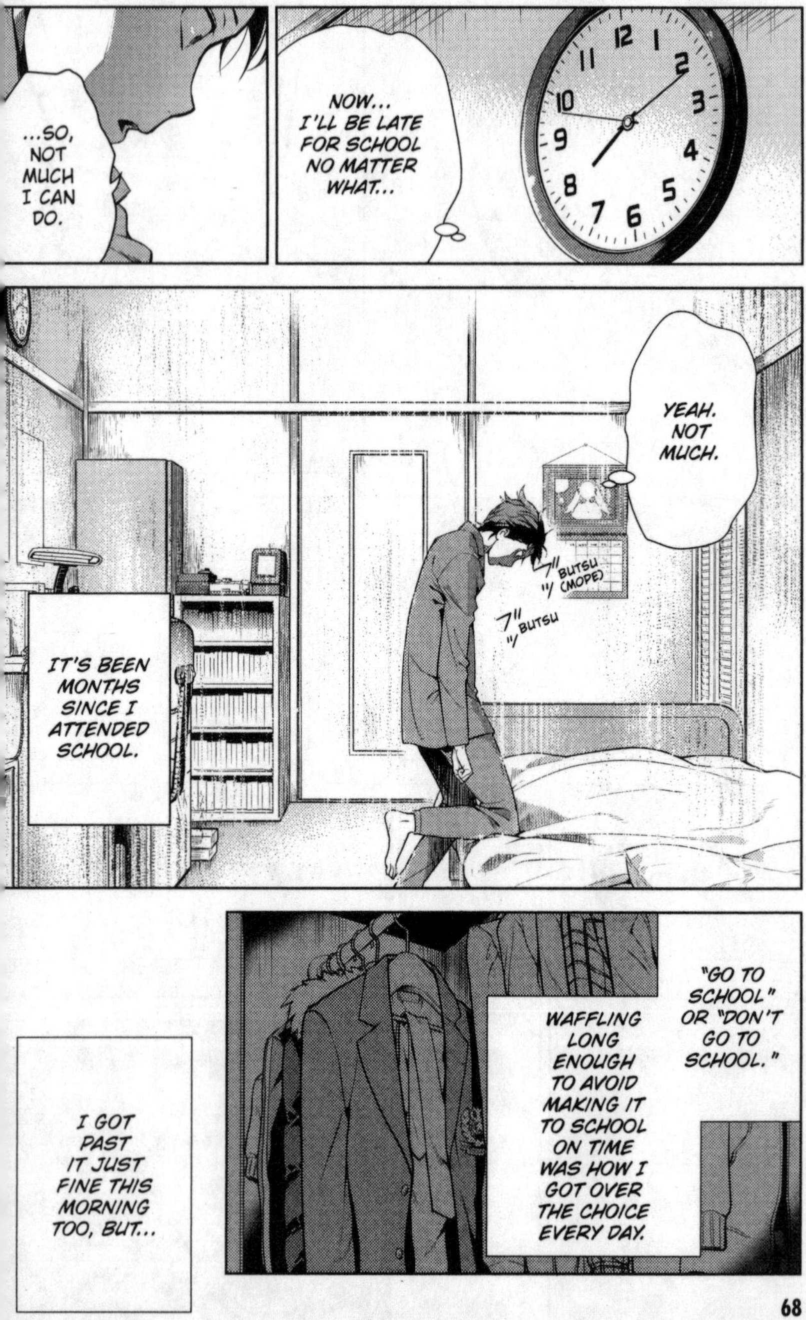
NOW... I'LL BE LATE FOR SCHOOL NO MATTER WHAT...
...SO, NOT MUCH I CAN DO.
YEAH. NOT MUCH.
BUTSU (MOPE)
BUTSU
IT'S BEEN MONTHS SINCE I ATTENDED SCHOOL.
"GO TO SCHOOL" OR "DON'T GO TO SCHOOL."
WAFFLING LONG ENOUGH TO AVOID MAKING IT TO SCHOOL ON TIME WAS HOW I GOT OVER THE CHOICE EVERY DAY.
I GOT PAST IT JUST FINE THIS MORNING TOO, BUT...

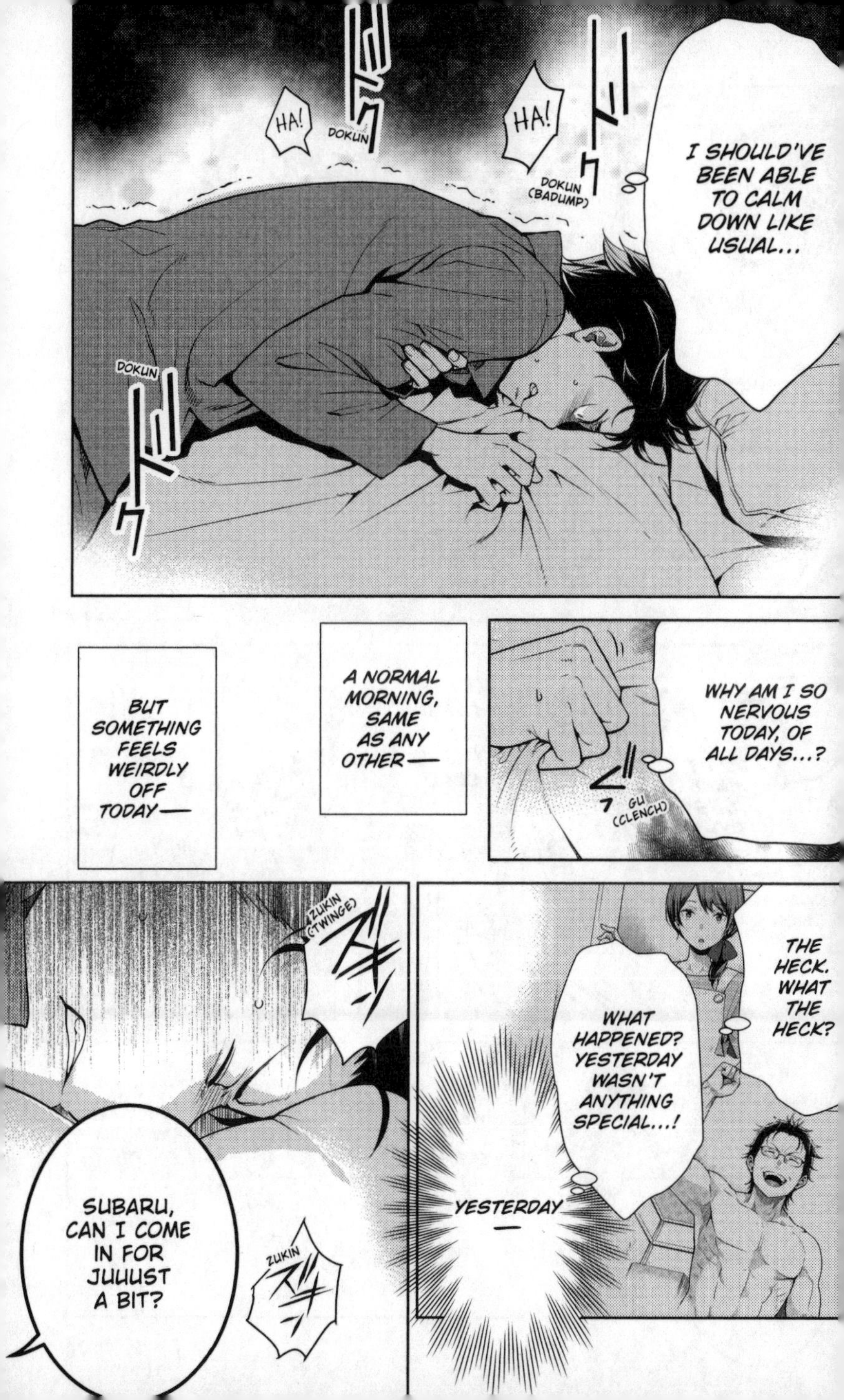
I SHOULD'VE BEEN ABLE TO CALM DOWN LIKE USUAL...
DOKUN (BADUMP)
HA!
DOKUN
HA!
DOKUN
WHY AM I SO NERVOUS TODAY, OF ALL DAYS...?
GU (CLENCH)
A NORMAL MORNING, SAME AS ANY OTHER—
BUT SOMETHING FEELS WEIRDLY OFF TODAY—
THE HECK. WHAT THE HECK?
WHAT HAPPENED? YESTERDAY WASN'T ANYTHING SPECIAL...!
YESTERDAY—
ZUKIN (TWINGE)
SUBARU, CAN I COME IN FOR JUUUST A BIT?
ZUKIN

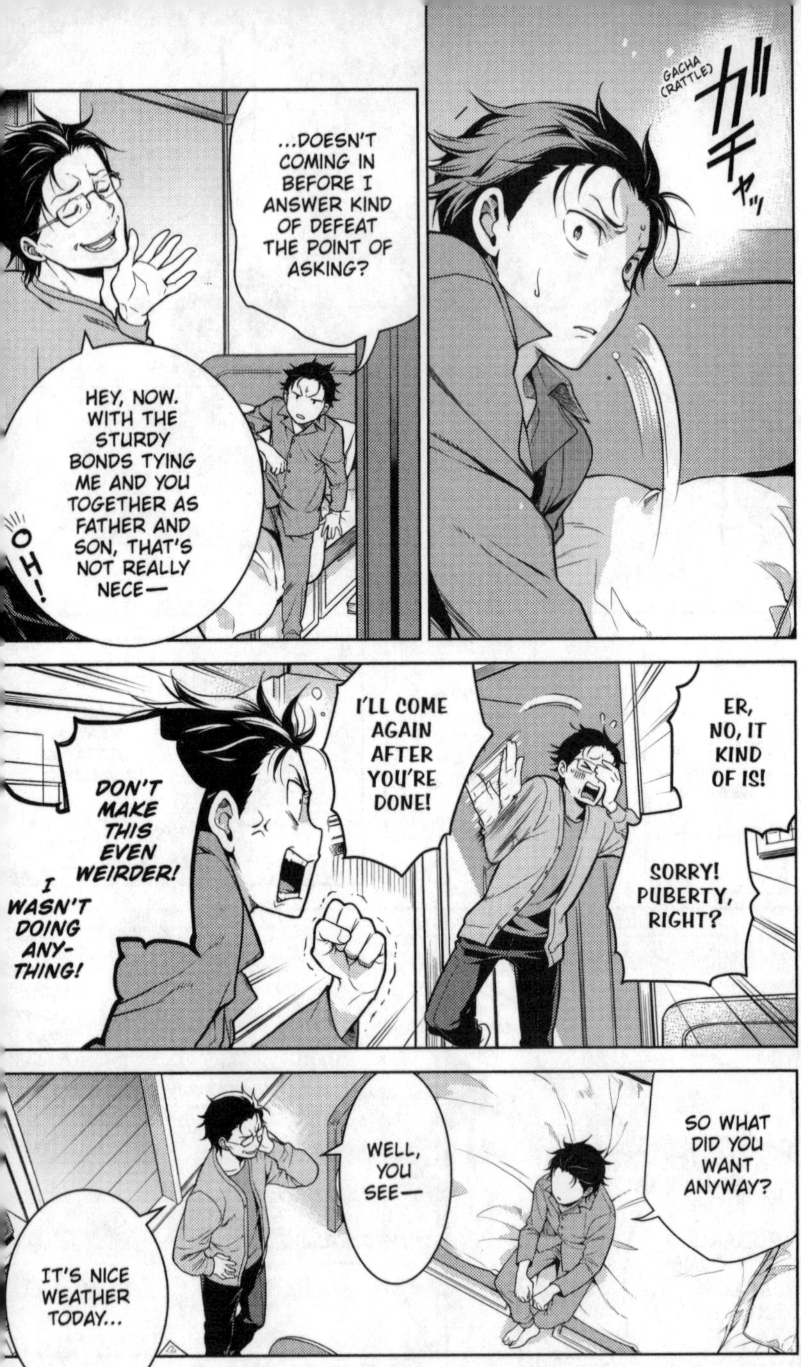

ガチャッ
GACHA (RATTLE)
...DOESN'T COMING IN BEFORE I ANSWER KIND OF DEFEAT THE POINT OF ASKING?
HEY, NOW. WITH THE STURDY BONDS TYING ME AND YOU TOGETHER AS FATHER AND SON, THAT'S NOT REALLY NECE—
OH!
ER, NO, IT KIND OF IS!
SORRY! PUBERTY, RIGHT?
I'LL COME AGAIN AFTER YOU'RE DONE!
DON'T MAKE THIS EVEN WEIRDER!
I WASN'T DOING ANYTHING!
SO WHAT DID YOU WANT ANYWAY?
WELL, YOU SEE—
IT'S NICE WEATHER TODAY...

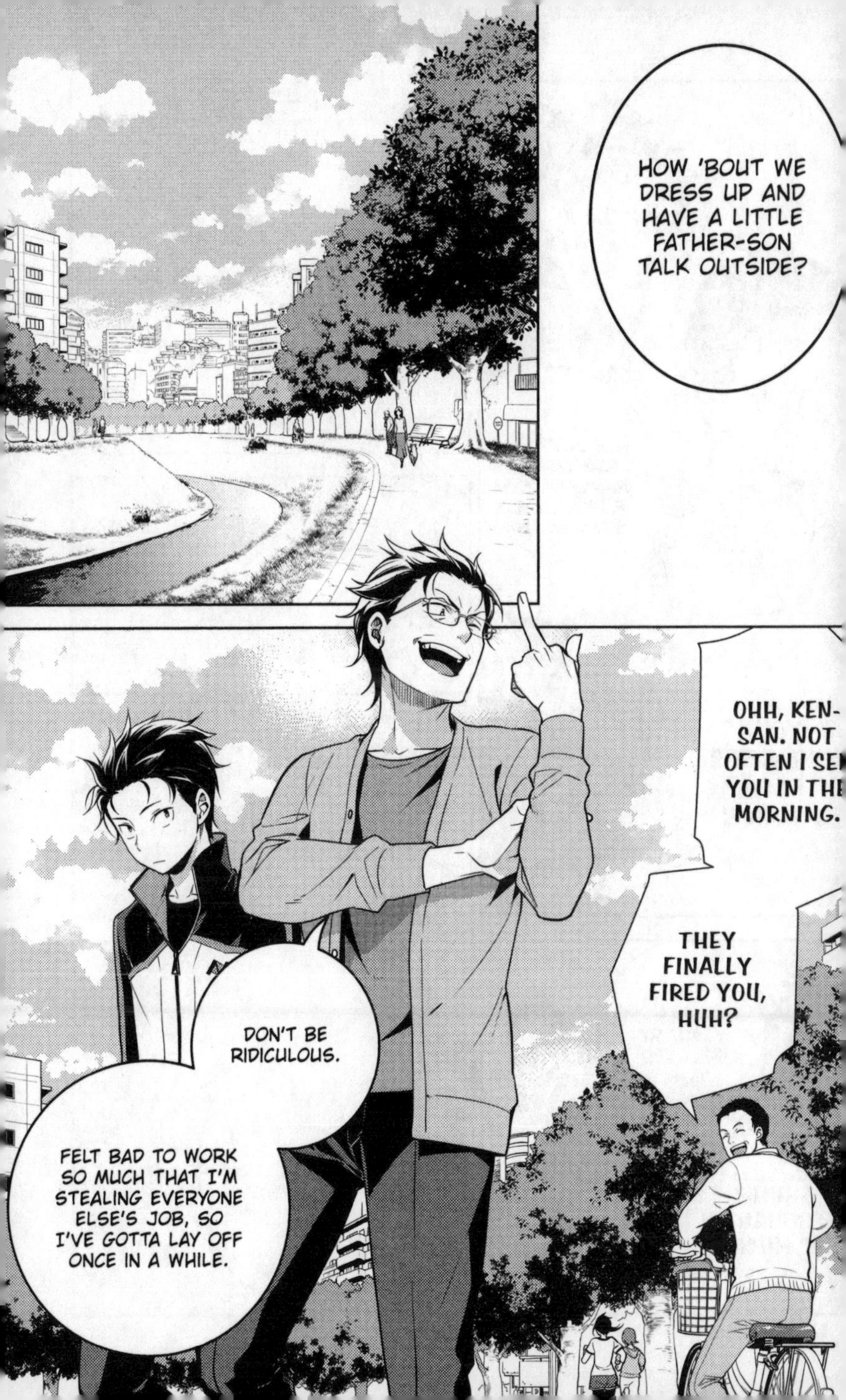
HOW 'BOUT WE DRESS UP AND HAVE A LITTLE FATHER-SON TALK OUTSIDE?
OHH, KEN-SAN. NOT OFTEN I SEE YOU IN THE MORNING.
THEY FINALLY FIRED YOU, HUH?
DON'T BE RIDICULOUS.
FELT BAD TO WORK SO MUCH THAT I'M STEALING EVERYONE ELSE'S JOB, SO I'VE GOTTA LAY OFF ONCE IN A WHILE.

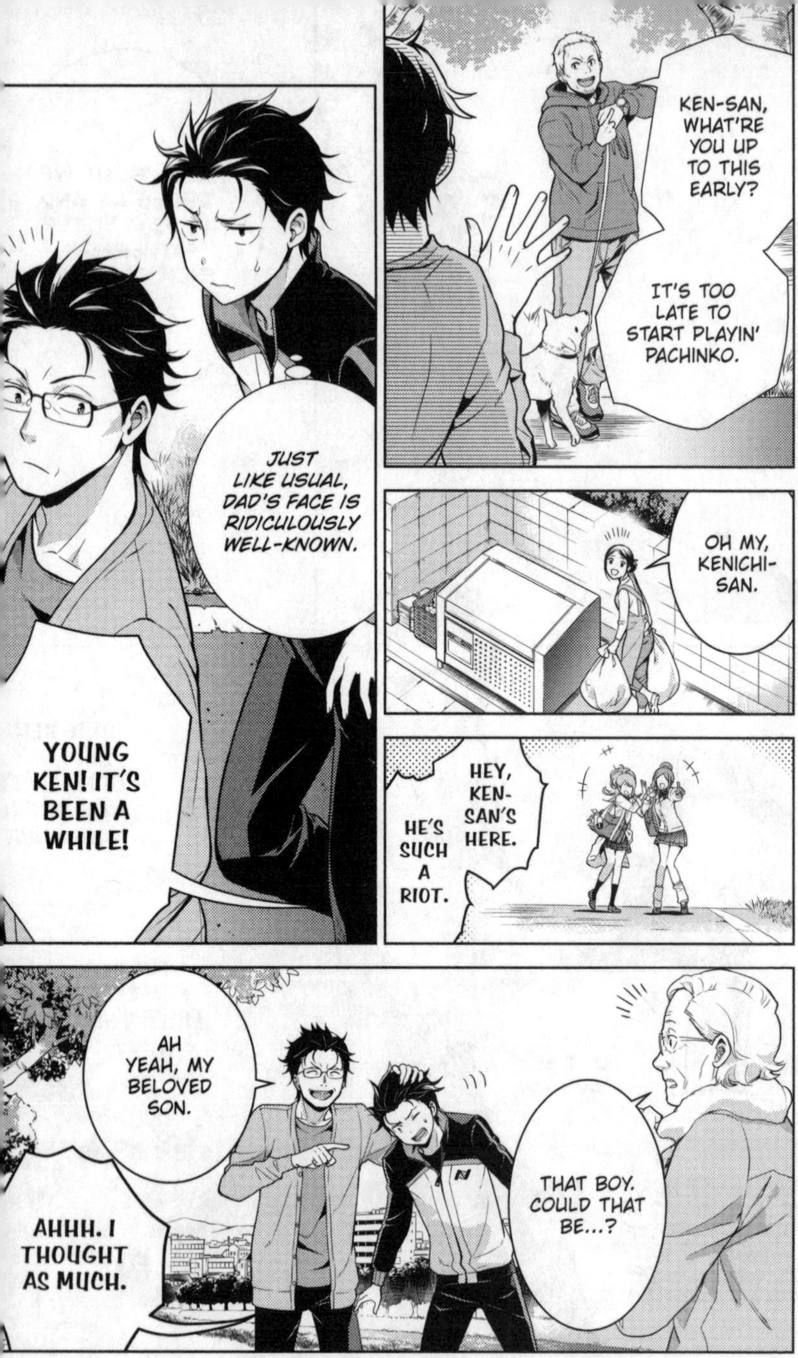
KEN-SAN, WHAT'RE YOU UP TO THIS EARLY?
IT'S TOO LATE TO START PLAYIN' PACHINKO.
OH MY, KENICHI-SAN.
HEY, KEN-SAN'S HERE.
HE'S SUCH A RIOT.
JUST LIKE USUAL, DAD'S FACE IS RIDICULOUSLY WELL-KNOWN.
YOUNG KEN! IT'S BEEN A WHILE!
THAT BOY. COULD THAT BE...?
AH YEAH, MY BELOVED SON.
AHHH. I THOUGHT AS MUCH.

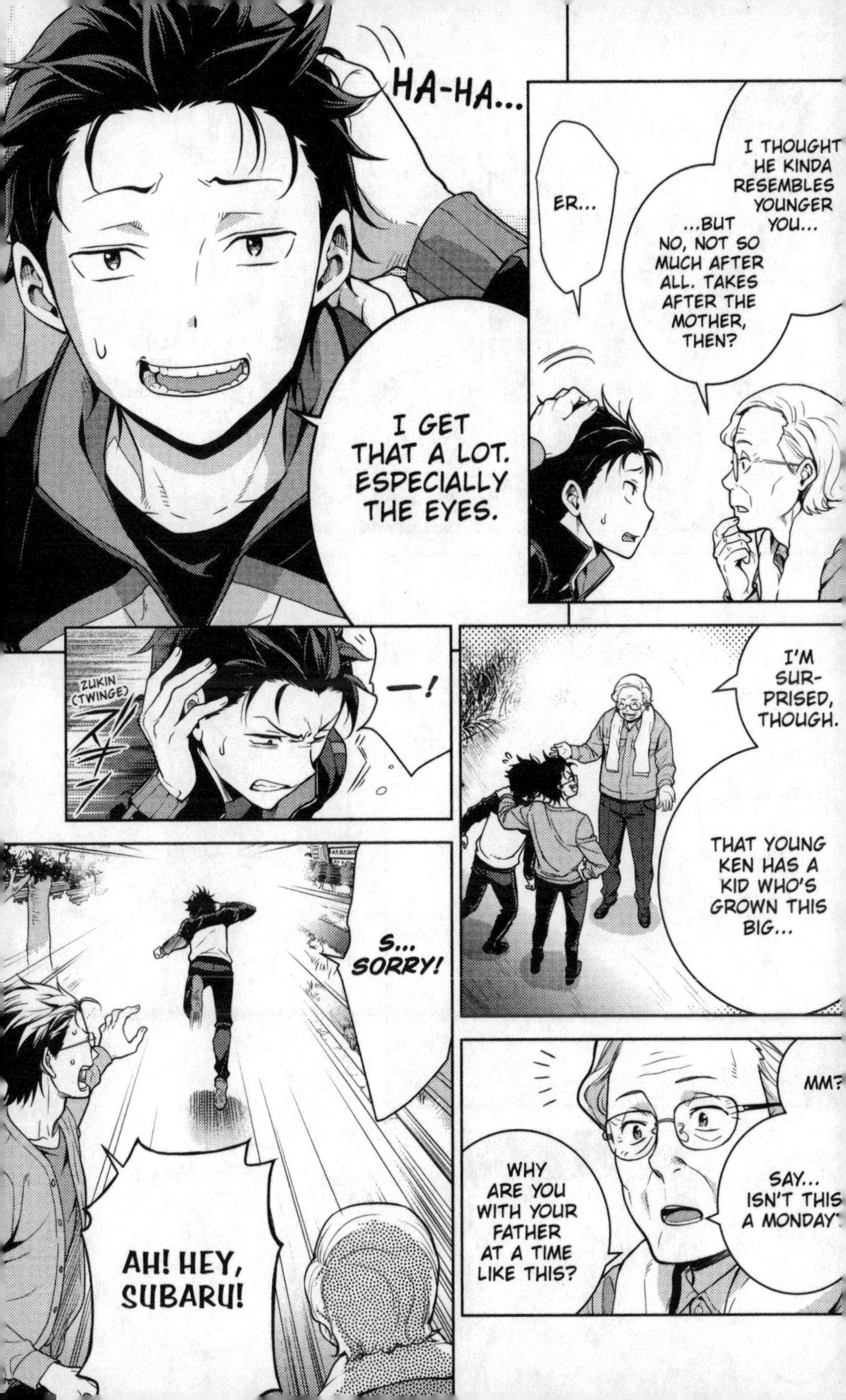
I THOUGHT HE KINDA RESEMBLES YOUNGER YOU...
...BUT NO, NOT SO MUCH AFTER ALL. TAKES AFTER THE MOTHER, THEN?
ER...
HA-HA...
I GET THAT A LOT. ESPECIALLY THE EYES.
I'M SUR-PRISED, THOUGH.
THAT YOUNG KEN HAS A KID WHO'S GROWN THIS BIG...
MM?
SAY... ISN'T THIS A MONDAY?
WHY ARE YOU WITH YOUR FATHER AT A TIME LIKE THIS?
ZUKIN (TWINGE)
—!
S... SORRY!
AH! HEY, SUBARU!

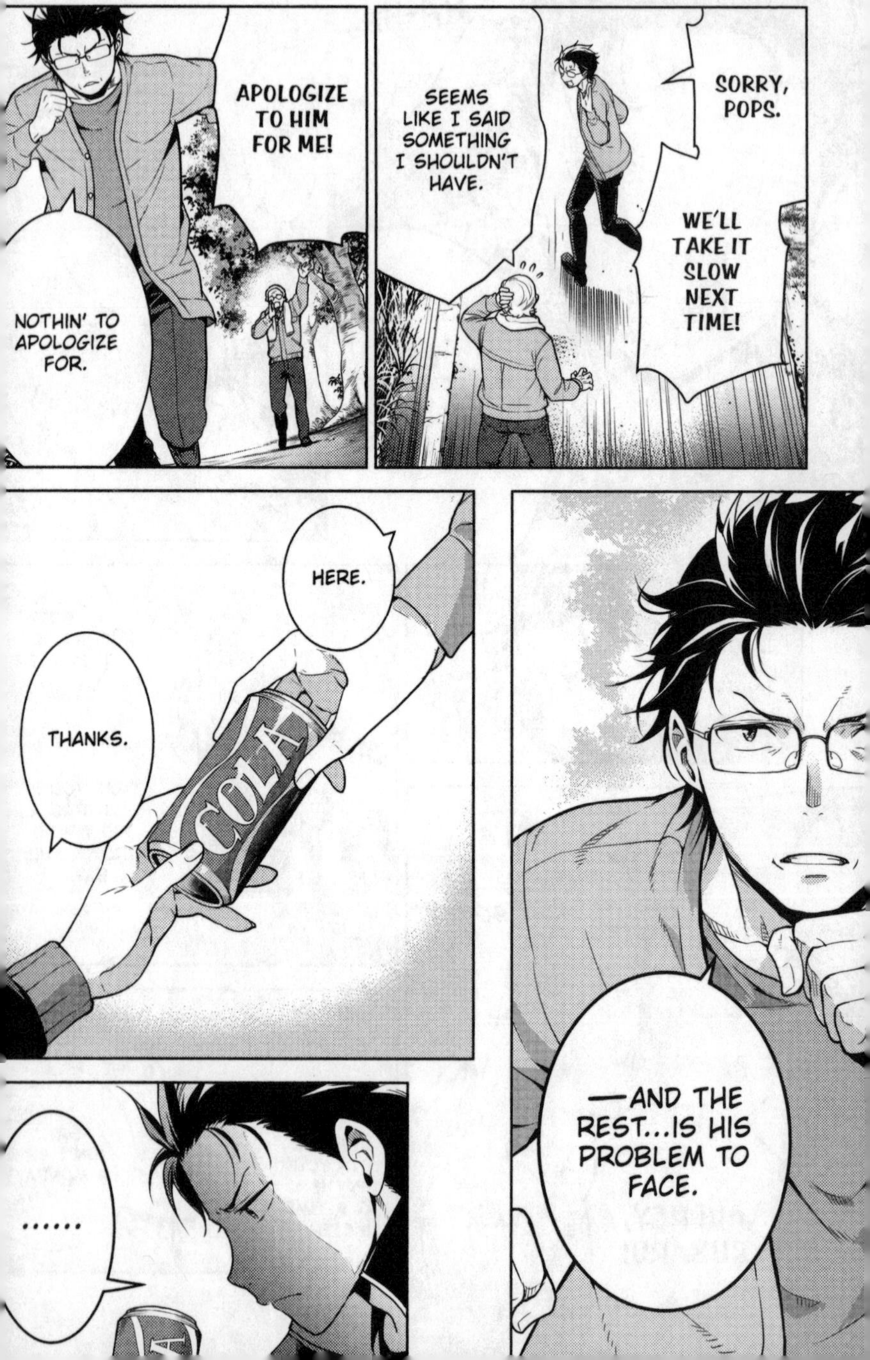
SORRY, POPS.
SEEMS LIKE I SAID SOMETHING I SHOULDN'T HAVE.
WE'LL TAKE IT SLOW NEXT TIME!
APOLOGIZE TO HIM FOR ME!
NOTHIN' TO APOLOGIZE FOR.
—AND THE REST...IS HIS PROBLEM TO FACE.
HERE.
THANKS.
COLA
......

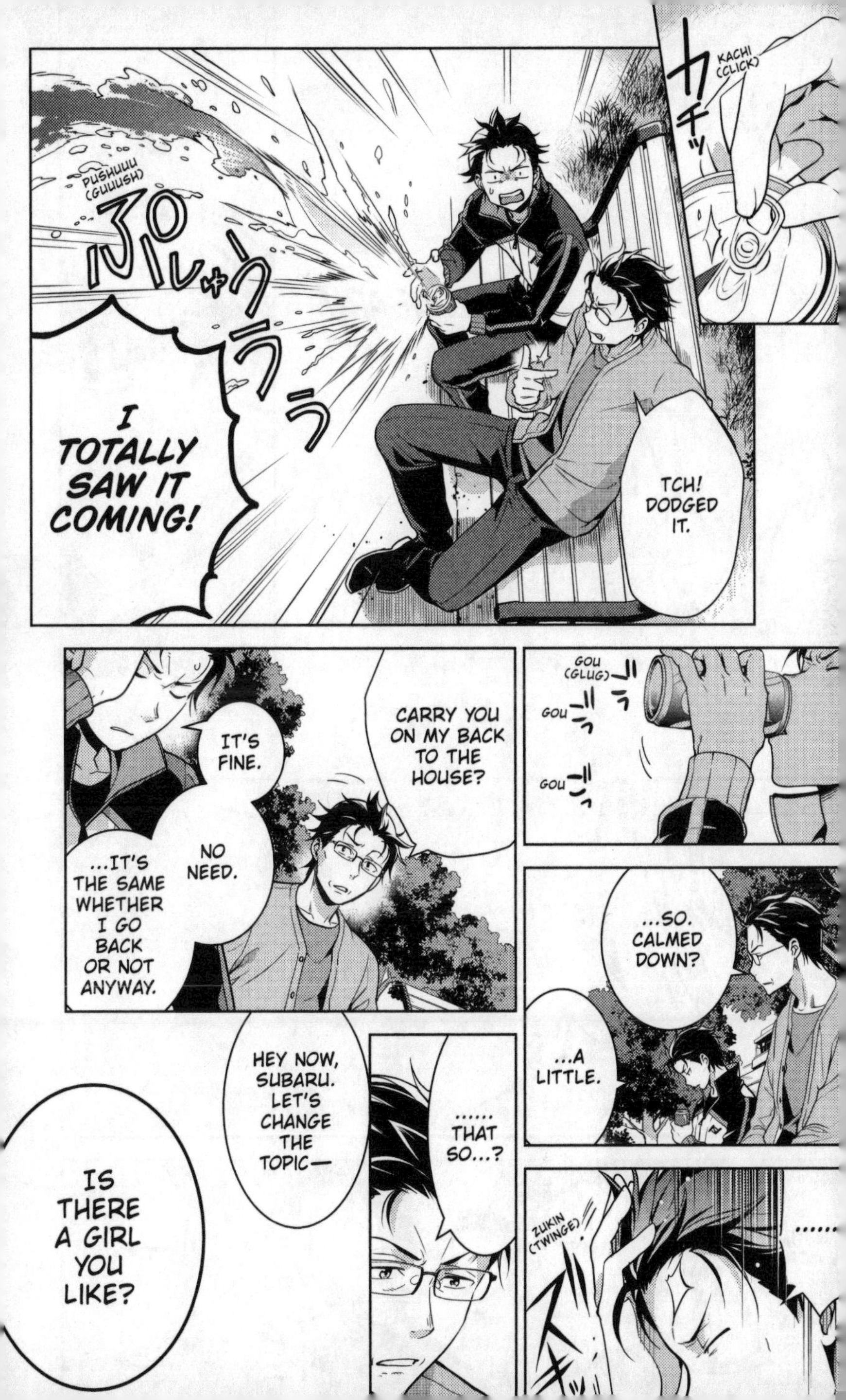
KACHI (CLICK)
PUSHUUU (GUUUSH)
TCH! DODGED IT.
I TOTALLY SAW IT COMING!
GOU (GLUG)
GOU
GOU
CARRY YOU ON MY BACK TO THE HOUSE?
IT'S FINE.
NO NEED.
...IT'S THE SAME WHETHER I GO BACK OR NOT ANYWAY.
...SO. CALMED DOWN?
...A LITTLE.
ZUKIN (TWINGE)
......
......THAT SO...?
HEY NOW, SUBARU. LET'S CHANGE THE TOPIC—
IS THERE A GIRL YOU LIKE?

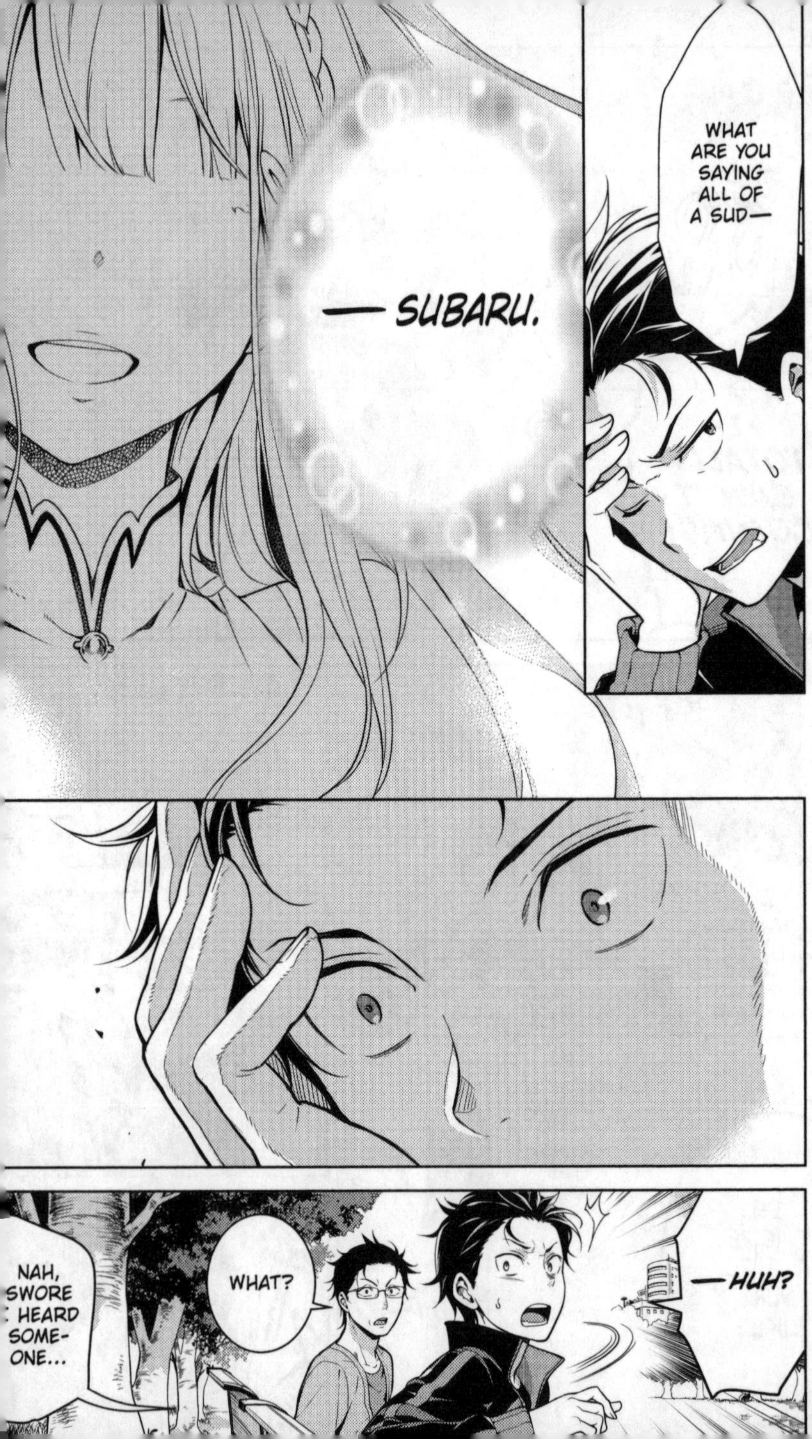
WHAT ARE YOU SAYING ALL OF A SUD—
—SUBARU.
—HUH?
WHAT?
NAH, SWORE HEARD SOME-ONE...

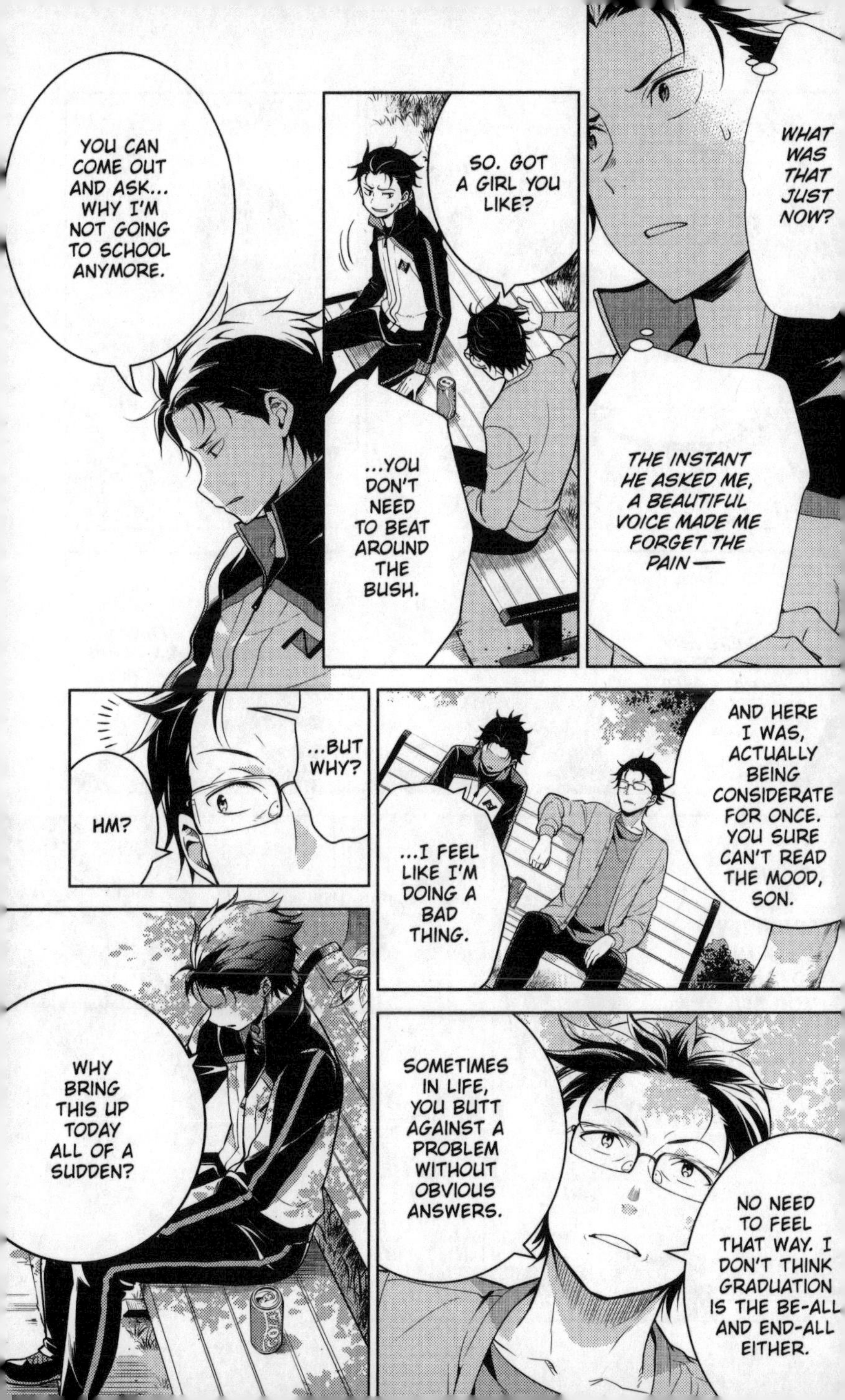
WHAT WAS THAT JUST NOW?
THE INSTANT HE ASKED ME, A BEAUTIFUL VOICE MADE ME FORGET THE PAIN—
SO. GOT A GIRL YOU LIKE?
...YOU DON'T NEED TO BEAT AROUND THE BUSH.
YOU CAN COME OUT AND ASK... WHY I'M NOT GOING TO SCHOOL ANYMORE.
AND HERE I WAS, ACTUALLY BEING CONSIDERATE FOR ONCE. YOU SURE CAN'T READ THE MOOD, SON.
...I FEEL LIKE I'M DOING A BAD THING.
...BUT WHY?
HM?
NO NEED TO FEEL THAT WAY. I DON'T THINK GRADUATION IS THE BE-ALL AND END-ALL EITHER.
SOMETIMES IN LIFE, YOU BUTT AGAINST A PROBLEM WITHOUT OBVIOUS ANSWERS.
WHY BRING THIS UP TODAY ALL OF A SUDDEN?

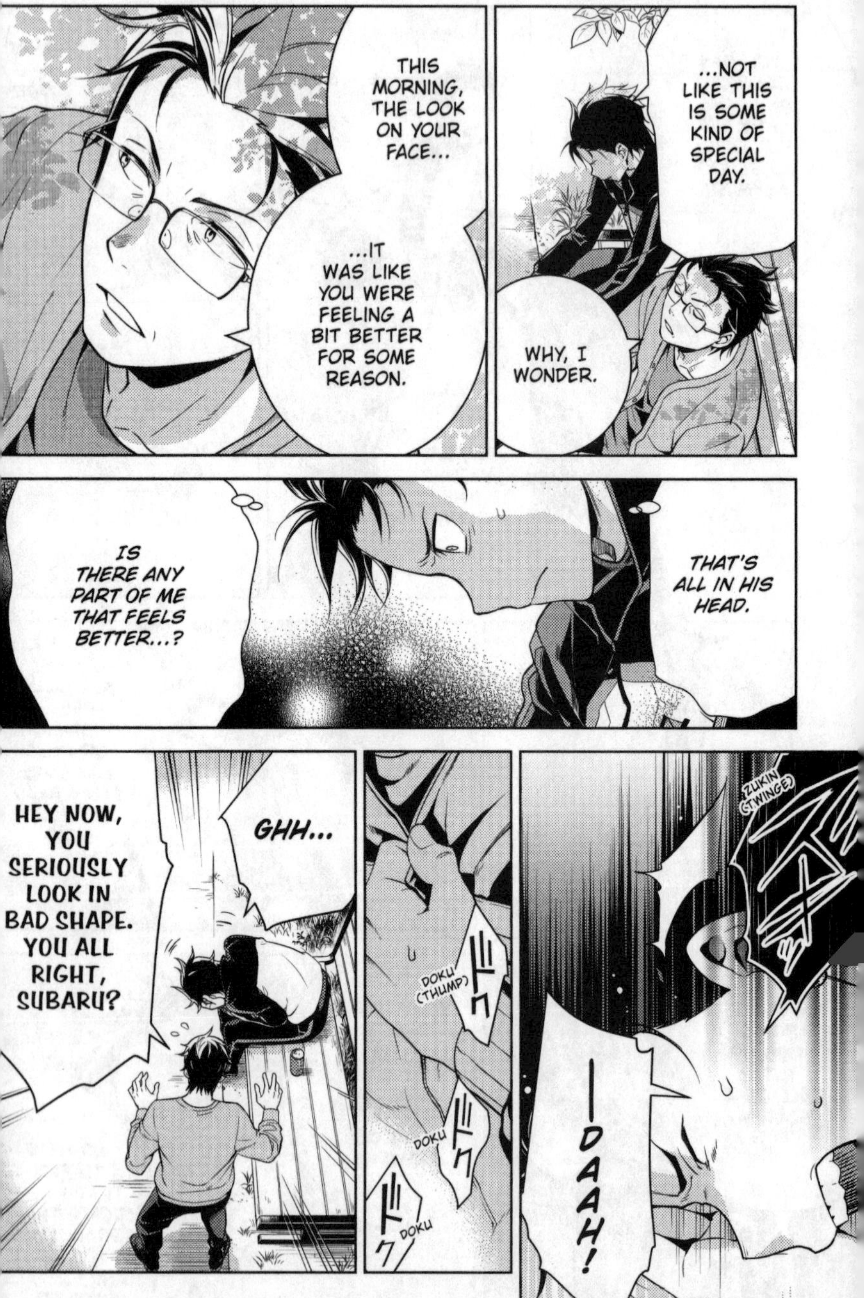
...NOT LIKE THIS IS SOME KIND OF SPECIAL DAY.
WHY, I WONDER.
THIS MORNING, THE LOOK ON YOUR FACE...
...IT WAS LIKE YOU WERE FEELING A BIT BETTER FOR SOME REASON.
THAT'S ALL IN HIS HEAD.
IS THERE ANY PART OF ME THAT FEELS BETTER...?
ZUKIN (TWINGE)
DAAH!
DOKU (THUMP)
DOKU
DOKU
GHH...
HEY NOW, YOU SERIOUSLY LOOK IN BAD SHAPE. YOU ALL RIGHT, SUBARU?

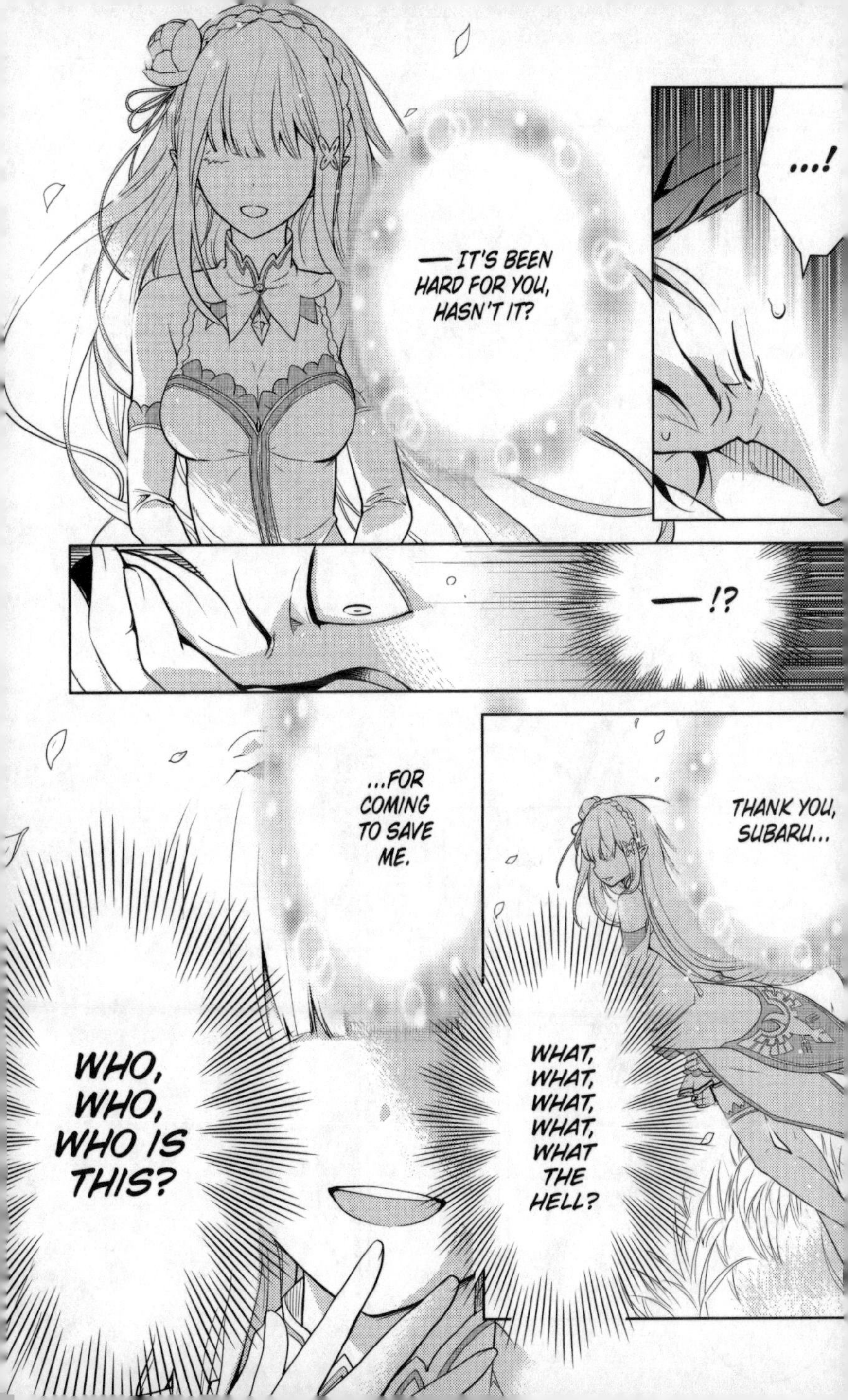
...!
—IT'S BEEN HARD FOR YOU, HASN'T IT?
—!?
THANK YOU, SUBARU...
...FOR COMING TO SAVE ME.
WHAT, WHAT, WHAT, WHAT, WHAT THE HELL?
WHO, WHO, WHO IS THIS?

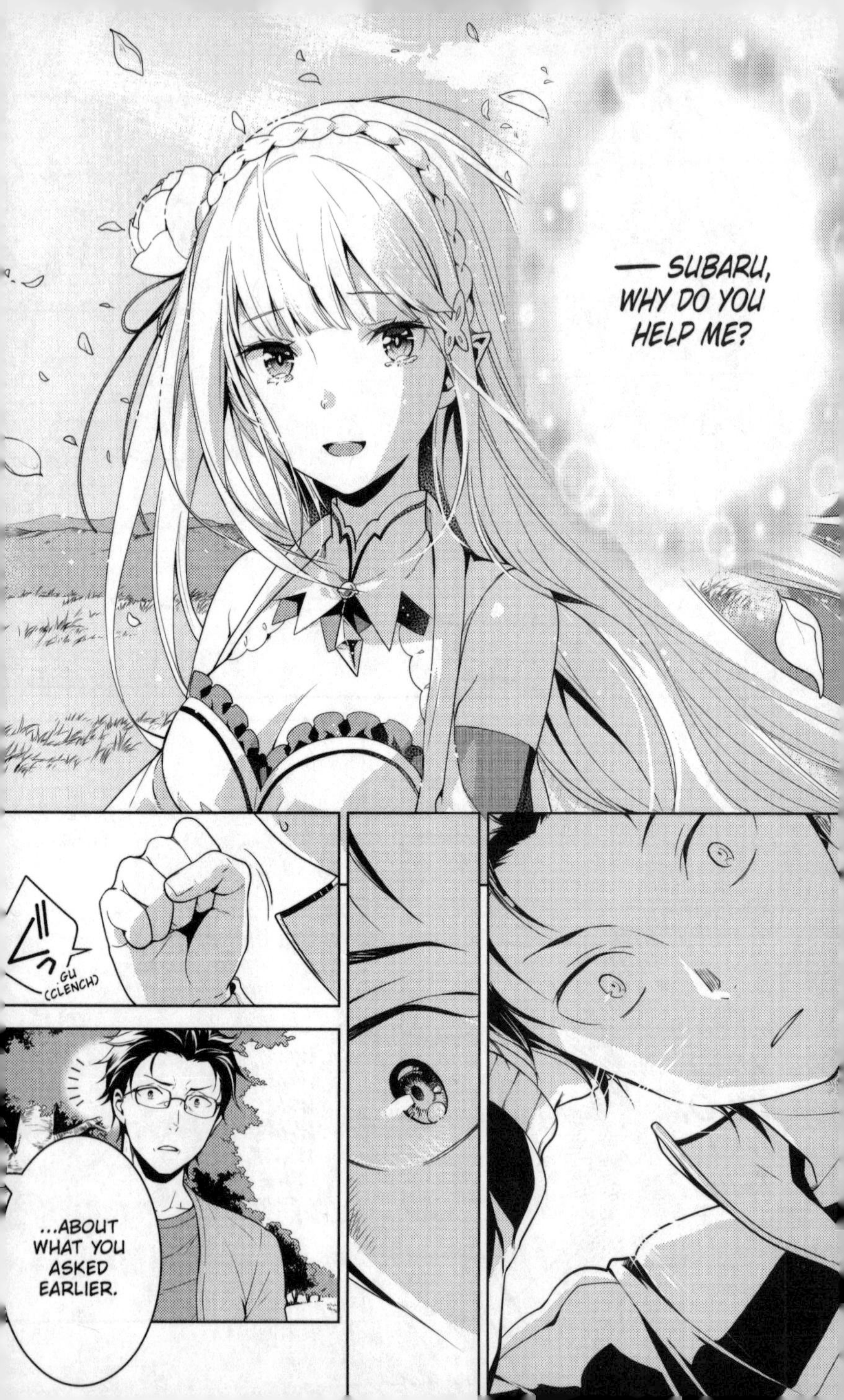
— SUBARU, WHY DO YOU HELP ME?
GU (CLENCH)
...ABOUT WHAT YOU ASKED EARLIER.

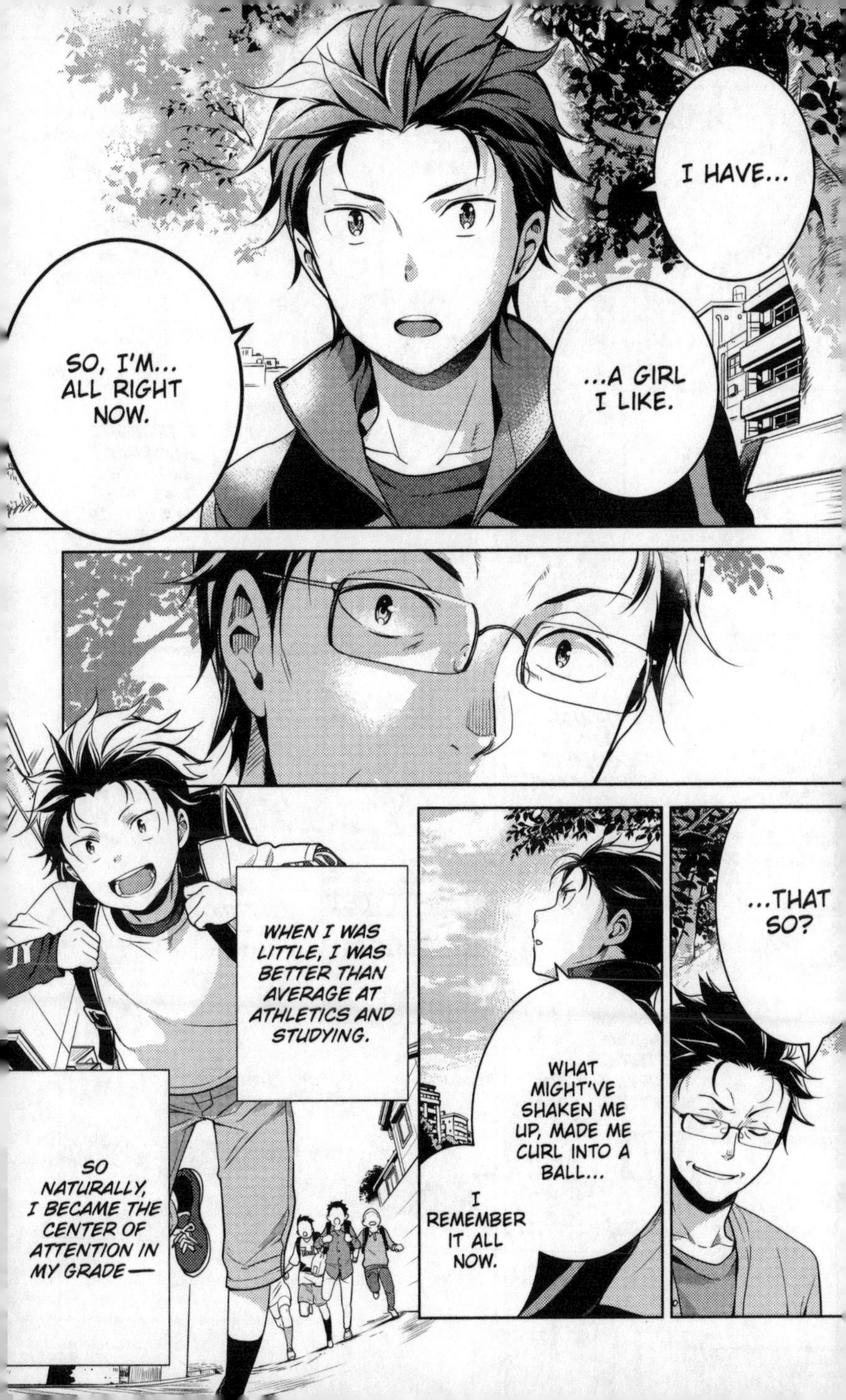
I HAVE...
...A GIRL I LIKE.
SO, I'M... ALL RIGHT NOW.
...THAT SO?
WHAT MIGHT'VE SHAKEN ME UP, MADE ME CURL INTO A BALL...
I REMEMBER IT ALL NOW.
WHEN I WAS LITTLE, I WAS BETTER THAN AVERAGE AT ATHLETICS AND STUDYING.
SO NATURALLY, I BECAME THE CENTER OF ATTENTION IN MY GRADE—

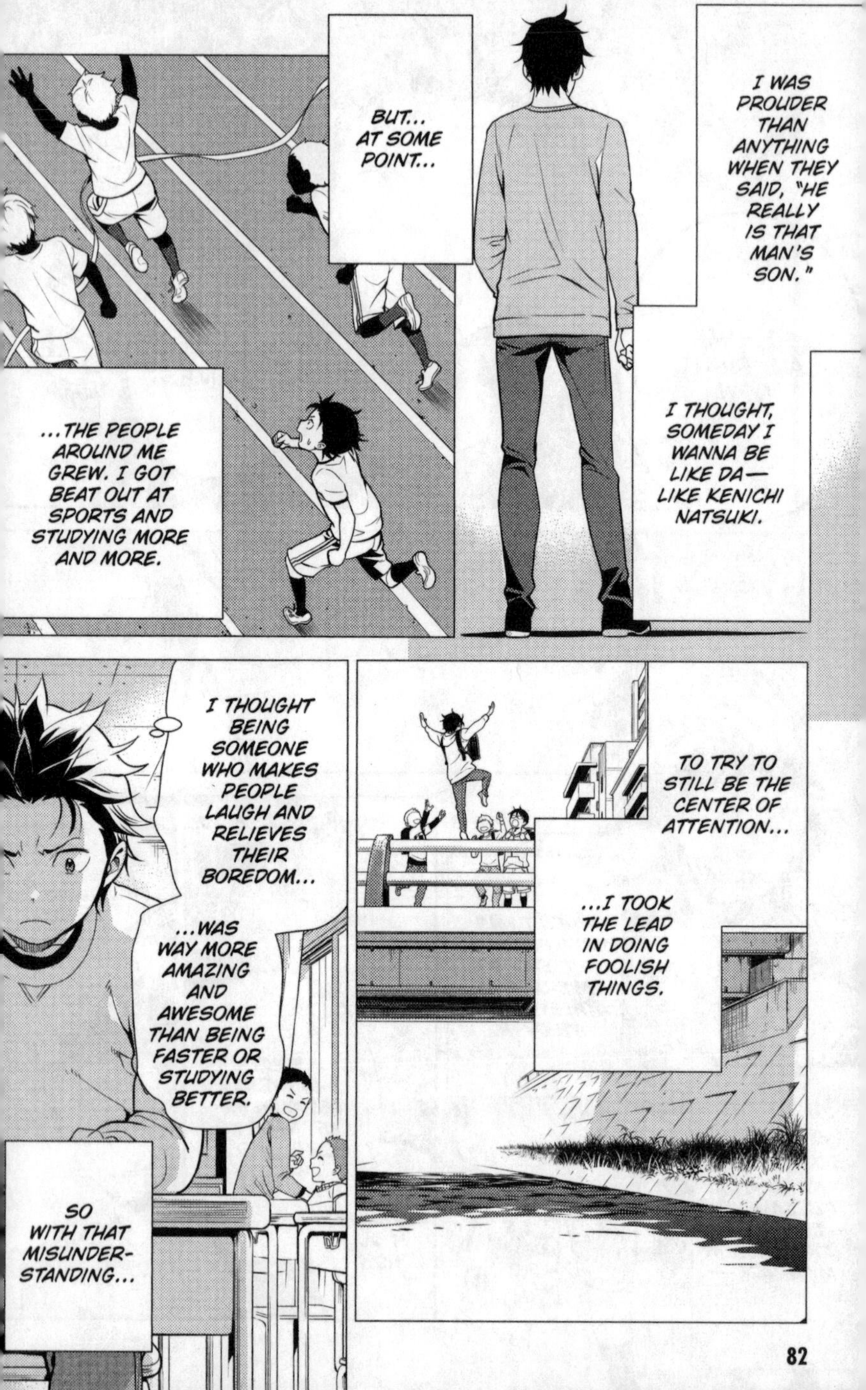
I WAS PROUDER THAN ANYTHING WHEN THEY SAID, "HE REALLY IS THAT MAN'S SON."
I THOUGHT, SOMEDAY I WANNA BE LIKE DA— LIKE KENICHI NATSUKI.
BUT... AT SOME POINT...
...THE PEOPLE AROUND ME GREW. I GOT BEAT OUT AT SPORTS AND STUDYING MORE AND MORE.
TO TRY TO STILL BE THE CENTER OF ATTENTION...
...I TOOK THE LEAD IN DOING FOOLISH THINGS.
I THOUGHT BEING SOMEONE WHO MAKES PEOPLE LAUGH AND RELIEVES THEIR BOREDOM...
...WAS WAY MORE AMAZING AND AWESOME THAN BEING FASTER OR STUDYING BETTER.
SO WITH THAT MISUNDER-STANDING...

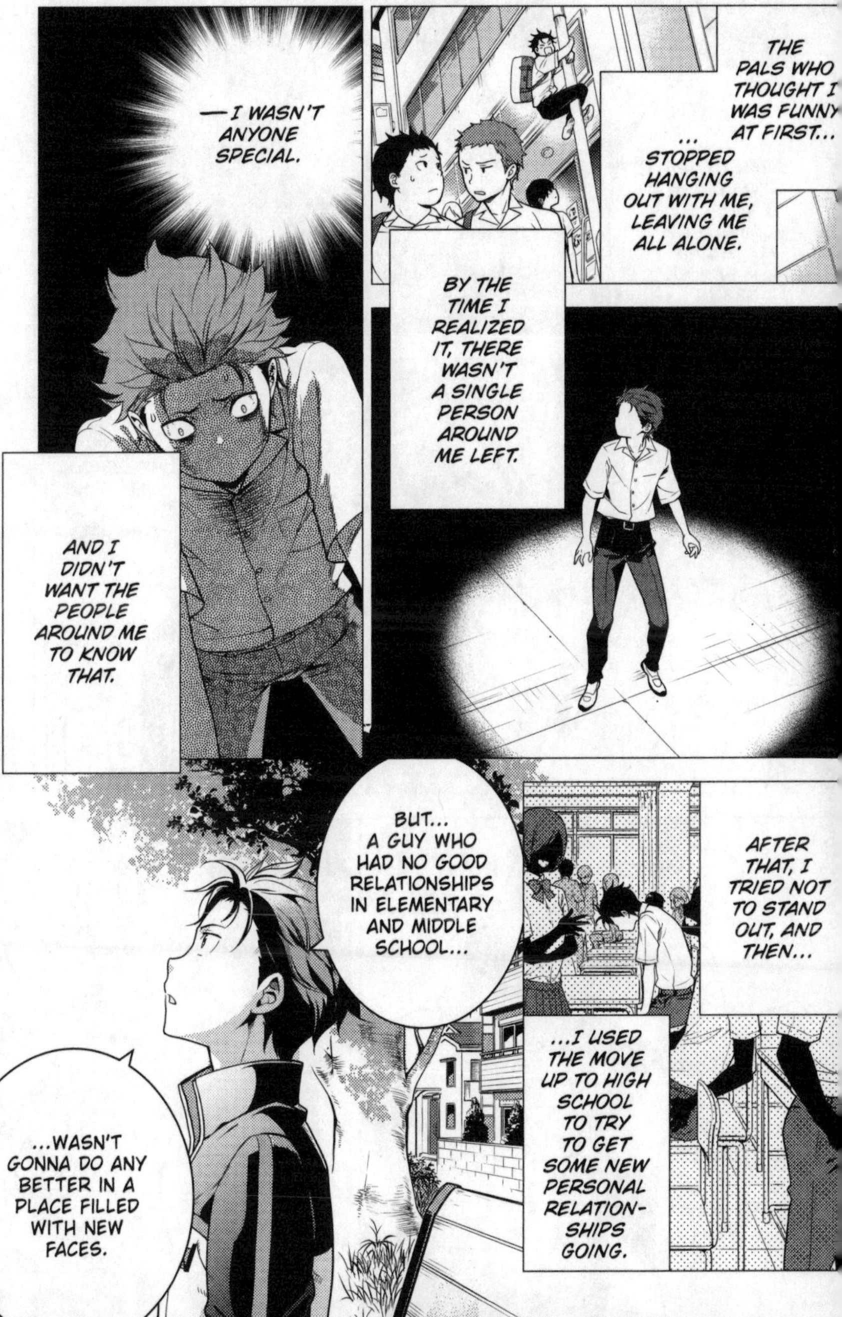
THE PALS WHO THOUGHT I WAS FUNNY AT FIRST...
...STOPPED HANGING OUT WITH ME, LEAVING ME ALL ALONE.
BY THE TIME I REALIZED IT, THERE WASN'T A SINGLE PERSON AROUND ME LEFT.
—I WASN'T ANYONE SPECIAL.
AND I DIDN'T WANT THE PEOPLE AROUND ME TO KNOW THAT.
AFTER THAT, I TRIED NOT TO STAND OUT, AND THEN...
...I USED THE MOVE UP TO HIGH SCHOOL TO TRY TO GET SOME NEW PERSONAL RELATION-SHIPS GOING.
BUT... A GUY WHO HAD NO GOOD RELATIONSHIPS IN ELEMENTARY AND MIDDLE SCHOOL...
...WASN'T GONNA DO ANY BETTER IN A PLACE FILLED WITH NEW FACES.

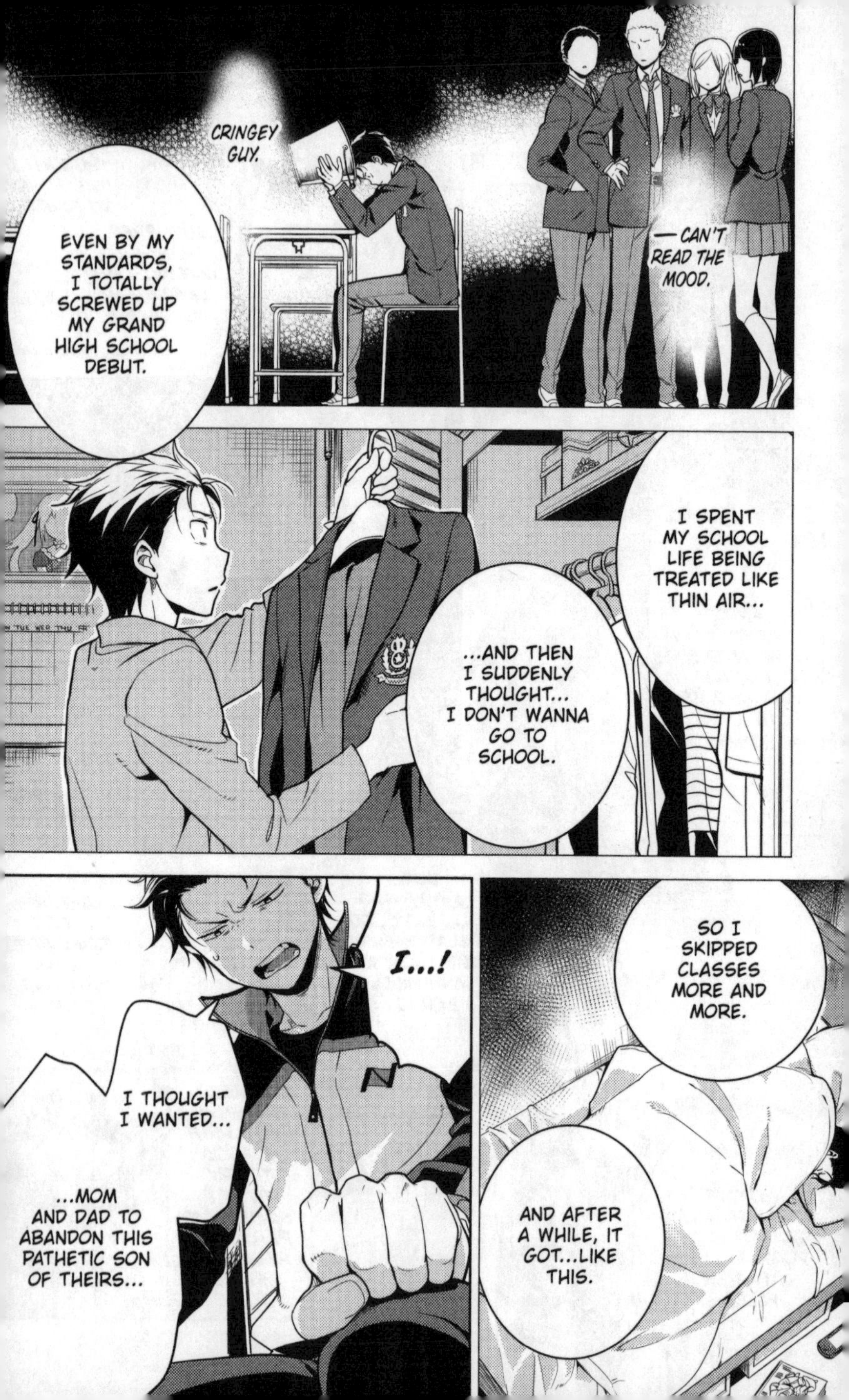
CRINGEY GUY.
—CAN'T READ THE MOOD.
EVEN BY MY STANDARDS, I TOTALLY SCREWED UP MY GRAND HIGH SCHOOL DEBUT.
I SPENT MY SCHOOL LIFE BEING TREATED LIKE THIN AIR...
...AND THEN I SUDDENLY THOUGHT... I DON'T WANNA GO TO SCHOOL.
SO I SKIPPED CLASSES MORE AND MORE.
AND AFTER A WHILE, IT GOT...LIKE THIS.
I...!
I THOUGHT I WANTED...
...MOM AND DAD TO ABANDON THIS PATHETIC SON OF THEIRS...

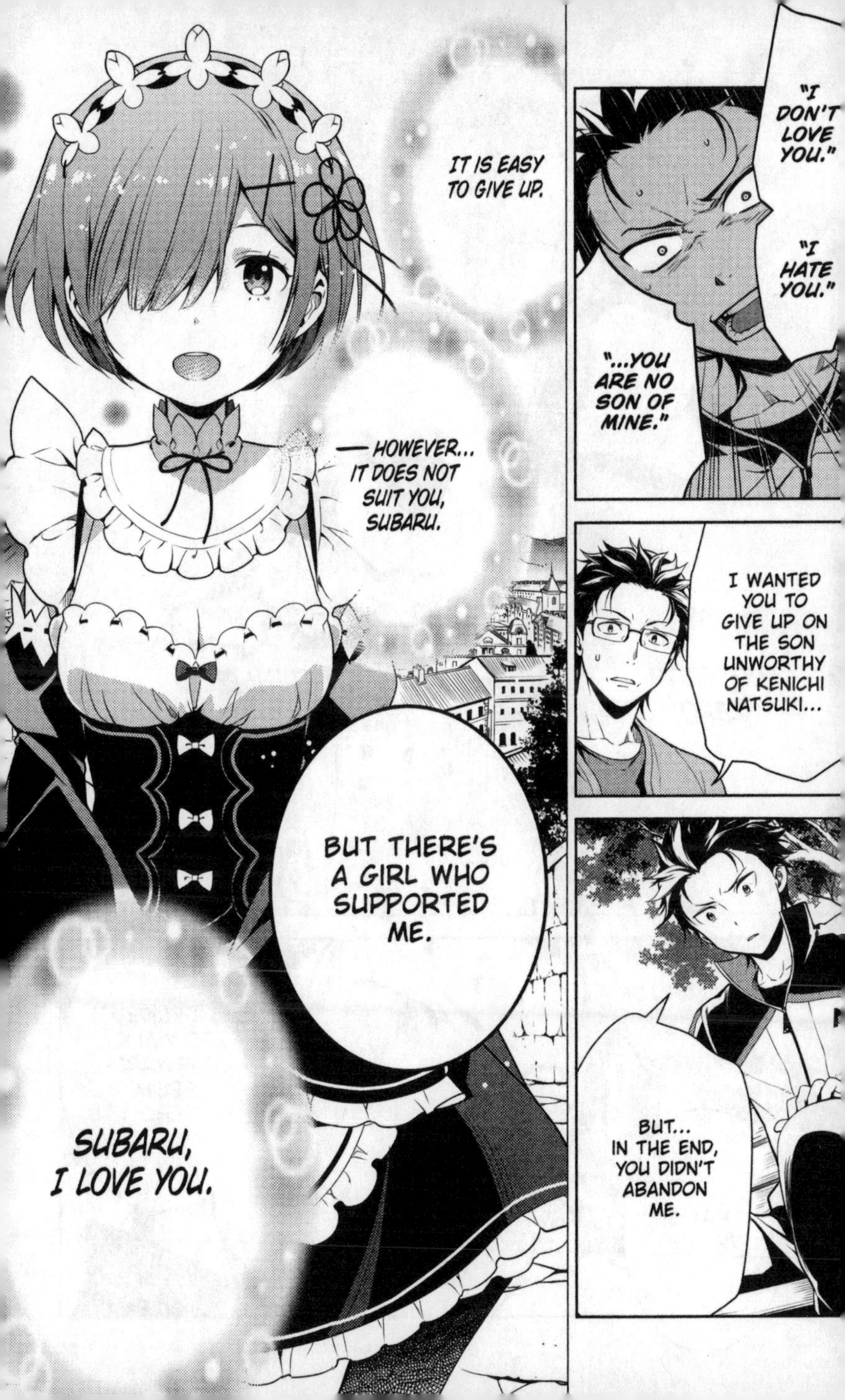
"I DON'T LOVE YOU."
"I HATE YOU."
"...YOU ARE NO SON OF MINE."
I WANTED YOU TO GIVE UP ON THE SON UNWORTHY OF KENICHI NATSUKI...
BUT... IN THE END, YOU DIDN'T ABANDON ME.
IT IS EASY TO GIVE UP.
—HOWEVER... IT DOES NOT SUIT YOU, SUBARU.
BUT THERE'S A GIRL WHO SUPPORTED ME.
SUBARU, I LOVE YOU.

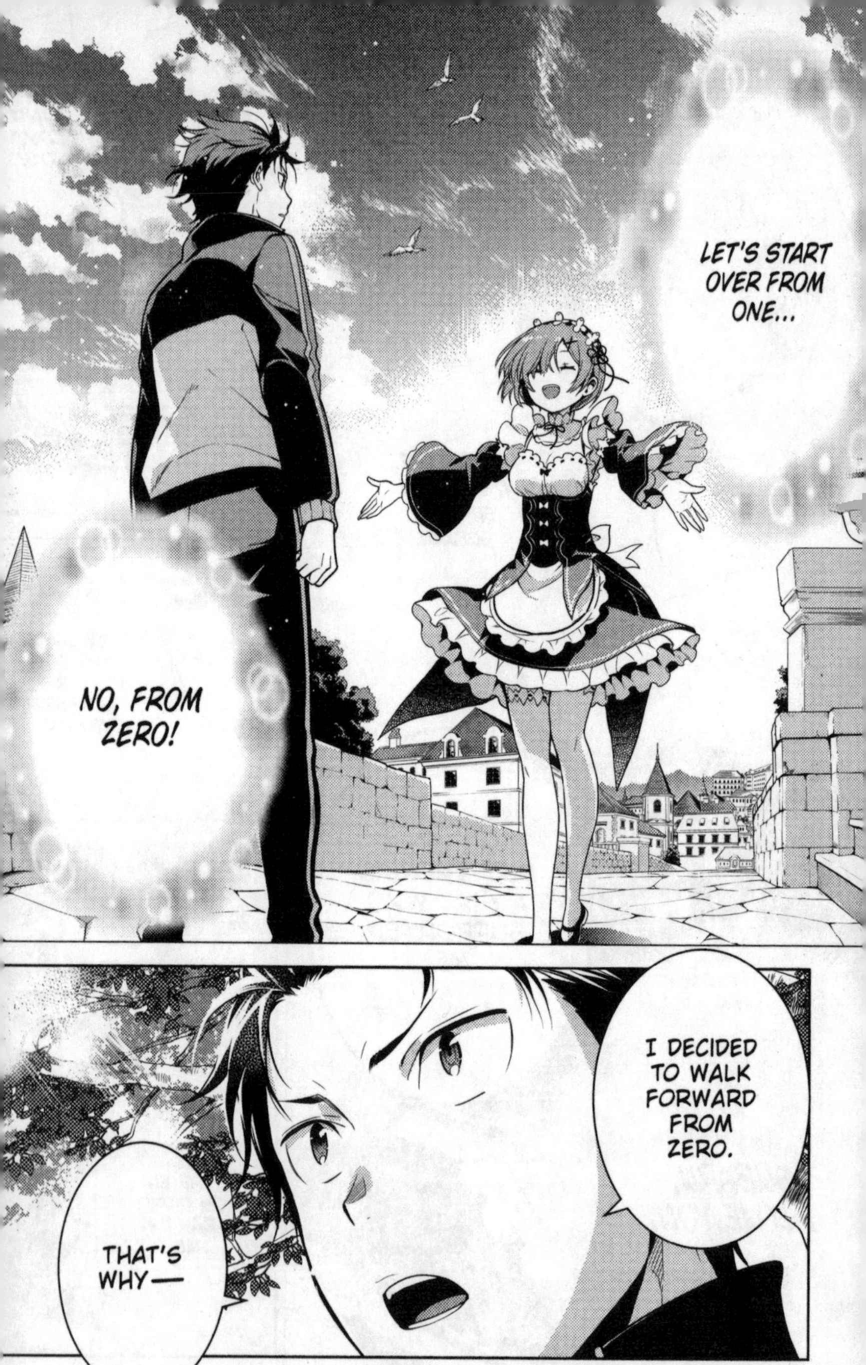
LET'S START OVER FROM ONE...
NO, FROM ZERO!
I DECIDED TO WALK FORWARD FROM ZERO.
THAT'S WHY—

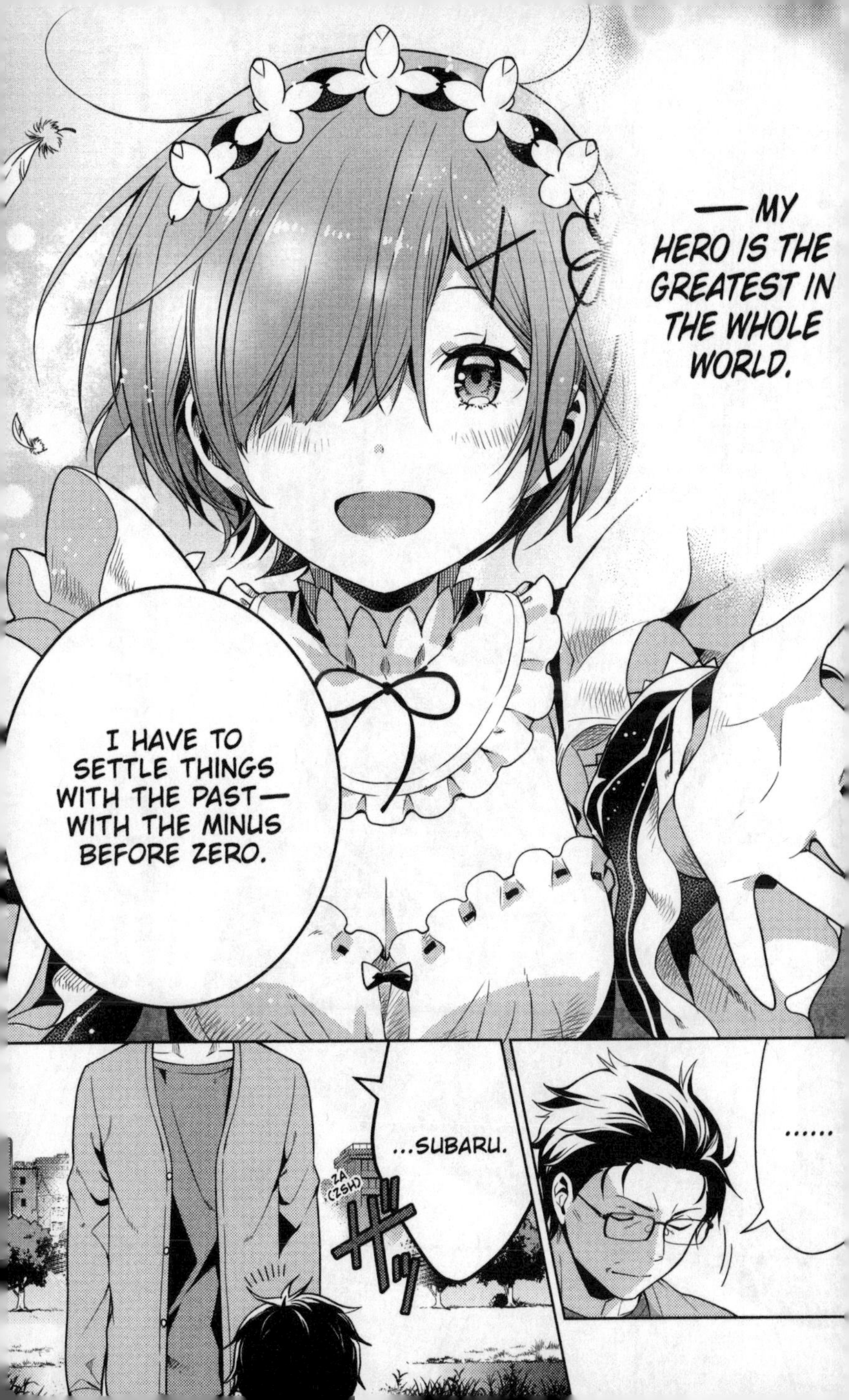
—MY HERO IS THE GREATEST IN THE WHOLE WORLD.
I HAVE TO SETTLE THINGS WITH THE PAST—WITH THE MINUS BEFORE ZERO.
......
...SUBARU.
ZA (ZSH)

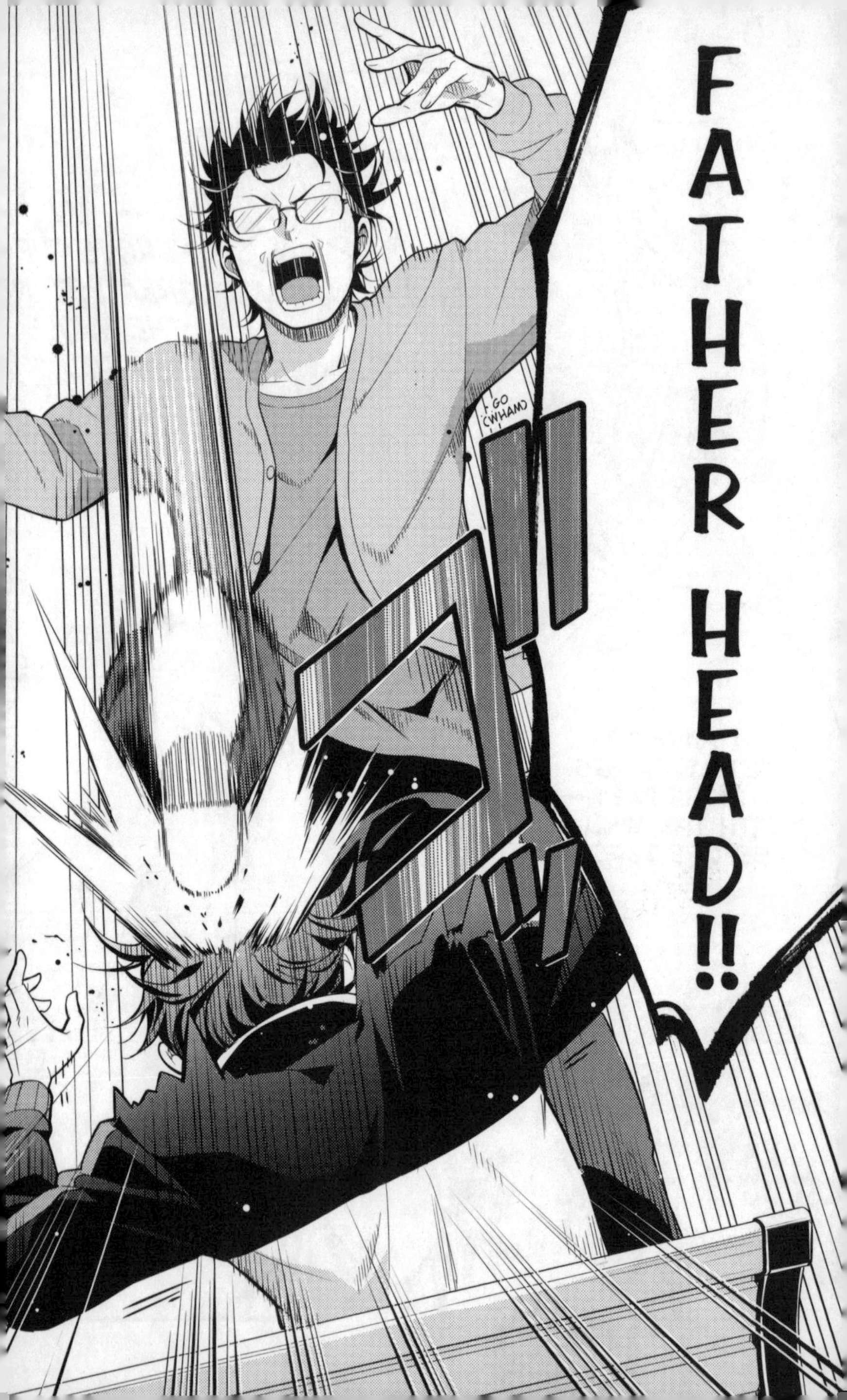
FATHER HEAD!!
GO (WHAM)

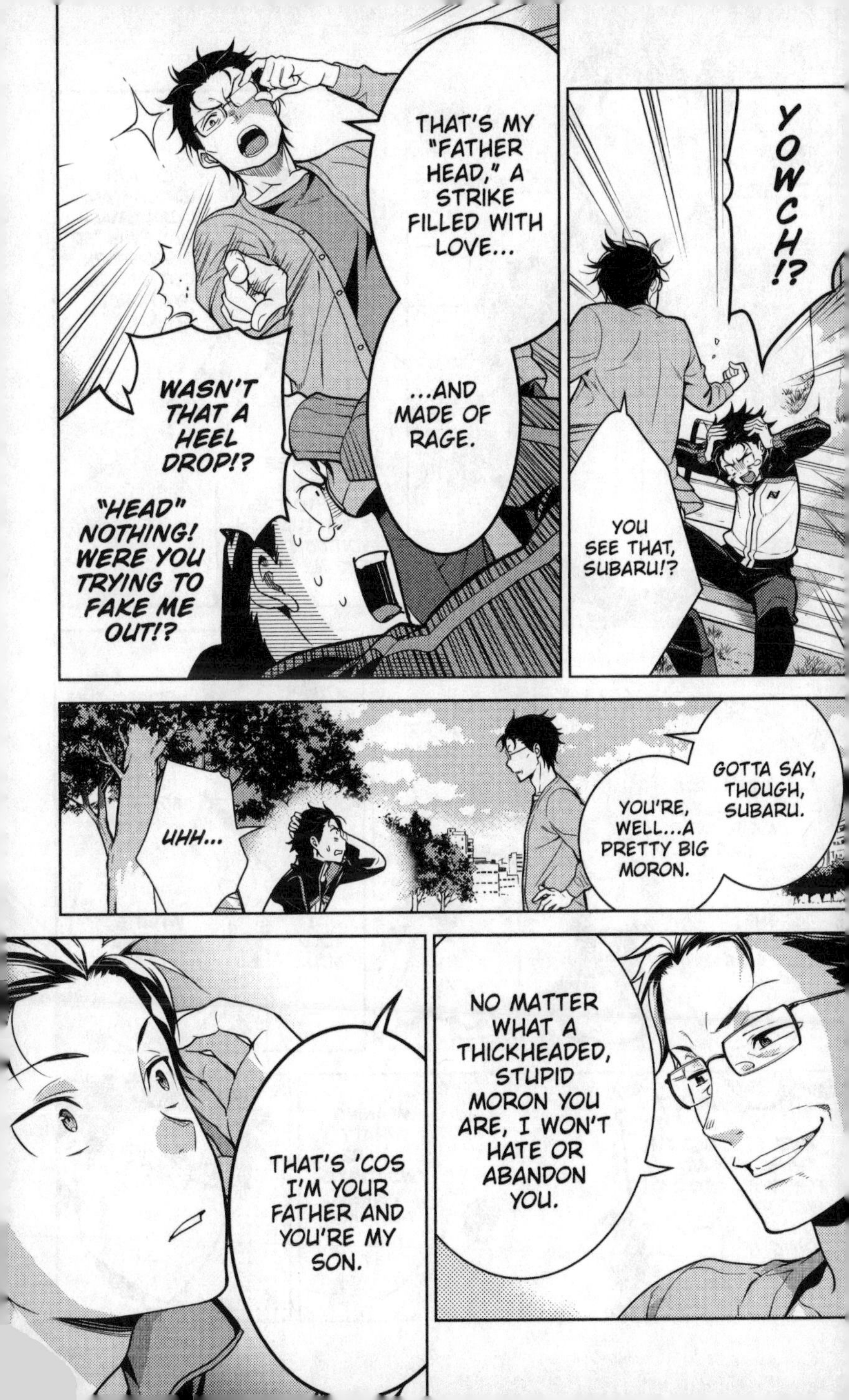
YOWCH!?
YOU SEE THAT, SUBARU!?
THAT'S MY "FATHER HEAD," A STRIKE FILLED WITH LOVE...
...AND MADE OF RAGE.
WASN'T THAT A HEEL DROP!?
"HEAD" NOTHING! WERE YOU TRYING TO FAKE ME OUT!?
GOTTA SAY, THOUGH, SUBARU.
YOU'RE, WELL...A PRETTY BIG MORON.
UHH...
NO MATTER WHAT A THICKHEADED, STUPID MORON YOU ARE, I WON'T HATE OR ABANDON YOU.
THAT'S 'COS I'M YOUR FATHER AND YOU'RE MY SON.

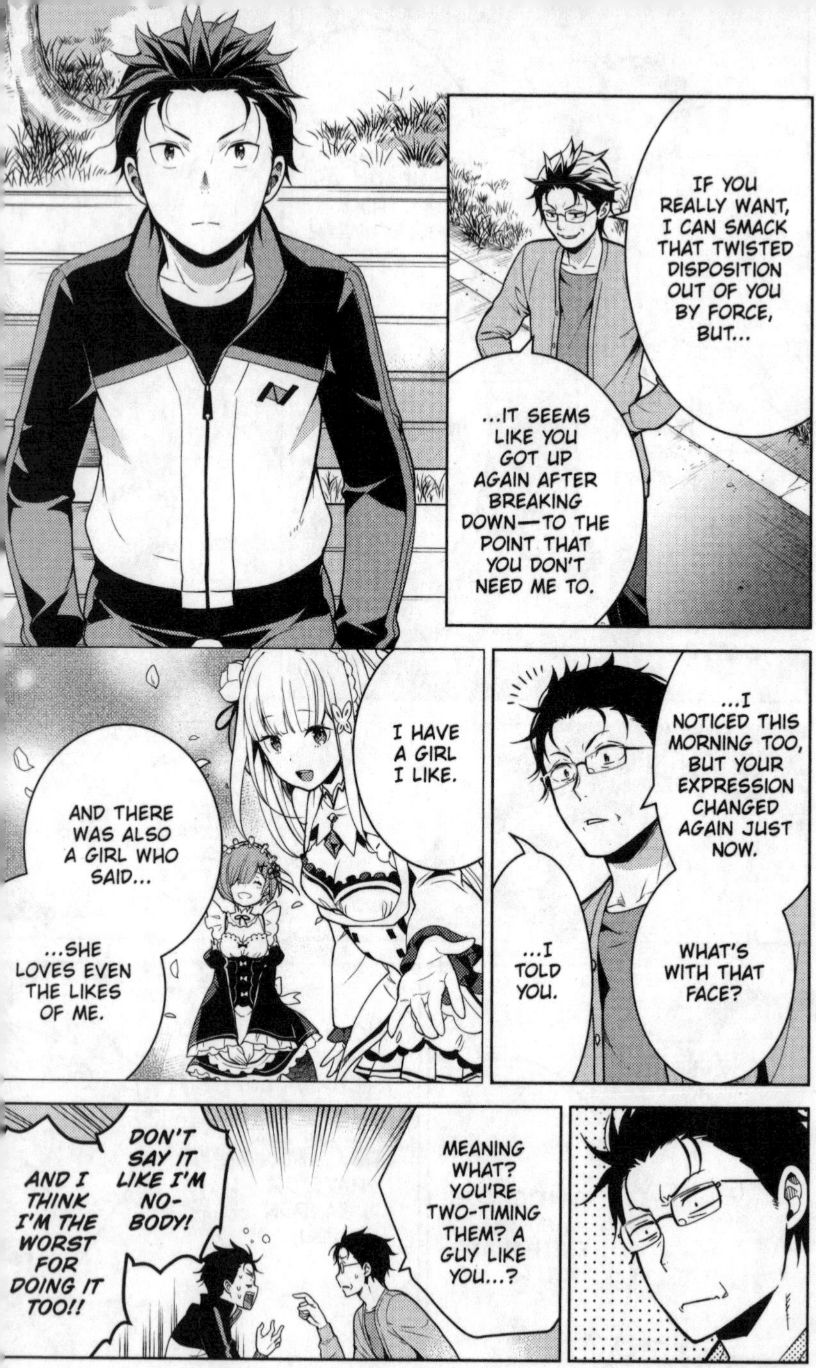
IF YOU REALLY WANT, I CAN SMACK THAT TWISTED DISPOSITION OUT OF YOU BY FORCE, BUT...
...IT SEEMS LIKE YOU GOT UP AGAIN AFTER BREAKING DOWN—TO THE POINT THAT YOU DON'T NEED ME TO.
...I NOTICED THIS MORNING TOO, BUT YOUR EXPRESSION CHANGED AGAIN JUST NOW.
WHAT'S WITH THAT FACE?
...I TOLD YOU.
I HAVE A GIRL I LIKE.
AND THERE WAS ALSO A GIRL WHO SAID...
...SHE LOVES EVEN THE LIKES OF ME.
MEANING WHAT? YOU'RE TWO-TIMING THEM? A GUY LIKE YOU...?
DON'T SAY IT LIKE I'M NO-BODY!
AND I THINK I'M THE WORST FOR DOING IT TOO!!

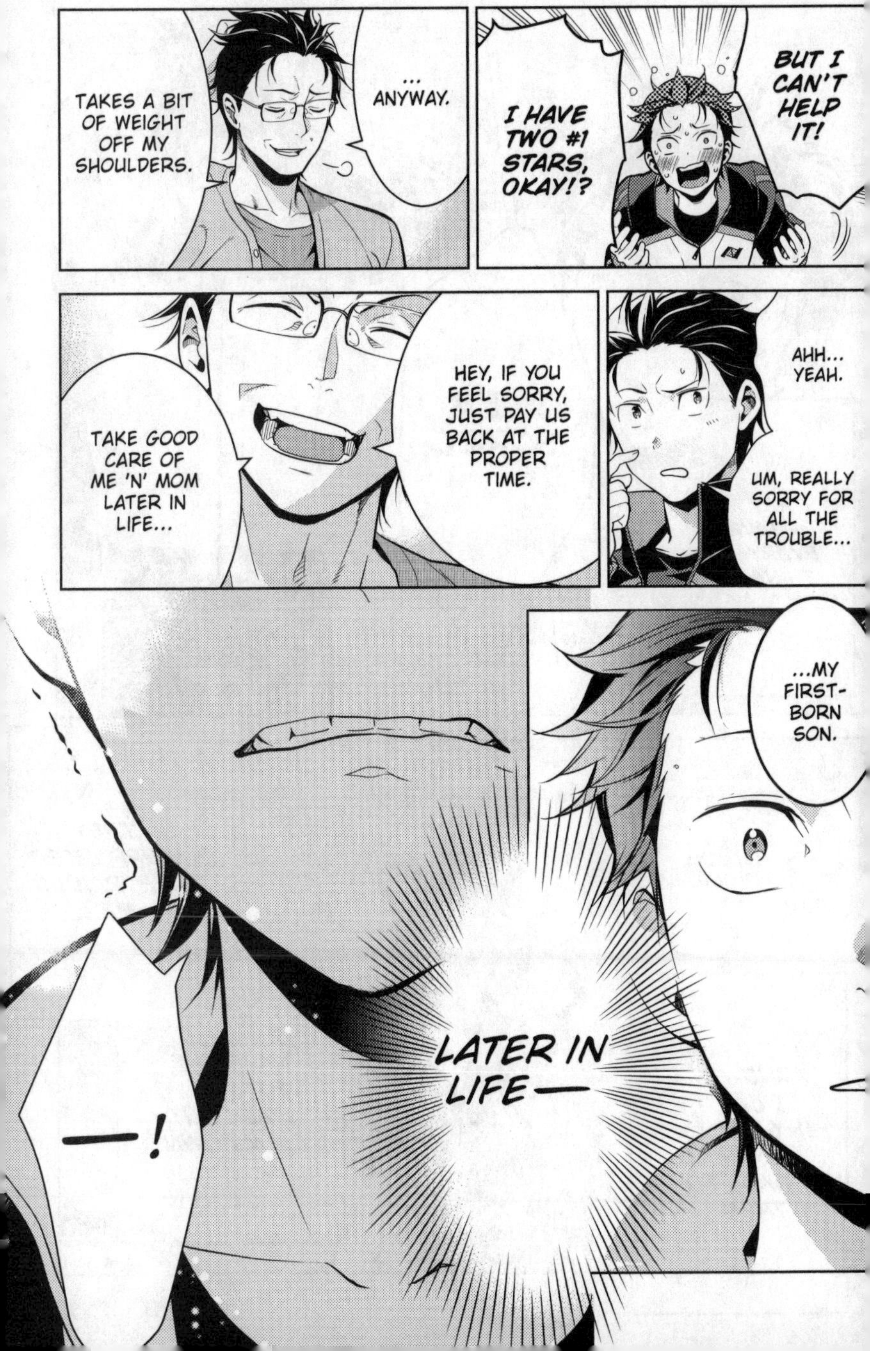
BUT I CAN'T HELP IT!
I HAVE TWO #1 STARS, OKAY!?
... ANYWAY.
TAKES A BIT OF WEIGHT OFF MY SHOULDERS.
AHH... YEAH.
UM, REALLY SORRY FOR ALL THE TROUBLE...
HEY, IF YOU FEEL SORRY, JUST PAY US BACK AT THE PROPER TIME.
TAKE GOOD CARE OF ME 'N' MOM LATER IN LIFE...
...MY FIRST-BORN SON.
LATER IN LIFE—
—!

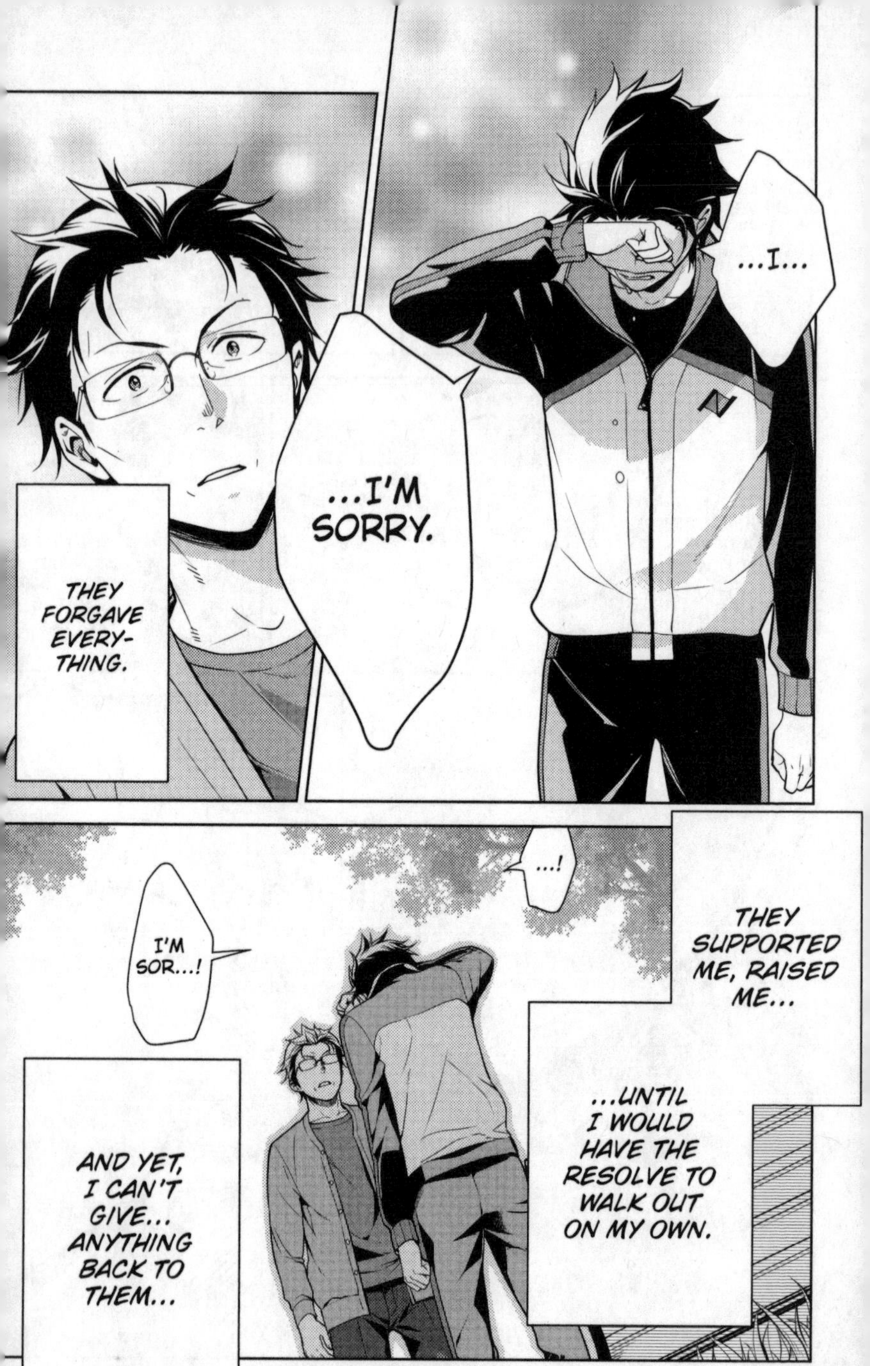
...I...
...I'M SORRY.
THEY FORGAVE EVERY-THING.
THEY SUPPORTED ME, RAISED ME...
...!
...UNTIL I WOULD HAVE THE RESOLVE TO WALK OUT ON MY OWN.
I'M SOR...!
AND YET, I CAN'T GIVE... ANYTHING BACK TO THEM...

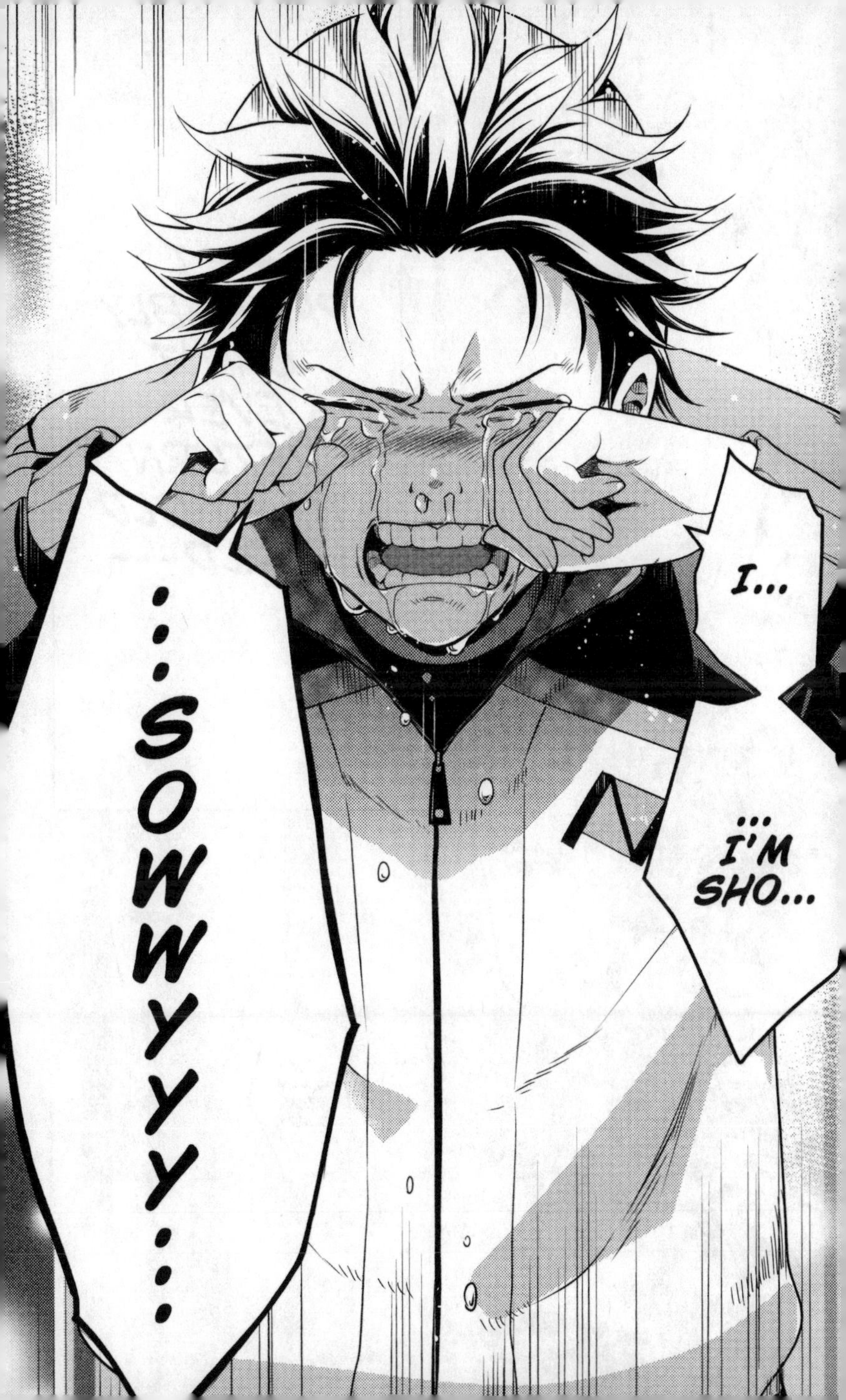
I...
...I'M SHO...
...SOWWYY...

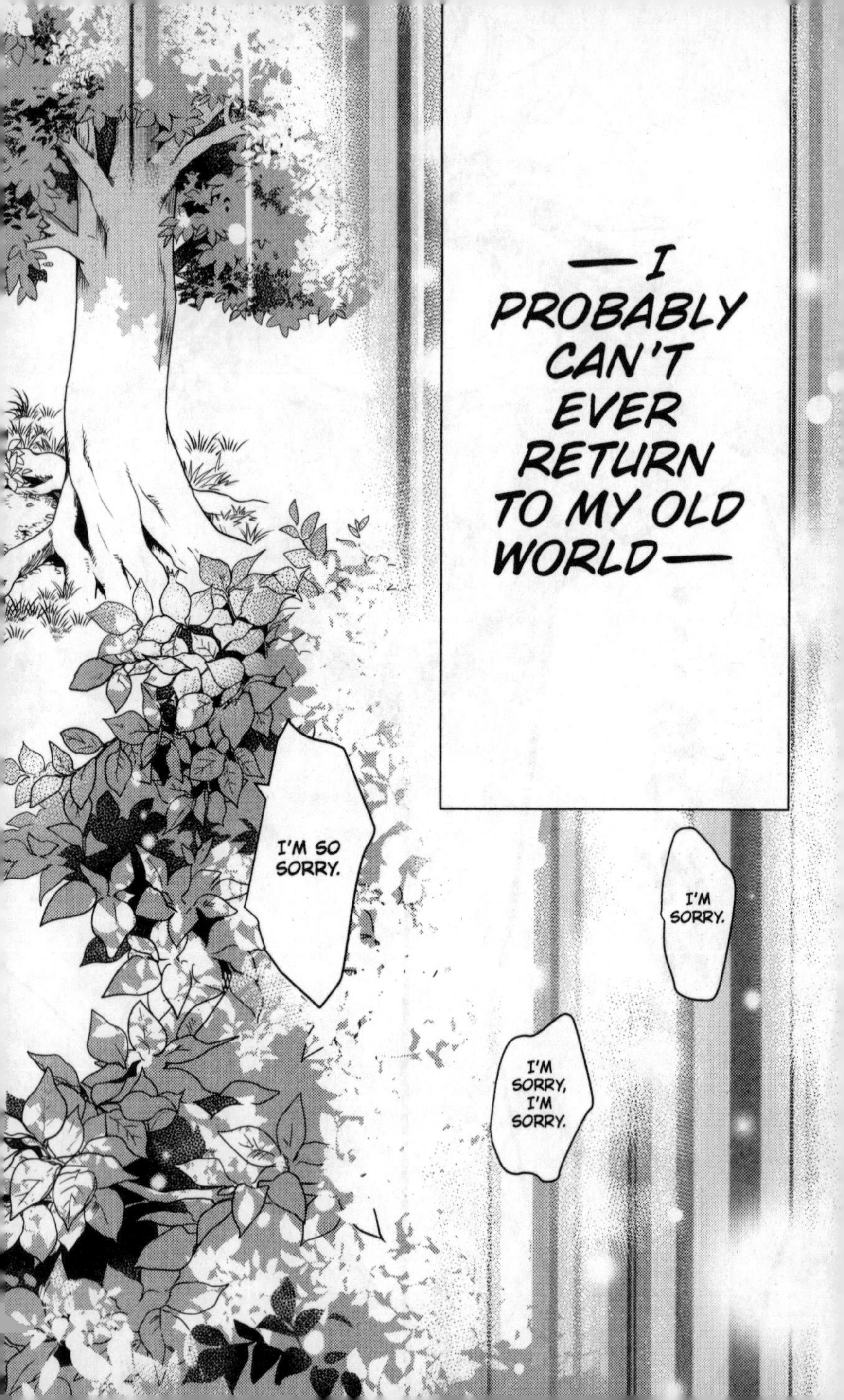
—I PROBABLY CAN'T EVER RETURN TO MY OLD WORLD—
I'M SORRY.
I'M SO SORRY.
I'M SORRY, I'M SORRY.

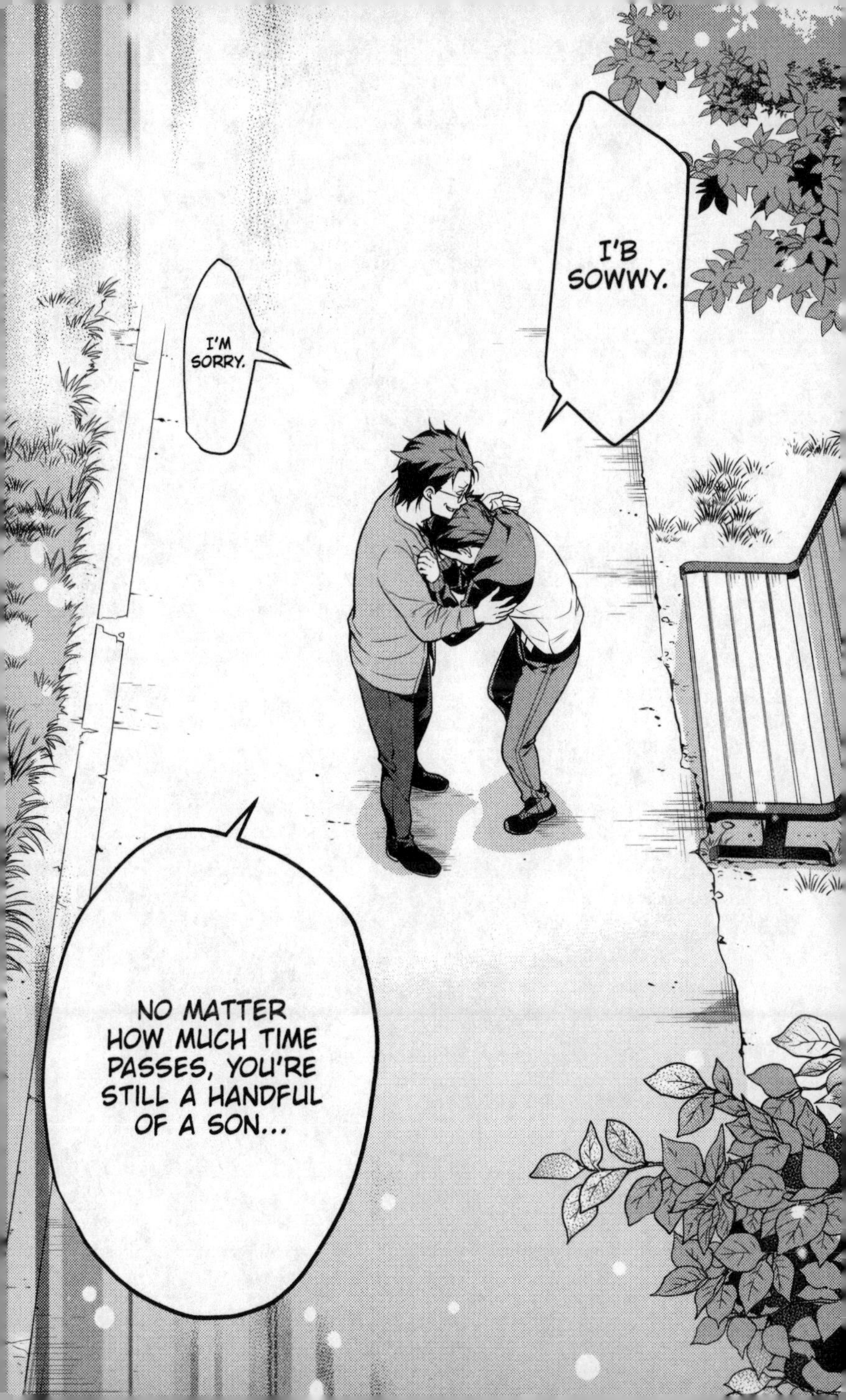
I'B SOWWY.
I'M SORRY.
NO MATTER HOW MUCH TIME PASSES, YOU'RE STILL A HANDFUL OF A SON...

Re:ZERO -Starting Life in Another World-

The only ability Subaru Natsuki gets when he's summoned to another world is time travel via his own death. But to save her, he'll die as many times as it takes.

Episode 7
A Long Good-Bye

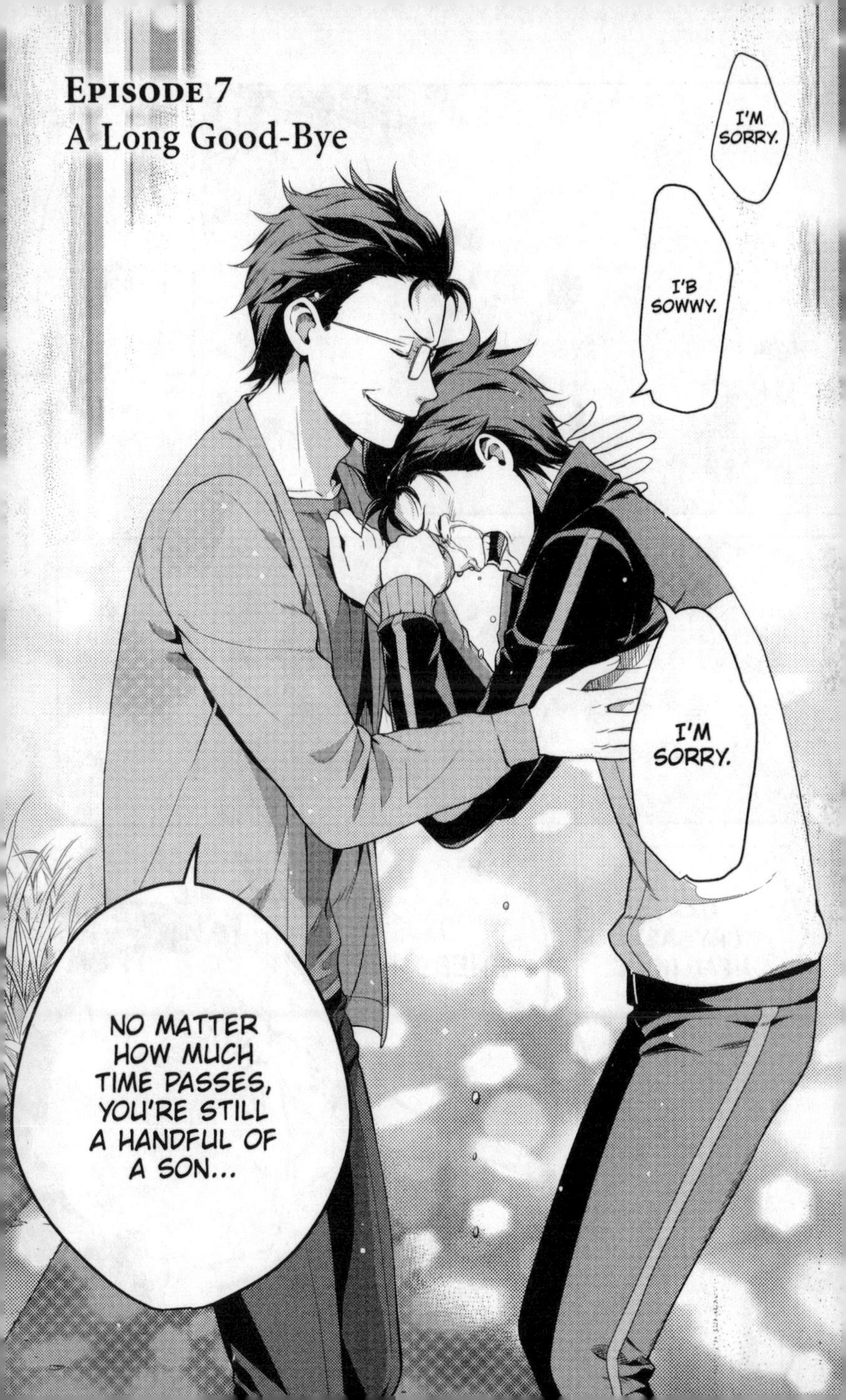
I'M SORRY.
I'B SOWWY.
I'M SORRY.
NO MATTER HOW MUCH TIME PASSES, YOU'RE STILL A HANDFUL OF A SON...

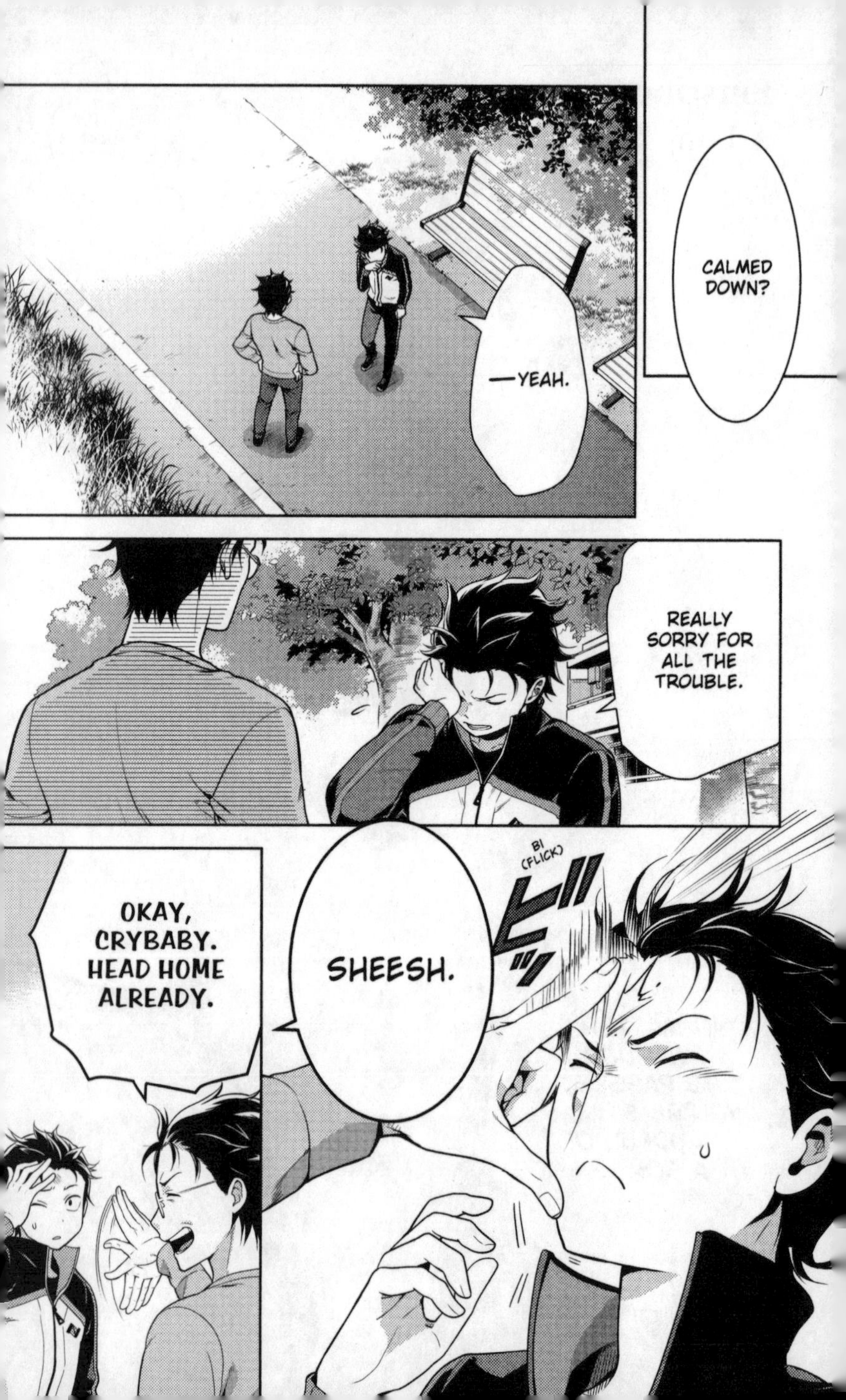

CALMED DOWN?
—YEAH.
REALLY SORRY FOR ALL THE TROUBLE.
ビッ
BI (FLICK)
SHEESH.
OKAY, CRYBABY. HEAD HOME ALREADY.

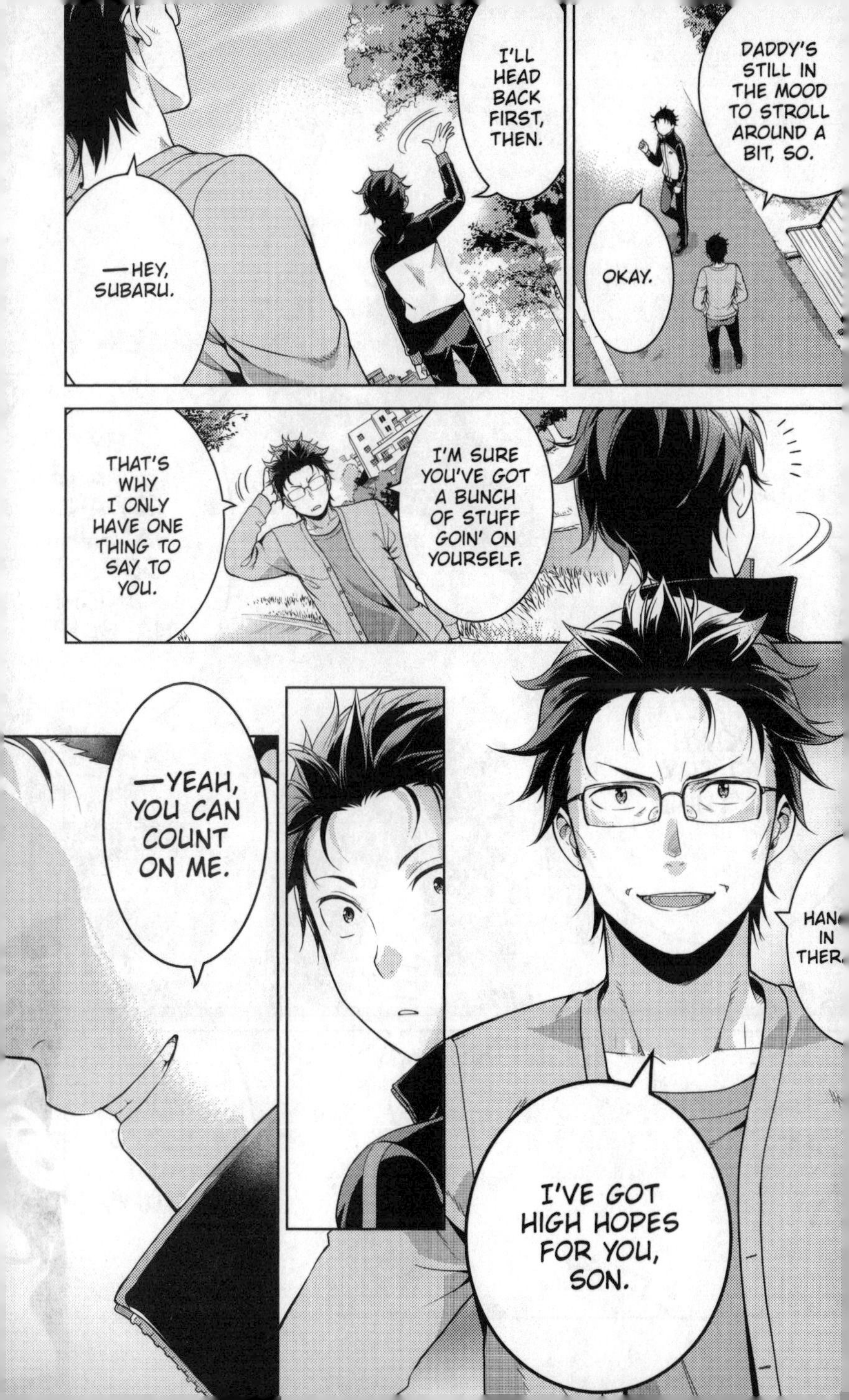
DADDY'S STILL IN THE MOOD TO STROLL AROUND A BIT, SO.
OKAY.
I'LL HEAD BACK FIRST, THEN.
—HEY, SUBARU.
I'M SURE YOU'VE GOT A BUNCH OF STUFF GOIN' ON YOURSELF.
THAT'S WHY I ONLY HAVE ONE THING TO SAY TO YOU.
HAN IN THER
I'VE GOT HIGH HOPES FOR YOU, SON.
—YEAH, YOU CAN COUNT ON ME.

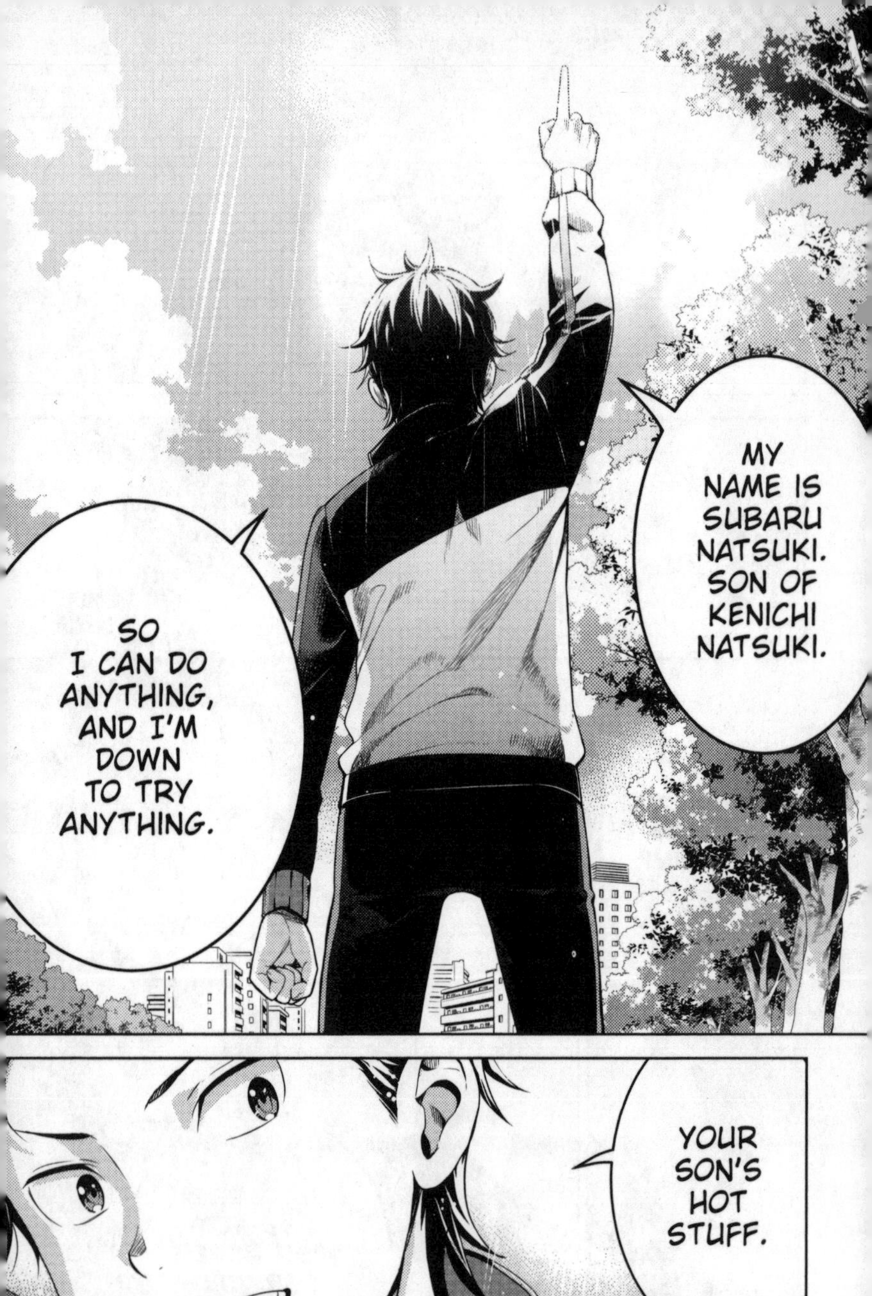
MY NAME IS SUBARU NATSUKI. SON OF KENICHI NATSUKI.
SO I CAN DO ANYTHING, AND I'M DOWN TO TRY ANYTHING.
YOUR SON'S HOT STUFF.

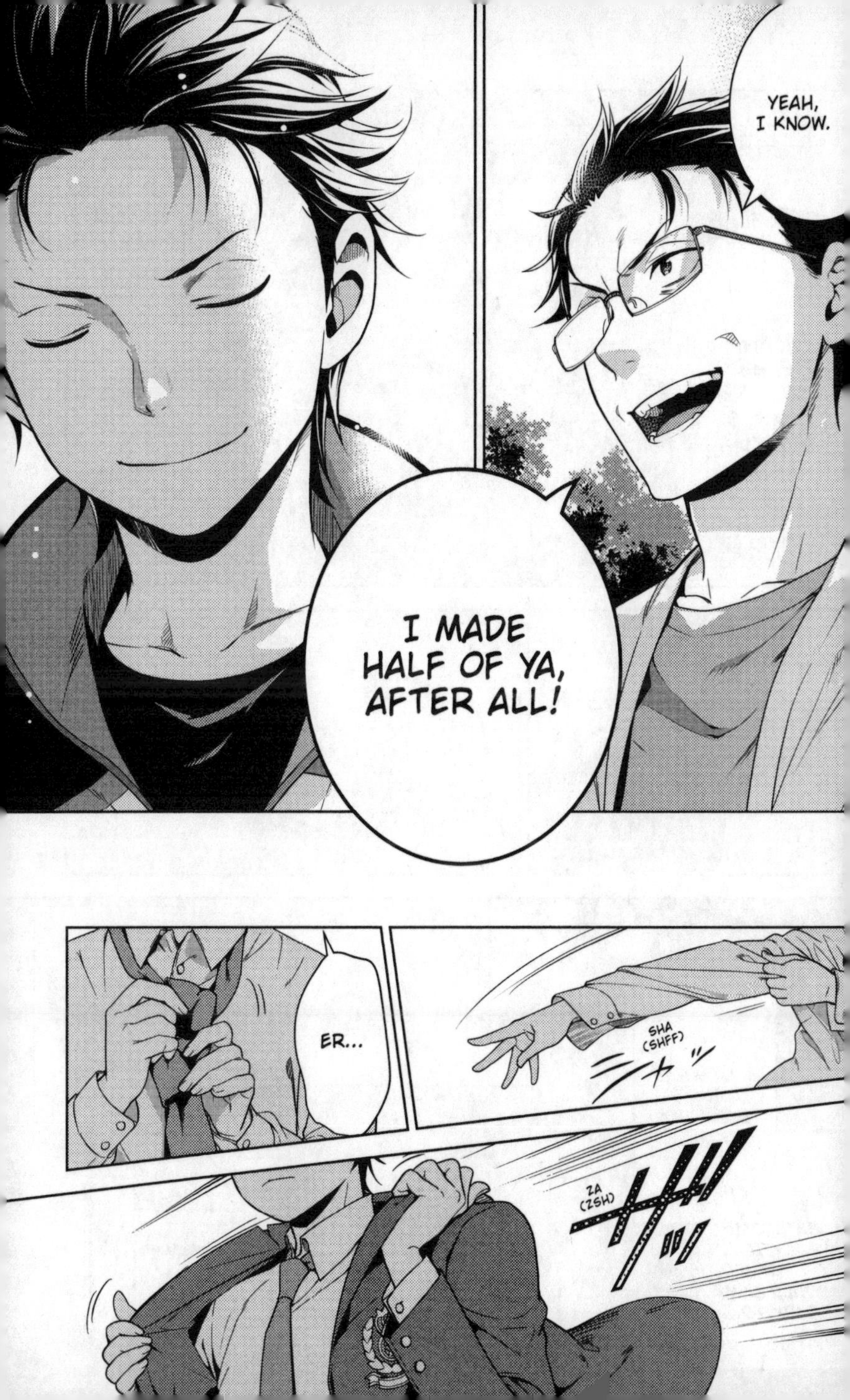
YEAH, I KNOW.
I MADE HALF OF YA, AFTER ALL!
SHA (SHFF)
ER...
ZA (ZSH)

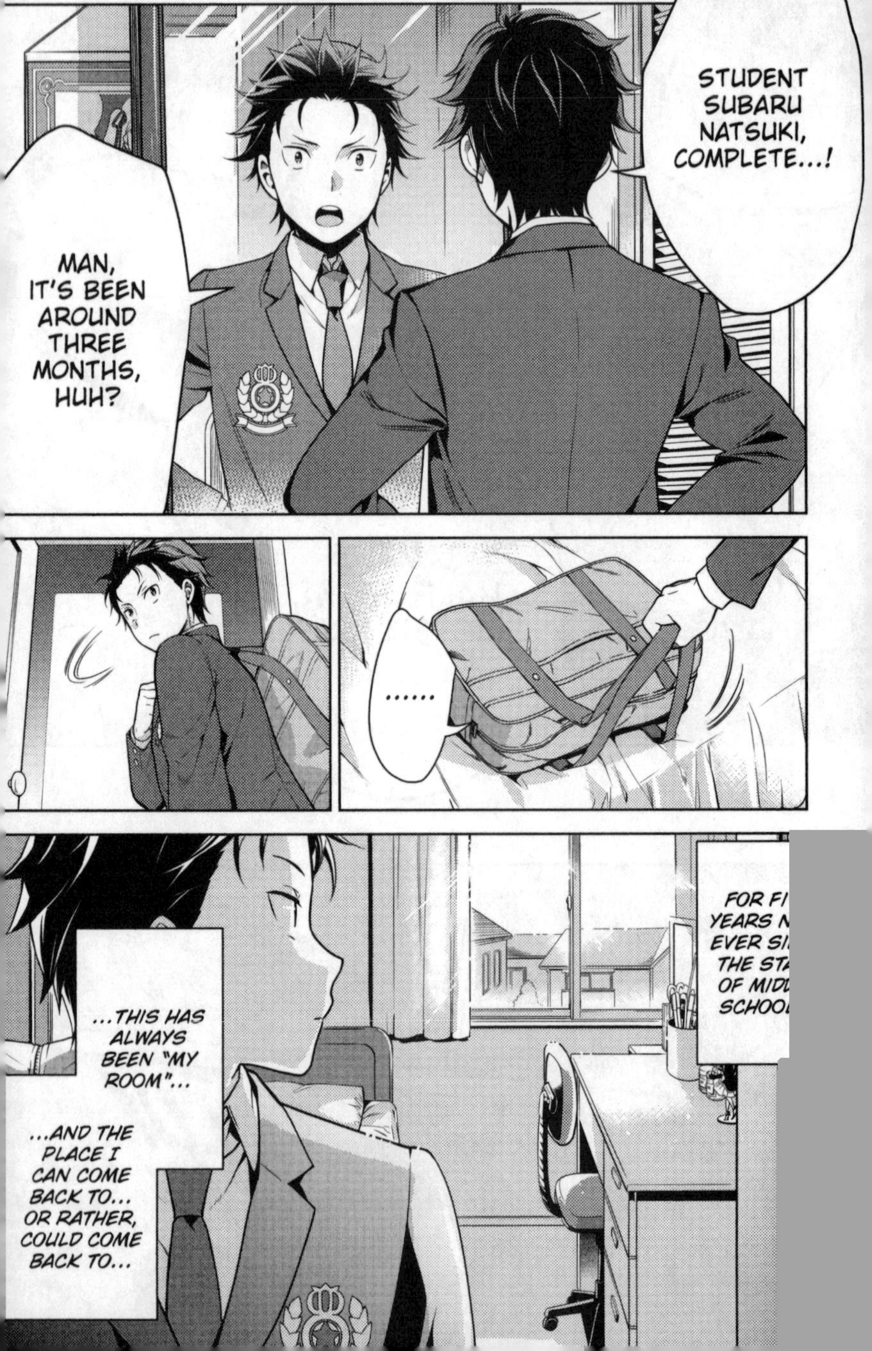
STUDENT SUBARU NATSUKI, COMPLETE...!
MAN, IT'S BEEN AROUND THREE MONTHS, HUH?
......
FOR FI YEARS N EVER SI THE STA OF MIDD SCHOO
...THIS HAS ALWAYS BEEN "MY ROOM"...
...AND THE PLACE I CAN COME BACK TO... OR RATHER, COULD COME BACK TO...

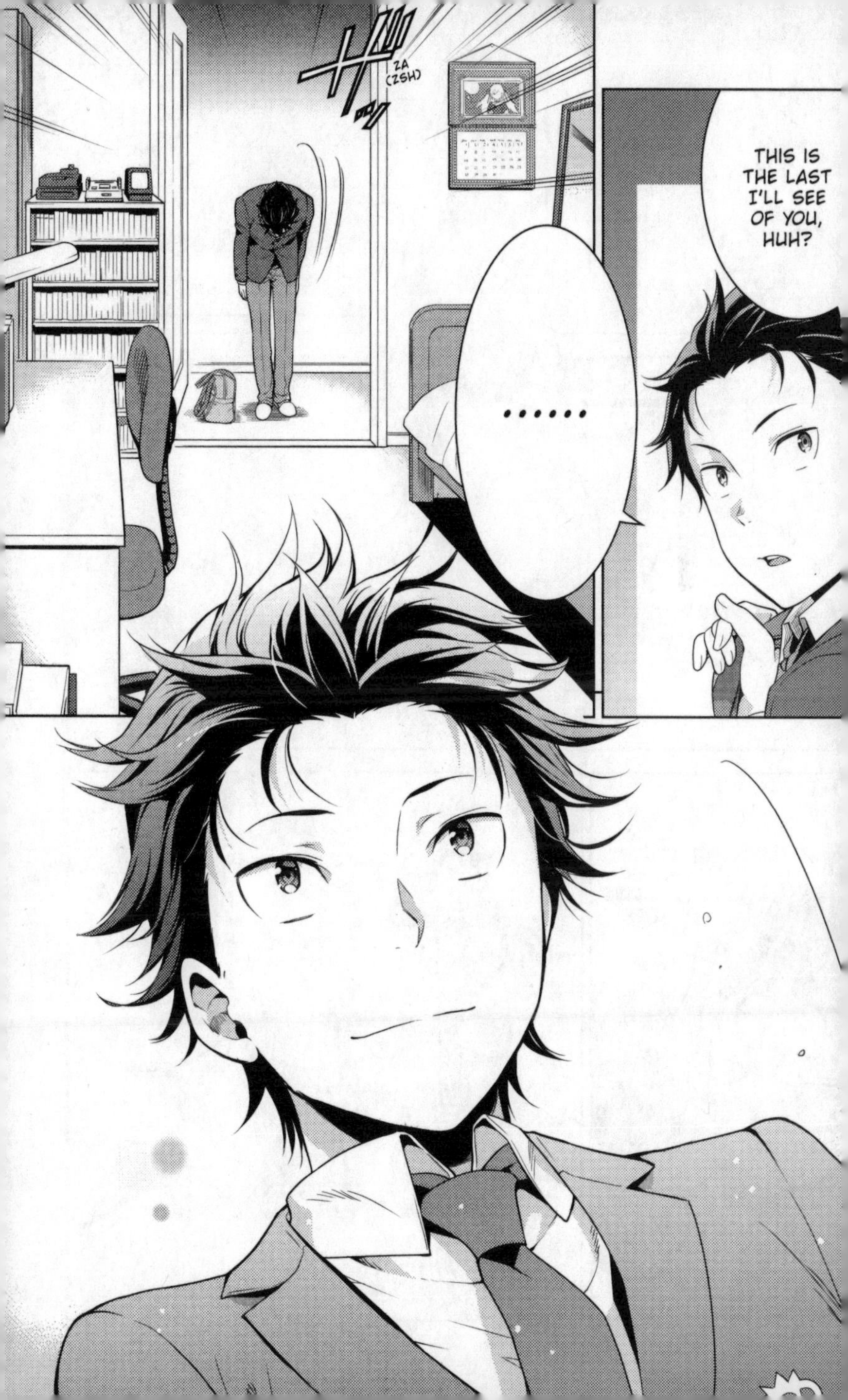
THIS IS THE LAST I'LL SEE OF YOU, HUH?
......
ZA (ZSH)

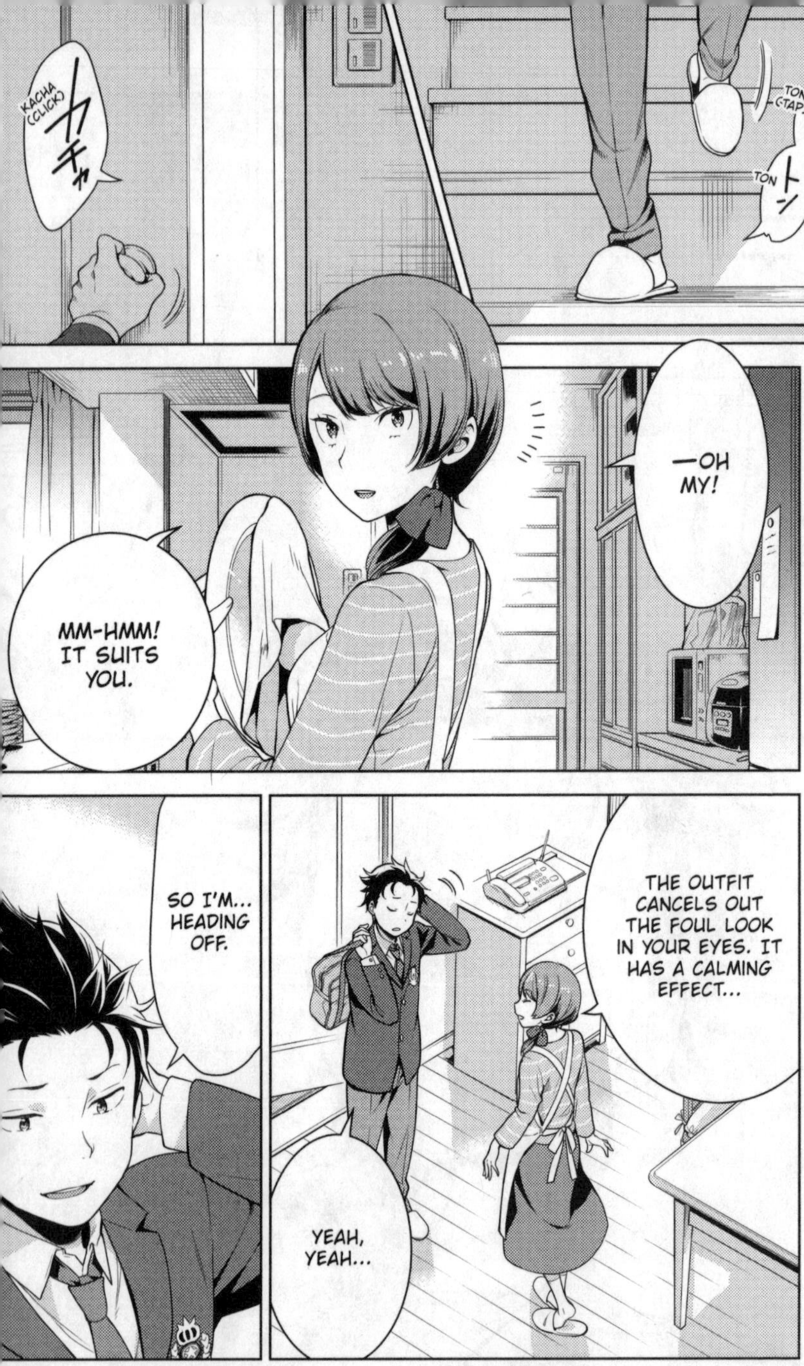
TON (TAP)
TON
KACHA (CLICK)
—OH MY!
MM-HMM! IT SUITS YOU.
THE OUTFIT CANCELS OUT THE FOUL LOOK IN YOUR EYES. IT HAS A CALMING EFFECT...
YEAH, YEAH...
SO I'M... HEADING OFF.

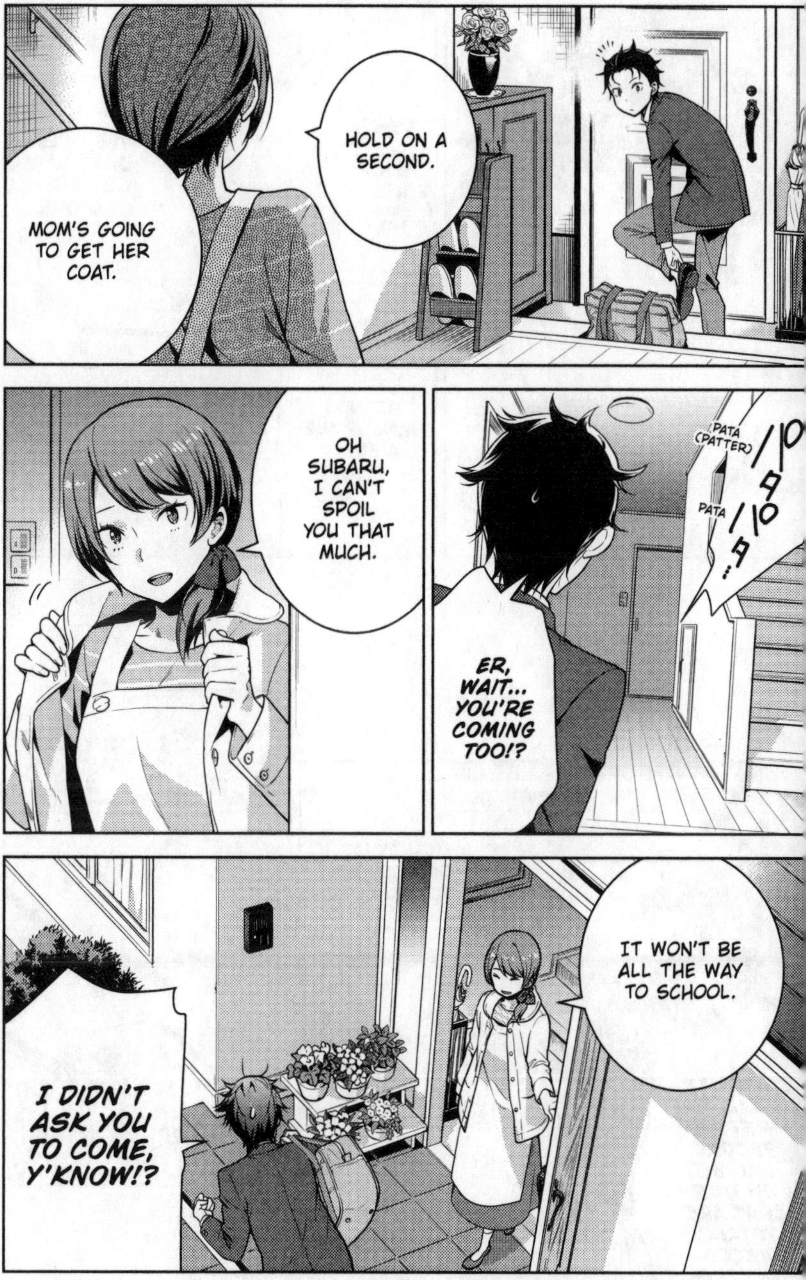
HOLD ON A SECOND.
MOM'S GOING TO GET HER COAT.
PATA (PATTER)
PATA
ER, WAIT... YOU'RE COMING TOO!?
OH SUBARU, I CAN'T SPOIL YOU THAT MUCH.
IT WON'T BE ALL THE WAY TO SCHOOL.
I DIDN'T ASK YOU TO COME, Y'KNOW!?

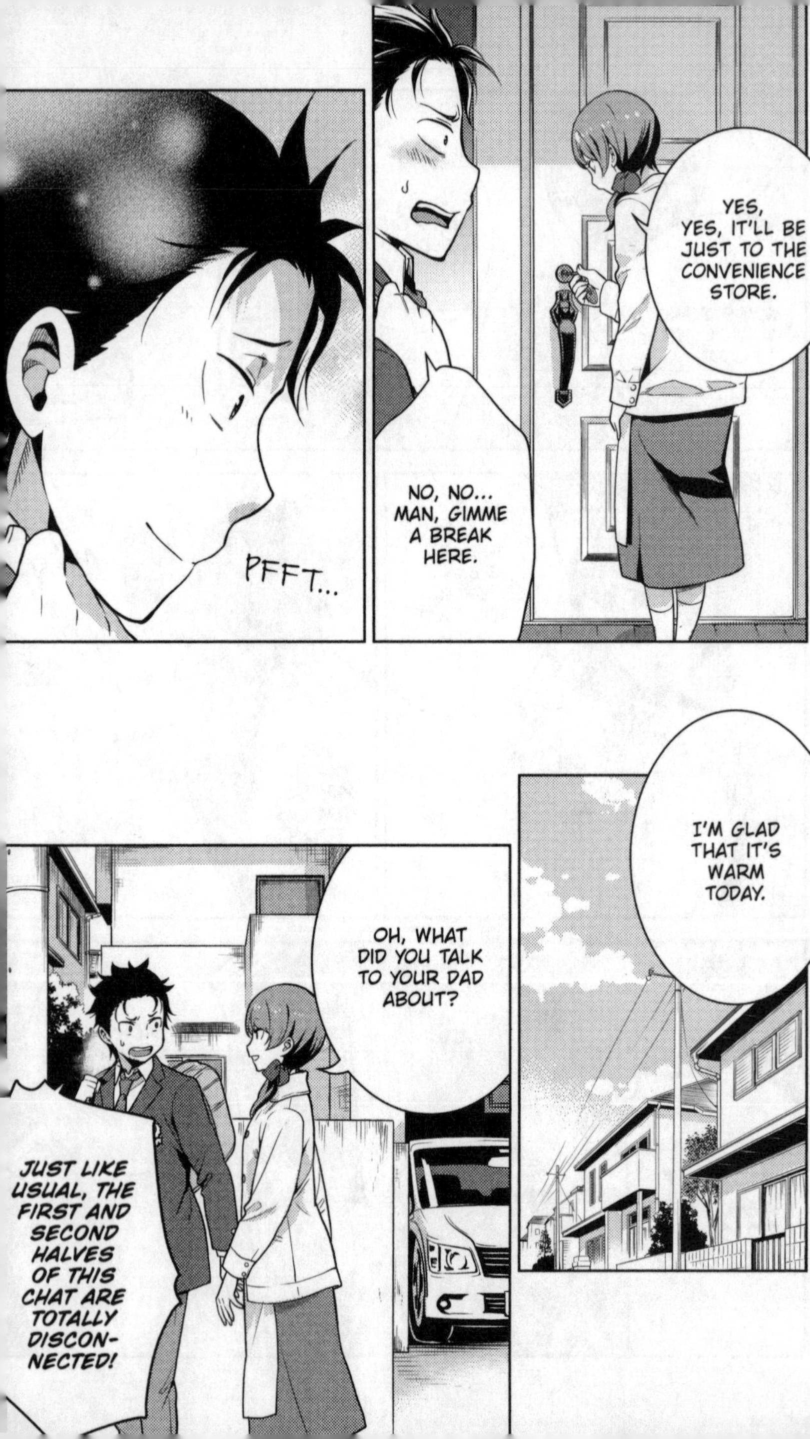
YES, YES, IT'LL BE JUST TO THE CONVENIENCE STORE.
NO, NO... MAN, GIMME A BREAK HERE.
PFFT...
I'M GLAD THAT IT'S WARM TODAY.
OH, WHAT DID YOU TALK TO YOUR DAD ABOUT?
JUST LIKE USUAL, THE FIRST AND SECOND HALVES OF THIS CHAT ARE TOTALLY DISCONNECTED!

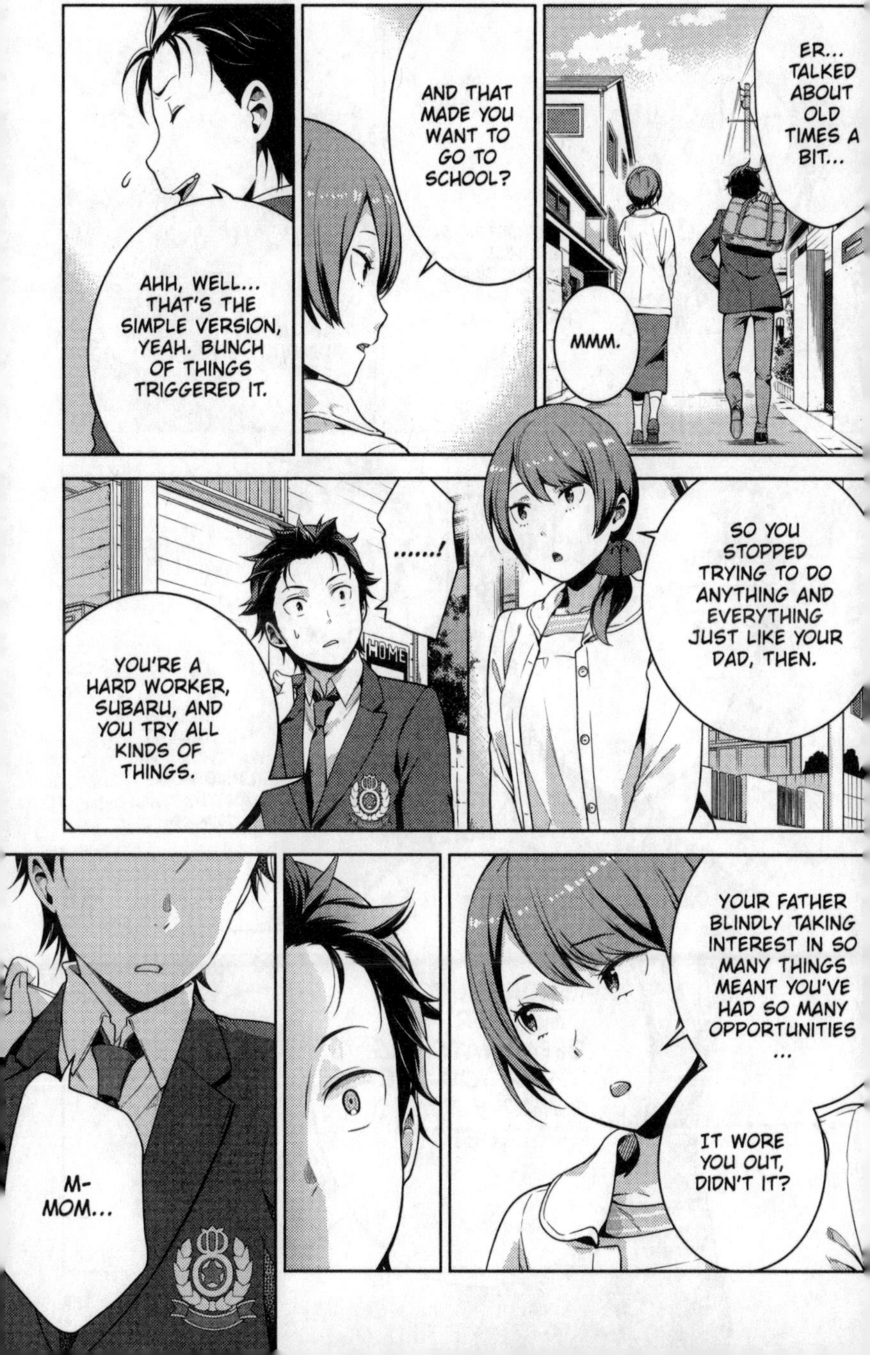
ER... TALKED ABOUT OLD TIMES A BIT...
MMM.
AND THAT MADE YOU WANT TO GO TO SCHOOL?
AHH, WELL... THAT'S THE SIMPLE VERSION, YEAH. BUNCH OF THINGS TRIGGERED IT.
SO YOU STOPPED TRYING TO DO ANYTHING AND EVERYTHING JUST LIKE YOUR DAD, THEN.
......!
HOME
YOU'RE A HARD WORKER, SUBARU, AND YOU TRY ALL KINDS OF THINGS.
YOUR FATHER BLINDLY TAKING INTEREST IN SO MANY THINGS MEANT YOU'VE HAD SO MANY OPPORTUNITIES ...
IT WORE YOU OUT, DIDN'T IT?
M- MOM...

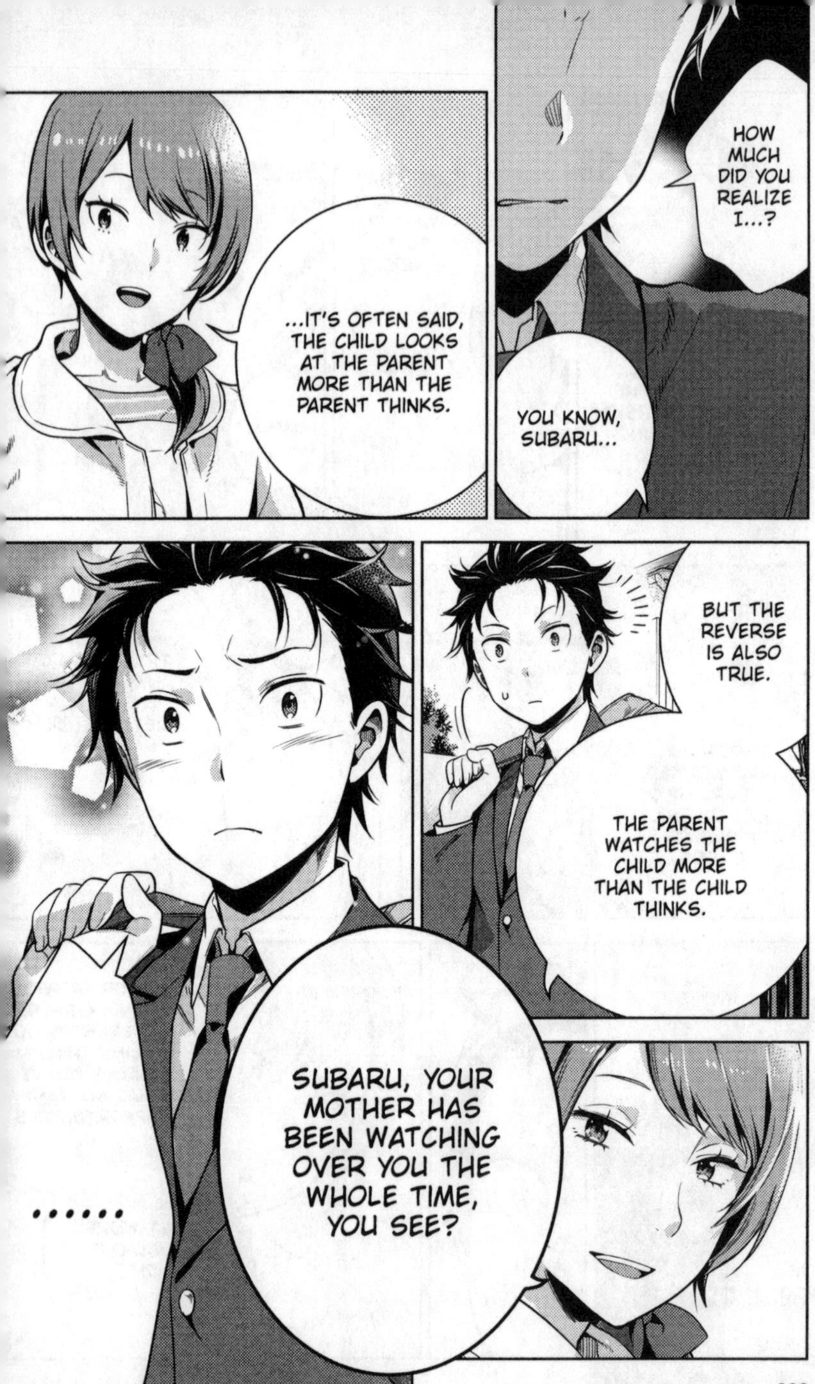
HOW MUCH DID YOU REALIZE I...?
YOU KNOW, SUBARU...
...IT'S OFTEN SAID, THE CHILD LOOKS AT THE PARENT MORE THAN THE PARENT THINKS.
BUT THE REVERSE IS ALSO TRUE.
THE PARENT WATCHES THE CHILD MORE THAN THE CHILD THINKS.
SUBARU, YOUR MOTHER HAS BEEN WATCHING OVER YOU THE WHOLE TIME, YOU SEE?
......

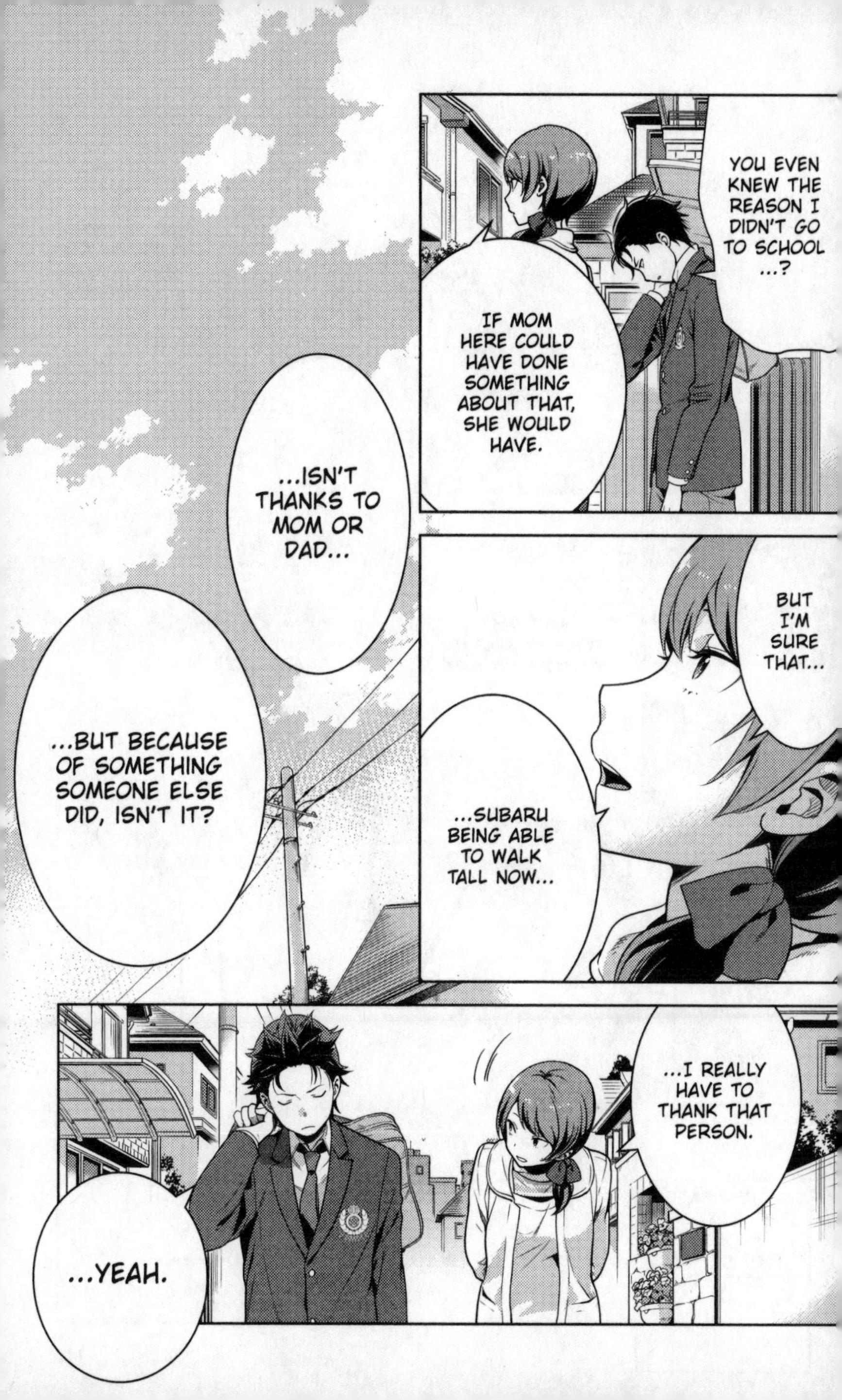
YOU EVEN KNEW THE REASON I DIDN'T GO TO SCHOOL ...?
IF MOM HERE COULD HAVE DONE SOMETHING ABOUT THAT, SHE WOULD HAVE.
BUT I'M SURE THAT...
...SUBARU BEING ABLE TO WALK TALL NOW...
...ISN'T THANKS TO MOM OR DAD...
...BUT BECAUSE OF SOMETHING SOMEONE ELSE DID, ISN'T IT?
...I REALLY HAVE TO THANK THAT PERSON.
...YEAH.

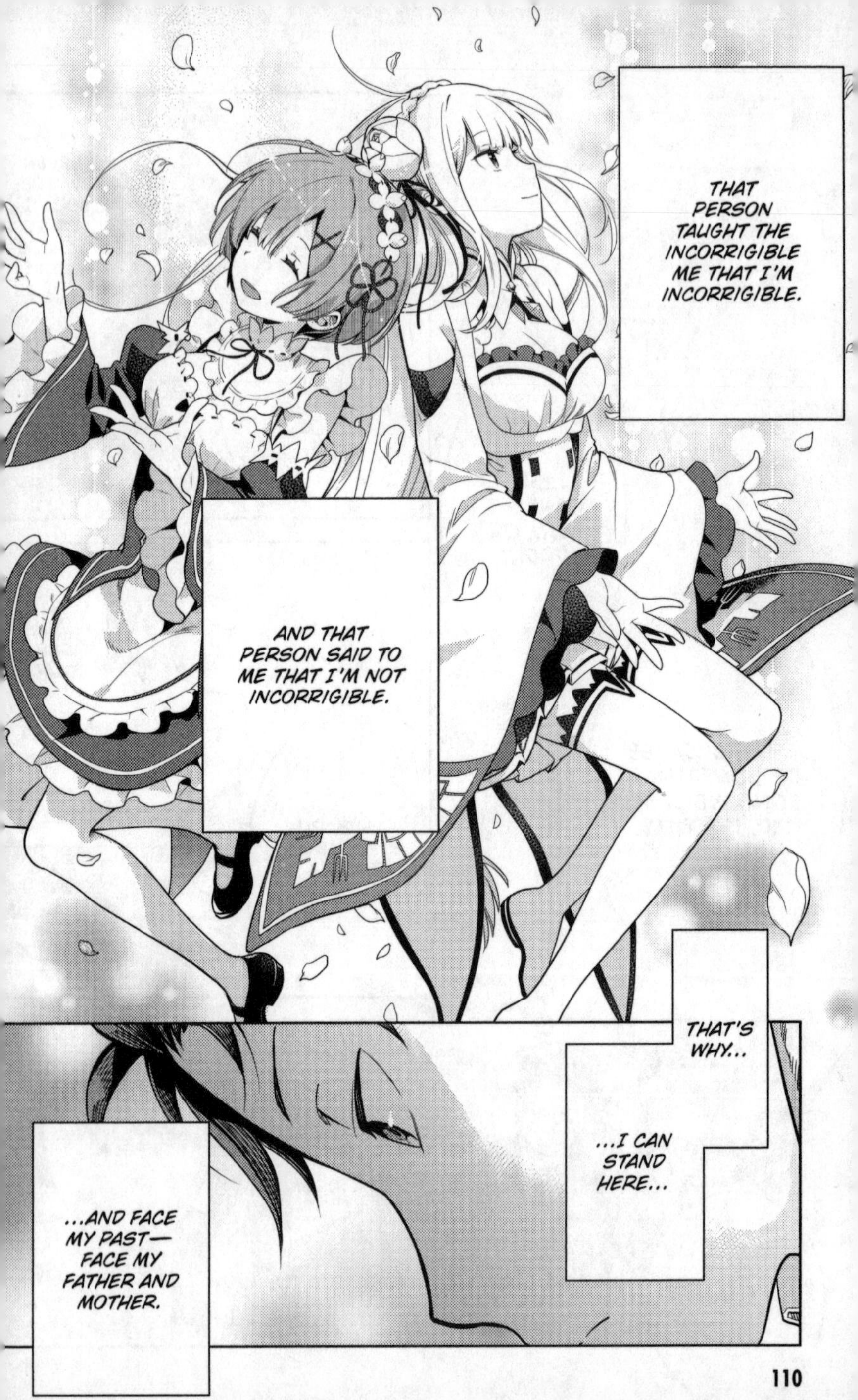
THAT PERSON TAUGHT THE INCORRIGIBLE ME THAT I'M INCORRIGIBLE.
AND THAT PERSON SAID TO ME THAT I'M NOT INCORRIGIBLE.
THAT'S WHY...
...I CAN STAND HERE...
...AND FACE MY PAST—FACE MY FATHER AND MOTHER.

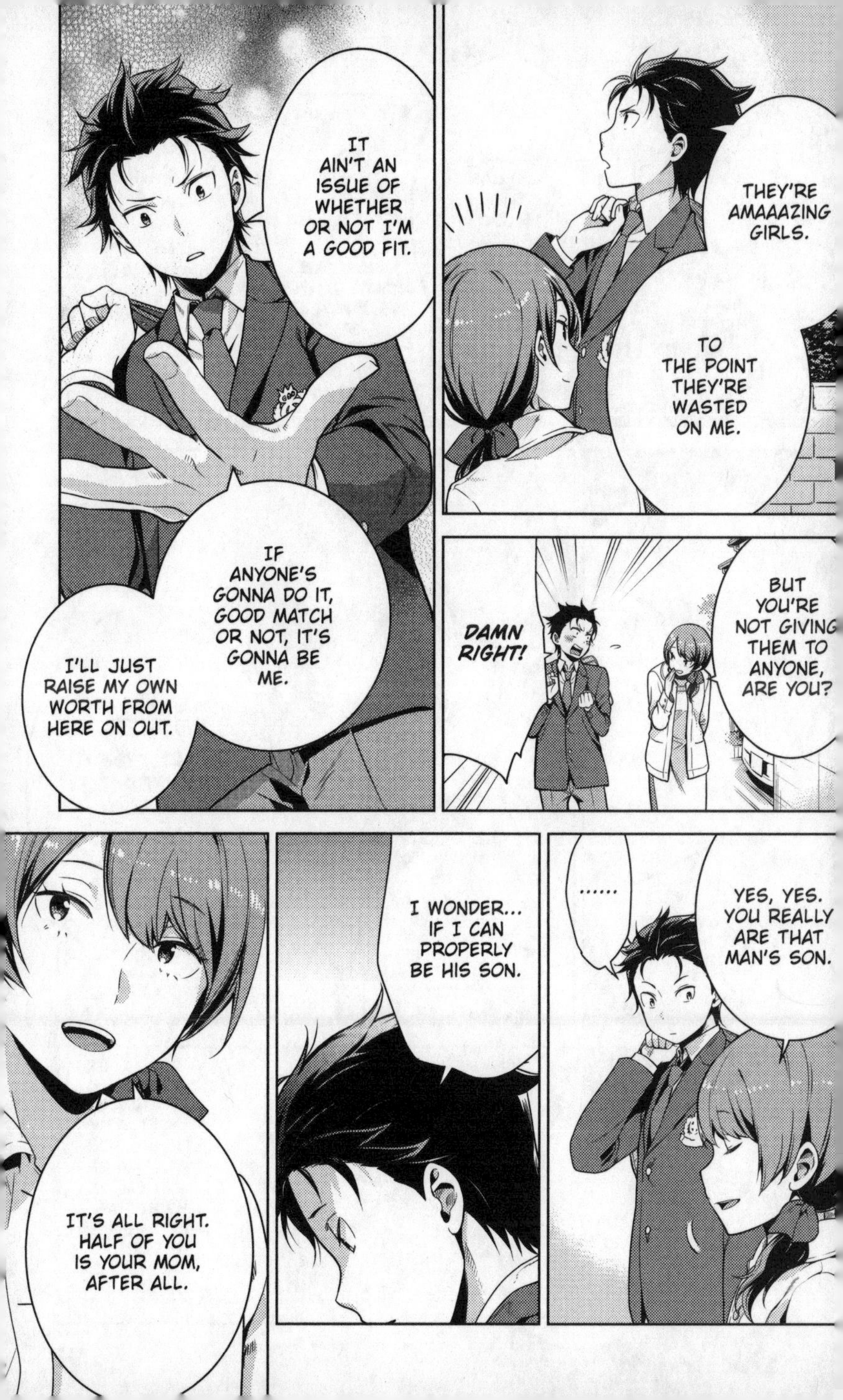
THEY'RE AMAAAZING GIRLS.
TO THE POINT THEY'RE WASTED ON ME.
BUT YOU'RE NOT GIVING THEM TO ANYONE, ARE YOU?
DAMN RIGHT!
IT AIN'T AN ISSUE OF WHETHER OR NOT I'M A GOOD FIT.
IF ANYONE'S GONNA DO IT, GOOD MATCH OR NOT, IT'S GONNA BE ME.
I'LL JUST RAISE MY OWN WORTH FROM HERE ON OUT.
YES, YES. YOU REALLY ARE THAT MAN'S SON.
......
I WONDER... IF I CAN PROPERLY BE HIS SON.
IT'S ALL RIGHT. HALF OF YOU IS YOUR MOM, AFTER ALL.

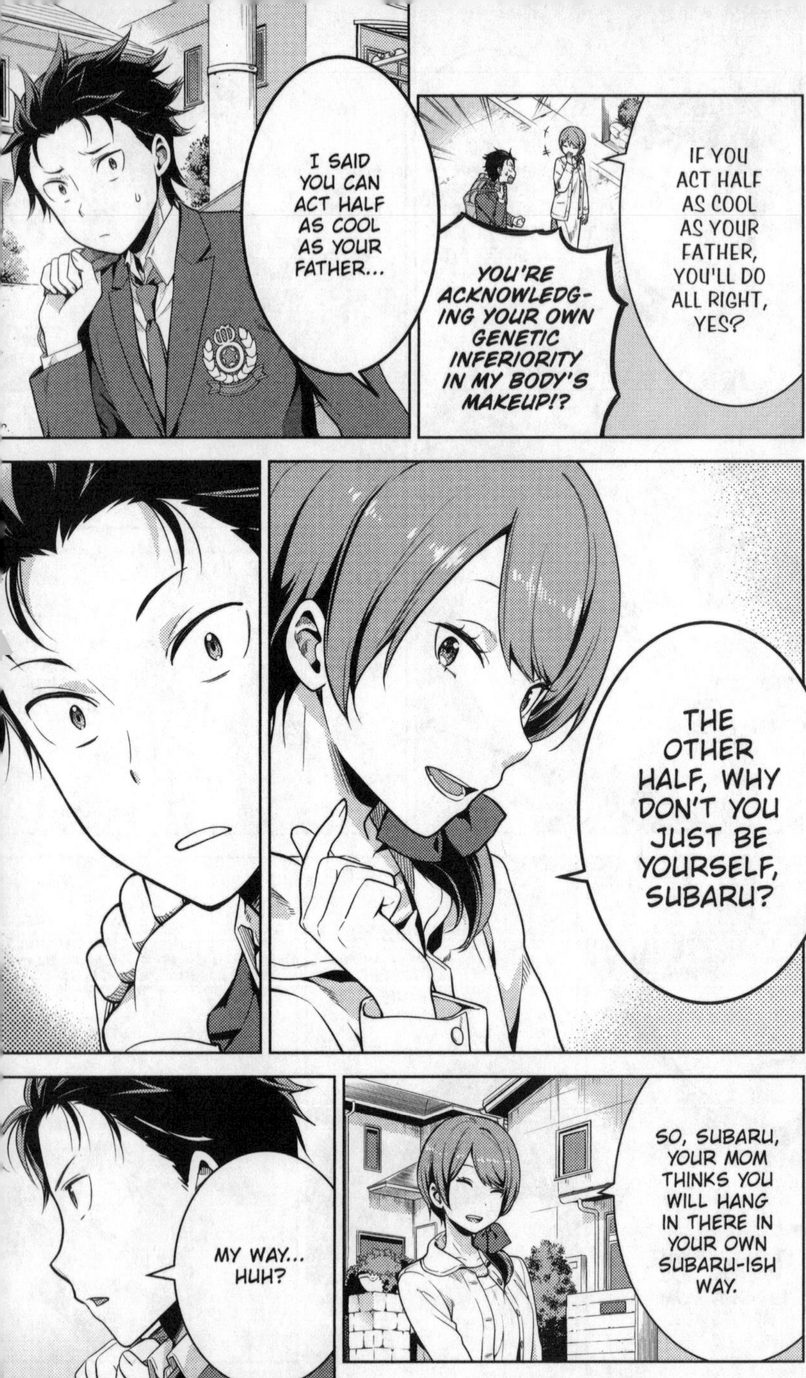
IF YOU ACT HALF AS COOL AS YOUR FATHER, YOU'LL DO ALL RIGHT, YES?
YOU'RE ACKNOWLEDG-ING YOUR OWN GENETIC INFERIORITY IN MY BODY'S MAKEUP!?
I SAID YOU CAN ACT HALF AS COOL AS YOUR FATHER...
THE OTHER HALF, WHY DON'T YOU JUST BE YOURSELF, SUBARU?
SO, SUBARU, YOUR MOM THINKS YOU WILL HANG IN THERE IN YOUR OWN SUBARU-ISH WAY.
MY WAY... HUH?

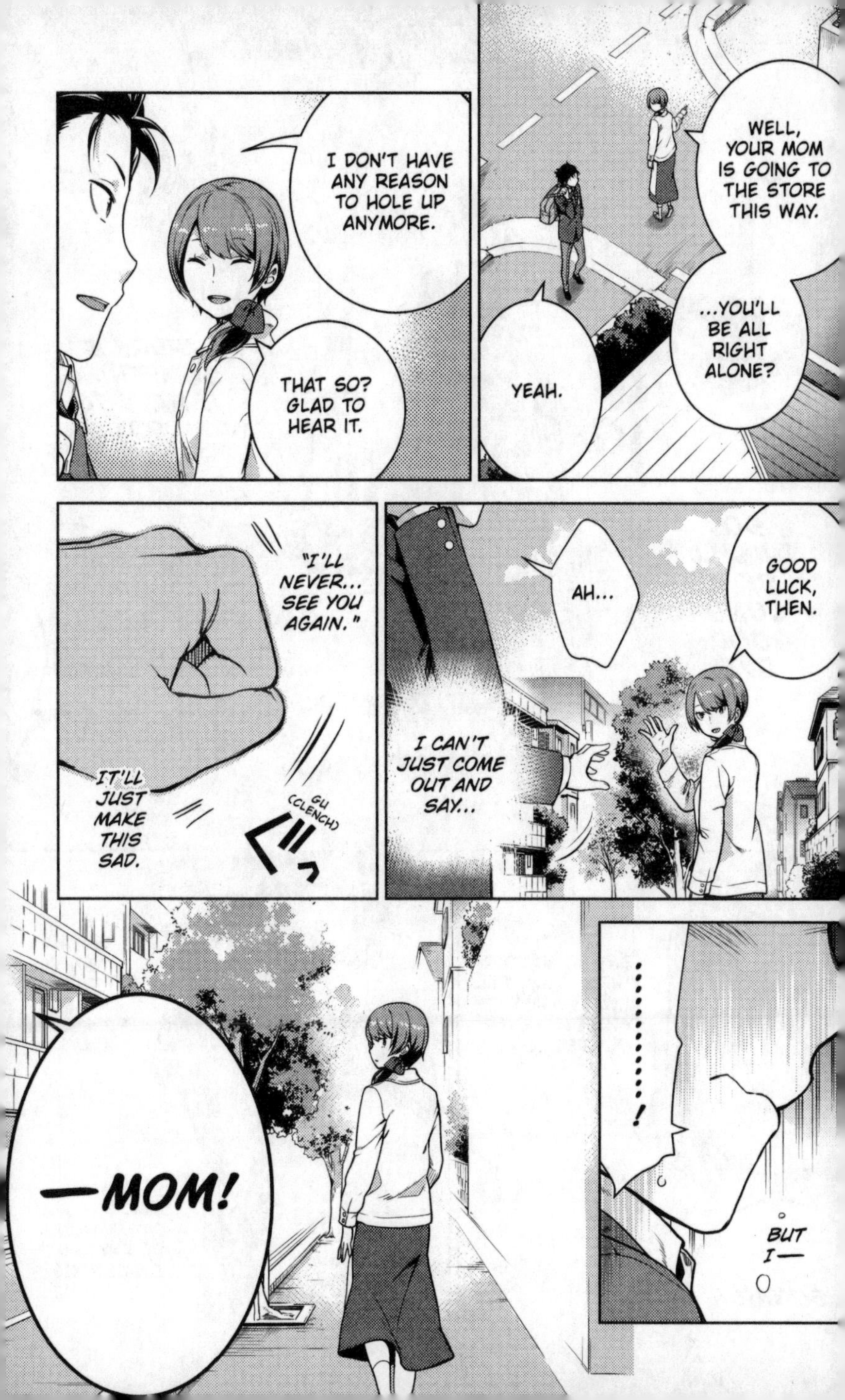
WELL, YOUR MOM IS GOING TO THE STORE THIS WAY.
...YOU'LL BE ALL RIGHT ALONE?
YEAH.
I DON'T HAVE ANY REASON TO HOLE UP ANYMORE.
THAT SO? GLAD TO HEAR IT.
GOOD LUCK, THEN.
AH...
I CAN'T JUST COME OUT AND SAY...
"I'LL NEVER... SEE YOU AGAIN."
GU (CLENCH)
IT'LL JUST MAKE THIS SAD.
..........!
BUT I—
—MOM!

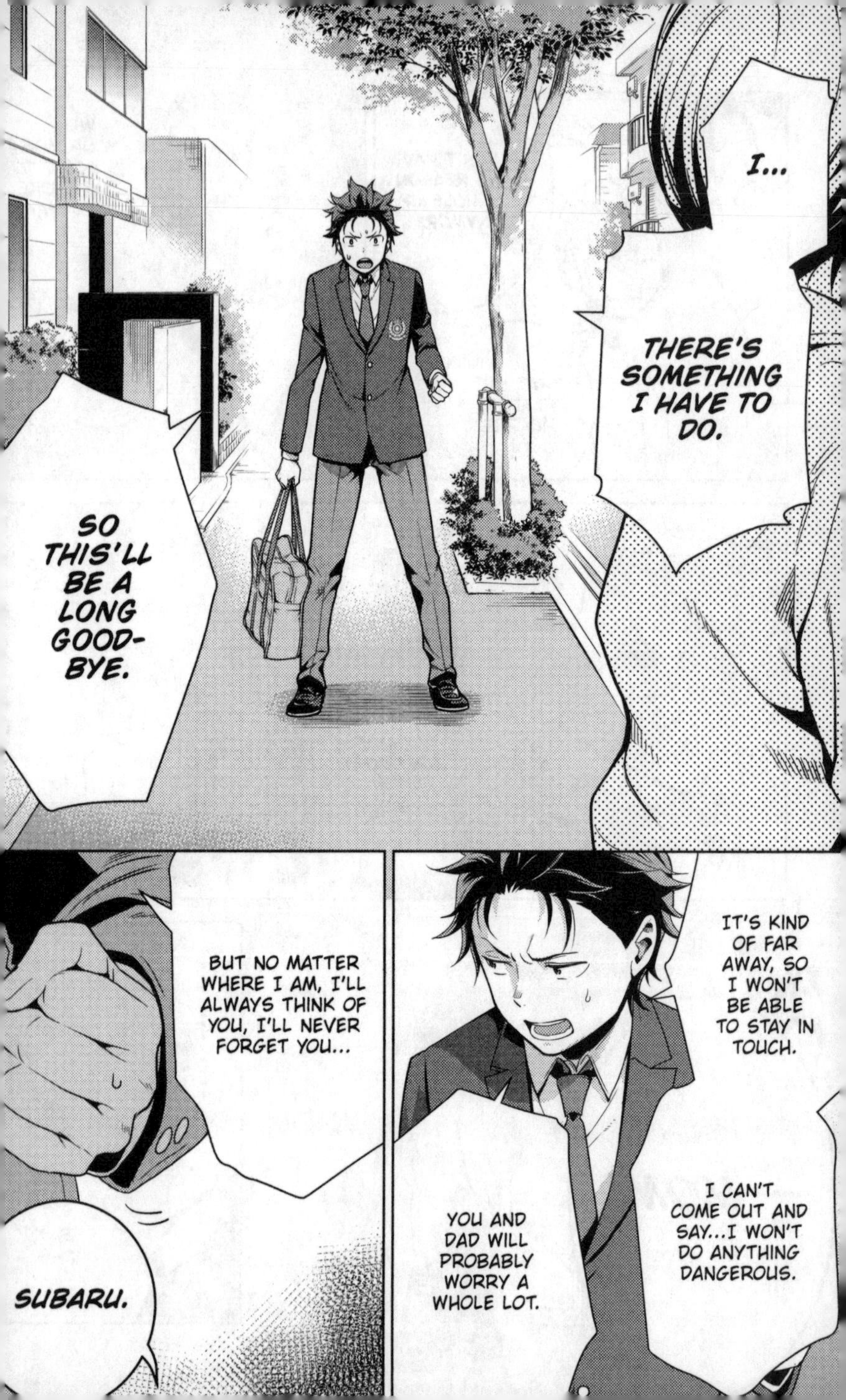
I...
THERE'S SOMETHING I HAVE TO DO.
SO THIS'LL BE A LONG GOOD-BYE.
IT'S KIND OF FAR AWAY, SO I WON'T BE ABLE TO STAY IN TOUCH.
I CAN'T COME OUT AND SAY...I WON'T DO ANYTHING DANGEROUS.
YOU AND DAD WILL PROBABLY WORRY A WHOLE LOT.
BUT NO MATTER WHERE I AM, I'LL ALWAYS THINK OF YOU, I'LL NEVER FORGET YOU...
SUBARU.

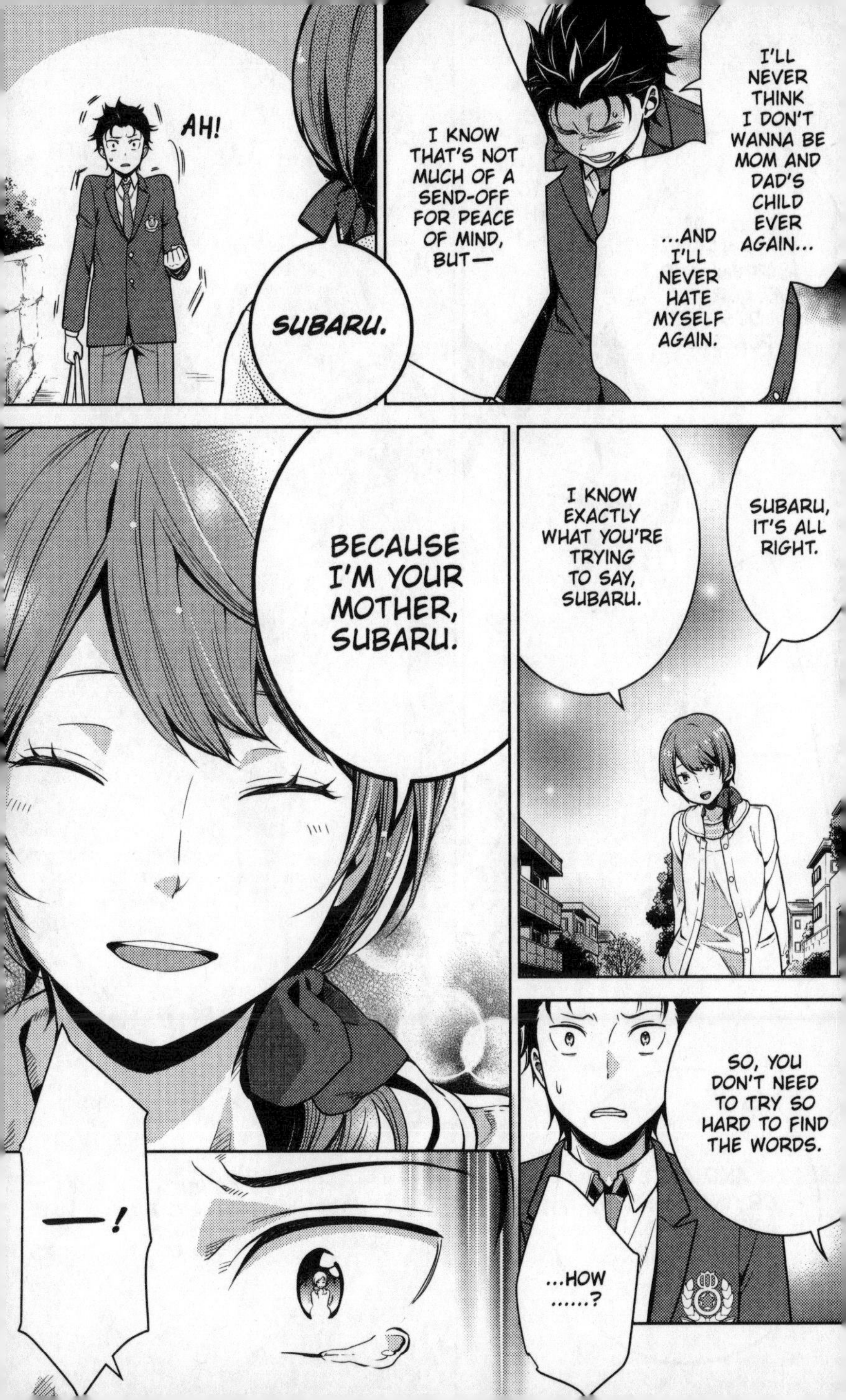

I'LL NEVER THINK I DON'T WANNA BE MOM AND DAD'S CHILD EVER AGAIN...
...AND I'LL NEVER HATE MYSELF AGAIN.
I KNOW THAT'S NOT MUCH OF A SEND-OFF FOR PEACE OF MIND, BUT—
SUBARU.
AH!
SUBARU, IT'S ALL RIGHT.
I KNOW EXACTLY WHAT YOU'RE TRYING TO SAY, SUBARU.
SO, YOU DON'T NEED TO TRY SO HARD TO FIND THE WORDS.
...HOW ......?
BECAUSE I'M YOUR MOTHER, SUBARU.
—!

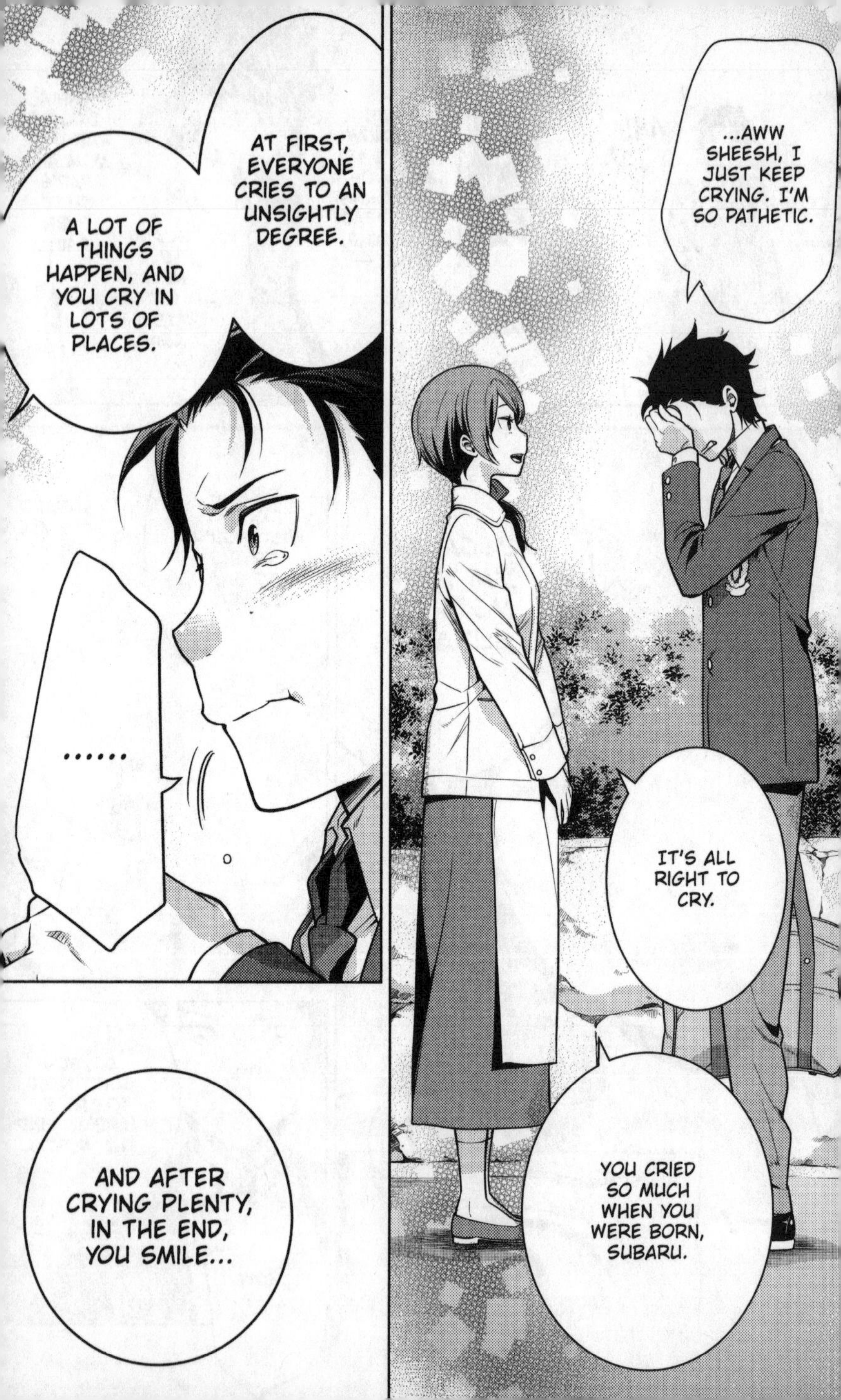
...AWW SHEESH, I JUST KEEP CRYING. I'M SO PATHETIC.
IT'S ALL RIGHT TO CRY.
YOU CRIED SO MUCH WHEN YOU WERE BORN, SUBARU.
AT FIRST, EVERYONE CRIES TO AN UNSIGHTLY DEGREE.
A LOT OF THINGS HAPPEN, AND YOU CRY IN LOTS OF PLACES.
......
AND AFTER CRYING PLENTY, IN THE END, YOU SMILE...

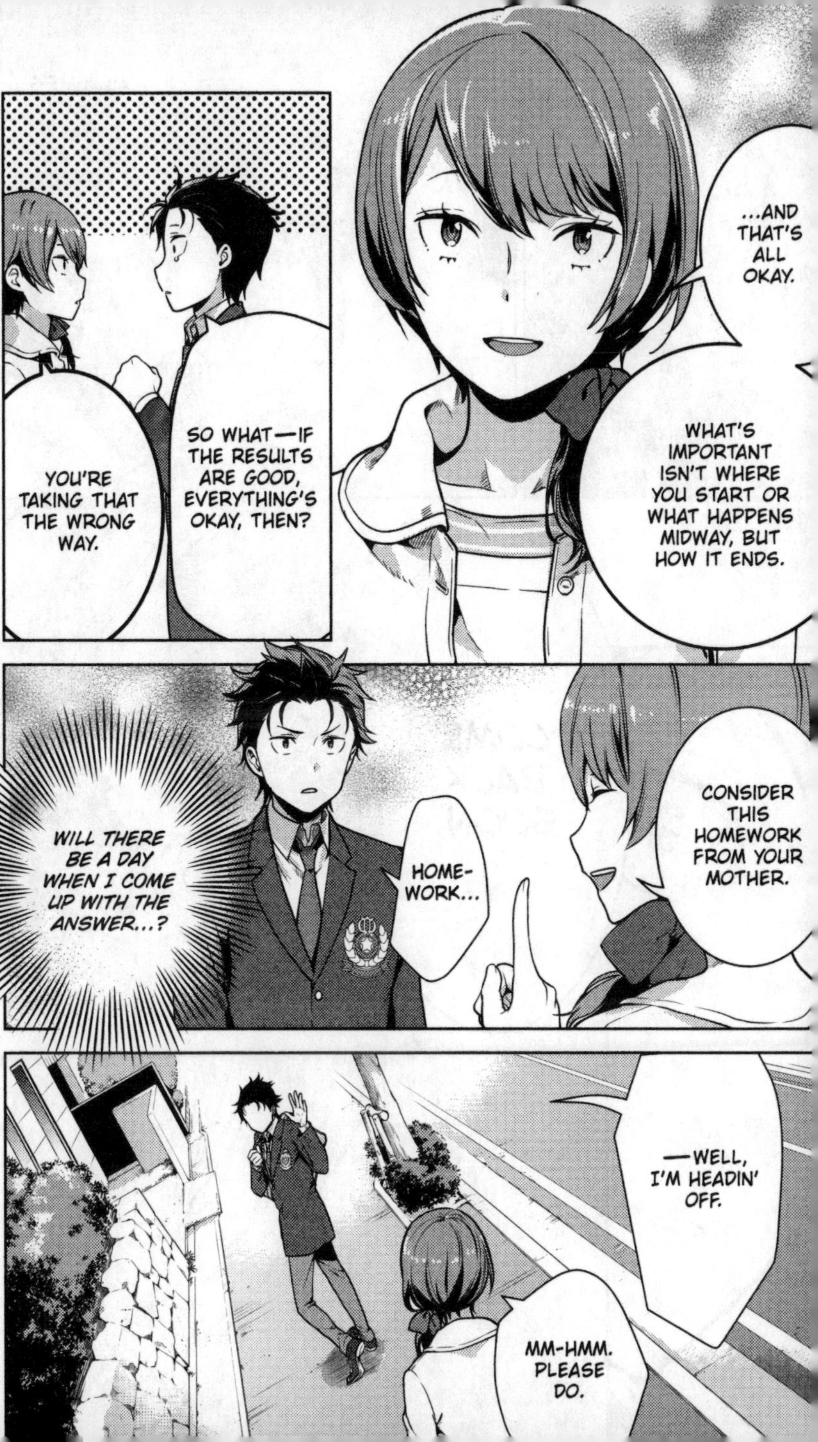
...AND THAT'S ALL OKAY.
WHAT'S IMPORTANT ISN'T WHERE YOU START OR WHAT HAPPENS MIDWAY, BUT HOW IT ENDS.
SO WHAT—IF THE RESULTS ARE GOOD, EVERYTHING'S OKAY, THEN?
YOU'RE TAKING THAT THE WRONG WAY.
CONSIDER THIS HOMEWORK FROM YOUR MOTHER.
HOME-WORK...
WILL THERE BE A DAY WHEN I COME UP WITH THE ANSWER...?
—WELL, I'M HEADIN' OFF.
MM-HMM. PLEASE DO.

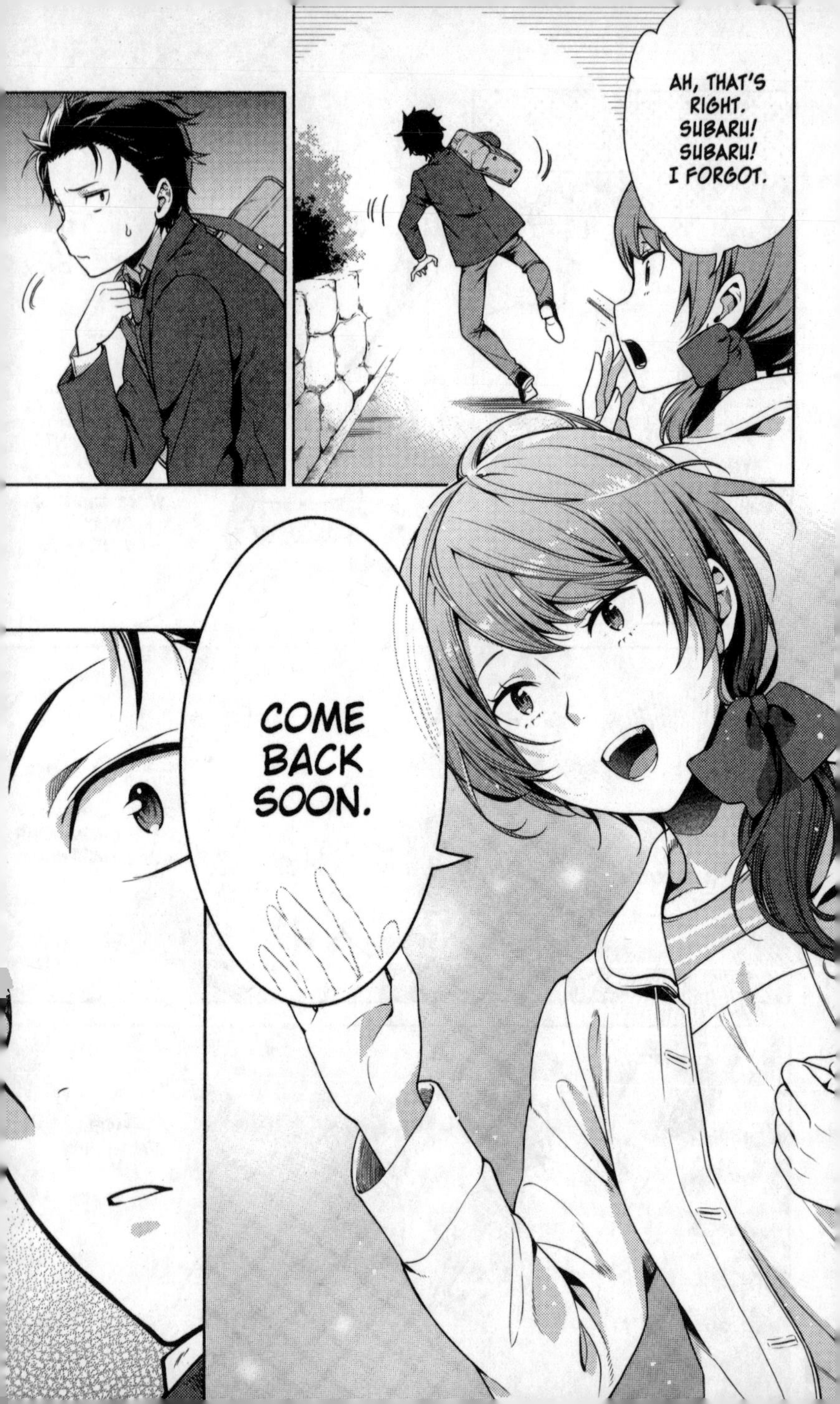
AH, THAT'S RIGHT. SUBARU! SUBARU! I FORGOT.
COME BACK SOON.

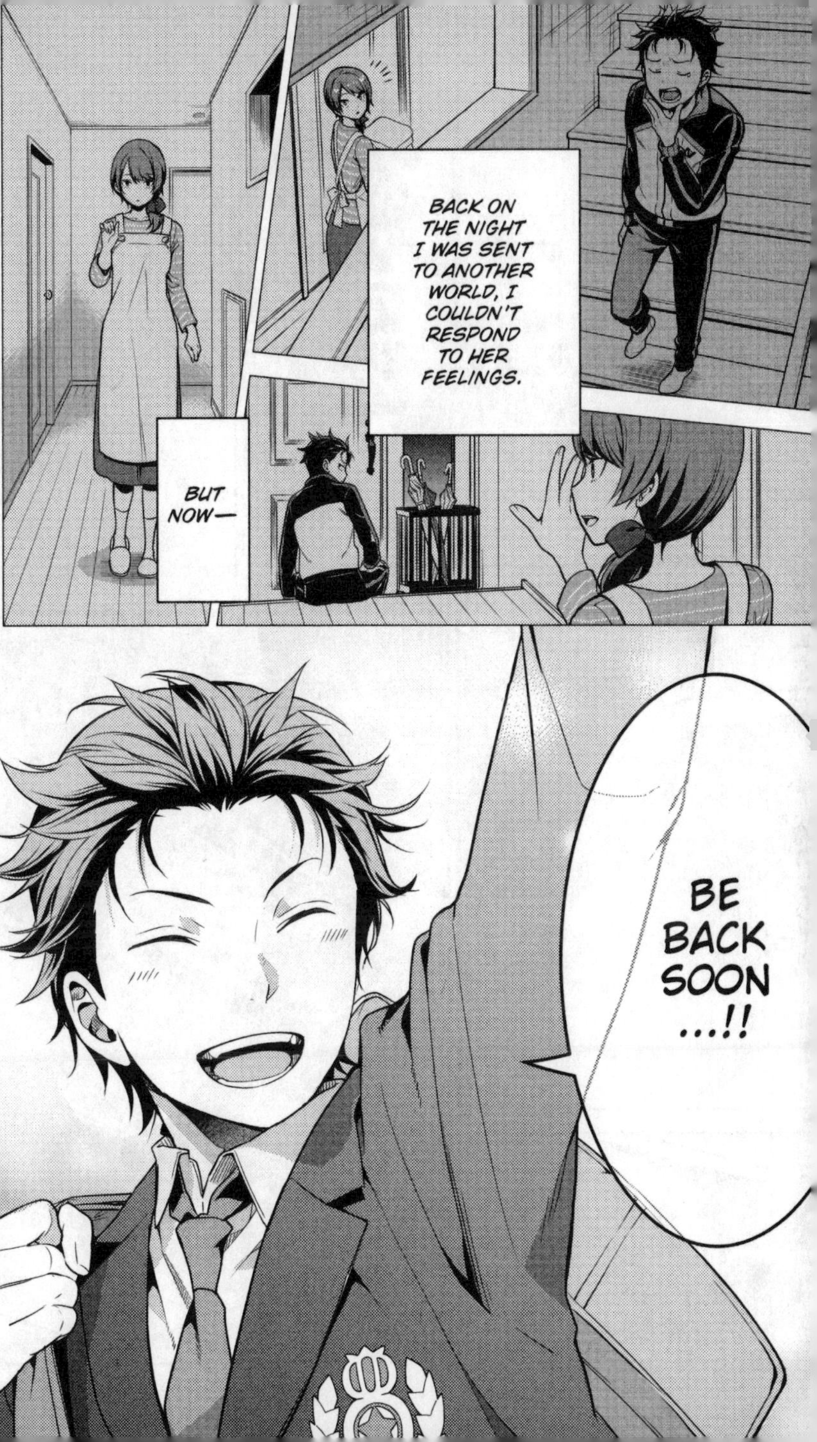
BACK ON THE NIGHT I WAS SENT TO ANOTHER WORLD, I COULDN'T RESPOND TO HER FEELINGS.
BUT NOW—
BE BACK SOON ...!!

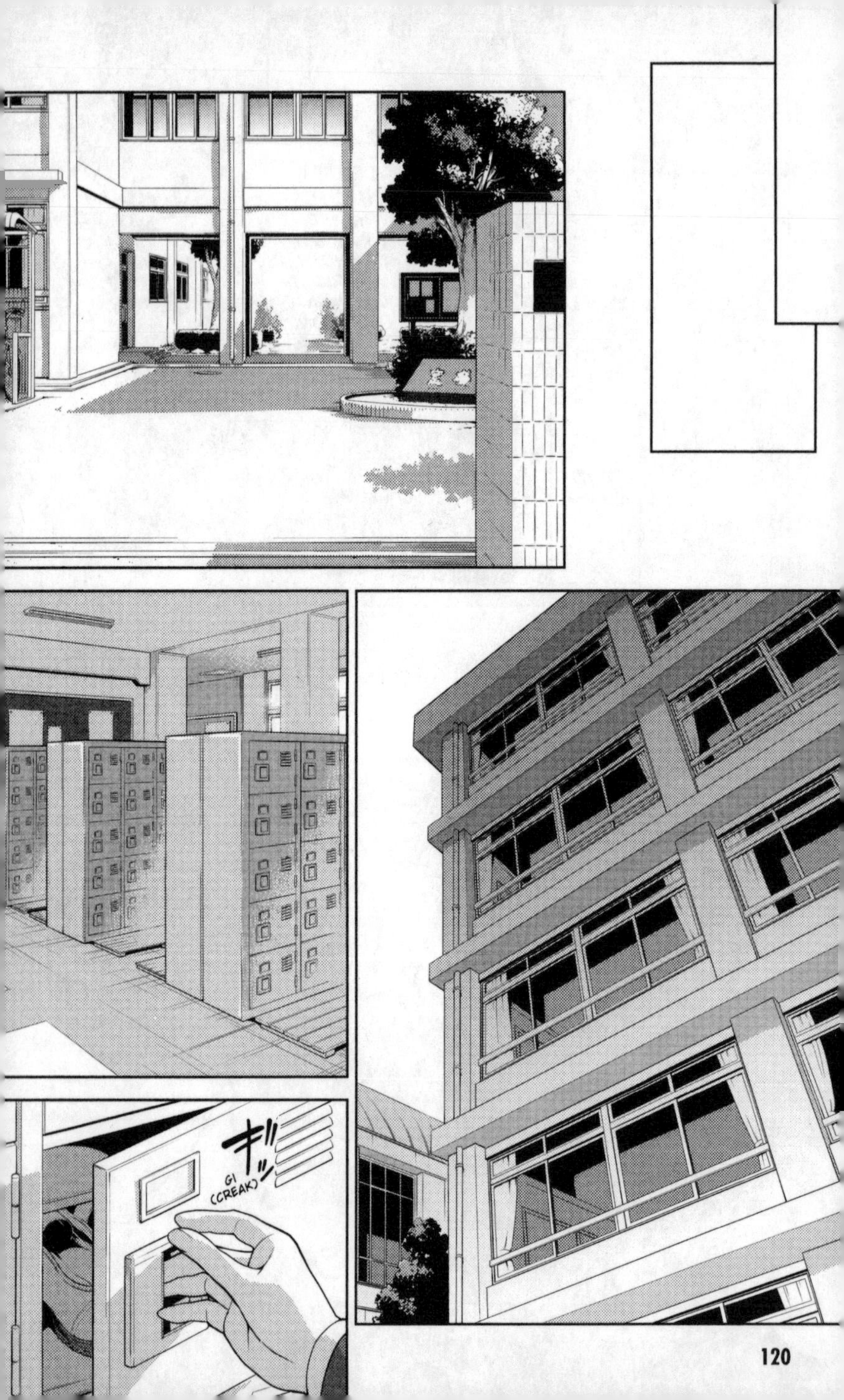
ギ
GI
(CREAK)

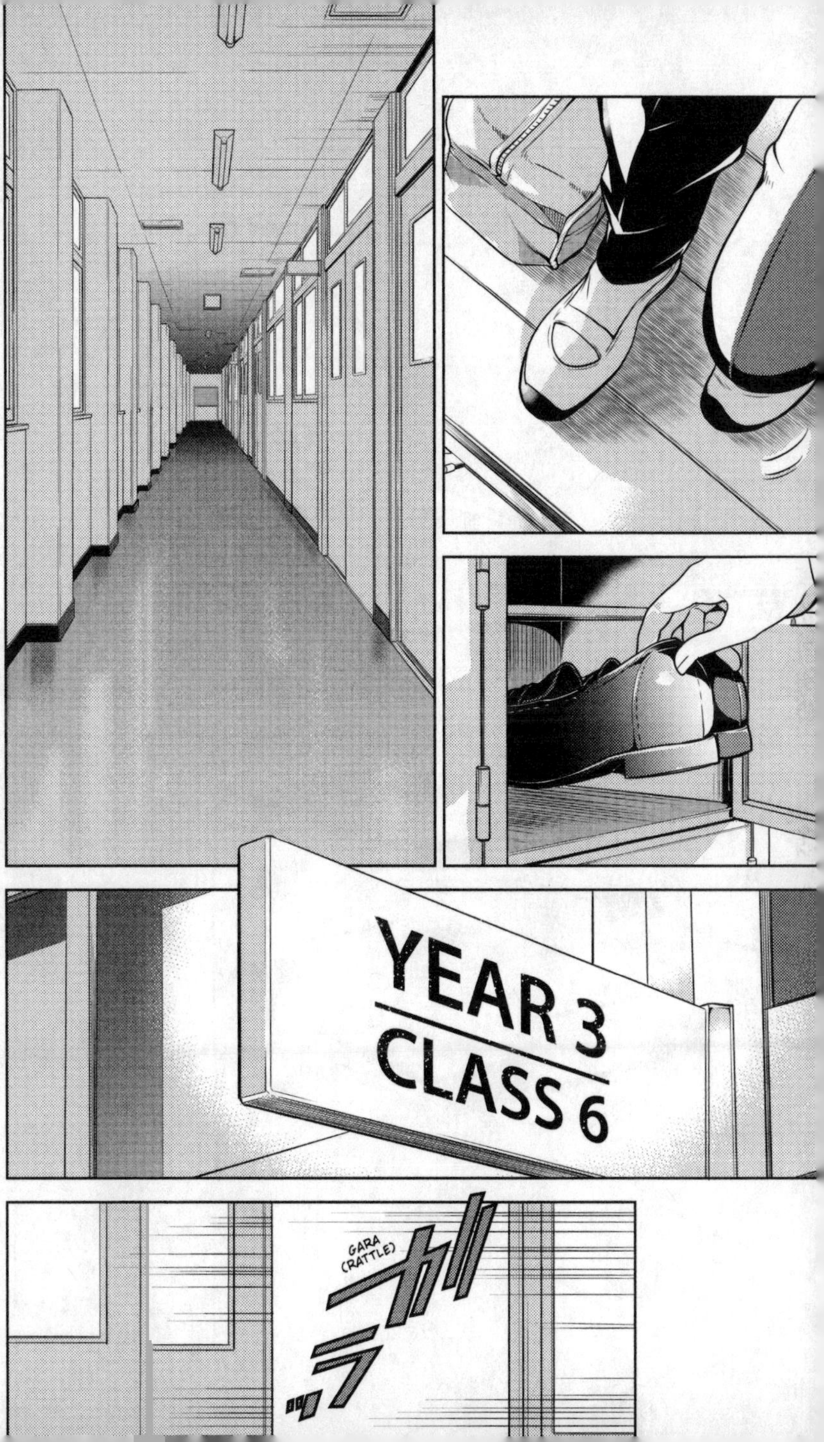
YEAR 3
CLASS 6
GARA (RATTLE)

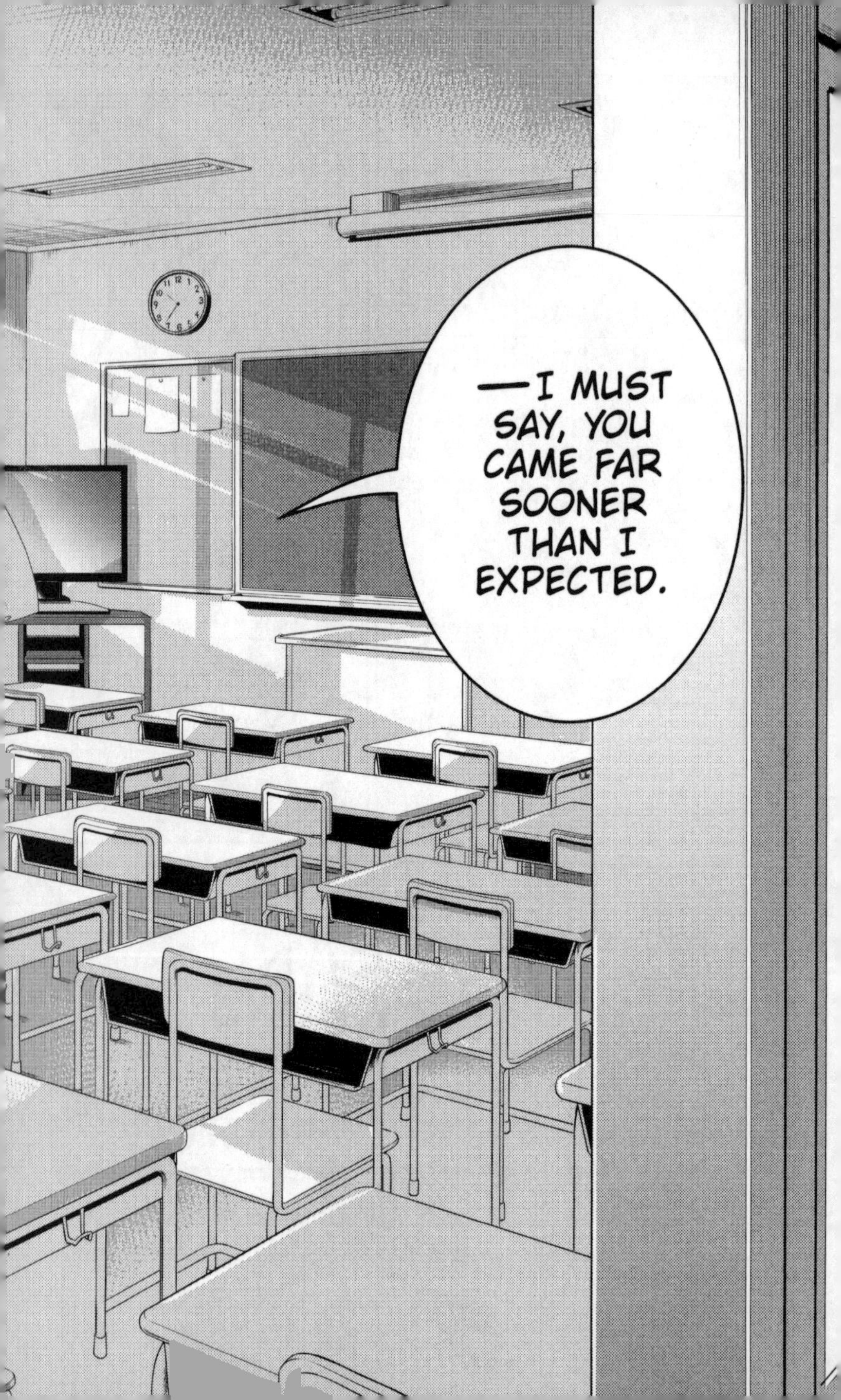
—I MUST SAY, YOU CAME FAR SOONER THAN I EXPECTED.

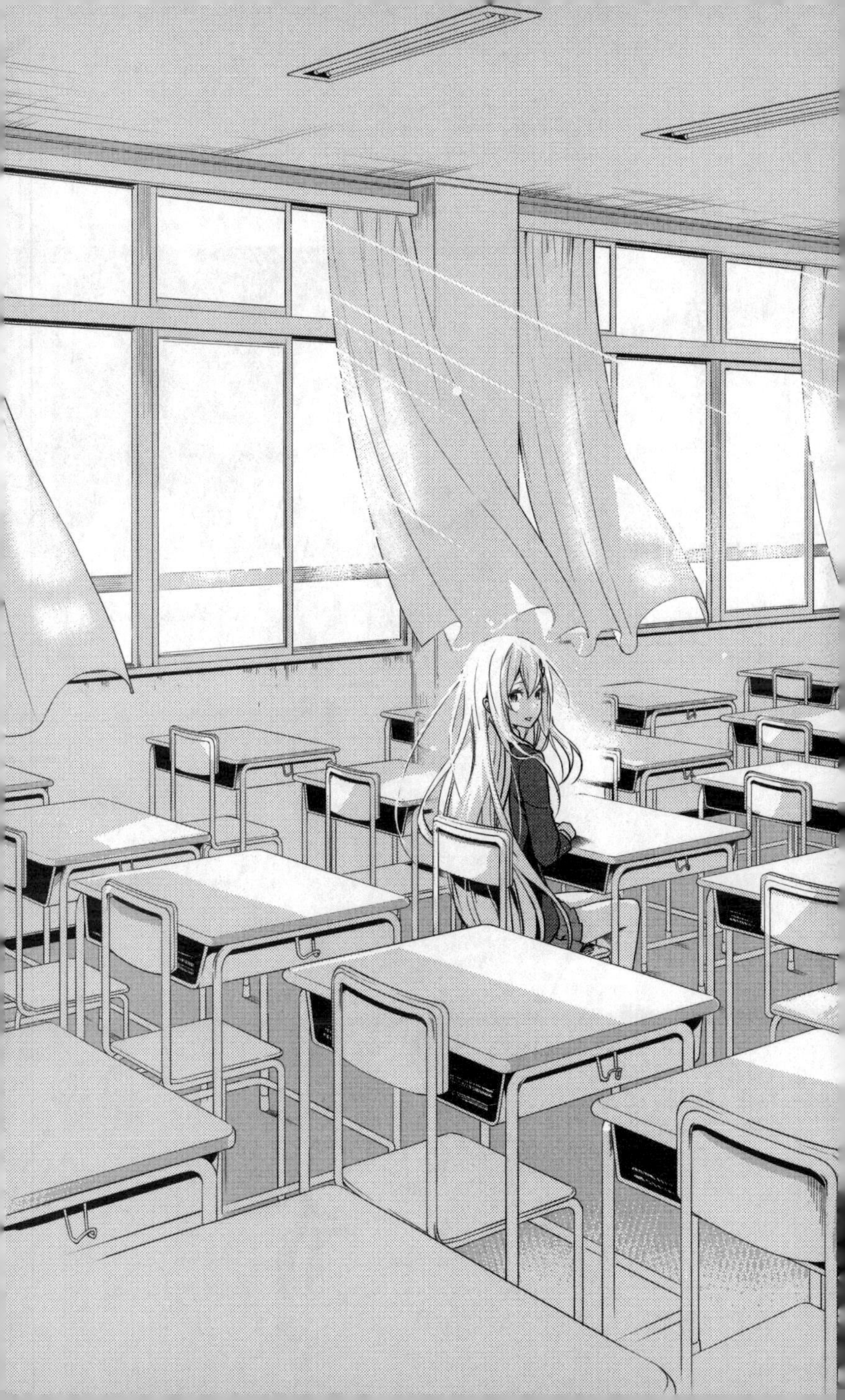

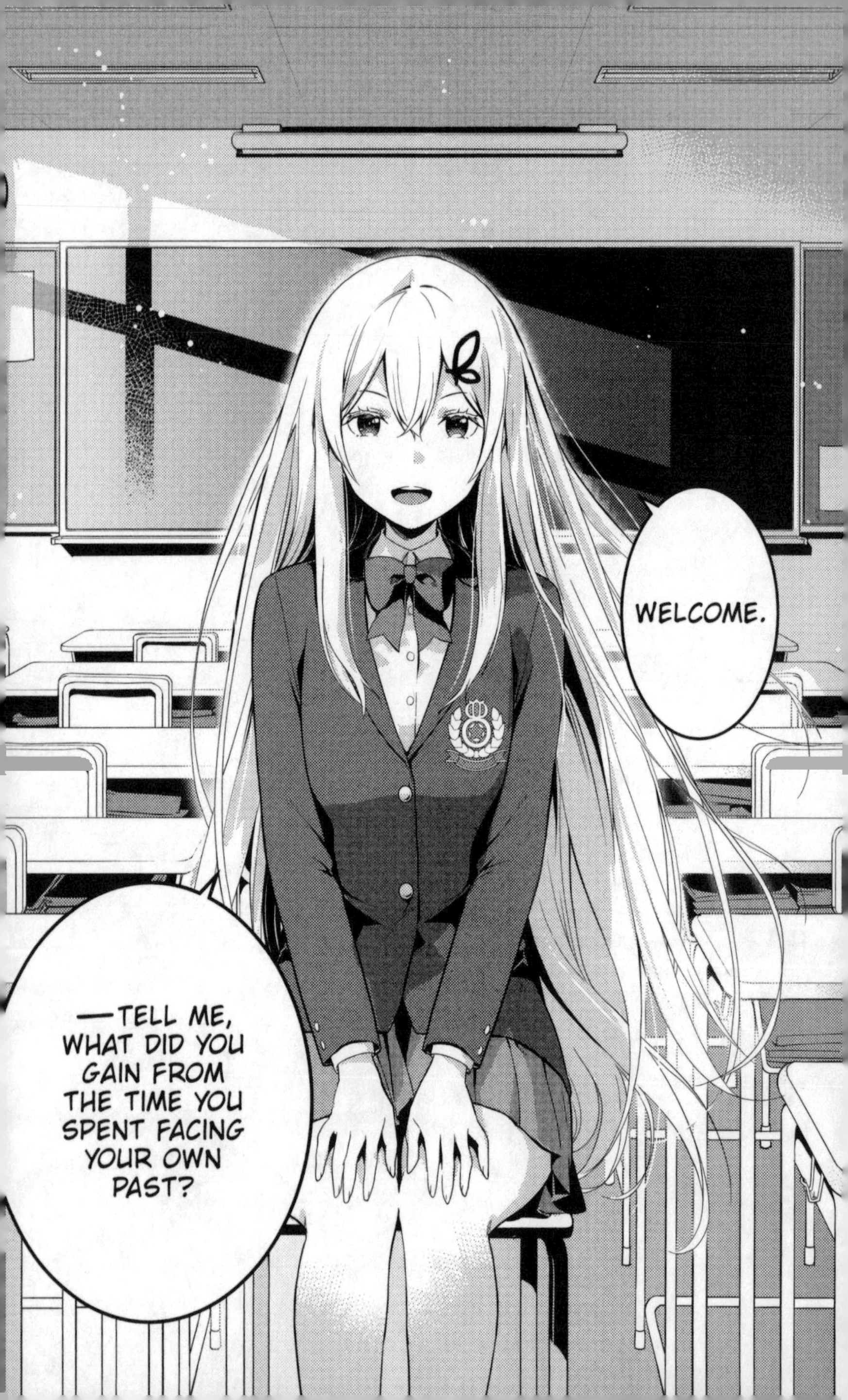
WELCOME.
—TELL ME, WHAT DID YOU GAIN FROM THE TIME YOU SPENT FACING YOUR OWN PAST?

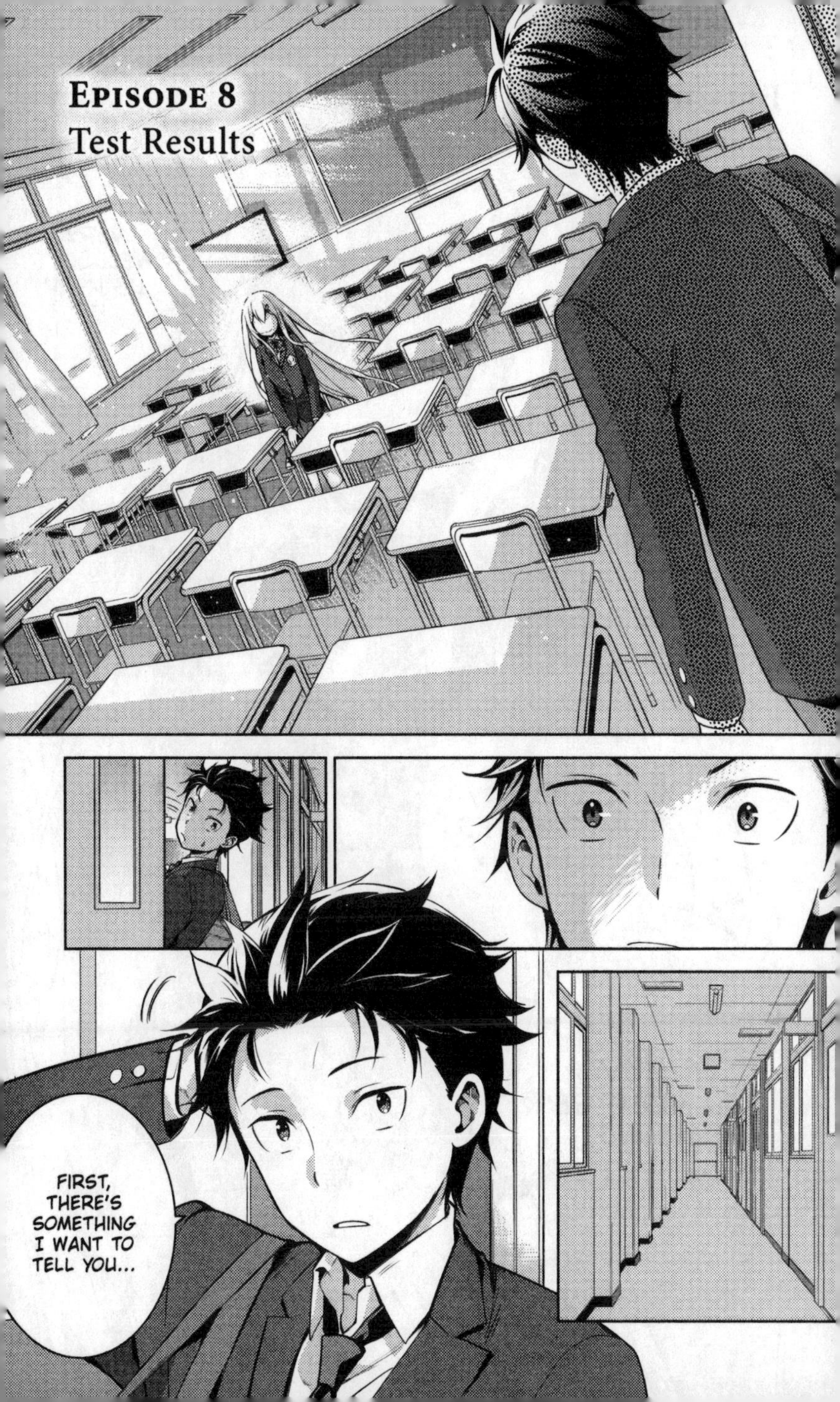
Episode 8
Test Results
FIRST, THERE'S SOMETHING I WANT TO TELL YOU...

Episode 8
Test results

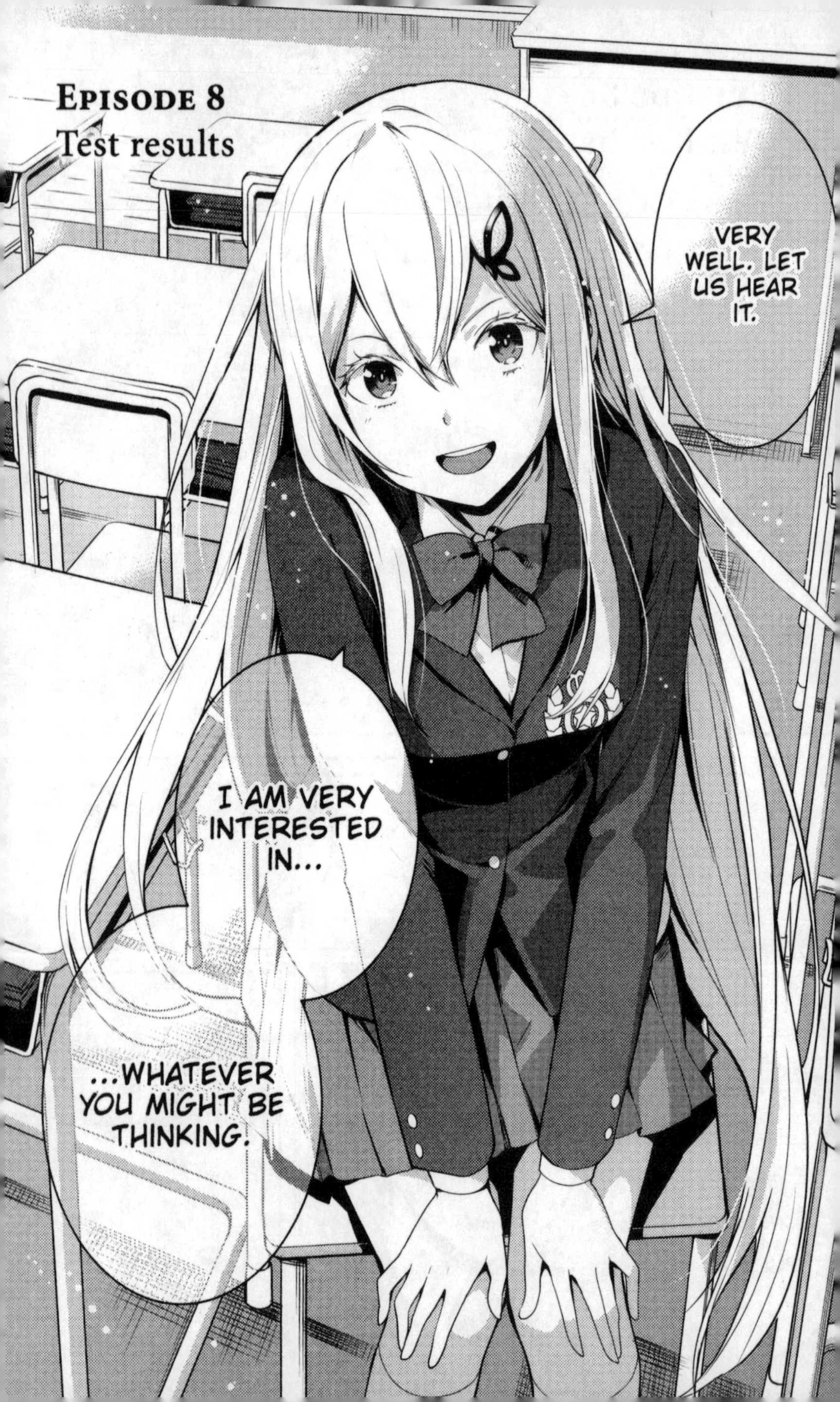

VERY WELL. LET US HEAR IT.
I AM VERY INTERESTED IN...
...WHATEVER YOU MIGHT BE THINKING.

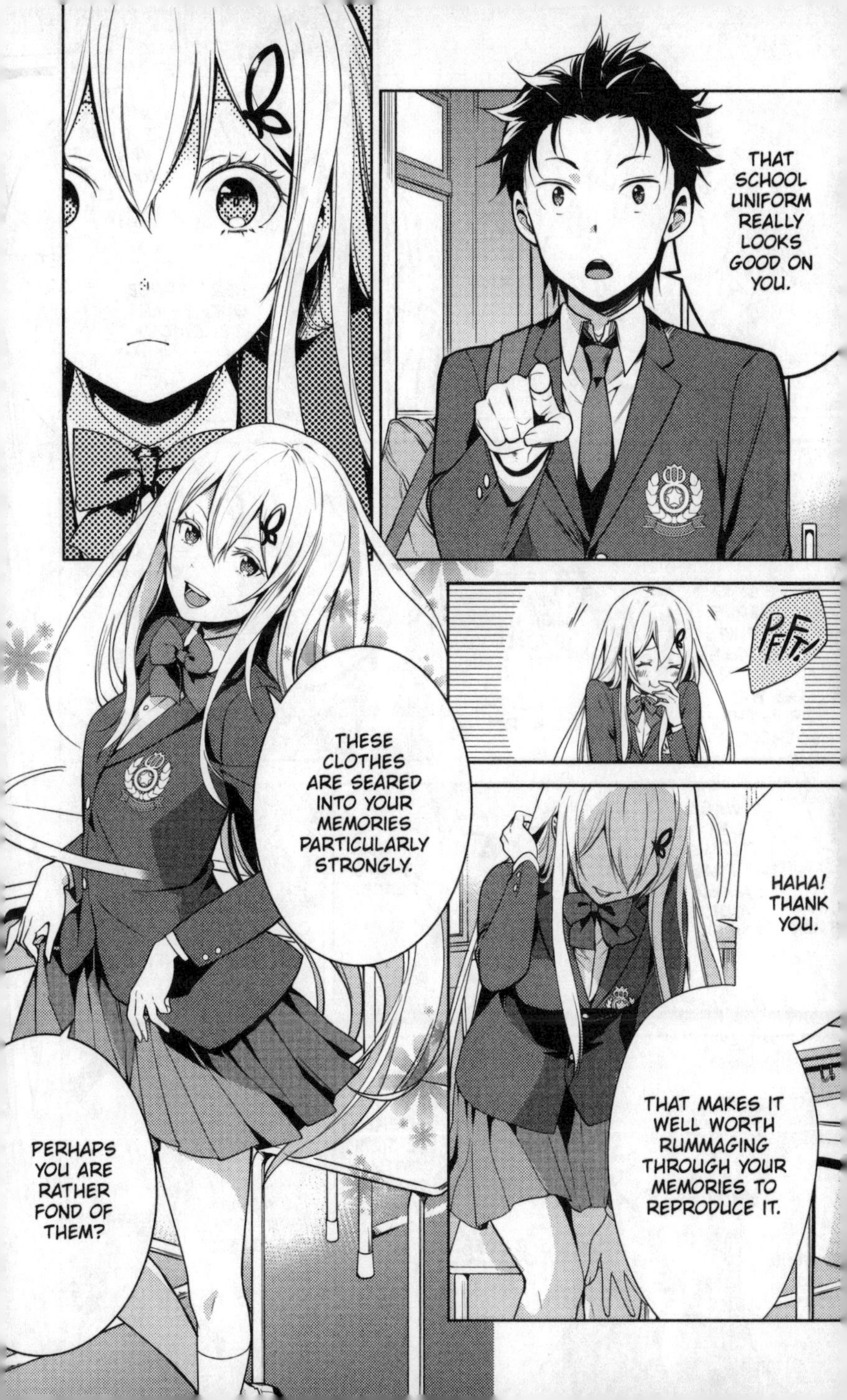
THAT SCHOOL UNIFORM REALLY LOOKS GOOD ON YOU.
PFFT!
HAHA! THANK YOU.
THAT MAKES IT WELL WORTH RUMMAGING THROUGH YOUR MEMORIES TO REPRODUCE IT.
THESE CLOTHES ARE SEARED INTO YOUR MEMORIES PARTICULARLY STRONGLY.
PERHAPS YOU ARE RATHER FOND OF THEM?

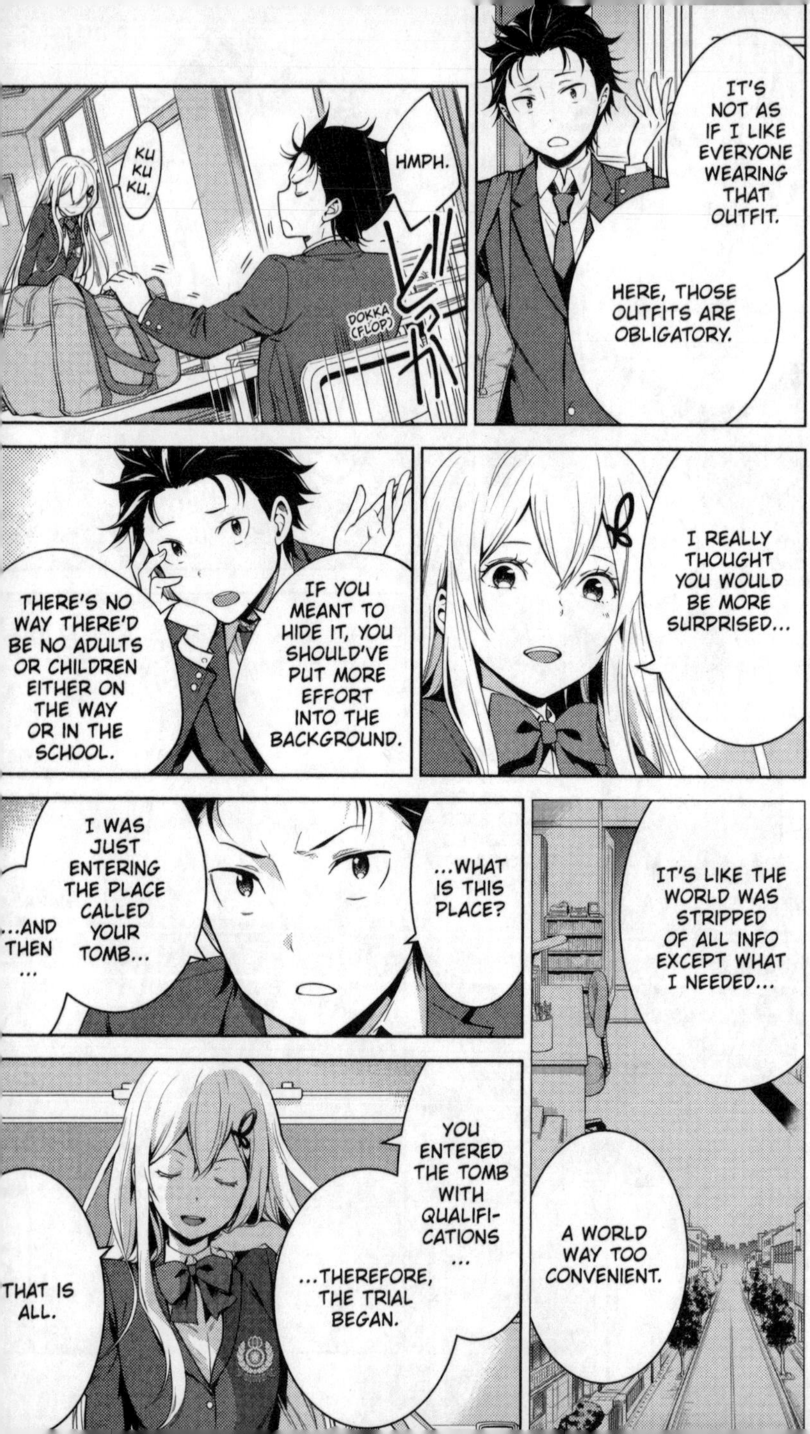
IT'S NOT AS IF I LIKE EVERYONE WEARING THAT OUTFIT.
HERE, THOSE OUTFITS ARE OBLIGATORY.
HMPH.
KU KU KU.
DOKKA (FLOP)
I REALLY THOUGHT YOU WOULD BE MORE SURPRISED...
IF YOU MEANT TO HIDE IT, YOU SHOULD'VE PUT MORE EFFORT INTO THE BACKGROUND.
THERE'S NO WAY THERE'D BE NO ADULTS OR CHILDREN EITHER ON THE WAY OR IN THE SCHOOL.
IT'S LIKE THE WORLD WAS STRIPPED OF ALL INFO EXCEPT WHAT I NEEDED...
A WORLD WAY TOO CONVENIENT.
...WHAT IS THIS PLACE?
I WAS JUST ENTERING THE PLACE CALLED YOUR TOMB...
...AND THEN ...
YOU ENTERED THE TOMB WITH QUALIFI-CATIONS ...
...THEREFORE, THE TRIAL BEGAN.
THAT IS ALL.

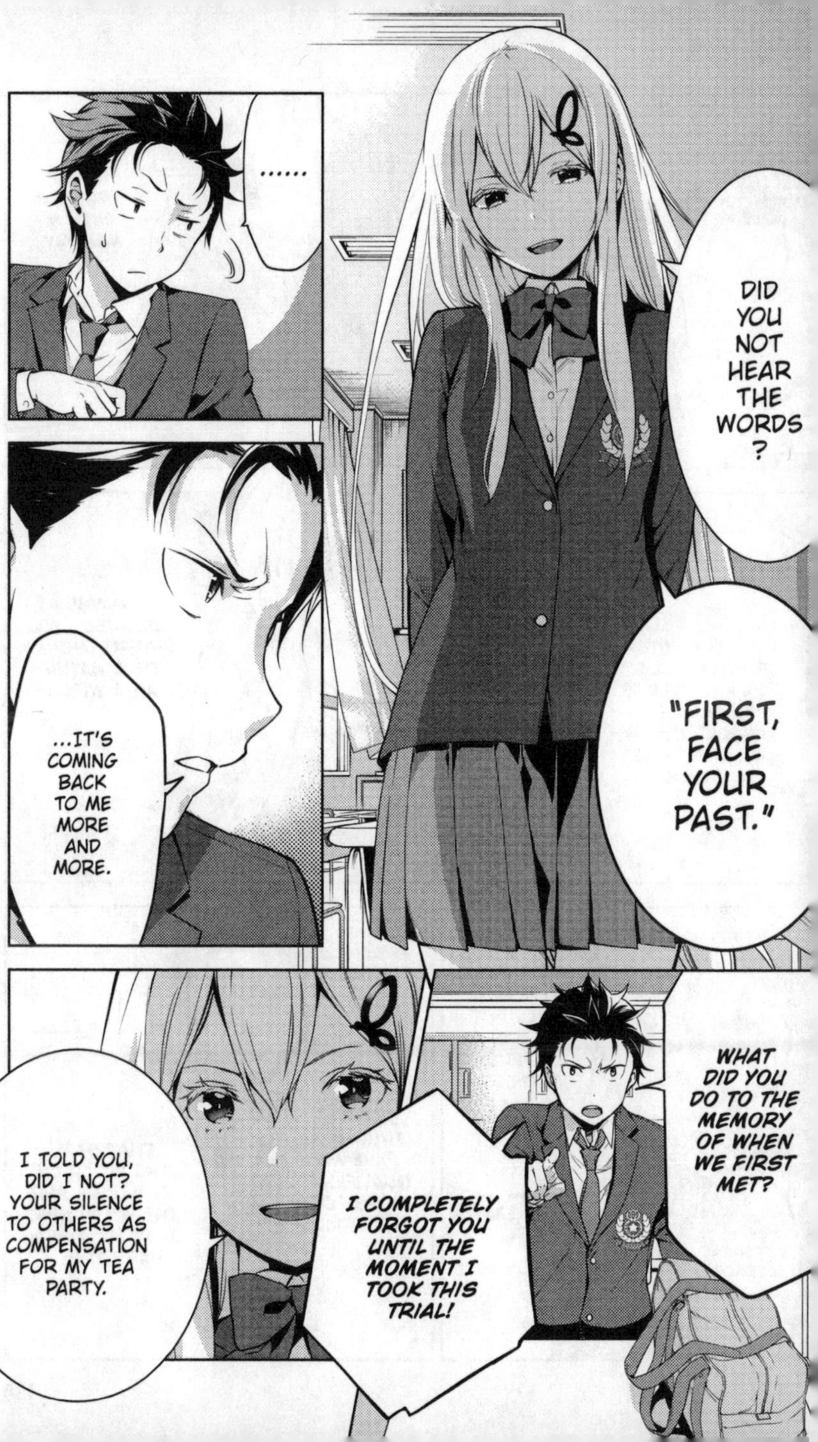
DID YOU NOT HEAR THE WORDS?
"FIRST, FACE YOUR PAST."
......
...IT'S COMING BACK TO ME MORE AND MORE.
WHAT DID YOU DO TO THE MEMORY OF WHEN WE FIRST MET?
I COMPLETELY FORGOT YOU UNTIL THE MOMENT I TOOK THIS TRIAL!
I TOLD YOU, DID I NOT? YOUR SILENCE TO OTHERS AS COMPENSATION FOR MY TEA PARTY.

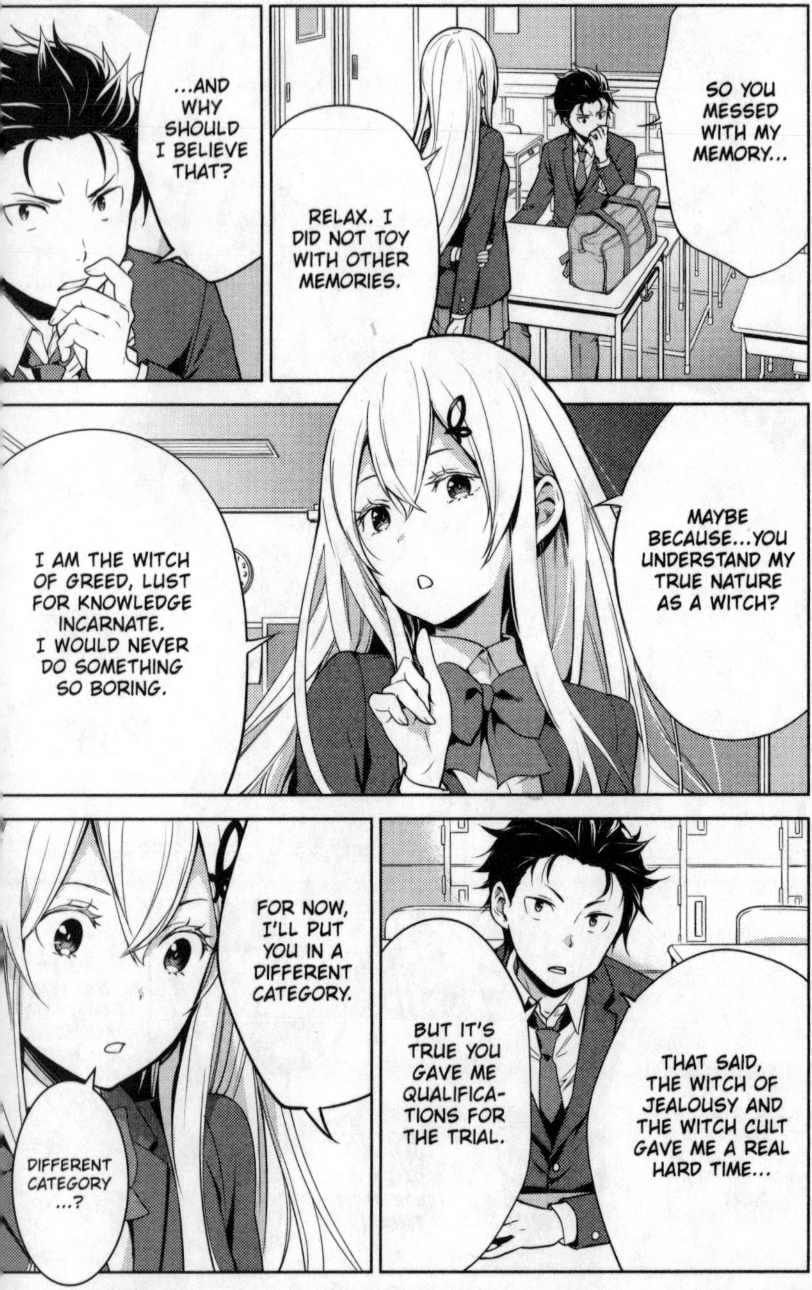
SO YOU MESSED WITH MY MEMORY...
RELAX. I DID NOT TOY WITH OTHER MEMORIES.
...AND WHY SHOULD I BELIEVE THAT?
MAYBE BECAUSE...YOU UNDERSTAND MY TRUE NATURE AS A WITCH?
I AM THE WITCH OF GREED, LUST FOR KNOWLEDGE INCARNATE. I WOULD NEVER DO SOMETHING SO BORING.
THAT SAID, THE WITCH OF JEALOUSY AND THE WITCH CULT GAVE ME A REAL HARD TIME...
BUT IT'S TRUE YOU GAVE ME QUALIFICATIONS FOR THE TRIAL.
FOR NOW, I'LL PUT YOU IN A DIFFERENT CATEGORY.
DIFFERENT CATEGORY ...?

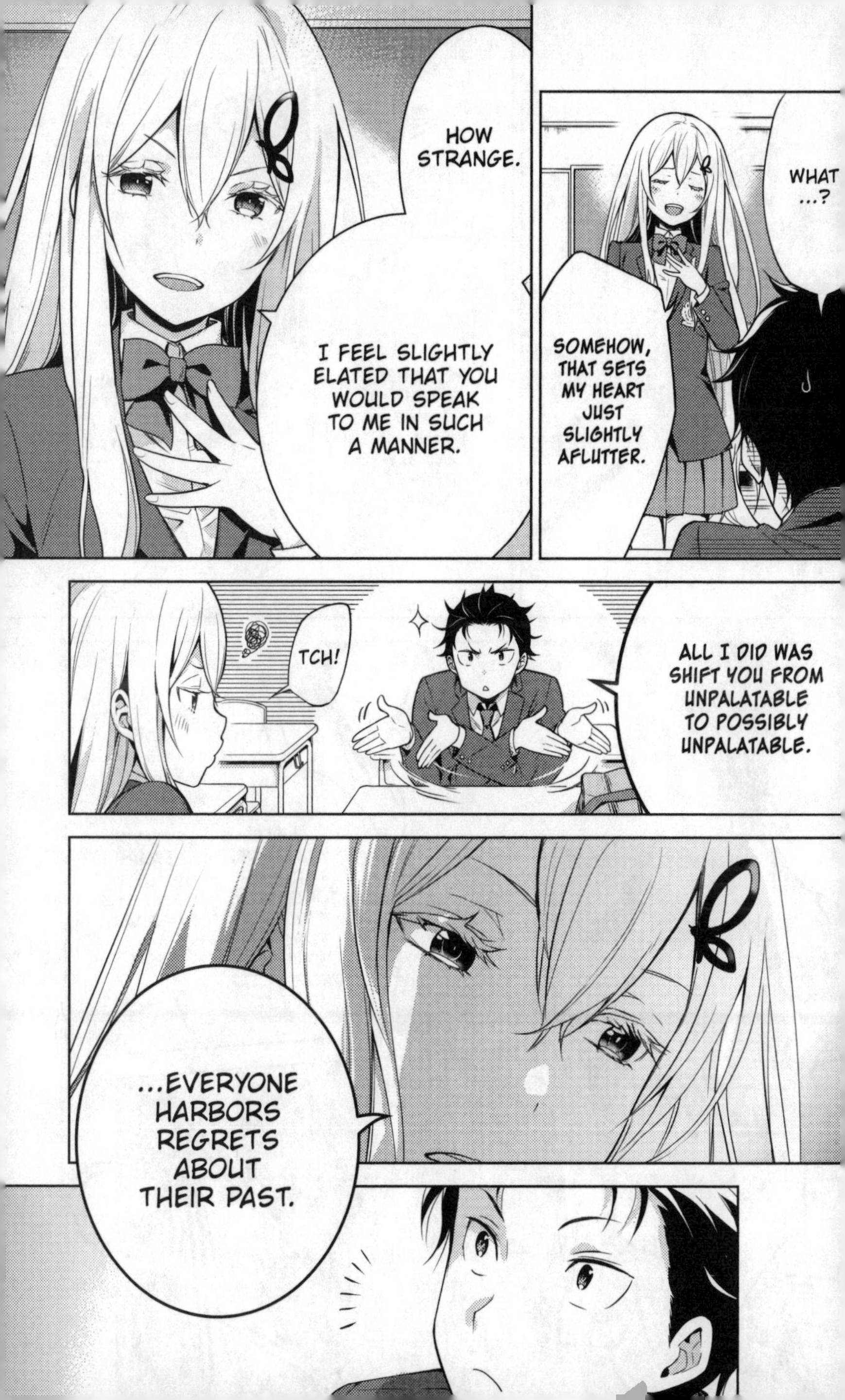
WHAT ...?
SOMEHOW, THAT SETS MY HEART JUST SLIGHTLY AFLUTTER.
HOW STRANGE.
I FEEL SLIGHTLY ELATED THAT YOU WOULD SPEAK TO ME IN SUCH A MANNER.
ALL I DID WAS SHIFT YOU FROM UNPALATABLE TO POSSIBLY UNPALATABLE.
TCH!
...EVERYONE HARBORS REGRETS ABOUT THEIR PAST.

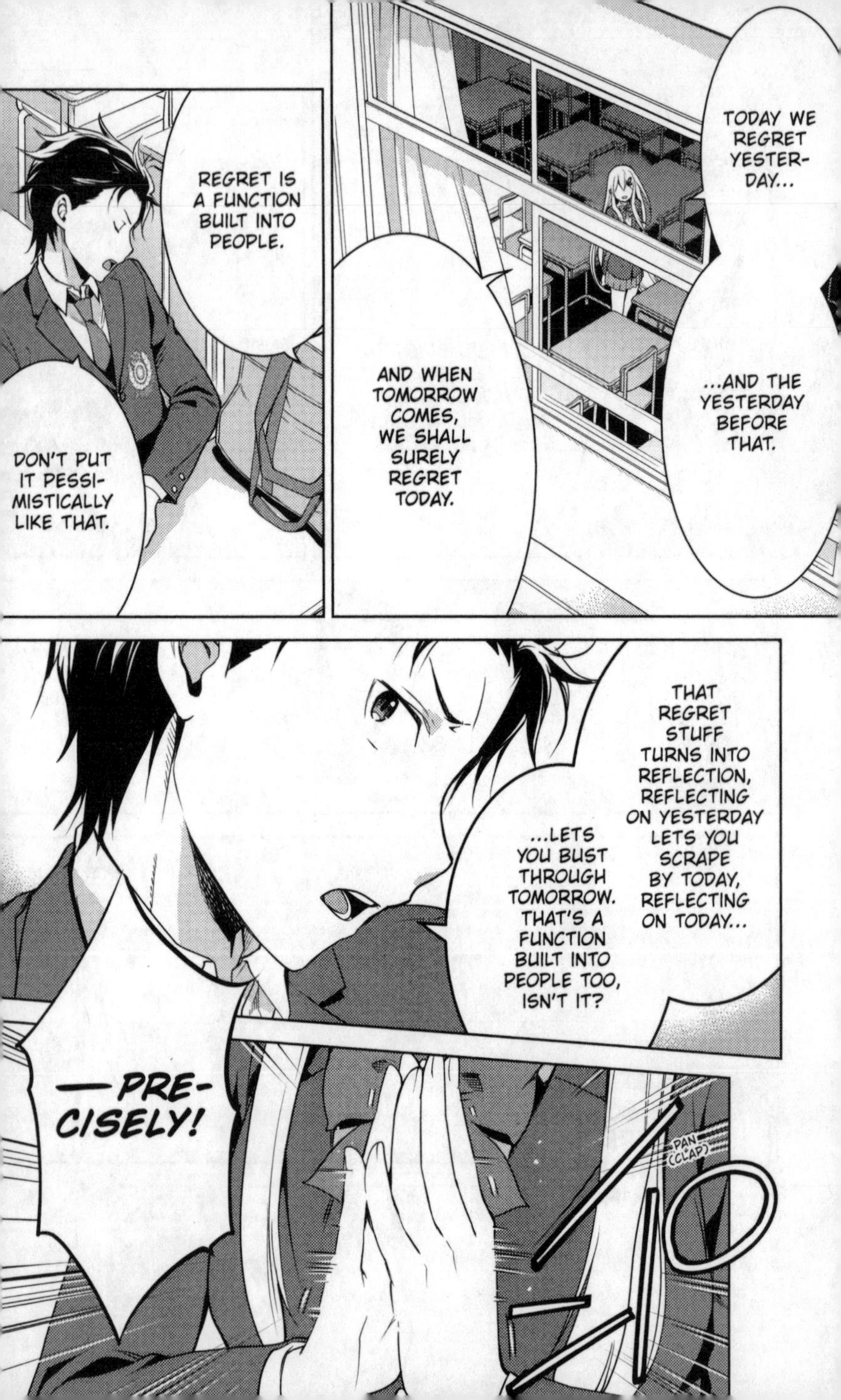
TODAY WE REGRET YESTER-DAY...
...AND THE YESTERDAY BEFORE THAT.
AND WHEN TOMORROW COMES, WE SHALL SURELY REGRET TODAY.
REGRET IS A FUNCTION BUILT INTO PEOPLE.
DON'T PUT IT PESSI-MISTICALLY LIKE THAT.
THAT REGRET STUFF TURNS INTO REFLECTION, REFLECTING ON YESTERDAY LETS YOU SCRAPE BY TODAY, REFLECTING ON TODAY...
...LETS YOU BUST THROUGH TOMORROW. THAT'S A FUNCTION BUILT INTO PEOPLE TOO, ISN'T IT?
PAN (CLAP)
—PRE-CISELY!

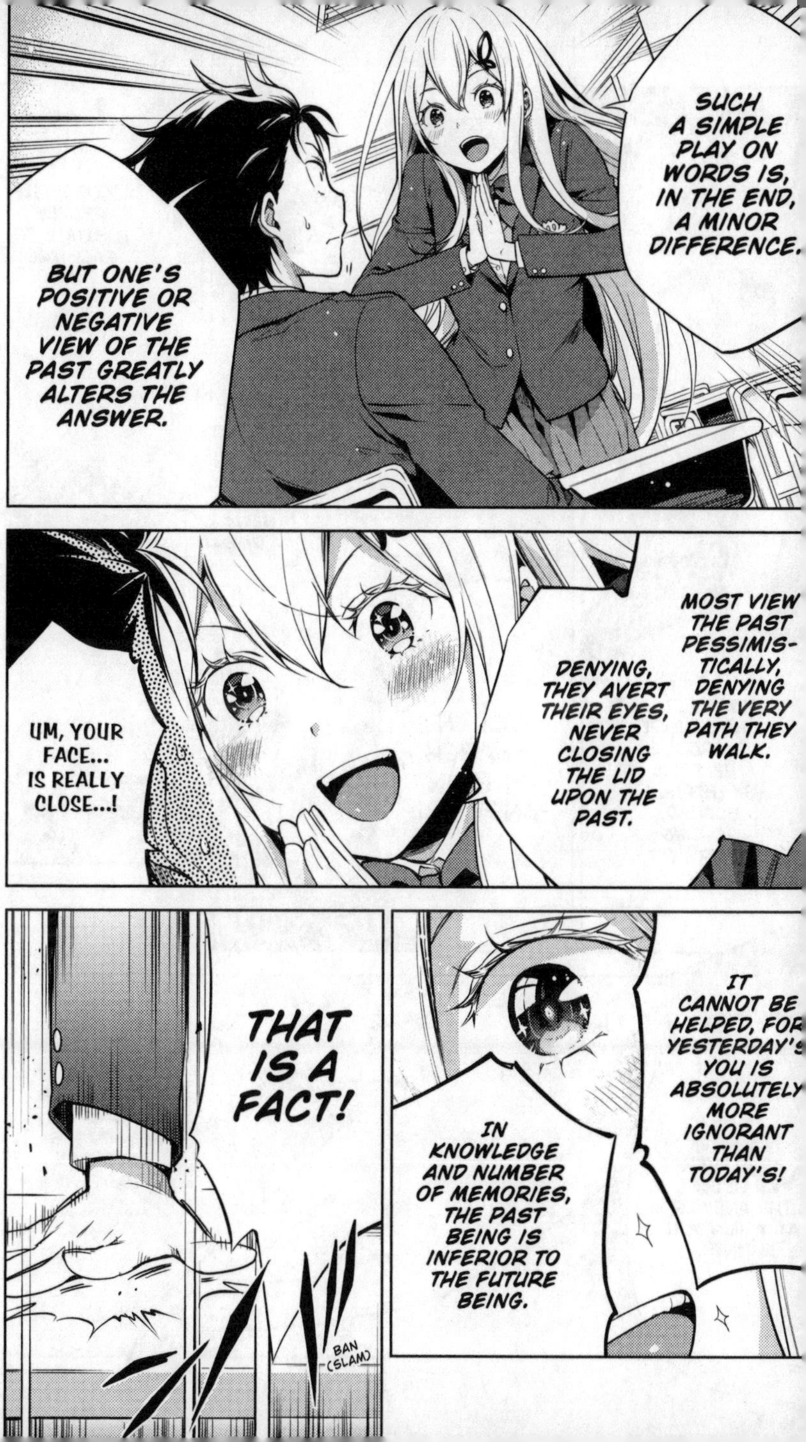
SUCH A SIMPLE PLAY ON WORDS IS, IN THE END, A MINOR DIFFERENCE.
BUT ONE'S POSITIVE OR NEGATIVE VIEW OF THE PAST GREATLY ALTERS THE ANSWER.
MOST VIEW THE PAST PESSIMIS-TICALLY, DENYING THE VERY PATH THEY WALK.
DENYING, THEY AVERT THEIR EYES, NEVER CLOSING THE LID UPON THE PAST.
UM, YOUR FACE... IS REALLY CLOSE...!
IT CANNOT BE HELPED, FOR YESTERDAY'S YOU IS ABSOLUTELY MORE IGNORANT THAN TODAY'S!
IN KNOWLEDGE AND NUMBER OF MEMORIES, THE PAST BEING IS INFERIOR TO THE FUTURE BEING.
THAT IS A FACT!
BAN (SLAM)

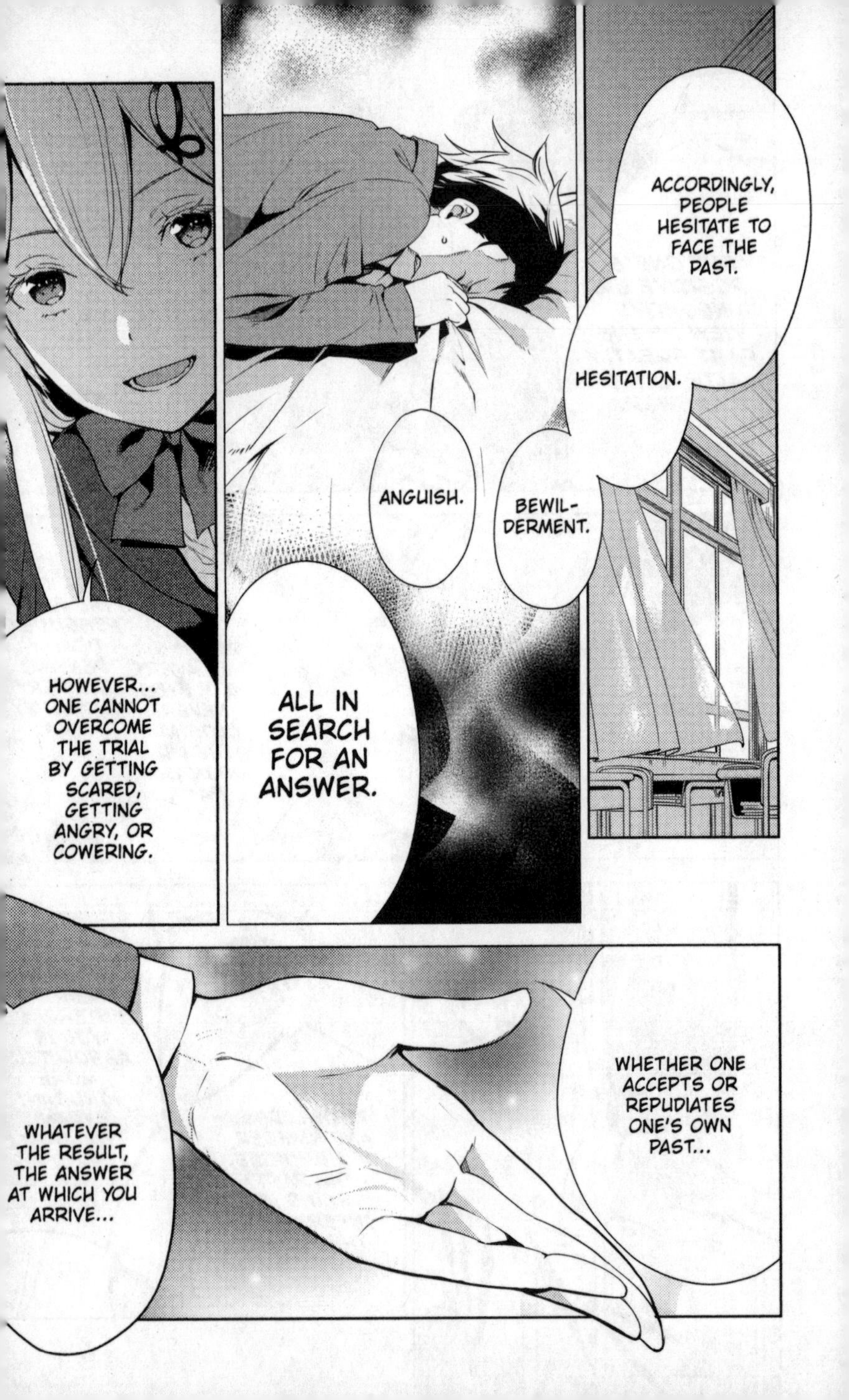
ACCORDINGLY, PEOPLE HESITATE TO FACE THE PAST.
HESITATION.
BEWILDERMENT.
ANGUISH.
ALL IN SEARCH FOR AN ANSWER.
HOWEVER... ONE CANNOT OVERCOME THE TRIAL BY GETTING SCARED, GETTING ANGRY, OR COWERING.
WHETHER ONE ACCEPTS OR REPUDIATES ONE'S OWN PAST...
WHATEVER THE RESULT, THE ANSWER AT WHICH YOU ARRIVE...

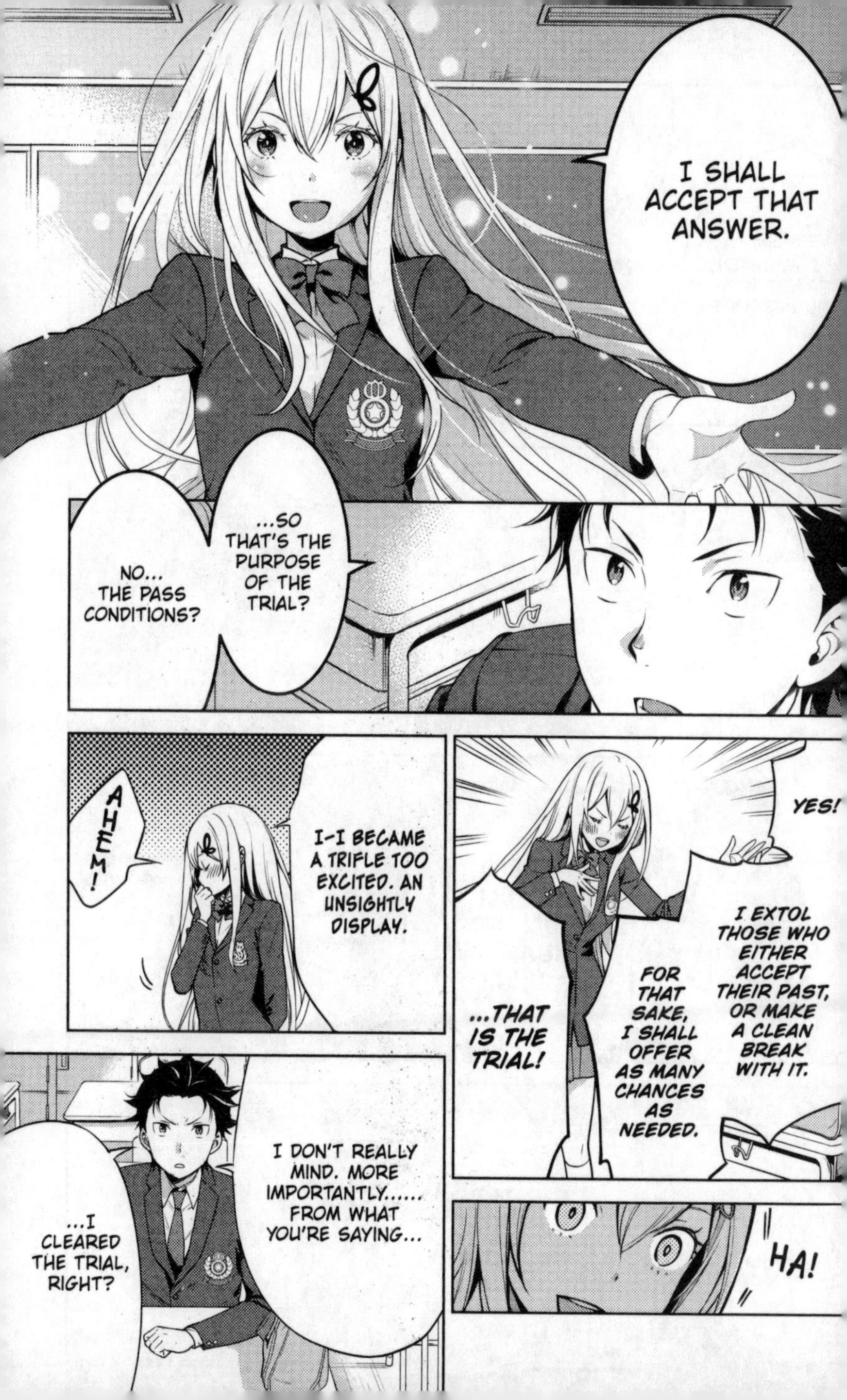
I SHALL ACCEPT THAT ANSWER.
...SO THAT'S THE PURPOSE OF THE TRIAL?
NO... THE PASS CONDITIONS?
YES!
I EXTOL THOSE WHO EITHER ACCEPT THEIR PAST, OR MAKE A CLEAN BREAK WITH IT.
FOR THAT SAKE, I SHALL OFFER AS MANY CHANCES AS NEEDED.
...THAT IS THE TRIAL!
AHEM!
I-I BECAME A TRIFLE TOO EXCITED. AN UNSIGHTLY DISPLAY.
I DON'T REALLY MIND. MORE IMPORTANTLY...... FROM WHAT YOU'RE SAYING...
...I CLEARED THE TRIAL, RIGHT?
HA!

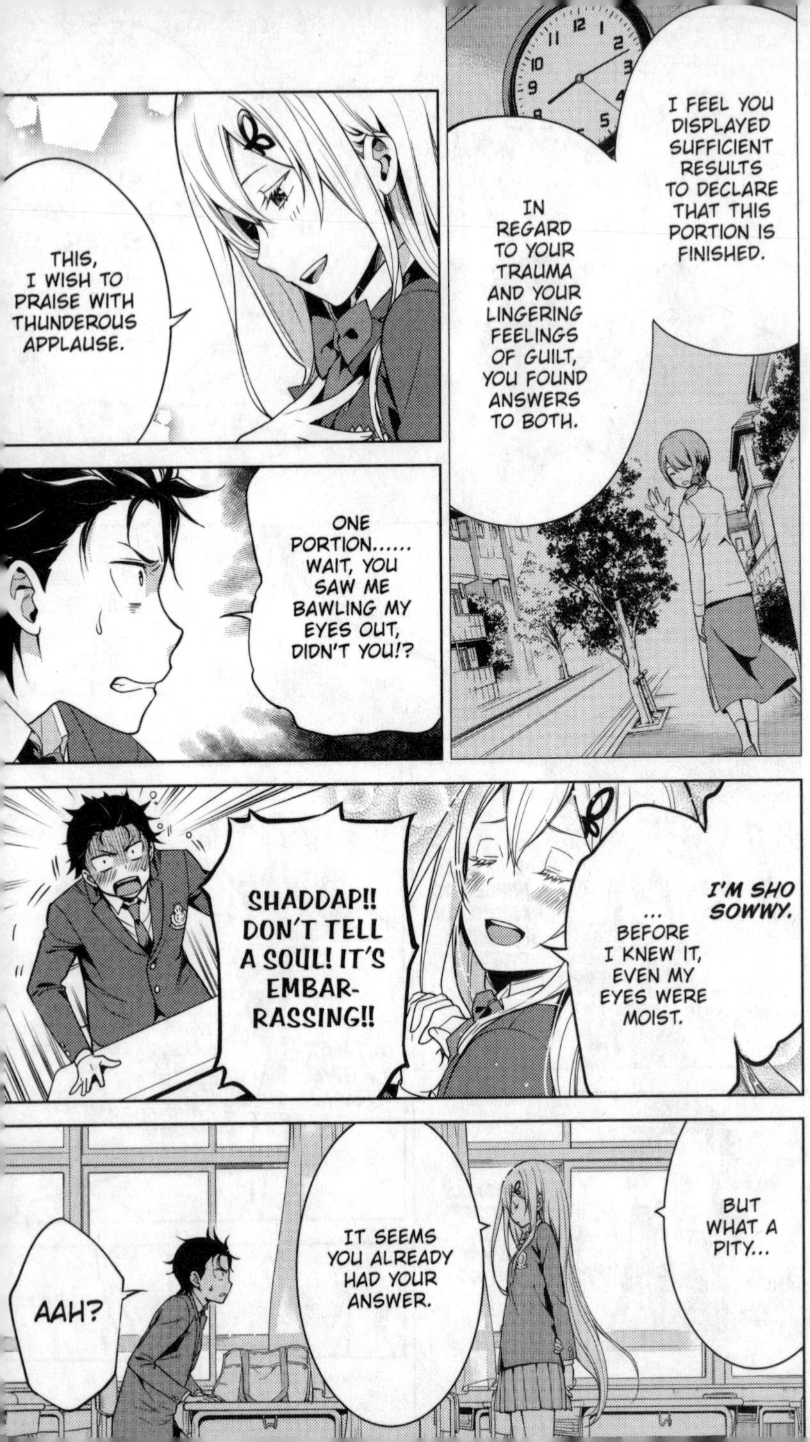
I FEEL YOU DISPLAYED SUFFICIENT RESULTS TO DECLARE THAT THIS PORTION IS FINISHED.
IN REGARD TO YOUR TRAUMA AND YOUR LINGERING FEELINGS OF GUILT, YOU FOUND ANSWERS TO BOTH.
THIS, I WISH TO PRAISE WITH THUNDEROUS APPLAUSE.
ONE PORTION...... WAIT, YOU SAW ME BAWLING MY EYES OUT, DIDN'T YOU!?
I'M SHO SOWWY.
... BEFORE I KNEW IT, EVEN MY EYES WERE MOIST.
SHADDAP!! DON'T TELL A SOUL! IT'S EMBAR-RASSING!!
BUT WHAT A PITY...
IT SEEMS YOU ALREADY HAD YOUR ANSWER.
AAH?

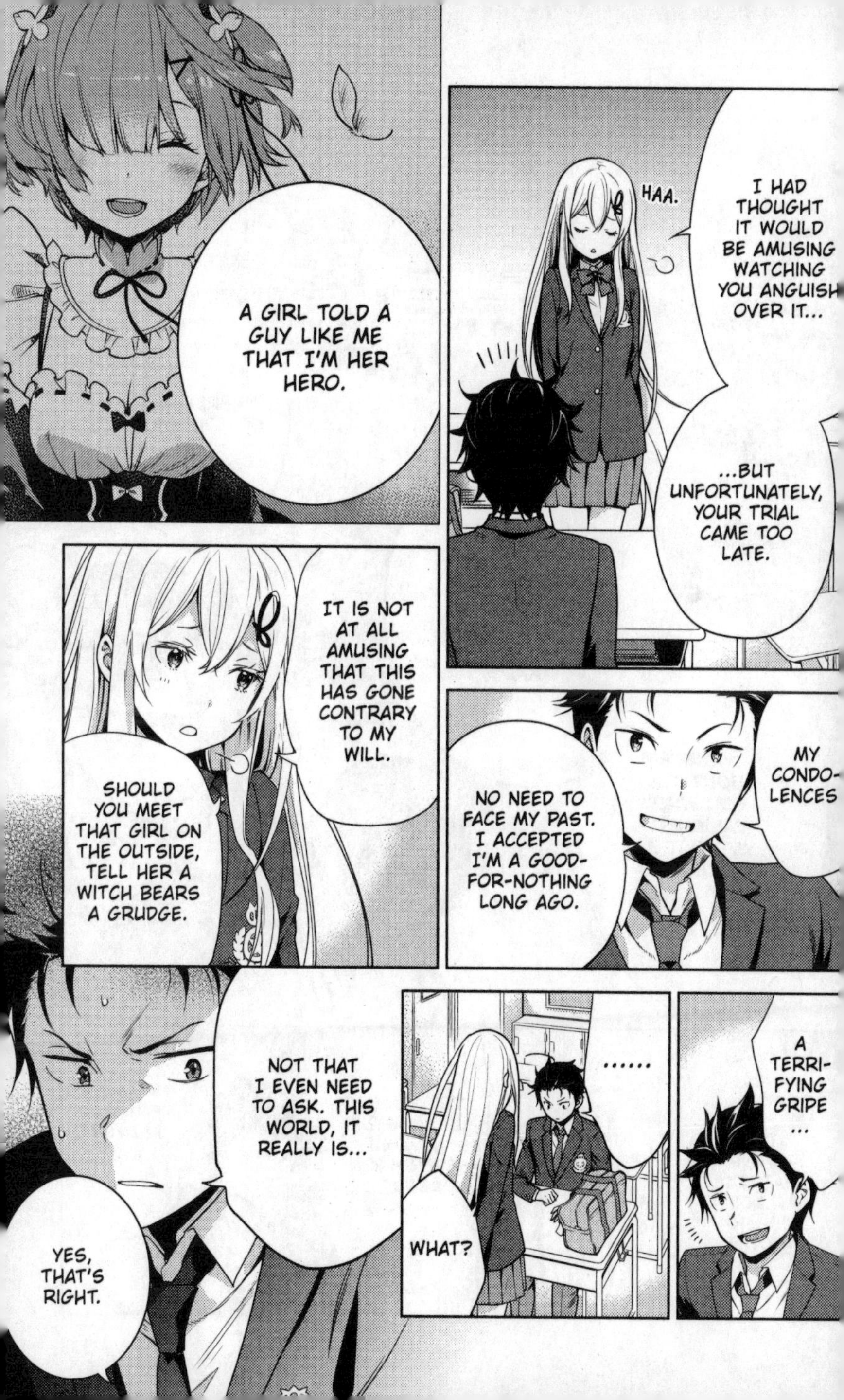
I HAD THOUGHT IT WOULD BE AMUSING WATCHING YOU ANGUISH OVER IT...
HAA.
...BUT UNFORTUNATELY, YOUR TRIAL CAME TOO LATE.
MY CONDOLENCES
NO NEED TO FACE MY PAST. I ACCEPTED I'M A GOOD-FOR-NOTHING LONG AGO.
A GIRL TOLD A GUY LIKE ME THAT I'M HER HERO.
IT IS NOT AT ALL AMUSING THAT THIS HAS GONE CONTRARY TO MY WILL.
SHOULD YOU MEET THAT GIRL ON THE OUTSIDE, TELL HER A WITCH BEARS A GRUDGE.
A TERRIFYING GRIPE...
......
WHAT?
NOT THAT I EVEN NEED TO ASK. THIS WORLD, IT REALLY IS...
YES, THAT'S RIGHT.

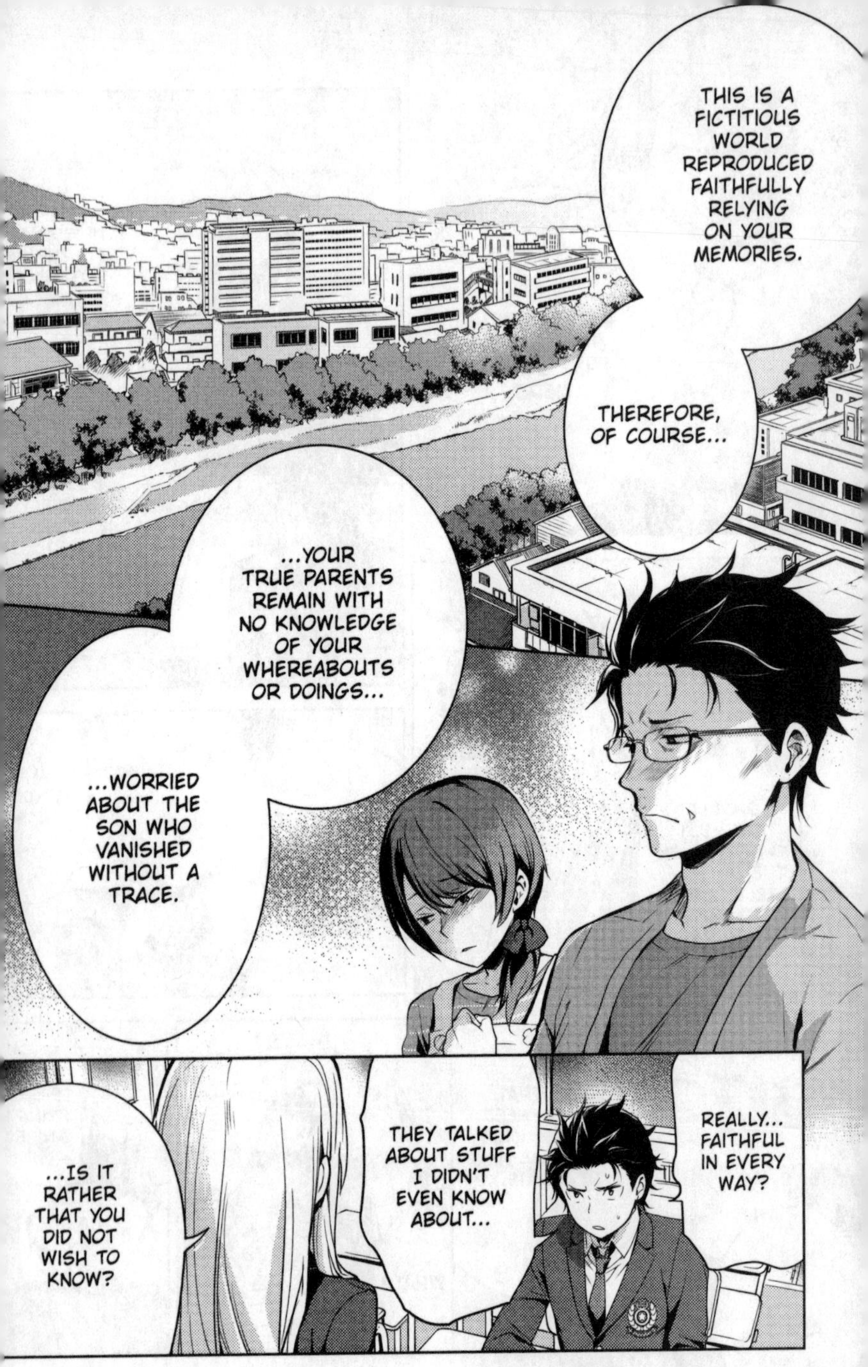
THIS IS A FICTITIOUS WORLD REPRODUCED FAITHFULLY RELYING ON YOUR MEMORIES.
THEREFORE, OF COURSE...
...YOUR TRUE PARENTS REMAIN WITH NO KNOWLEDGE OF YOUR WHEREABOUTS OR DOINGS...
...WORRIED ABOUT THE SON WHO VANISHED WITHOUT A TRACE.
REALLY... FAITHFUL IN EVERY WAY?
THEY TALKED ABOUT STUFF I DIDN'T EVEN KNOW ABOUT...
...IS IT RATHER THAT YOU DID NOT WISH TO KNOW?

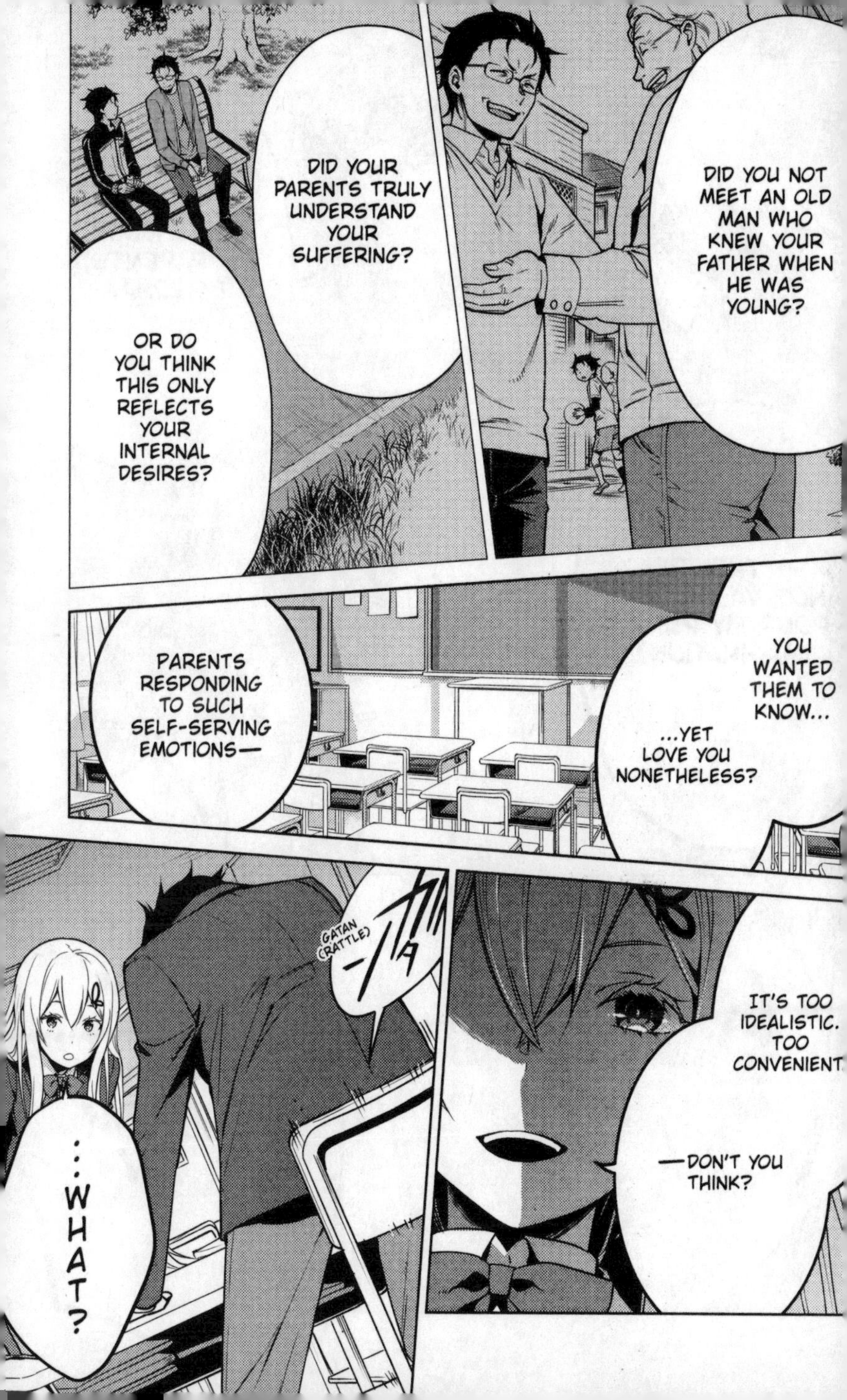
DID YOU NOT MEET AN OLD MAN WHO KNEW YOUR FATHER WHEN HE WAS YOUNG?
DID YOUR PARENTS TRULY UNDERSTAND YOUR SUFFERING?
OR DO YOU THINK THIS ONLY REFLECTS YOUR INTERNAL DESIRES?
YOU WANTED THEM TO KNOW...
...YET LOVE YOU NONETHELESS?
PARENTS RESPONDING TO SUCH SELF-SERVING EMOTIONS—
IT'S TOO IDEALISTIC. TOO CONVENIENT.
—DON'T YOU THINK?
GATAN (RATTLE)
...WHAT?

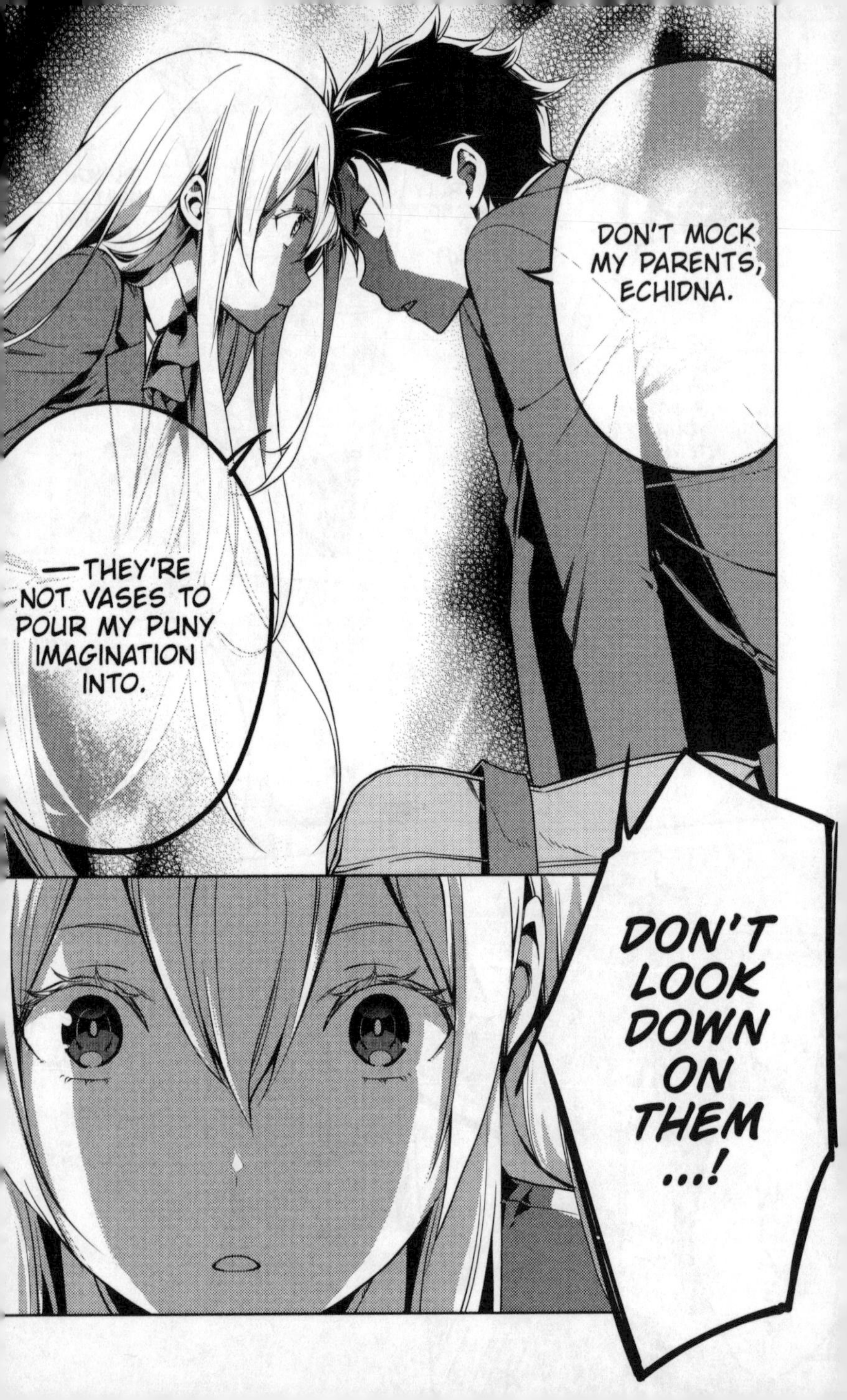
DON'T MOCK MY PARENTS, ECHIDNA.
—THEY'RE NOT VASES TO POUR MY PUNY IMAGINATION INTO.
DON'T LOOK DOWN ON THEM ...!

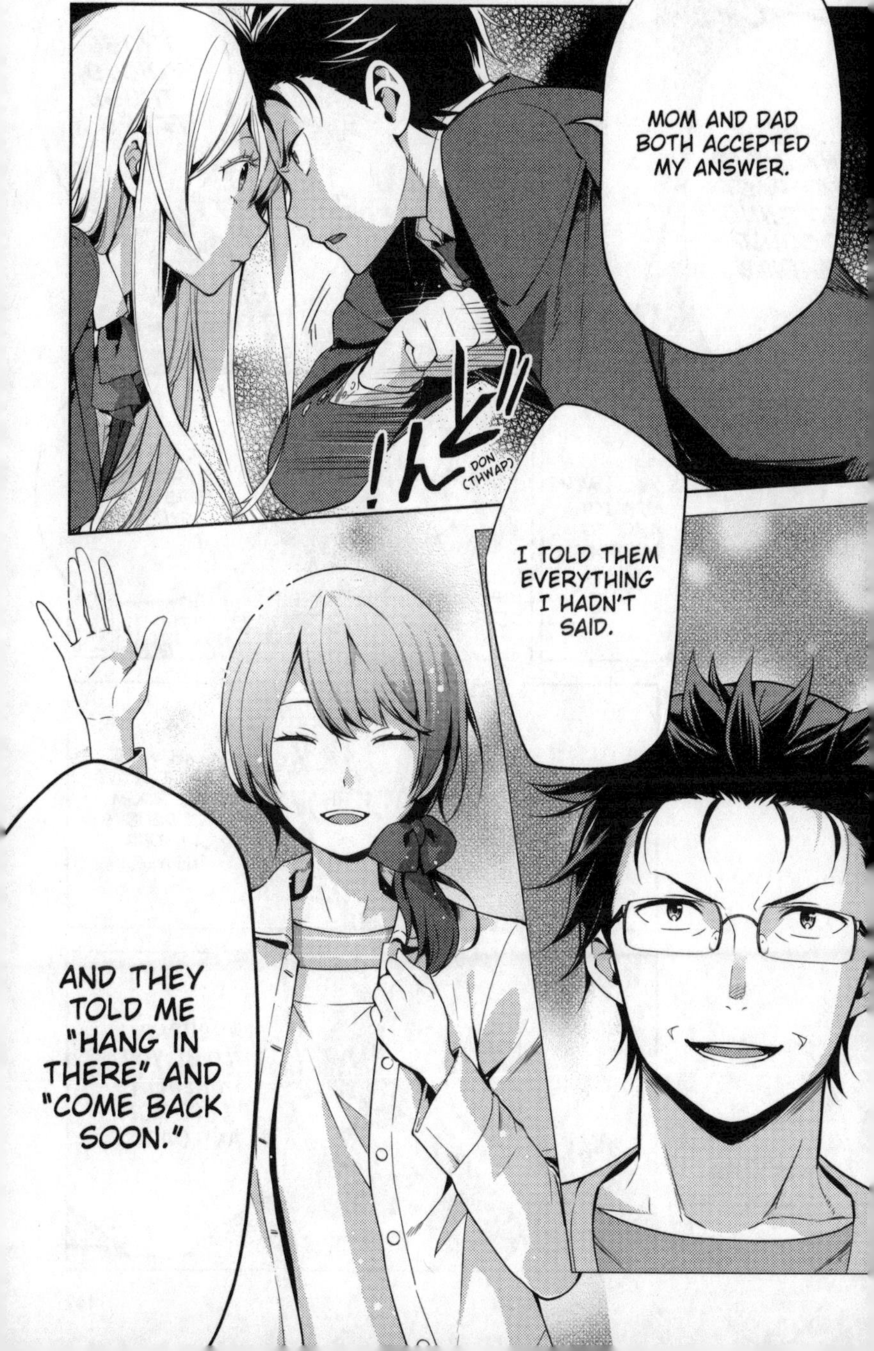
MOM AND DAD BOTH ACCEPTED MY ANSWER.
DON (THWAP)
I TOLD THEM EVERYTHING I HADN'T SAID.
AND THEY TOLD ME "HANG IN THERE" AND "COME BACK SOON."

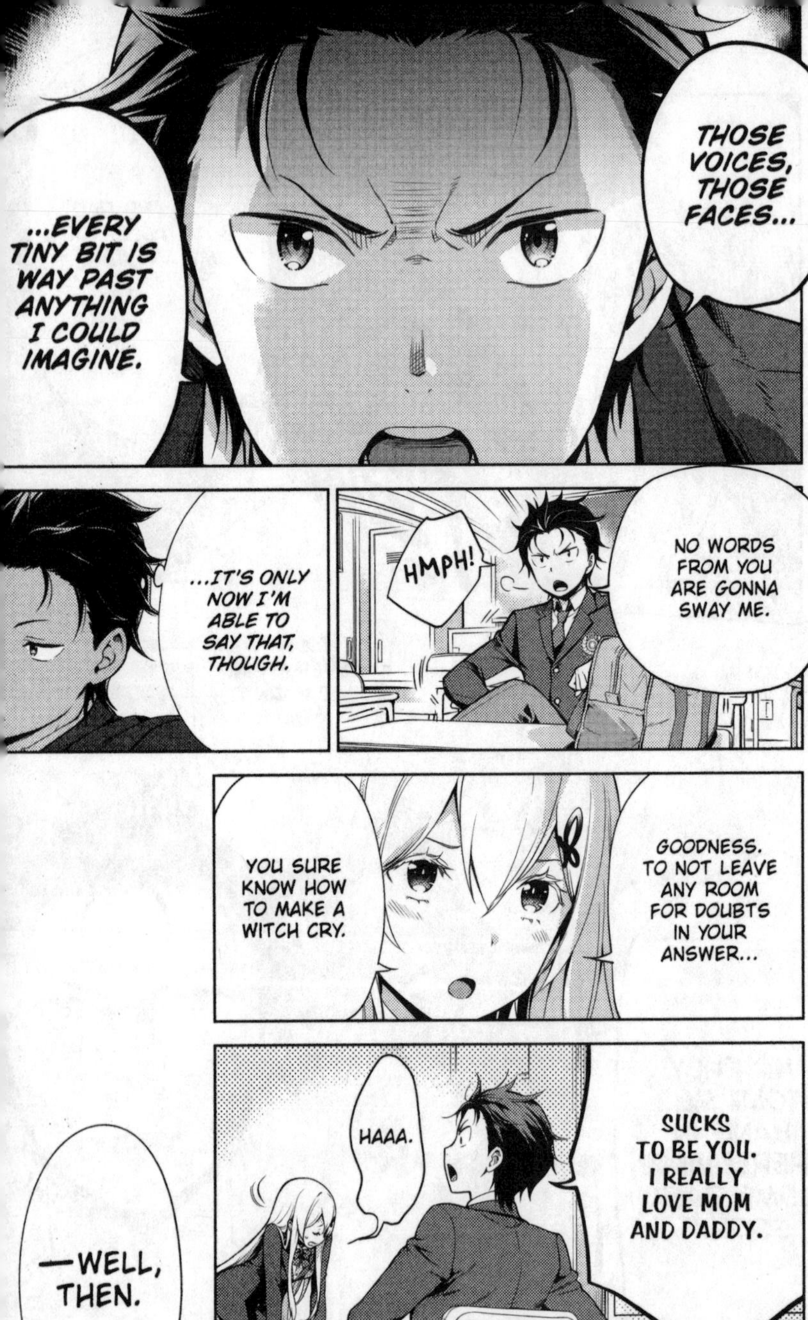
THOSE VOICES, THOSE FACES...
...EVERY TINY BIT IS WAY PAST ANYTHING I COULD IMAGINE.
NO WORDS FROM YOU ARE GONNA SWAY ME.
HMPH!
...IT'S ONLY NOW I'M ABLE TO SAY THAT, THOUGH.
GOODNESS. TO NOT LEAVE ANY ROOM FOR DOUBTS IN YOUR ANSWER...
YOU SURE KNOW HOW TO MAKE A WITCH CRY.
SUCKS TO BE YOU. I REALLY LOVE MOM AND DADDY.
HAAA.
—WELL, THEN.

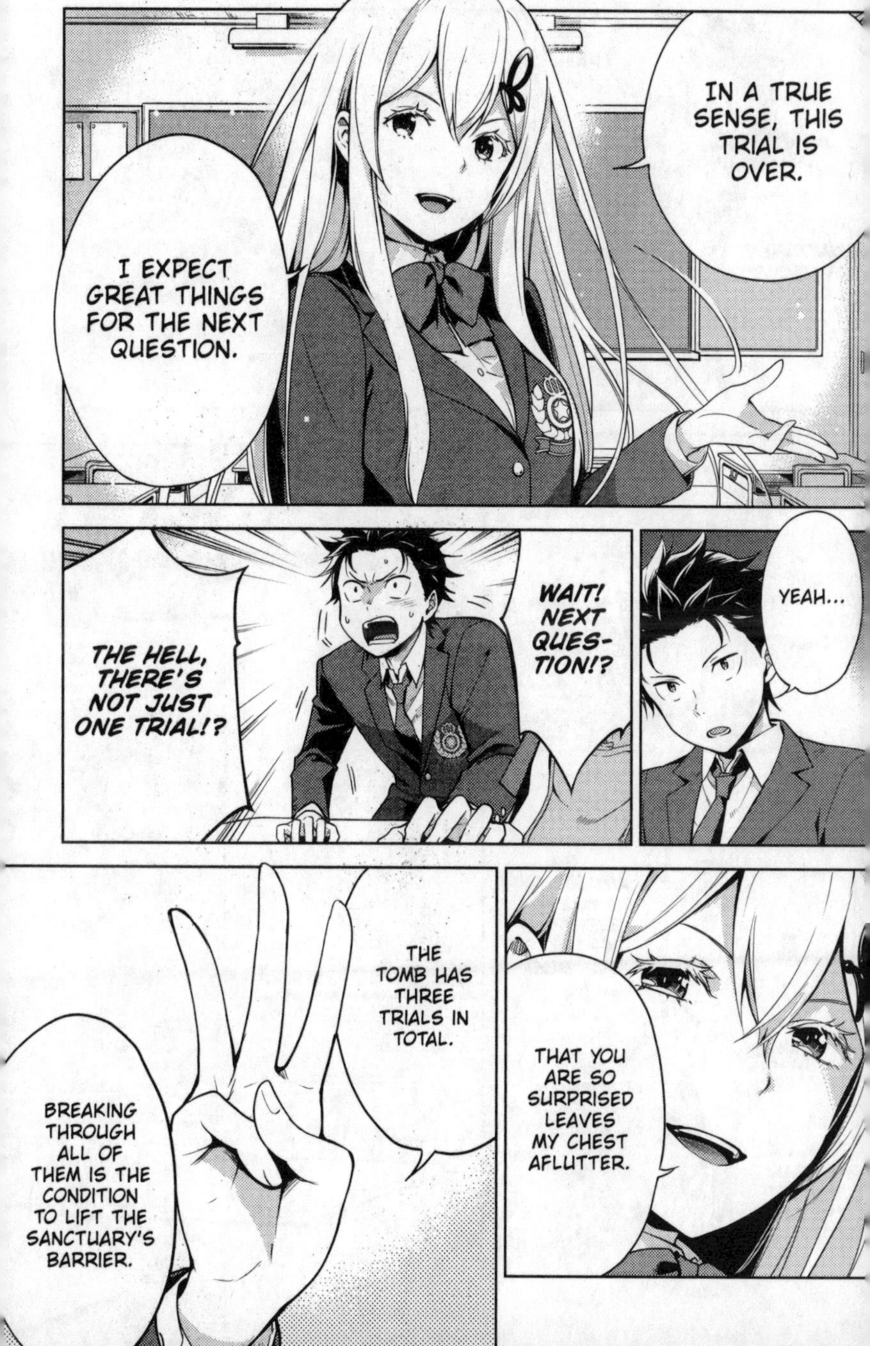
IN A TRUE SENSE, THIS TRIAL IS OVER.
I EXPECT GREAT THINGS FOR THE NEXT QUESTION.
YEAH...
WAIT! NEXT QUES-TION!?
THE HELL, THERE'S NOT JUST ONE TRIAL!?
THAT YOU ARE SO SURPRISED LEAVES MY CHEST AFLUTTER.
THE TOMB HAS THREE TRIALS IN TOTAL.
BREAKING THROUGH ALL OF THEM IS THE CONDITION TO LIFT THE SANCTUARY'S BARRIER.

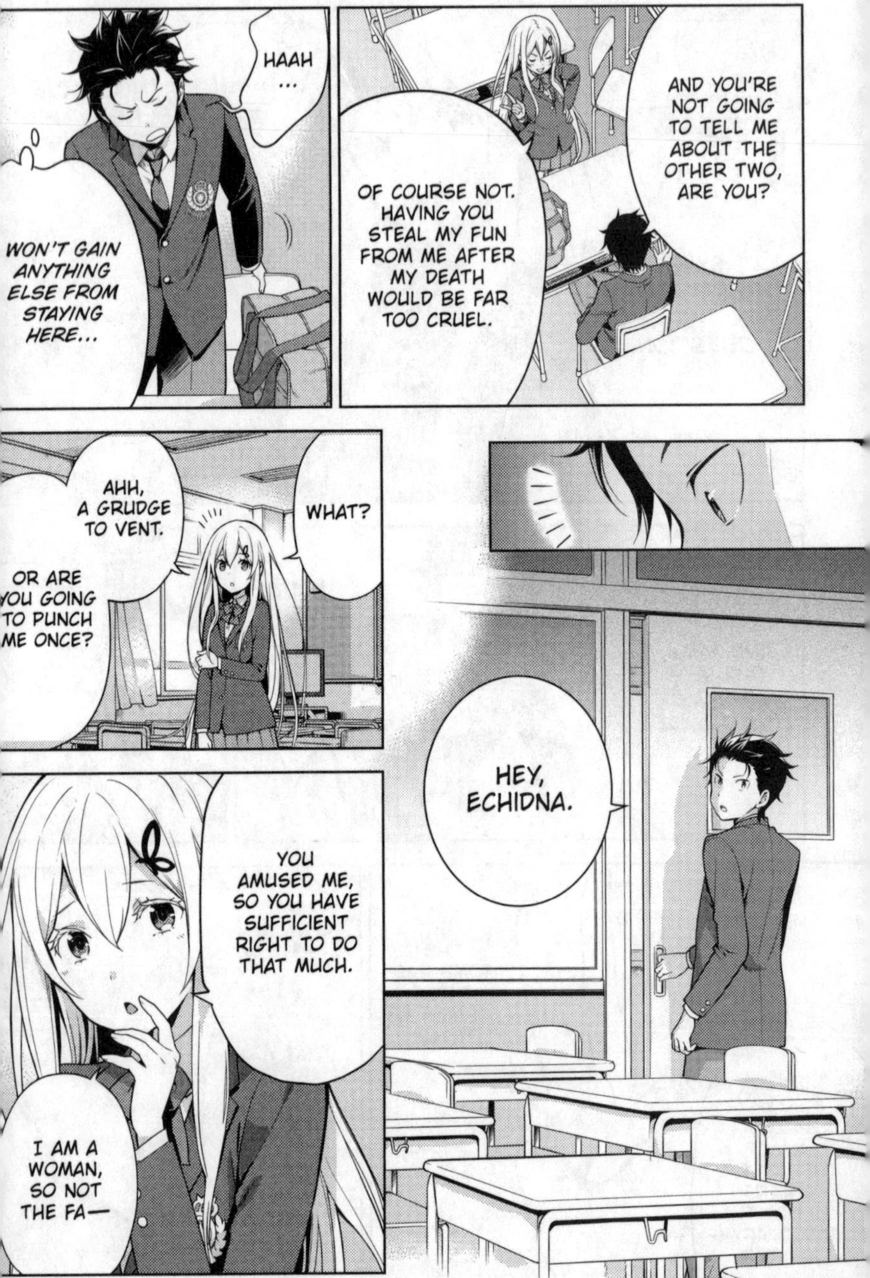
AND YOU'RE NOT GOING TO TELL ME ABOUT THE OTHER TWO, ARE YOU?
OF COURSE NOT. HAVING YOU STEAL MY FUN FROM ME AFTER MY DEATH WOULD BE FAR TOO CRUEL.
HAAH...
WON'T GAIN ANYTHING ELSE FROM STAYING HERE...
HEY, ECHIDNA.
WHAT?
AHH, A GRUDGE TO VENT.
OR ARE YOU GOING TO PUNCH ME ONCE?
YOU AMUSED ME, SO YOU HAVE SUFFICIENT RIGHT TO DO THAT MUCH.
I AM A WOMAN, SO NOT THE FA—

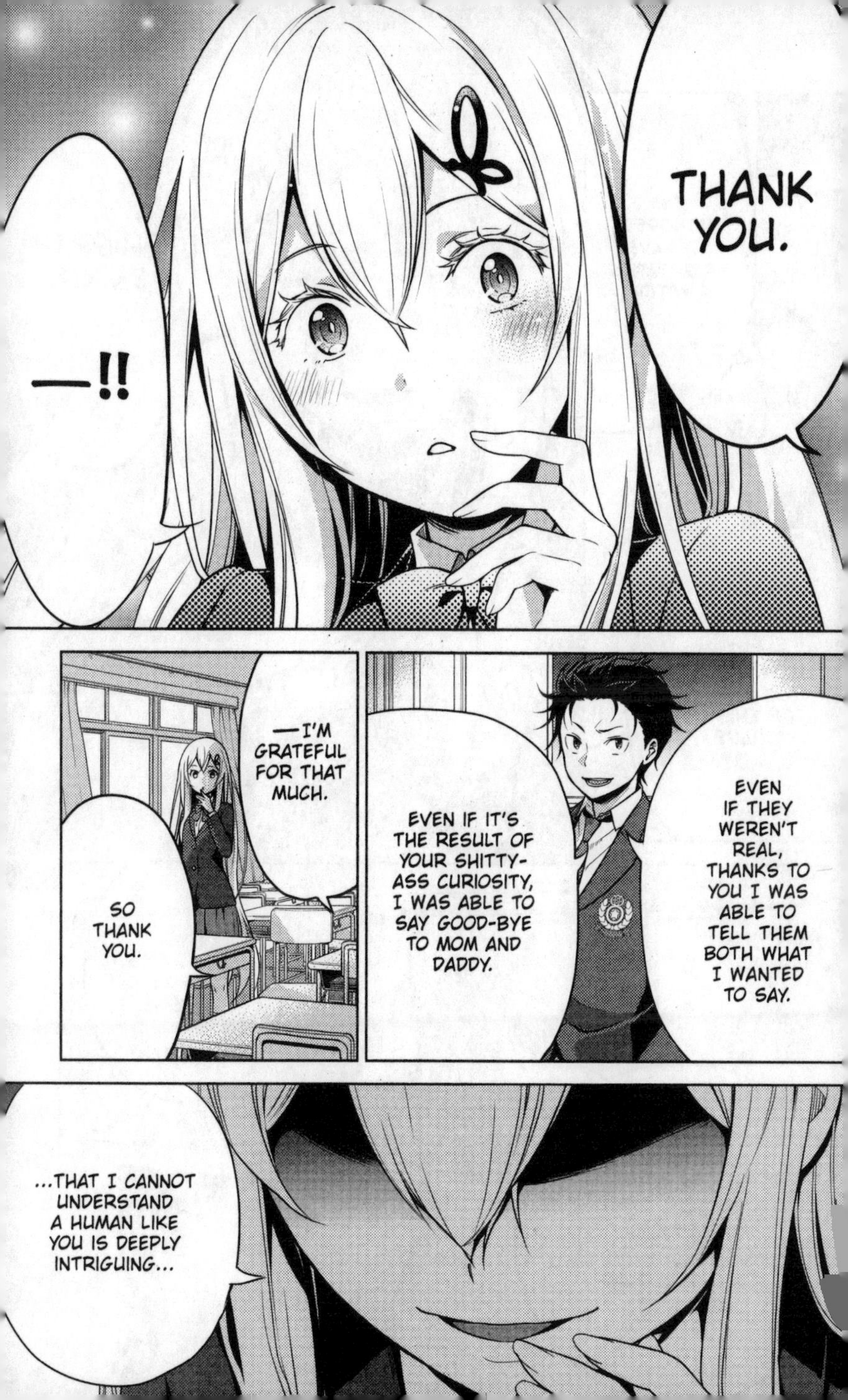
THANK YOU.
—!!
EVEN IF THEY WEREN'T REAL, THANKS TO YOU I WAS ABLE TO TELL THEM BOTH WHAT I WANTED TO SAY.
EVEN IF IT'S THE RESULT OF YOUR SHITTY-ASS CURIOSITY, I WAS ABLE TO SAY GOOD-BYE TO MOM AND DADDY.
—I'M GRATEFUL FOR THAT MUCH.
SO THANK YOU.
...THAT I CANNOT UNDERSTAND A HUMAN LIKE YOU IS DEEPLY INTRIGUING...

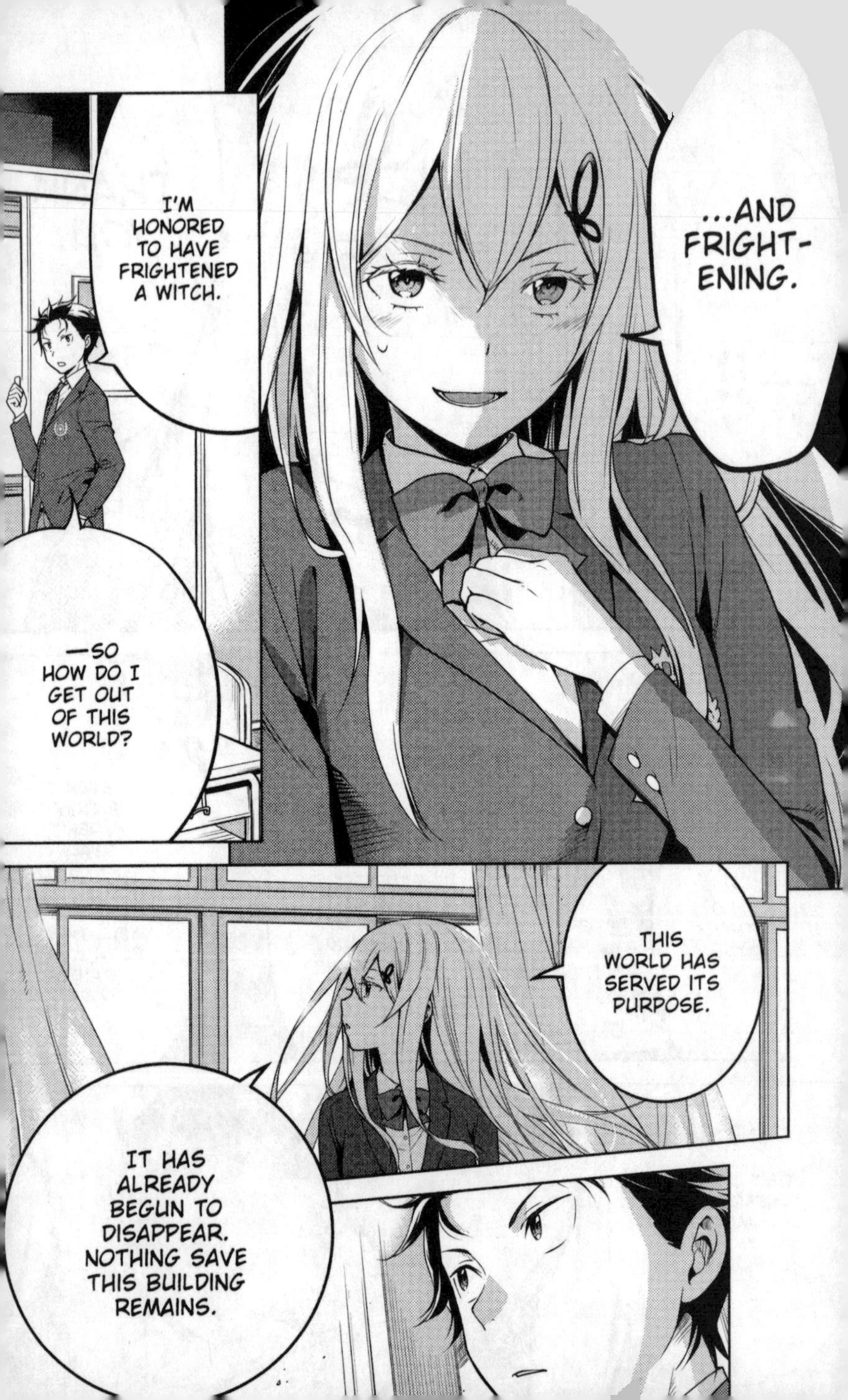
...AND FRIGHT-ENING.
I'M HONORED TO HAVE FRIGHTENED A WITCH.
—SO HOW DO I GET OUT OF THIS WORLD?
THIS WORLD HAS SERVED ITS PURPOSE.
IT HAS ALREADY BEGUN TO DISAPPEAR. NOTHING SAVE THIS BUILDING REMAINS.

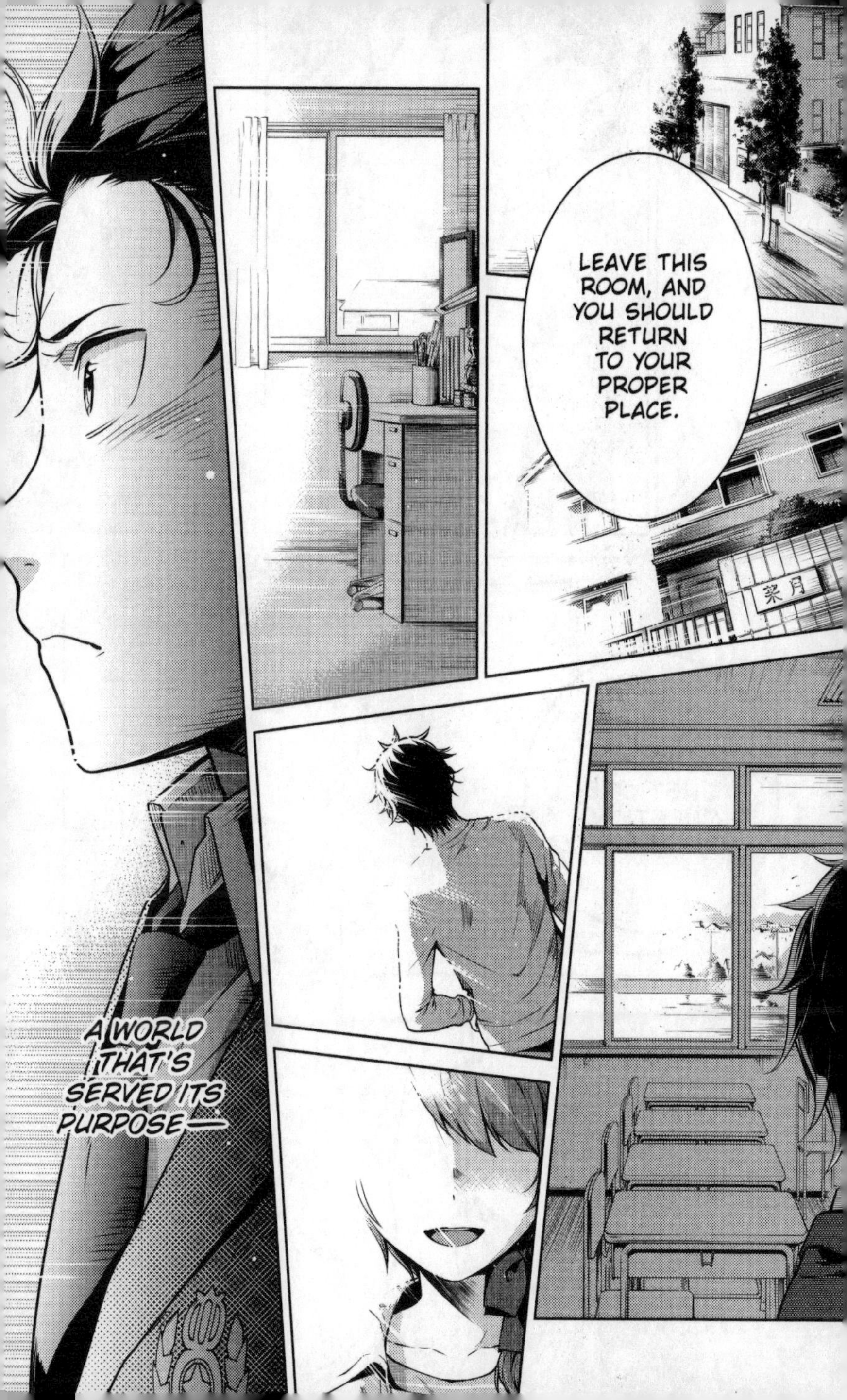
LEAVE THIS ROOM, AND YOU SHOULD RETURN TO YOUR PROPER PLACE.
菜月
A WORLD THAT'S SERVED ITS PURPOSE—

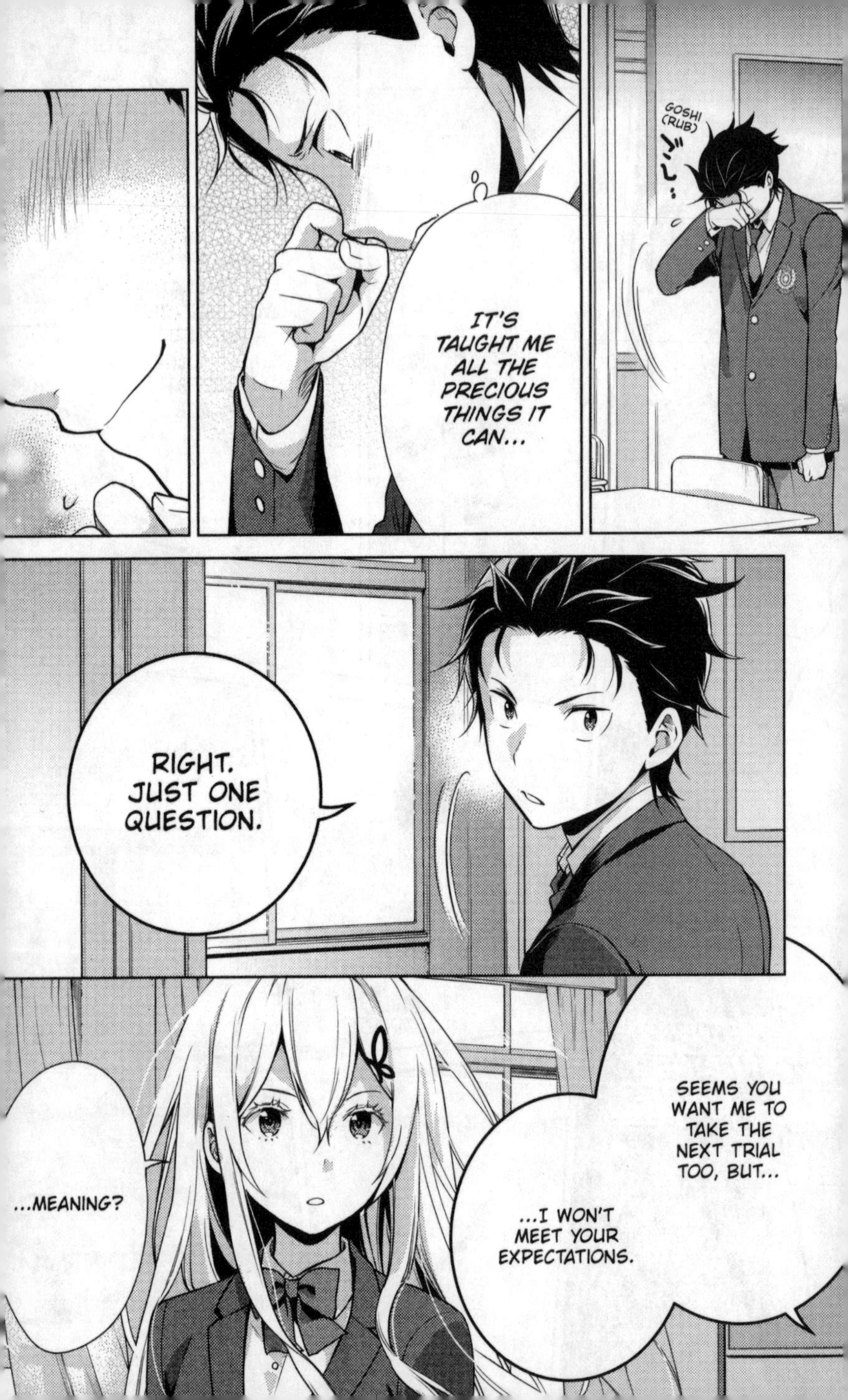
GOSHI (RUB)
IT'S TAUGHT ME ALL THE PRECIOUS THINGS IT CAN...
RIGHT. JUST ONE QUESTION.
SEEMS YOU WANT ME TO TAKE THE NEXT TRIAL TOO, BUT...
...I WON'T MEET YOUR EXPECTATIONS.
...MEANING?

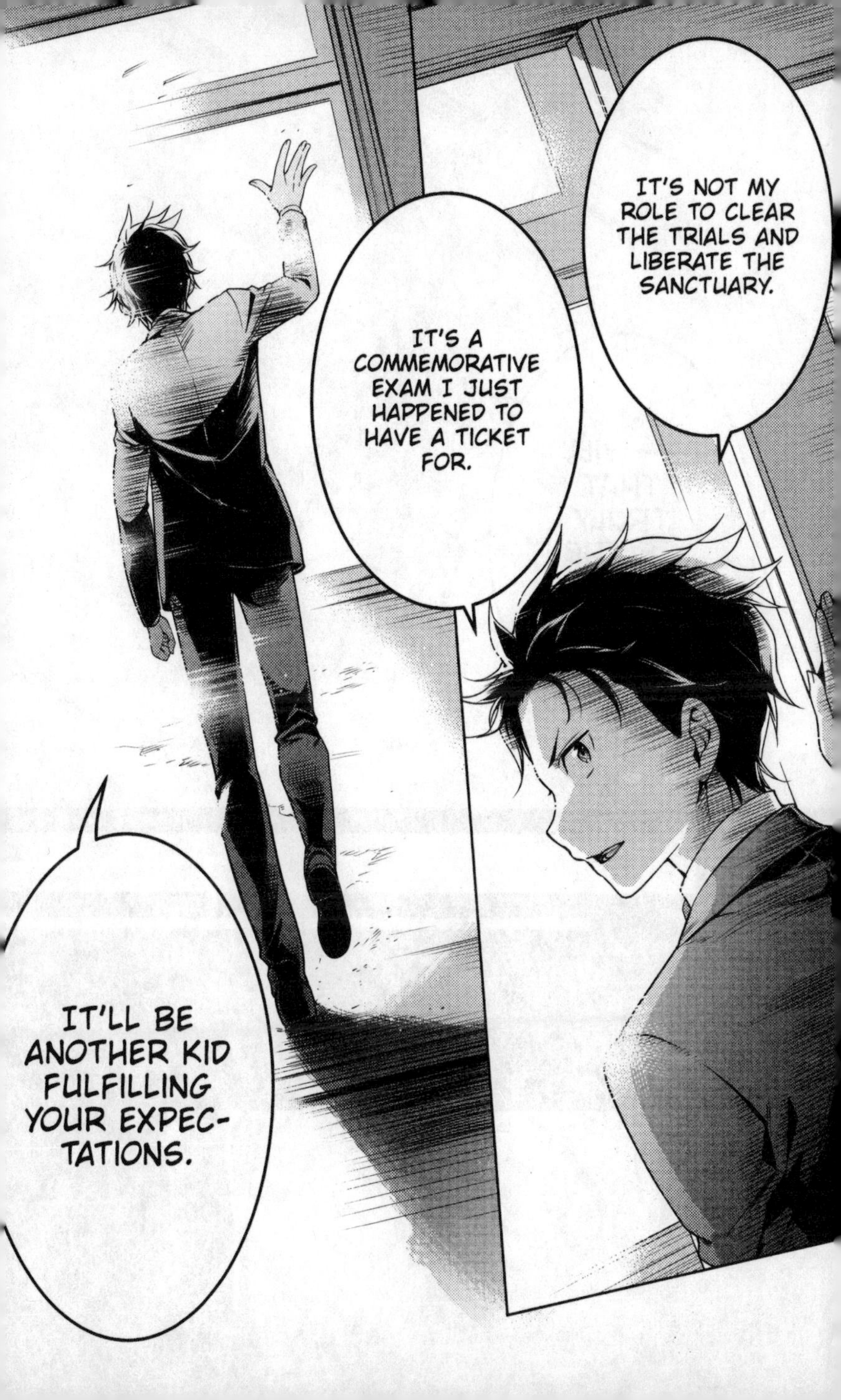
IT'S NOT MY ROLE TO CLEAR THE TRIALS AND LIBERATE THE SANCTUARY.
IT'S A COMMEMORATIVE EXAM I JUST HAPPENED TO HAVE A TICKET FOR.
IT'LL BE ANOTHER KID FULFILLING YOUR EXPEC-TATIONS.

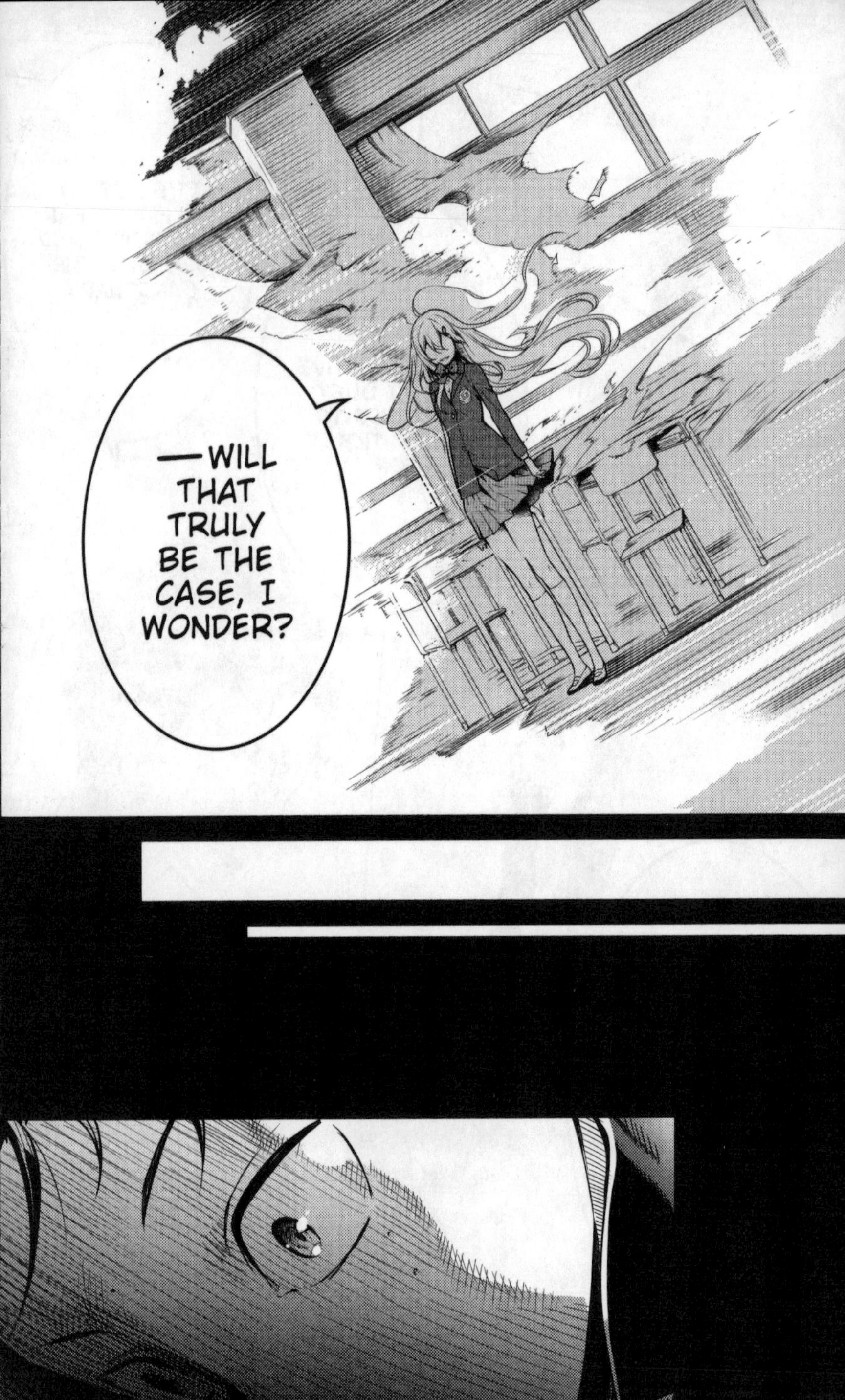
—WILL THAT TRULY BE THE CASE, I WONDER?

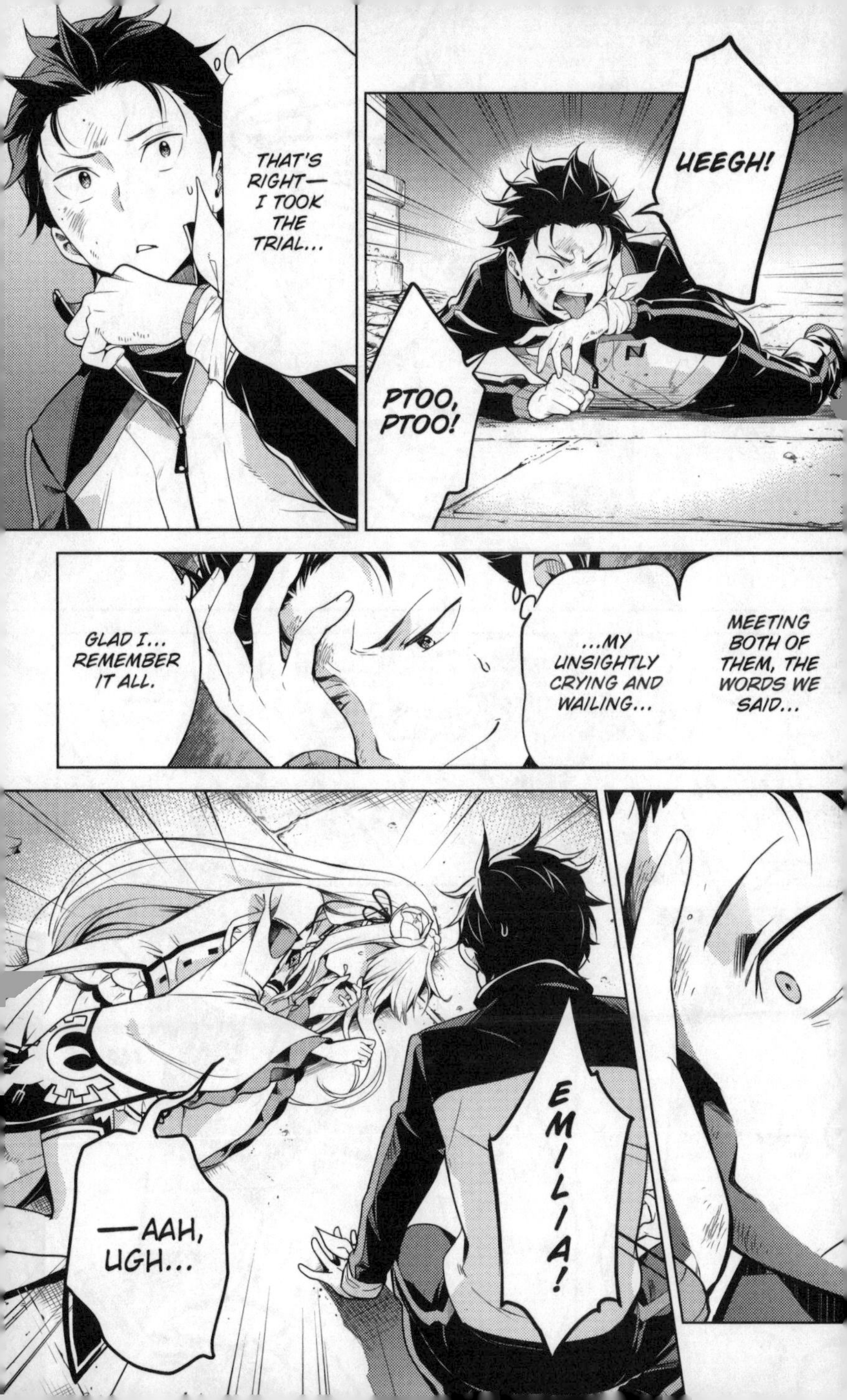
UEEGH!
PTOO, PTOO!
THAT'S RIGHT— I TOOK THE TRIAL...
MEETING BOTH OF THEM, THE WORDS WE SAID...
...MY UNSIGHTLY CRYING AND WAILING...
GLAD I... REMEMBER IT ALL.
EMILIA!
—AAH, UGH...

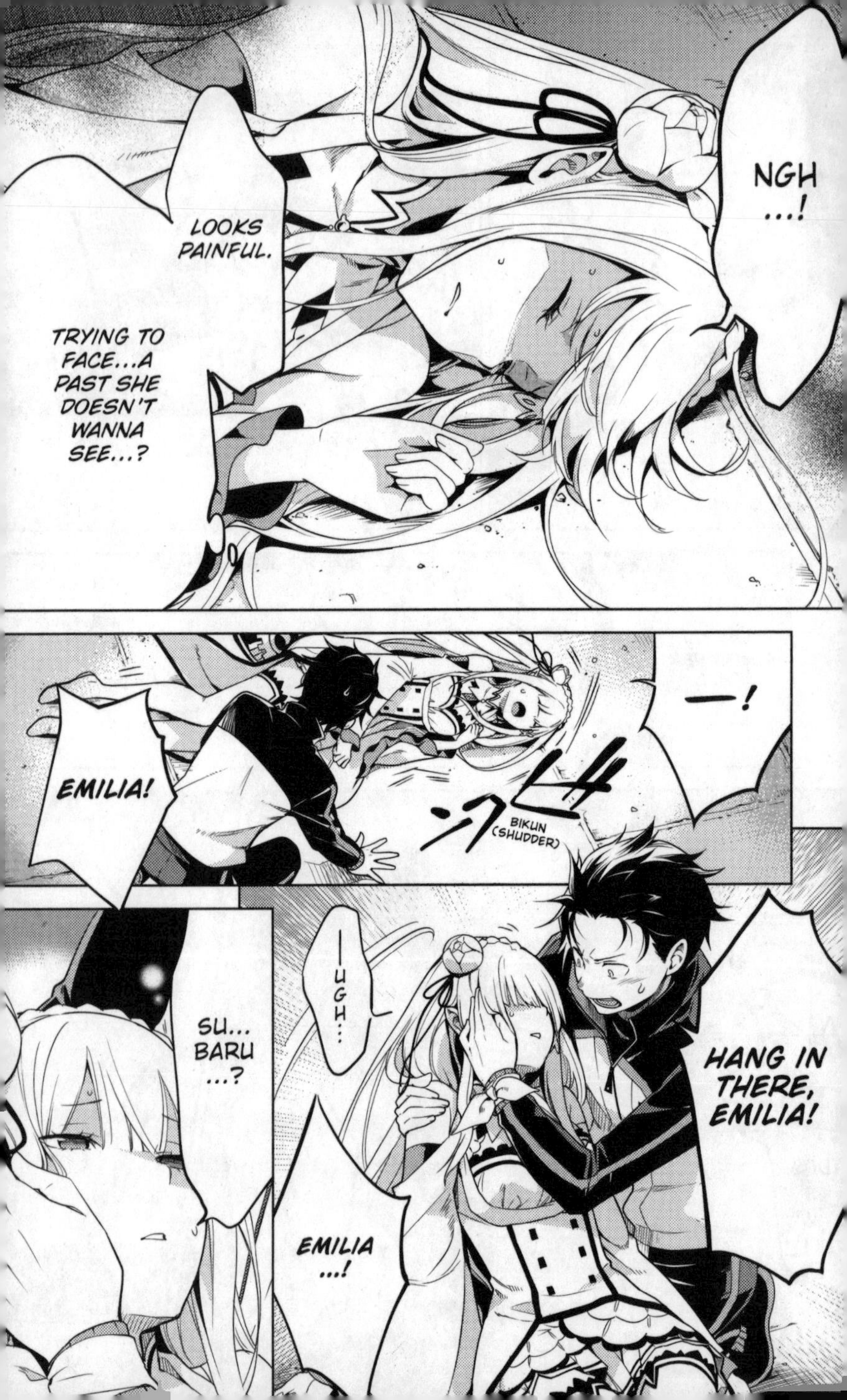
NGH ...!
LOOKS PAINFUL.
TRYING TO FACE...A PAST SHE DOESN'T WANNA SEE...?
—!
BIKUN (SHUDDER)
EMILIA!
HANG IN THERE, EMILIA!
UGH...
EMILIA ...!
SU... BARU ...?

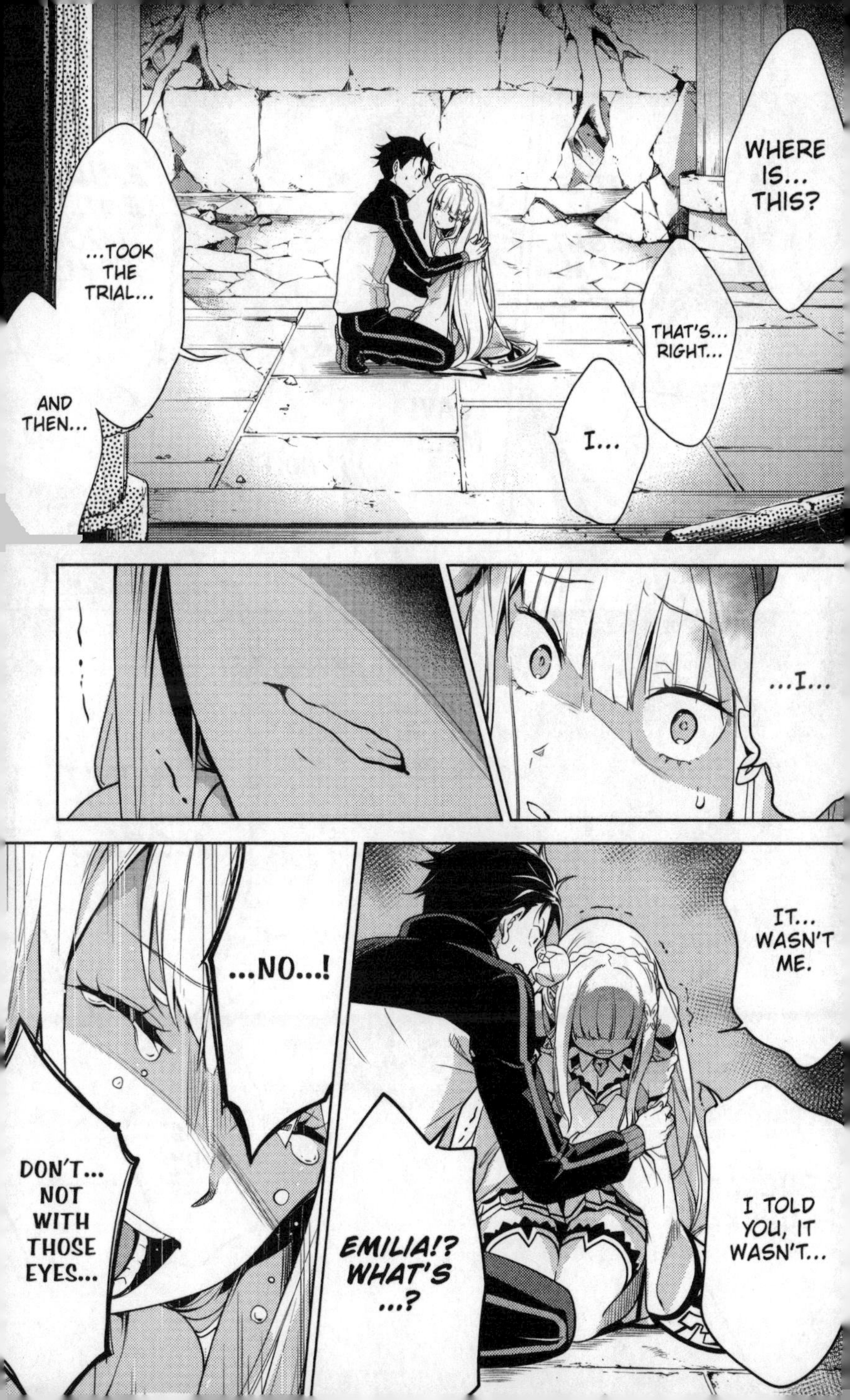
WHERE IS... THIS?
THAT'S... RIGHT...
I...
...TOOK THE TRIAL...
AND THEN...
...I...
IT... WASN'T ME.
I TOLD YOU, IT WASN'T...
EMILIA!? WHAT'S ...?
...NO...!
DON'T... NOT WITH THOSE EYES...

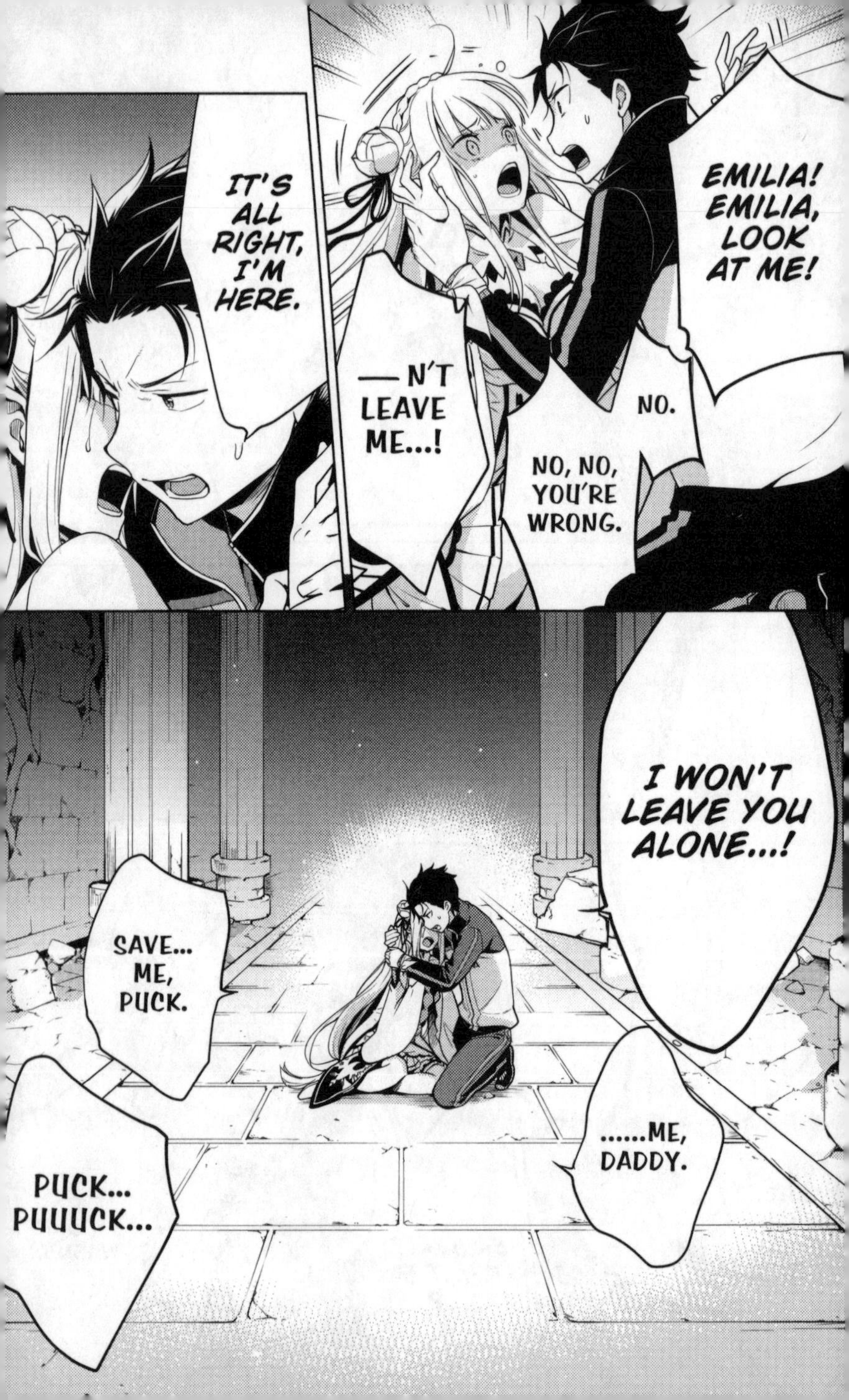
EMILIA! EMILIA, LOOK AT ME!
NO.
NO, NO, YOU'RE WRONG.
—N'T LEAVE ME...!
IT'S ALL RIGHT, I'M HERE.
I WON'T LEAVE YOU ALONE...!
SAVE... ME, PUCK.
......ME, DADDY.
PUCK... PUUUCK...

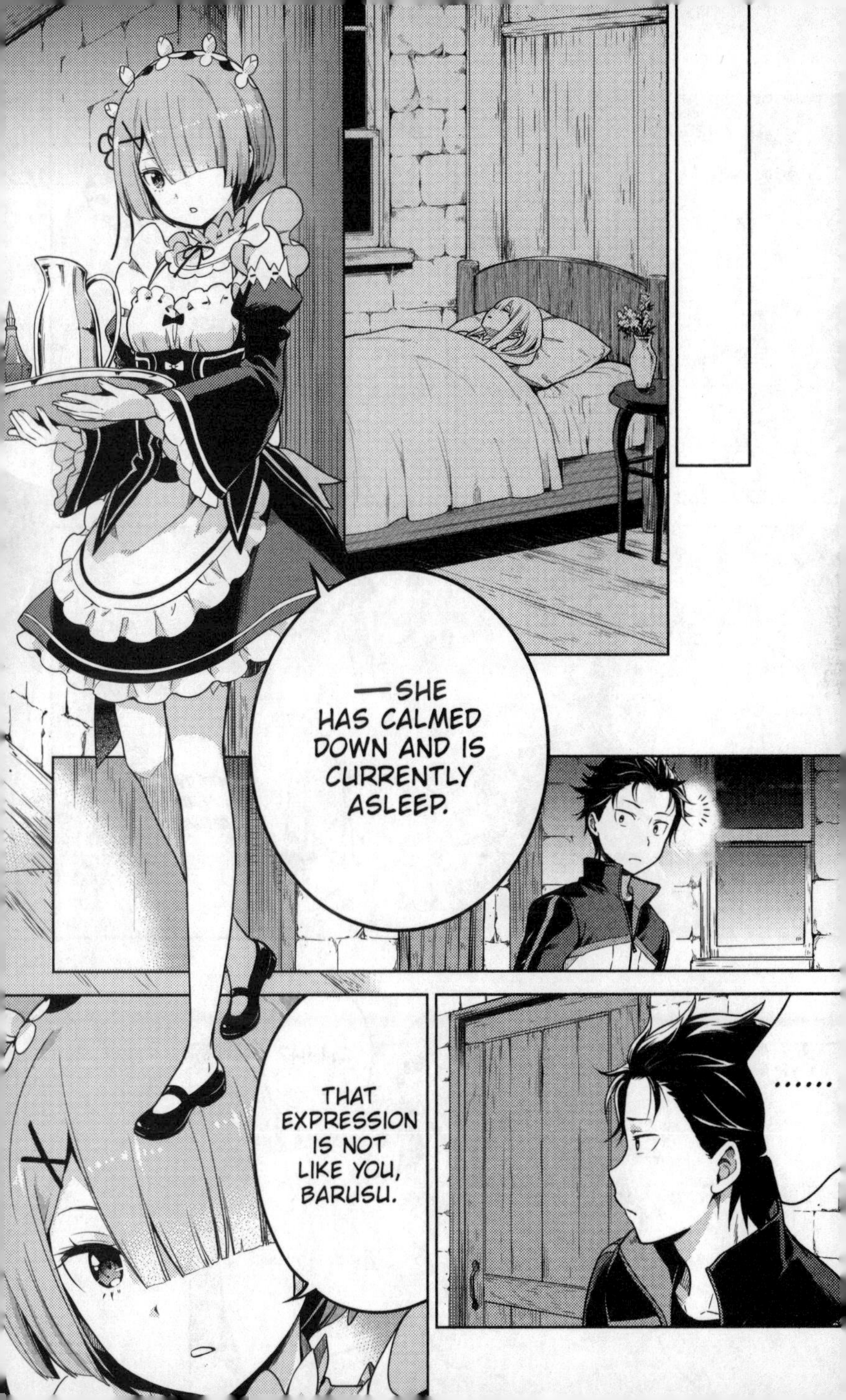
—SHE HAS CALMED DOWN AND IS CURRENTLY ASLEEP.
......
THAT EXPRESSION IS NOT LIKE YOU, BARUSU.

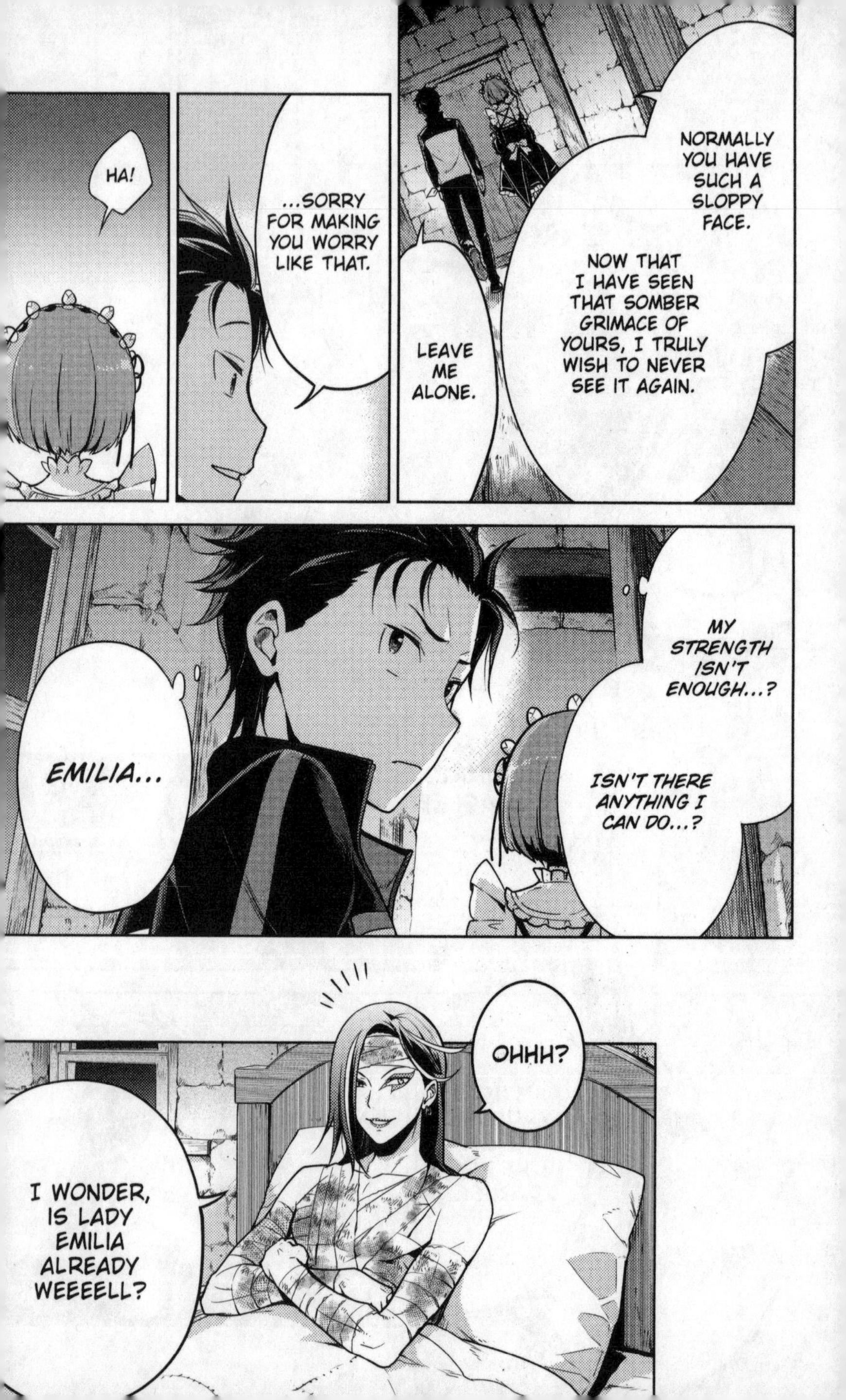
NORMALLY YOU HAVE SUCH A SLOPPY FACE.
NOW THAT I HAVE SEEN THAT SOMBER GRIMACE OF YOURS, I TRULY WISH TO NEVER SEE IT AGAIN.
LEAVE ME ALONE.
...SORRY FOR MAKING YOU WORRY LIKE THAT.
HA!
MY STRENGTH ISN'T ENOUGH...?
ISN'T THERE ANYTHING I CAN DO...?
EMILIA...
OHHH?
I WONDER, IS LADY EMILIA ALREADY WEEEELL?

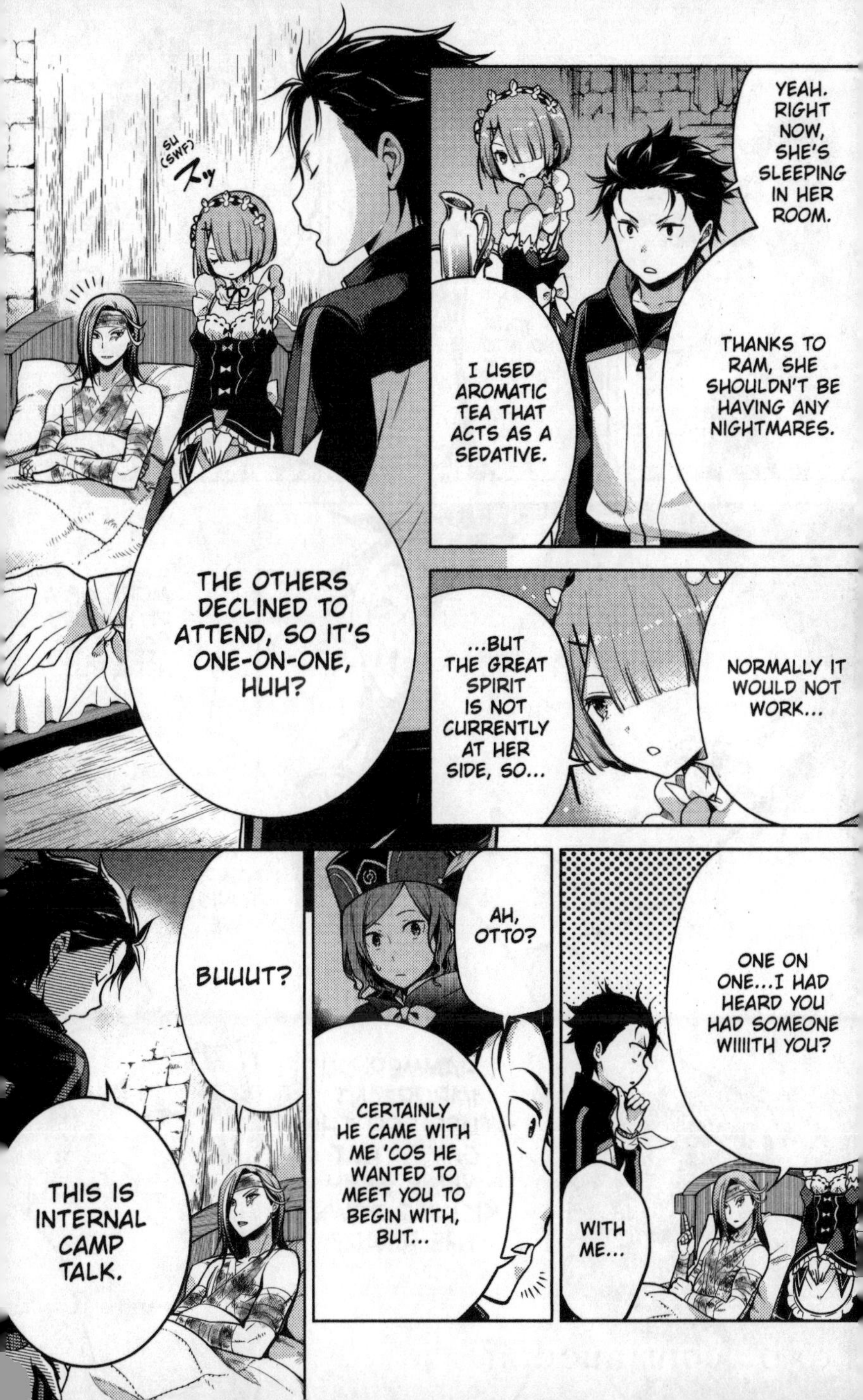
YEAH. RIGHT NOW, SHE'S SLEEPING IN HER ROOM.
THANKS TO RAM, SHE SHOULDN'T BE HAVING ANY NIGHTMARES.
I USED AROMATIC TEA THAT ACTS AS A SEDATIVE.
NORMALLY IT WOULD NOT WORK...
...BUT THE GREAT SPIRIT IS NOT CURRENTLY AT HER SIDE, SO...
SU (SWF)
THE OTHERS DECLINED TO ATTEND, SO IT'S ONE-ON-ONE, HUH?
ONE ON ONE...I HAD HEARD YOU HAD SOMEONE WIIIITH YOU?
WITH ME...
AH, OTTO?
CERTAINLY HE CAME WITH ME 'COS HE WANTED TO MEET YOU TO BEGIN WITH, BUT...
BUUUT?
THIS IS INTERNAL CAMP TALK.

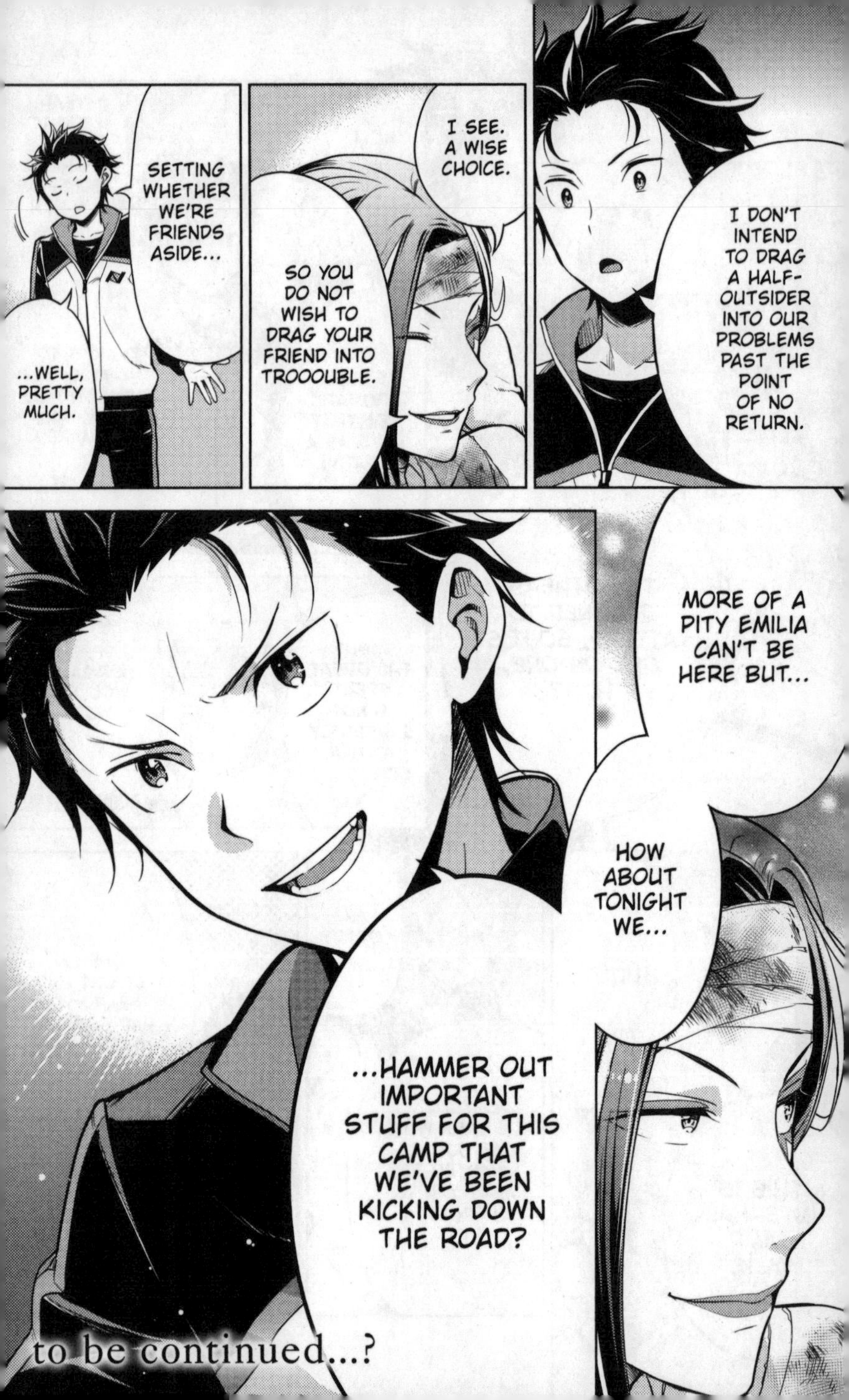
I DON'T INTEND TO DRAG A HALF-OUTSIDER INTO OUR PROBLEMS PAST THE POINT OF NO RETURN.
I SEE. A WISE CHOICE.
SO YOU DO NOT WISH TO DRAG YOUR FRIEND INTO TROOOUBLE.
SETTING WHETHER WE'RE FRIENDS ASIDE...
...WELL, PRETTY MUCH.
MORE OF A PITY EMILIA CAN'T BE HERE BUT...
HOW ABOUT TONIGHT WE...
...HAMMER OUT IMPORTANT STUFF FOR THIS CAMP THAT WE'VE BEEN KICKING DOWN THE ROAD?
to be continued...?

Re:ZERO -

-Starting Life in Another World-

Haruno Atori-sensei, Yu Aikawa-sensei, congratulations on Volume 2 of *Chapter 4* of *Re:ZERO –Starting Life in Another World–* going on sale!

Volume 2 of the *Chapter 4* comic adaptation is out so quickly! This time, just as the subtitle "The Sanctuary and the Witch of Greed" proclaims, the setting is the Sanctuary and begins with the Witch of Greed. It is a tale of a variety of major characters moving and acting according to their own motives. This includes Subaru Natsuki, the main character of *Re:ZERO*, but at any rate, many characters are concealing what they really think. And since this is a tale where these inner workings are revealed over the course of the Return by Death loop, I think that makes the composition extremely, enormously complex!

After slipping away from over there, he is unable to stand over here; whittled down over here, he cannot accomplish anything over there...I'm waiting with bated breath for the readers to be greatly entertained by the turbulent developments in chapters to come! Oh, as the original author, of course I'm cooperating in any way I can, but as the original author, it is simply exquisite to see my own works drawn by other people!

So, along with all of the readers, I await the next chapter on hands and knees! What will happen next!? It'll be the death of Subaru!

Re:ZERO -Starting Life in Another World- Chapter 4: The Sanctuary and the Witch of Greed

From the Author of the Original Work,
Tappei Nagatsuki

Illustration by Shinichirou Otsuka

CONGRATS ON VOL.2 GOING ON SALE!

ECHIDNA'S SO CUTE, HUH!?

Thank you very much for reading Volume 2.

So the Trials finally begin... this development makes my heart thump with every panel.

Please give your best regards next volume too!

Y. AIKAWA
@aikawayou

LAST FALL, I WENT WITH ATORI-SAN...
THE BACKGROUND AND STUFF IS GREAT FOR REFERENCE.
...TO SEE THE FROZEN BOND AT THE THEATER.
TEENSY YOUNG EMILIA IS REALLY ADORABLE.
PUCK
MOFU
もふ
MOFU (FLUFFY)
もふ
LOVE THE VOICE TOO
KINDA LONELY NOT HAVING PUCK IN CHAPTER 4!!
THAT!
I SUPPOSE IT IS—!
TOTALLY THAT!

Re:ZERO –Starting Life in Another World– Chapter 4: The Sanctuary and the Witch of Greed
Adaptation Afterword (Yu Aikawa)

Afterword

Hello.
This is Atori. I'm in charge of art.

Thank you very much for reading this book.

Subaru's original world came up in Vol. 2, and I had fun drawing the school stuff: his uniform, his school building, and so forth.

Also, School Uniform Echidna is so wonderful!

If all of you enjoyed reading this, that makes me happy. You're always a huge help.

To Yu Aikawa-sensei who's responsible for the adaptation and storyboards;
Kuru-san the assistant;
Tappei Nagatsuki-sensei the original author;
everyone else involved in this book; and all the readers who have read this far, thank you very much.

-2020, Haruno Atori

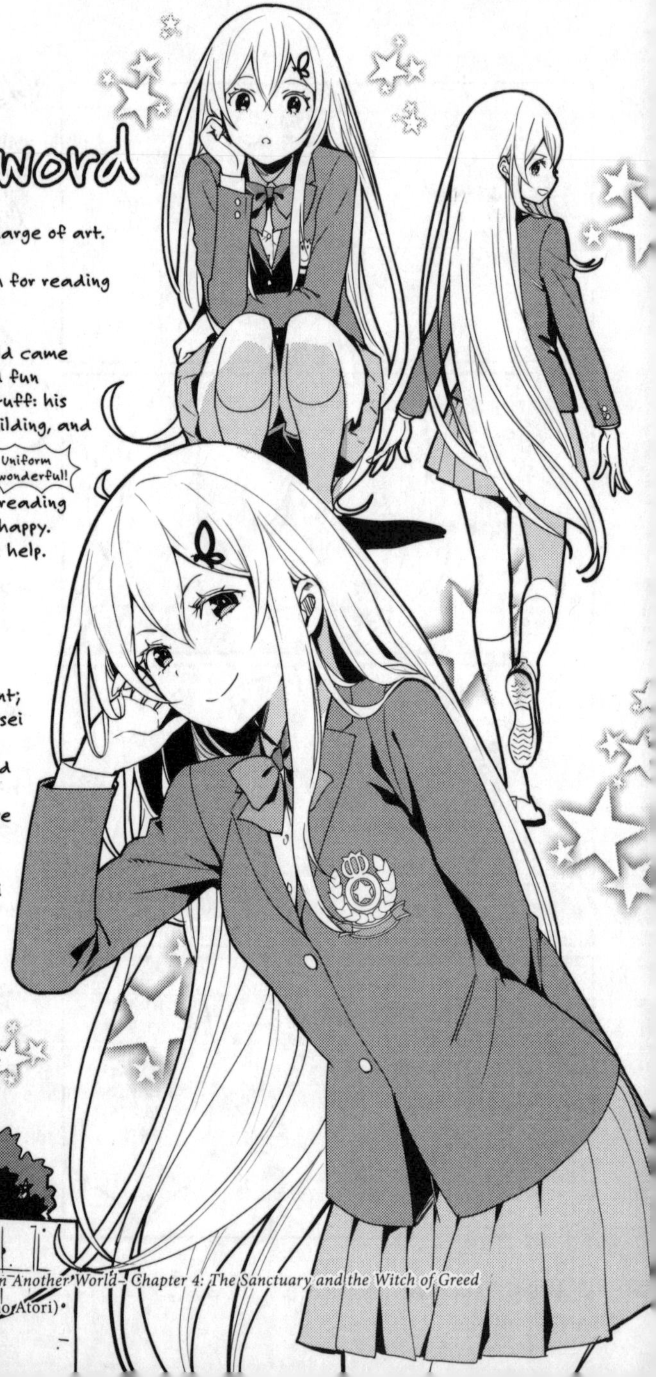

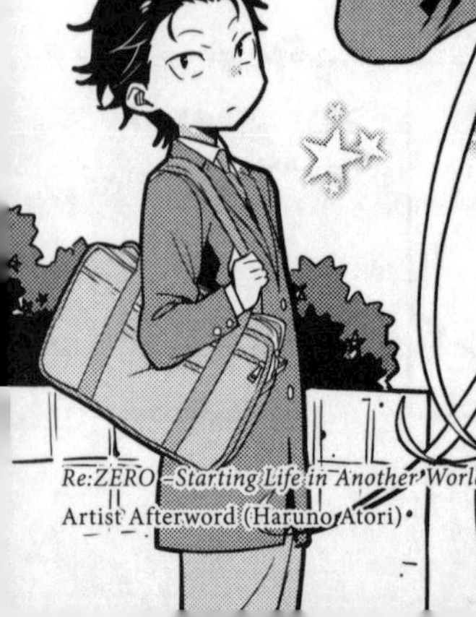

Re:ZERO -Starting Life in Another World- Chapter 4: The Sanctuary and the Witch of Greed
Artist Afterword (Haruno Atori)

Re:ZeRo

-Starting Life in Another World-

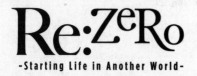

RE:ZERO -STARTING LIFE IN ANOTHER WORLD- ②
Chapter 4: The Sanctuary and the Witch of Greed

Art: Haruno Atori
Adaptation: Yu Aikawa
Original Story: Tappei Nagatsuki
Character Design: Shinichirou Otsuka

Translation: Jeremiah Bourque
Lettering: Rochelle Gancio

RE:ZERO KARA HAJIMERU ISEKAI SEIKATSU DAIYONSHO
Seiiki to Goyoku no Majo Vol. 2
© Haruno Atori 2020
© Yu Aikawa 2020
© Tappei Nagatsuki 2020
First published in Japan in 2020 by KADOKAWA CORPORATION, Tokyo. English translation rights arranged with KADOKAWA CORPORATION, Tokyo through TUTTLE-MORI AGENCY, Inc.

English translation © 2021 by Yen Press, LLC

Yen Press
150 West 30th Street, 19th Floor
New York, NY 10001

Visit us at yenpress.com
facebook.com/yenpress
twitter.com/yenpress
yenpress.tumblr.com
instagram.com/yenpress

First Yen Press Edition: July 2021

Yen Press is an imprint of Yen Press, LLC.
The Yen Press name and logo are trademarks of Yen Press, LLC.

The publisher is not responsible for websites (or their content) that are not owned by the publisher.

Library of Congress Control Number: 2016936537

ISBNs: 978-1-9753-2311-0 (paperback)
978-1-9753-2312-7 (ebook)

10 9 8 7 6 5 4 3 2 1

BVG

Printed in the United States of America